"Both intriguing and encyclopedic. . . . Schacter . . . brings a masterful erudition and objectivity to *Searching For Memory*. . . . Many . . . fascinating aspects of memory and memory research [are] woven together by Schacter into a readable narrative." —Alan Stone, *American Journal of Psychiatry*

"Schacter has synthesized a broad overview of the ways that our brains store and, all too often, distort the past. . . . Schacter argues passionately for a better appreciation of both the power and the limitation of our mental records." —*Scientific American*

"Schacter tells bizarre tales of harmed brains in the Oliver Sacks mode, stories that challenge our assumption that our minds are unitary wholes. . . . His many careful distinctions in the recovered-memory controversy are both valuable and sane." —John Crowley, *Washington Post Book World*

"A broad and readable excursion through a range of memory phenomena, drawing extensively on [Schacter's] own work at the interface of academic and clinical interests." —John Morton, *New Scientist*

"An engrossing and lively account of the complex interplay of physiology and psychology that supports our memory systems. . . . The book dismantles many myths . . . a fascinating overview." —Maureen Zent, *Memphis Commercial Appeal*

"Schacter . . . takes us on a journey ranging from the subtle biochemical probes used to decipher memory formation in sea slugs to the latest neuroimaging techniques used to light up human brains. . . . Anyone interested in a summary of this burgeoning new field will be well rewarded." —Joseph Glenmullen, *Boston Globe*

"*Searching for Memory* is a rich and engaging account of current neuroscientific approaches to understanding human memory. The author draws on original art and everyday experience, as well as cutting-edge research, to explore a central paradox of memory: The aspects that make it fragile do not diminish its power." —*BrainWork*

"In short, a highly readable, intellectually rich, and altogether memorable work." —*Kirkus Reviews*

"[A] convincing and always well-argued account of the different types of memory that have recently been distinguished. . . . This is an excellent book on an important topic: it is exceptionally well written; its examples of defects in memory are fascinating." —Stuart Sutherland, *New York Times Book Review*, a "Notable Book of the Year"

"An acute and poetic observer of human nature, Daniel Schacter has brought together a powerful and original synthesis of current work on memory, and a poignant evocation of memory's 'fragile power,' in a book that manages to be at once weighty and delightful. *Searching for Memory* ponders every aspect of memory: how different forms of memory may be weakened or obliterated with disease; how, far below the level of consciousness, implicit memory allows us to perceive, speak and act; how memories are transmitted, and transformed, by culture and art; how memories—and selves—are built through experience and continually reconstructed throughout life."
—Oliver Sacks, M.D., author of *An Anthropologist on Mars*

"Fascinating work." —*Science News*

"In his comprehensive *Searching for Memory*, Daniel Schacter provides an authoritative synthesis of scientific findings (many from his own research), an evocative compilation of relevant works of art, and a convincing account of the human experience of memory."
—Howard Gardner, Project Zero, Harvard University Graduate School of Education, and author of *Leading Minds*

"If you ever have doubts about the reliability of your recollections and if you want to understand why memory can play unexpected tricks on all of us, this is the book for you. Drawing on a wealth of findings from memory research, and aided by careful scholarship and a sharp focus, Daniel Schacter convincingly undermines the myth of remembrance as the objective replica of things past. And as he does, he succeeds in illuminating the scaffolding behind the creative mental reconstructions which let us search for lost time. A notable achievement."
—Antonio R. Damasio, M.D., Ph.D., M.W.Van Allen Professor of Neurology, University of Iowa, and author of *Descartes' Error*

"A full, rich picture of how human memory works, an elegant, captivating tour de force ... this wonderfully enlightening survey enlarges our understanding of the mind's potential." —*Publishers Weekly*, starred review

"Dan Schacter ... has written a compelling, readable overview of what scientists know about human memory. ... This book is mandatory reading for anyone interested in psychology, biology, or simply the human lot. . . . Schacter has performed a difficult and commendable task, distilling a huge amount of information into a convenient format."
—Mark Pendergrast, *Philadelphia Inquirer*

Searching for Memory

The Brain, the Mind, and the Past

DANIEL L. SCHACTER

Basic Books
A Member of the Perseus Books Group

Designed by Elliott Beard

Library of Congress Cataloging-in-Publication Data

    Searching for memory : the brain, the mind, and the past /
Daniel L. Schacter. — 1st ed.
    Includes bibliographical references and index.
    ISBN 0-465-02502-1 (cloth)
    ISBN 0-465-07552-5 (paper)
    1. Memory. 2. Recollection (Psychology). 3. Memory
disorders. I. Title.
go371.S29   1996
153.1'2—dc20   96-19521

00 01 ❖/RRD 10 9

For my mother, Harriet

Great is the power of memory, a fearful thing, O my God, a deep and boundless manifoldness; and this thing is the mind, and this am I myself.

—Augustine, *The Confessions of Saint Augustine*

"I know it can't've *been* like that, but that's what I remember."

—Pat Barker, *Regeneration*

As I used to say to my clients, "Memory is life."

—Saul Bellow, *The Bellarosa Connection*

CONTENTS

ACKNOWLEDGMENTS

THE SEEDS OF THIS BOOK were sown in 1975, when I worked as a research assistant for Dr. Herbert Crovitz at a Veterans Administration Hospital in Durham, North Carolina. There I tested brain-damaged patients who were utterly incapable of remembering new information for more than a few seconds. One man conversed easily when we first met and seemed more or less like anyone else. But when I left the room and returned several minutes later, he had totally forgotten we had ever met. Startled and intrigued by such dramatic disorders, I developed a deep and enduring interest in memory that I have pursued for the past two decades.

I have had much help along the way. Herb Crovitz ignited my interest in memory, and Endel Tulving nurtured it during my years in graduate school and ever since. I have been fortunate to work closely with many fine psychologists and neuroscientists during the past two decades. For their contributions to research described in this book, I am indebted to Marilyn Albert, Nat Alpert, Barbara Church, Lynn Cooper, Tim Curran, Elizabeth Glisky, Peter Graf, Joanne Harbluk, John Kihlstrom, Bill Milberg, Morris Moscovitch, Mary Jo Nissen, Michael Polster, Scott Rauch, Eric Reiman, Cary Savage, Endel Tulving, Anne Uecker, Mieke Verfaellie, and Paul Wang—to name only some of my collaborators. I have received pointers and advice concerning phenomena and issues addressed in these pages from numerous colleagues, including Steve Ceci, Mary Harvey, Jake Jabobs, Eric Kandel, Michelle Leichtman, Elizabeth Loftus, James McGaugh, Richard McNally, Roddy Roediger, and Larry Squire. The members of the memory working group in Harvard's Mind/Brain/Behavior initiative—Emory Brown, Joseph Coyle, Jordan Fieldman, Gerald Fischbach, Jerry Green, Jerome Kagan, Elaine Scarry, and Lawrence Sullivan—have helped me to think through issues addressed in this book during numerous stimulating discussions. I am especially grateful to colleagues and students who provided perceptive comments on various drafts of the entire manuscript: Laird Cermak, Tim Curran, Stephen Kosslyn, Wilma Koutstaal, Ken Norman, Kevin Ochsner, and Robin Rosenberg. For tracking down references all over the Boston area, I thank Gayle Bessenoff and Lissa Galluccio, and for keeping track of the ever-increasing bibliography, I am grateful to Mara Gross and Kim Nelson. Maura Wogan provided helpful advice concerning pragmatic aspects of this endeavor. My wife, Susan McGlynn, not only provided useful feedback on the evolving manuscript, but also put up with too many occasions when my need to write just one more page kept me from family duties. Her love and support throughout this project have helped me more than she can imagine.

I am fortunate that my research has been supported by various public and private agencies, and I am deeply grateful to all of them: Air Force Office for Scientific Research, Connaught Foundation, Charles A. Dana Foundation, McDonnell-Pew Program in Cognitive Neuroscience, National Institute on Aging, National Institute of Neurological Diseases and Stroke, National Institute of Mental Health, and Natural Sciences and Engineering Research Council of Canada. Much of that research has involved people with shattered memories. I am especially thankful for all the time and effort expended by patients and their families during participation in our research projects. To protect their privacy, I have used fictitious names or initials for patients who took part in my studies, and have also changed some background information about them.

Although this book is primarily about the scientific study of memory, I have also drawn on the inspiration of artists. In the course of acquiring a collection of artworks in which memory is a central theme, I have been unfailingly impressed by the dedication and humanity that so many artists bring to their work. I am grateful that they have allowed me to share their creations and tell their stories. All artworks reproduced in this book, except for Magritte's "The Menaced Assassin," are from my personal collection.

At Basic Books, I have been fortunate to work with a number of skilled professionals. Jo Ann Miller, now with John Wiley and Sons, provided wise counsel and insightful editorial guidance from the inception of this book until near its end. Susan Rabiner stepped in during the latter phases of the project with grace, enthusiasm, and intelligence, helping to improve the final product significantly. Linda Carbone kept finding ways to help me communicate more clearly and succinctly, even when this project intruded on her early days of motherhood; I greatly appreciate her commitment.

My greatest debt is to my family, Susan, Hannah, and Emily, the source of my most vital memories.

INTRODUCTION
Memory's Fragile Power

IN GABRIEL GARCÍA MÁRQUEZ'S epic novel *One Hundred Years of Solitude*, a strange plague invades the small village of Macondo, causing the inhabitants to lose aspects of their memories. The symptoms develop in stages. Each villager loses the ability to call up childhood recollections, then the names and functions of objects, later the identity of other people, and finally "even the awareness of his own being."

A silversmith, frightened when he cannot come up with the word *anvil* to describe the tool he has always worked with, frantically goes about placing written labels on every item in his home. Inspired by the method's seeming success, José Arcadio Buendía attempts to label everything in the village:

> He . . . marked the animals and plants: *cow, goat, pig, hen, cassava, caladium, banana.* Little by little, studying the infinite possibilities of loss of memory, he realized that the day might come when things would be recognized by their inscriptions but that no one would remember their use. Then he was more explicit. . . . *This is the cow. She must be milked every morning so that she will produce milk, and the milk must be boiled in order to be mixed with coffee to make coffee and milk.*[1]

Distressed at the thought of a life of endless labeling, Buendía makes a heroic last attempt to save the memory of the villagers: he

1

tries to develop a memory machine that will store written entries of all the experiences and knowledge accumulated in each person's life. After devising fourteen thousand entries for the machine, mercifully, Buendía is freed from this nightmare by a stranger who cures him of the plague. With a cure comes the full restoration of his memory. Only then does he recognize the stranger as an old and dear friend.

The novel dramatizes a world without memory: a world in which even close friends and family members seem like strangers; a world in which symbolic forms of communication are useless, and most of the tasks on which society depends cannot be performed; and, perhaps most tellingly, a world in which our sense of personal identity and self-awareness is stripped away. The narrator in Saul Bellow's *The Bellarosa Connection,* who runs a memory-improvement institute, sums it up for his clients: "Memory is life."[2]

Yet, except for those annoying moments when memory fails or when someone we know is afflicted with memory loss, most of us are barely aware that just about everything we do or say depends on the smooth and efficient operation of our memory systems. Stop and think for a moment about what is involved in just one simple task: arranging to meet a friend at a restaurant. For starters, you must be able to bring to mind your friend's name and phone number as well as the information needed to execute the call. Then you must use your memory of voices to identify the person who answers the phone as your friend. Throughout, to hold up your end of the conversation and to understand what is being said to you, you must constantly access an internal dictionary of words, sounds, meanings, and syntax. At some point you must search through memories of visits to restaurants, or recommendations of new ones, in order to determine which restaurant would be a good choice. You must be able to call up details of your friend's personality, special interests, and anything else that will contribute to harmony and avoid provocation or confrontation. Later, you must call upon knowledge and skills that remind you how to get physically from here to there. Finally, you must be fully aware of what else is going on in your life so that you do not schedule the meeting for a time when you already have something planned.

We perform these feats of memory naturally, even though the tasks require the virtually perfect operation of memory-retrieval systems with processes so complex that even the most advanced computer would not be able to carry out the assignment as easily and effectively as we do. Now consider that we rely on these systems to perform similar feats countless times each and every day of our lives.

Like other biologically based capabilities, memory is generally well adapted to such everyday demands of life, because it has evolved over countless generations in response to the pressures of natural selection. A foraging animal who can remember locations where food has been found has an important survival advantage over a competitor with less accurate recall; an inhabitant of the jungle who can recognize quickly the signs of a dangerous predator stands a better chance of escape than a competitor with slower or foggier recognition processes. Indeed, we can guess that many features of memory survived the rigors of evolution precisely because they helped animals and people survive and reproduce; any memory system that consistently produced serious distortions would not be likely to survive many generations.[3] While far from perfect at meeting all human needs, our own memory systems do a remarkably good job of handling the staggering variety of demands we place upon them.

Yet memory's reputation has been tarnished lately. We hear disturbing reports of false traumatic memories in therapy patients. We read strange stories of people who vividly recall alien abductions. And we learn that scientists have come up with simple ways to induce some of us to remember clearly events that never happened!

Does this suggest that as accurate as memory is in most situations, it is less consistently reliable than we once believed it to be? Or that its reliability is conditional, highly accurate in some situations or under some conditions—perhaps when our well-being or even our survival is at stake—but less so in other circumstances? Or that it is highly reliable in allowing us to recall a general sketch of moments from the past, but much less reliable in its recall of specific detail?

We've all had firsthand experience with memory's imperfections. I once asked a colleague how long it had been since he shaved his beard. He replied in bewilderment that he had always been clean-shaven. Each of us had perfect confidence in his own memory, yet the two were in conflict. Likewise, all of us have had the uncomfortable experience of being unable to pull up a word or a name we once knew well, failing to recognize a face that ought to seem familiar, or drawing a blank when a friend reminds us of something we supposedly did together. Why is it, we may ask, that trying to remember the past is sometimes like trying to capture a darting phantom? Is this evidence of the imperfection of evolution? Or, rather, of the side effects of its advantages? Imagine having immediate access to everything you ever knew or experienced. Is protection from the chaos that would result the price we pay for the occasional inability to retrieve information we need or want at the moment?

Researchers studying memory have begun to grapple in earnest with these and other equally intriguing questions about how we remember the past. For example, to study emotion, researchers often ask their subjects to call up the saddest or happiest moment of their lives. Remarkably, it has been observed that the act of remembering sad episodes can bring people to tears within moments, and remembering happy incidents can induce an almost immediate sense of elation. Why does memory have such power in our lives?[4]

To begin to answer the questions I've raised, we must first try to understand what memory is. Twenty years ago, when I first entered the field of memory research, it was fashionable for cognitive psychologists to compare memories to computer files that are placed in storage and pulled out when needed. Back then, nobody thought that the study of memory should include the subjective experience of remembering. We now believe with some degree of certainty that our memories are not just bits of data that we coldly store and retrieve, computerlike. Artists and writers, of course, have long been aware of the importance of subjective experience in memory, and I am often struck by their prescient comments about what memory has meant to them in their creative work.

For instance, in Matthew Stadler's novel *Landscape: Memory,* the story's protagonist, Maxwell Kosegarten, starts to paint a landscape he saw several years earlier. The painting develops slowly, over time, as Maxwell retrieves and explores his memory again and again. As he paints, he confronts the discrepancy between the view of memory as a static reproduction and what his own experience is telling him. He writes:

> if my memory ought to be an accurate replica of the original experience, if that was so, my painting was hopelessly inaccurate. It was a bad painting of a fuzzy memory. But I preferred to think that memory is never frozen, nor should it be. My painting was a successful rendering of the dynamic memory that had simply begun with the original event. . . . My painting, I figured, was so very accurate in its depiction of this memory that it would inevitably look wrong when compared to the original model.[5]

Philosophers and writers have sought to penetrate memory's mysteries for centuries, and scientists have struggled with remembering and forgetting for more than one hundred years. For much of this time, progress has been slow, but the study of memory has undergone dramatic changes during the past couple of decades, some even revolutionary. Most important, we have now come to believe that memory is not a single or unitary faculty of the mind, as was long assumed. Instead, it is composed of a variety of distinct and dissociable processes and systems. Each system depends on a particular constellation of networks in the brain that involve different neural structures, each of which plays a highly specialized role within the system. New breakthroughs in brain imaging allow us to see, for the first time, how these specific parts of the brain contribute to different memory processes.

In this book I identify and discuss different types of memory that enable us to hold information for brief periods of time, to learn skills and acquire habits, to recognize everyday objects, to retain conceptual information, and to recollect specific events. Acting in concert, these memory systems allow us to accomplish the tasks of our day-to-day lives while also supplying our intellect and emotions with ideas and feelings from the past that allow us to act with purpose and live rich emotional lives. But memory involves more than just our remembrance of things past. As we have come to learn that memory is not one single thing, we've opened up a whole new world of implicit, nonconscious memory that underlies our abilities to carry out effortlessly such tasks as riding a bicycle or playing a piano, without having to direct each movement consciously every time we attempt the task. Many of us think of this type of memory as being stored in our fingers, but new research is uncovering that specific brain systems are involved in the nonconscious effects of the past on the present.

We now know enough about how memories are stored and retrieved to demolish another long-standing myth: that memories are passive or literal recordings of reality. Many of us still see our memories as a series of family pictures stored in the photo album of our minds. Yet it is now clear that we do not store judgment-free snapshots of our past experiences but rather hold on to the meaning, sense, and emotions these experiences provided us. Although serious errors and distortions occur relatively infrequently, they furnish significant clues about how we remember the past because they arise from, and provide a window on, some of the fundamental properties of our memory systems.

One especially important such property is that we cannot separate our memories of the ongoing events of our lives from what has happened to us previously. Imagine that for a set time period, two people were tied together so that each could witness only what the other saw, read only what the other read, learn only what the other learned, and have only the emotional experiences the other experienced. Unless these two people were identical personalities with identical pasts, their memories of the time period could be vastly different. What has happened to us in the past determines what we take out of our daily encounters in life; memories are records of how we have experienced events, not replicas of the events themselves. Experiences are encoded by brain networks whose connections have already been shaped by previous encounters with the world. This preexisting knowledge powerfully influences how we encode and store new memories, thus contributing to the nature, texture, and quality of what we will recall of the moment.

Not surprisingly, these insights and others have taught us much about the vulnerability of memory—why our recollections are sometimes predisposed to corruption by suggestive influences, and how we sometimes distort the past for no immediately apparent reason. And we are beginning to understand why some memories have the power to induce us to cry, to laugh, or to tremble. We are still far from being able to say that we have a complete picture of how human memory works, but after centuries with little success, we are starting to find places for many pieces of the puzzle.

One reason for the emerging synthesis is that students of the brain and the mind, after years of going separate ways, have come together to develop an integrated approach that has transformed the study of memory: cognitive neuroscience. A mere two decades ago, the study of memory was carried out by separate tribes of cognitive psychologists, clinicians, and neuroscientists. Cognitive psychologists studied memory in the laboratory, but showed scant interest in the world of memory outside the lab and little or none in the brain.

Clinicians—psychologists, neurologists, and psychiatrists—described fascinating disorders of memory, but were unfamiliar with the elegant techniques used by cognitive psychologists to dissect memory. Neuroscientists studied memory by removing particular parts of animals' brains and then observing the effects. Most of them hardly noticed the findings and ideas of cognitive psychologists or clinicians.

In the 1980s, cognitive psychologists began to emerge from the confines of the laboratory. Some studied memory in everyday life, adding a new richness to their work. Others began to test patients with memory disorders, bringing their vast arsenal of experimental tools to bear on understanding baffling cases of amnesia. Clinicians interested in memory loss drew increasingly on the techniques and theories developed by cognitive psychologists, and used new methods for visualizing the brain, such as magnetic resonance imaging (MRI), to provide precise characterizations of brain damage in their patients. At the same time, neuroscience made stunning progress, facilitated by technical breakthroughs that allowed increasingly refined explorations of the brain and by the development of powerful new theories using neural networks. More and more neuroscientists began to relate their findings with rats and monkeys to human memory. And during just the past few years, new functional neuroimaging techniques, such as positron emission tomography (PET scanning), have allowed us to see the brain in action while people remember. Cognitive psychologists, clinicians, and neuroscientists are all now contributing to pathbreaking neuroimaging research that is providing a novel window on memory and brain. A synthesis has emerged during the past two decades that is exciting and vast in scope.

I decided to write this book because I believe it is time to tell the tale from the perspective of someone who has been part of it. For much of my career I have attempted to link cognitive psychology, clinical observations, and neuroscience into a cohesive approach to understanding memory. Here I try to paint the big picture of memory as I have come to see it.

But my goal in writing this book goes beyond describing the new synthesis in memory research and relating some of my own discoveries and ideas, to include consideration of a puzzle that many of these findings highlight. Memory, that complex and usually reliable asset, can sometimes deceive us badly. Yet even though memory can be highly elusive in some situations and dead wrong in others, it still forms the foundation for our most strongly held beliefs about ourselves. A head-injury patient I once interviewed who had lost many treasured memories felt that he had also lost his sense of self. He became so obsessed with the missing pages of his past that he could think or talk of little else.

"I can't review my life," he kept telling me.

This important duality—memory's many limitations on the one hand and its pervasive influence on the other—is at the heart of this book because it is central to understanding how the past shapes the present. I refer to it as fragile power, and it has affected increasing numbers of us in recent years. An intense controversy has exploded in therapy settings, courtrooms, and the popular media as people claim, with passionate conviction, to have recovered long lost memories of sexual abuse during childhood. Are some of these allegations based on illusory "memories" created, rather than uncovered, in psychotherapy? We have also seen a steady parade of child care workers and others convicted for abusing young children. Did these children really experience the horrors they report, or did repeated questioning create memories of events that never occurred?

Memory's fragile power is evident in other sectors of society, too. As the aging population lives longer, more and more families are affected by the corresponding increase in cases of Alzheimer's disease. Here, the devastating progression of memory disorder highlights both our extraordinary dependence on memory and its remarkable sensitivity to changes in brain function. And in perhaps the most poignant example of all, fifty years after the horrors of the Nazi killing grounds, so-called revisionist groups have attempted to recast society's collective memory of the Holocaust by dismissing the recollections of survivors and questioning the mountains of factual evidence and footage of the most despicable event of modern times.

These examples remind us that trying to understand memory's fragile power is not just an exercise in intellectual curiosity; it is also essential for understanding some of the most compelling issues of our times. In this book I relate insights from modern memory research to these and other important manifestations of memory in our day-to-day lives. Chapter 1 examines subjective experiences of remembering. It was once believed that remembering a past experience is merely a matter of bringing to mind a stored record of the event, but recent research has overturned this persisting myth. We will see how even the seemingly simple act of calling to mind a memory of a particular past experience—what you did last Saturday night or where you went on your first date—is constructed from influences operating in the present as well as from information you have stored about the past.

In chapter 2 I explain some of the fundamental processes that give rise to our memories. I will show how understanding the nature of encoding can help us to fathom the spectacular feats of memory of a long-distance runner who could recall long strings of digits and an autistic savant who had an extraordinary ability to remember visual patterns but little else. I will illustrate the complexities of the retrieval process when I introduce a brain-damaged boy who could recall his recent experiences through writing but not talking. And we will see how PET scanning studies are beginning to alter our thinking about how the brain accomplishes encoding and retrieval. I have taken part in some of this research and will report the latest developments from the cutting edge of an exciting frontier.

Chapter 3 examines how we construct our autobiographies from fragments of experience that change over time. We will see that memories are not stored in any single location in the brain, as some researchers used to believe, nor are they distributed throughout the entire brain, as others contended. Different parts of the brain hold on to different aspects of an experience, which are in turn linked together by a special memory system hidden deep within the inner recesses of our brains. New conceptions of autobiographical memory will help us to make sense of what happened to a brain-damaged man haunted by a delusional memory that he is still fighting World War II, and provide insights into the experiences of a novelist who told the story of her life to a dying daughter.

How accurate are the tales we tell about our lives? In chapter 4, I explore the relation between memory and reality and consider what happens when the connection between the two is severed. Accumulating evidence suggests that we are usually correct about the general character of our pasts, but are susceptible to various kinds of biases and distortions when we recount specific experiences. We are especially prone to misremembering the source of our memories, as in the story I relate of a woman who confused a man she had seen on television with the man who had raped her. Studies of patients with neurological damage have begun to reveal what parts of the brain allow us to sort out memories of actual events from fantasies or imaginings.

We have also learned important lessons from brain-damaged adults who have lost large chunks of their pasts—some because they cannot form new memories, others because they can't retrieve old ones. In chapter 5 we will see that studies of these amnesic patients have led to an idea with profound implications: memory is not a self-contained entity, as many researchers once believed, but instead depends on a variety of different systems in the brain.

The study of amnesic patients has also helped to open up the previously hidden world of *implicit memory*—when past experiences unconsciously influence our perceptions, thoughts, and actions. When I first began doing research, psychologists studied *explicit memory* for recent experiences by asking people deliberately to recall or recognize words or other materials they had been shown a few minutes earlier. But in the early 1980s, a series of stunning experiments showed that people can be influenced by recent experiences even when they are unable to recall or recognize them explicitly. As we will see in chapter 6, brain-damaged patients who lack explicit memory for recent events nonetheless retain implicit memory for them. Most of us know little about implicit memory, because it operates outside our awareness. But it is a pervasive influence in all our lives, and I will show how it affects everyday situations involving legal battles over intellectual property and disputes about plagiarized ideas.[6]

The power of memory is most forcefully illustrated by the profound effects of emotionally traumatic events, which I explore in chapter 7. I introduce men and women who have experienced terrible traumas that they could never forget: narrowly escaping a life-threatening fire, years of abuse in a Nazi concentration camp, or terrifying wartime incidents. And I discuss how recent discoveries in neuroscience have begun to illuminate the underpinnings of these potent recollections. Yet even though traumatic events are generally better remembered than ordinary experiences, these memories, like more mundane ones, are complex constructions—not literal recordings of reality.

Emotional trauma does not, however, always lead to vivid recall; sometimes emotionally intense experiences result in far-reaching amnesias. Chapter 8 considers mystifying cases of psychogenic amnesia, such as a young man who suddenly lost nearly all of his personal past after a psychological trauma. I examine what happens when people develop amnesia for shocking events, like a murderer who forgets committing a brutal crime. I also consider the controversial phenomenon of multiple personality, now referred to as dissociative identity disorder. Does this disorder provide an important window on memory and identity? Or, as skeptics claim, are multiple personalities now observed so frequently that we must question their validity? Having studied patients with dissociated identities, I agree with the critics that dubious diagnosis and treatment are serious problems, but I do not believe that all such cases can be explained in this way. I will discuss some of these perplexing cases in light of recent discoveries about the effects of stress-related hormones on the brain.

Questions concerning trauma and amnesia are central to the bitter debate over repressed memories of childhood sexual abuse, which I examine in chapter 9. This controversy is often thought of as a winner-take-all battle royal between advocates of recovered memories and proponents of false memories. I believe that we need to step back from the rhetoric, and recognize that this is an unfortunate oversimplification of an issue with many intermingled parts that need to be disentangled. Although it is likely that some therapists have helped to create illusory memories of abuse, it also seems clear that some recovered memories are accurate.

I conclude by considering what happens to memory as we age. We have learned that cell loss in some parts of the brain that are crucial for memory is either trivial or nonexistent, and that different kinds of memory are affected differently by aging. We have promising leads about what parts of the brain are hit hardest by aging and new insights into what this means for memory. Even as I write these words, my own research group and others are carrying out studies of aging memory with PET scans that are providing a direct window on memory and the aging brain that has never been previously available. Looking at memory in older individuals, I hope to show, offers valuable insights into the nature of memory's fragile power.

Science is typically more concerned with understanding mechanisms than with appreciating personal meanings, but to fathom memory's fragile power we must pay attention to both. Thus I delve into the personal stories of patients who have developed amnesia as a consequence of neurological or psychological trauma, and I tell of writers and artists whose lives have been affected to an unusual degree by attempts to recapture their pasts or by traumatic memories.

I also make use of artworks that focus on the nature or function of memory. All art relies on memory in a general sense—every work of art is affected, directly or indirectly, by the personal experiences of the artist—but some artists have made the exploration of memory a major subject of their work. I have come to appreciate that artists can convey with considerable potency some of the personal, experiential aspects of memory that are difficult to communicate as effectively in words.[7] Scientific research is the most powerful way to find out how memory works, but artists can best illuminate the impact of memory in our day-to-day lives. Throughout the book, I will include and describe artworks that communicate effectively, sometimes poignantly, relevant aspects of memory.

Two artists, Catherine McCarthy and Christel Dillbohner, distill the essence of memory's fragile power in highly personal works that commemorate the loss of a brother. McCarthy's "Children in the Wood" (figure 1) and Dillbohner's "Excursions VI" (figure 2) each contain images of faded memories that still wield considerable emotional power. Both artists seem to be saying that the past can be both evanescent and potent. We will try to understand the reasons why as we confront and explore the fragile power of human memory.

FIGURE 1

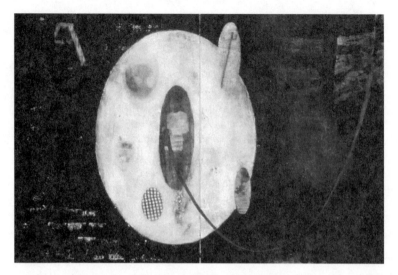

Catherine McCarthy, "Children in the Wood," 1992. 40 x 60". Diptych, oil, and varnish on canvas. Nielsen Gallery, Boston.

The artist, shown as a young girl, clutches a ribbon that travels through a dark space, connecting her to a barely visible fragment of a young boy's leg at the top of the canvas. It is a partial image of her brother, who died unexpectedly when he was young. The ribbon seems to symbolize the power of emotional memories that persist from the past and still tie the artist to her brother. She also surrounds herself with a white oval that itself contains a series of faint pictures, perhaps memories from McCarthy's childhood. A couple of the images are recognizable: an isolated telephone pole and a locomotive engine. Others are little more than formless blurs, testaments to childhood episodes that remain beyond the grasp of conscious recollection. Next to the oval is barely visible text from a favorite childhood fairy tale, "Children in the Wood." The words in the story are blurred and veiled, like much else from the distant past.

FIGURE 2

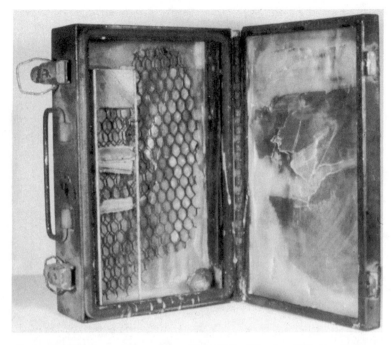

Christel Dillbohner, "Excursions VI," 1993. 8½ x 5 x 2½". Seeds, wax, and tar in box. Courtesy of the artist.

Dillbohner makes extensive use of old and discarded objects as visual symbols of memory, such as this tattered case standing open on its side. One inside panel holds fragments of objects—a ladder, a filter, and two seeds—whereas the other contains a thin layer of paper and a filmy wax. Materializing from a tear in the paper, like a memory emerging into consciousness, is a ghostly yet affecting old photograph of Dillbohner's brother, who died at an early age. By encasing the memory-laden photo and the object remains inside the case, the artist alludes to fragmentary but compelling memories that we all carry with us.

ONE

ON REMEMBERING

"A Telescope Pointed at Time"

"MY FIRST LOOK at the Boston Garden was 52 years ago and it wasn't love at first sight," the *Boston Globe* sportswriter Will McDonough commented on the venerable arena before its closing in 1995. "To me, the place always has been a dump and I can't wait to get rid of it. But not the memories. Those belong to me." McDonough went on to recount some of his most vivid recollections of the famed building: the time that pipes burst during a hockey game, flooding the stands with water; the day that a little-known man named Chuck Cooper became the first black player ever to participate in a National Basketball Association game; and the All-Star contest that was placed in jeopardy because basketball players threatened to strike. Although the Boston Garden will be reduced to rubble, McDonough still has his memories, and he probably always will. He is not alone. The *Boston Globe* headline stated: "After 66 years the Boston Garden soon will be gone, but what will remain with us forever are the memories."[1]

Occasions such as the closing of the Boston Garden underscore that we carry in our minds the remains of distant experiences that tie us to the past in a special way. Places that have long ceased to exist and people who have disappeared from our lives continue to survive in our recollections, sometimes as ghostlike phantoms we can barely fathom and sometimes as crystal-clear portraits with all the vibrancy of the here and now. Our memories belong to us. They are uniquely ours, not quite like those of anybody else. We feel this way in part because our memories are rooted in the ongoing series of episodes and incidents that uniquely constitute our everyday lives. We read the morning paper, stroll in the park, or talk with a friend, and we are in some way changed, transiently or perhaps permanently, by the experience. We go through an immense number of distinct episodes during a lifetime, but we can explicitly remember only a small fraction of them. As the narrator in Saul Bellow's *The Bellarosa Connection* says when asked about a long past event that he does not recall, "Lady, this is one of a trillion incidents in a life like mine. Why should I recollect it?"[2]

Our subjective sense of remembering the past is such a familiar and frequent part of our inner lives that we may fail to see any need to examine it. When I ask you to recall what you did last Saturday night, it may take a few seconds for you to generate a memory, but before long you are probably reexperiencing some aspects of that evening. As you think back, you may feel as though you are shining a spotlight on images, sounds, and emotions that are slumbering somewhere in the vast storehouse of memory. As innocent and plausible as this idea may seem, however, it is fundamentally misleading. Our experience of remembering an event does, of course, partly depend on information about the event that has been stored in our brains. But there are other contributors to the subjective sense of remembering, and to appreciate memory's fragile power we will need to understand them.

EXPERIENCING THE PAST
The Rememberer

Cognitive scientists commonly speak of human memory as a kind of information-processing device—a computer that stores, retains, and retrieves information. Although this sort of analogy does capture some of memory's important properties, it leaves no room for the subjective experience of remembering incidents and episodes from our pasts. Try to remember the most recent wedding you attended. Sights and sounds from the event probably come to mind, as well as the names and faces of people who were there. But there is more to the experience than merely retrieving different kinds of information: there is also a conviction that this episode is part of your personal history, related to events that came before and have occurred since. You may remember things that you thought or felt as the bride and groom spoke their vows, your surprise at how well or poorly an old acquaintance looked, or how much you enjoyed dancing to tunes you had not heard since you were young.

We are constantly making use of information acquired in the past. In order to type these sentences into my computer, I must retrieve words and grammatical rules that I learned long ago, yet I do not have any sub-jective experience of "remembering" them. Every time you start your car and begin to drive, you are calling on knowledge and skills you acquired years earlier, but you do not feel as though you are revisiting your past. As we will see, these uses of the past call on two of the brain's major memory systems: *semantic memory*, which contains conceptual and factual knowledge, and *procedural memory*, which allows us to learn skills and acquire habits. But there is something special about the subjective experience of explicitly remembering past incidents that separates it from other uses of memory, something that is often overlooked in sci-entific analyses that portray memory as a device for storing and retriev-ing information. In order to be experienced as a memory, the retrieved information must be recollected in the context of a particular time and place and with some reference to oneself as a participant in the episode. The psychologist Endel Tulving has argued that this kind of remem-bering depends on a special system called *episodic memory*, which allows us explicitly to recall the personal incidents that uniquely define our lives. Any analysis of episodic memory must consider the subjective experience of the person who does the remembering, referred to by Tulving as the *rememberer*. Stressing the intimate relationship between the rememberer and the remembered, Tulving observes that: "The par-ticular state of consciousness that characterizes the experience of remembering includes the rememberer's belief that the memory is a more or less true replica of the original event, even if only a fragmented and hazy one, as well as the belief that the event is part of his own past. Remembering, for the rememberer, is mental time travel, a sort of reliv-ing of something that happened in the past."[3]

The idea of remembering as "mental time travel" highlights some-thing that is truly remarkable: as rememberers, we can free ourselves from the immediate constraints of time and space, reexperiencing the past and projecting ourselves into the future at will. What we ordinar-ily think of as an exotic feat that could be accomplished only in sci-ence fiction is something we all engage in each and every day of our lives. Try to remember, for instance, the following three events: a child-hood birthday party; an incident from your first job; and the last thing you did before you went to bed last night. Within a matter of seconds, you have revisited parts of your past that are separated by years—

perhaps decades—and you did not need any fancy equipment to make this journey in time.

Visual artists have created evocative depictions of the subjective experiences of the rememberer. For example, in the nineteenth century, portrait painters showed people engaged in introspective acts of remembering, and conveyed the poignancy of their recollective experiences through emotion-filled facial expressions, supporting context, and titles suggestive of charged memories. A modern work that speaks eloquently to the nature of the rememberer's experience is "Looking for Yesterday," by the Massachusetts artist Candace Walters. (See figure 1.1.) A young woman's partial figure emerges from a suspended picture frame, eyes gazing into a distance that is not visible to the viewer. She seems to be engaged in an emotion-filled act of remembering. The woman hovers between two realities, partly in the frame and partly out of it—perhaps a metaphor for the rememberer's simultaneous existence in past and present.

Another contemporary work, New York artist Nancy Goldring's "The Traveler Remembers: Beigescape" (see figure 1.2), also evokes the rememberer's dual existence in past and present.

Artistic depictions of the rememberer are suggestive and even provocative. But scientists who study memory have only lately begun to study subjective experiences of remembering. For much of this century, the study of memory—like that of other areas of psychology—adhered to the tenets of behaviorism, which held that subjective mental experience is not a proper domain for scientific study. Then came the rise of cognitive psychology during the 1960s and 1970s, driven by an information-processing metaphor in which subjective experiences of remembering had no place. Philosophers offered eloquent introspective accounts of what remembering is like, but scientists generally ignored them.[4] When Tulving wrote about subjective experiences of the rememberer more than a decade ago, he had hardly any good evidence to go on. Now, accumulating scientific research is starting to tell a surprising story about the inner world of the rememberer, one that violates our intuitions about the sources of the experiences we explicitly remember every day of our lives.

MEMORY'S POINT OF VIEW

Try again to remember the most recent wedding you attended. Once you have fixed a scene in your mind, ask yourself the following

FIGURE 1.1

Candace Walters, "Looking for Yesterday," 1992. 11 x 8½". Oil stick and collage on paper. Clark Gallery, Lincoln, Massachusetts.

The title of this work suggests a search for the past, and a tear rolling down the woman's cheek implies that the past can never be fully recaptured. The piece reflects Walters's own attempts to remember events and feelings from childhood summers spent in rural Virginia. She paints a fragment of the countryside behind the young woman, a tantalizing yet elusive piece of the past that the rememberer seeks to find. "My roots are Southern," the artist comments. "My painting is devoted to the memory of porch swings and floating suns. My work is an escape into time travel, a spiritual journey and glimpse into something more."[5]

FIGURE 1.2

Nancy Goldring, "The Traveler Remembers: Beigescape," 1987. 15 x 18". Ektacolor print. Jayne H. Baum Gallery, New York.

Goldring gives visual form to the idea that remembering involves mental time travel. In the piece, which combines drawing and photographic images, a woman (the traveler) gazes out a window, apparently engaged in an act of recollection. Behind her, the collection of ghostly figures, intersecting gridlike structures, and a dreamy landscape are visual allusions to the people and places she has encountered during her travels, currently existing as fragmentary images in memory.

questions: Do you see yourself in the scene? Or do you see the scene through your eyes, as if you were there and looking outward, so that you yourself are not an object in the scene? Chances are that you will remember the wedding in the latter format, from a perspective similar to the one you had during the original event. Now try to remember back to your first day in kindergarten. Chances are that you will see yourself in the memory this time.

These two modes of remembering are referred to as *field* and *observer* memories, respectively. Sigmund Freud, one of the first to write about the field/observer distinction, believed that it held important implications for his psychoanalytic theories. Freud contended that observer memories—which we view as a detached observer—are necessarily altered versions of the original episode, because our initial perception of an event takes place from a field perspective. Noting the frequency of the observer perspective in his patients' childhood recollections, Freud believed that he had strong evidence for the reconstructive nature of early memories.[6]

The first serious investigation of field and observer memories was reported in 1983 by the cognitive psychologists Georgia Nigro and Ulric Neisser. They asked people to remember various situations, such as "watching a horror movie" or "being in an accident or near-accident," and queried them about their recollections. The majority of recollections were classified as field memories, but a significant minority (over 40 percent) were classified as observer memories. We tend to see ourselves as actors in the older memories (much as Freud maintained), whereas we tend to reexperience more recent memories from something like the original perspective.

Nigro and Neisser then asked some people to remember events from their personal past while focusing on the feelings associated with each episode, and asked others to remember events while focusing on the objective circumstances surrounding the remembered episodes. Remarkably, people experienced more field memories when focusing on feelings, whereas they experienced more observer memories when focusing on objective circumstances. Think about this result in relation to our wedding example. It implies that if I ask you to focus on "objective circumstances" (who attended, what they wore), you would be more likely to experience an observer memory, whereas if I ask you to focus on how you felt, you would be more likely to experience a field memory. This means that an important part of your recollective experience—whether or not you see yourself as a participant in a remembered event—is, to a large extent, constructed or invented at the time of attempted recall. The way you remember an event depends on your purposes and goals at the time that you attempt to recall it. You help to paint its picture during the act of remembering.[7]

In a more recent study, people recollected experiences from different times in their lives and classified them as field or observer memories; then they estimated the emotional intensity of the original experience and the intensity of the emotion they felt as they recollected it. When asked again to recall the memories, some people were told to switch from the field to the observer point of view. These people now said that the original experience was less emotional than they had indicated earlier, and also that they experienced less emotional intensity during the act of remembering than they had earlier. There was little change when the same perspective was adopted on the two occasions, or when perspective was switched from observer to field.[8]

Think about these findings in relation to our wedding memory. Suppose that when I first asked you to remember the wedding, you experienced a field memory of the bride and groom sharing their first dance. You remembered feeling a great deal of happiness at the time, and you felt the same way as you reexperienced the event. If I ask you now to recollect the experience again from the field perspective, your feelings will be similar. But suppose instead I ask you to try to recollect the bride and groom's first dance as an observer memory: that is, with you as a participant in the memory, perhaps sitting at your table as you watch the couple on the dance floor. The findings that I just considered suggest that you will now experience the memory as less emotionally intense than you did before, and you will experience your current level of emotional arousal as less than you did before. This surprising, even startling, observation again suggests that the emotional intensity of a memory is determined, at least in part, by the way in which you, the rememberer, go about remembering the episode. And the emotions that you attribute to the past may sometimes arise from the way in which you set out to retrieve a memory in the present.

REMEMBERING AND KNOWING THE PAST

Return again to our wedding episode. The first person you encounter at the reception is your dear Aunt Helen, whom you have not seen for some time. You immediately recognize the aging face, remember her name and identity, and recall that it has been exactly three years since you saw her last, at a similar family occasion. The person next to her strikes you as familiar, but, much to your consternation, you cannot recall his name, what he does, or where you might have seen him before. You are absolutely certain that you know him, but as he extends his hand, all you can do is hope that he will identify himself. And he does: it is the groom's friend Bill, whom you met at a party over a year earlier.

We have all had subjective experiences similar to these at different times in our lives. Sometimes we recall our personal past by recollecting a wealth of information about a person or place, other times by just knowing that someone or something is familiar. Psychologists have begun to explore these two forms of subjective experience, which are referred to as *remembering* and *knowing* the past. Several studies have shown that recall of visual information about the physical setting or context of an event is crucial to having a "remember" experience. In one, college students were given a beeper that sounded unpredictably several times a day. Each time the beeper went off, they recorded what was happening (except when it sounded at inopportune times). When the students were later asked to remember these events, the episodes they recalled most accurately and confidently included visual images of what had occurred during the episode. The subjective sense of remembering almost invariably involved some sort of visual reexperiencing of an event.[9]

Why does retrieving visual images tend to make us feel strongly that we are remembering a real event? Part of the reason is that some of the same brain regions are involved in both visual imagery and visual perception.[10] Since we usually rely on these areas to perceive the external world, it should not be surprising that when we use them to create visual images, the images may feel like the mental residue of actual events. These observations have an important implication: creating visual images may lead us to believe that we are remembering an event even when the incident never happened.[11] By appreciating that subjective experiences of remembering are enhanced when we conjure up visual images, we can better understand incidents in which people appear to be recalling horrific events that never occurred.

Though it is clearly important, visual reexperiencing is probably not the sole basis of the subjective sense of remembering. We are also likely to feel that we are remembering something from the past when we can recall associations and ideas that occurred to us during the initial episode. For example, a recent article by a distinguished philosopher discusses at length some ideas about memory and conscious experience. As I read the article, I made many mental notes about points where I agreed with the analysis and points where I disagreed. If you now ask me about the article, I can state with full confidence that I clearly *remember* having read it. But I do not have any specific visual images of exactly where I was when I read it, what the article looked like, and so forth. I remember having read the article because I recall my specific thoughts and reactions to it.[12]

On the other hand, if we are distracted or preoccupied as an event unfolds, we may later have great difficulty remembering the details of what happened, although we may still have a general memory of it. Knowing but not remembering can sometimes be embarrassing. I once attended a reception in my honor before giving a lecture about memory to a large audience. I was introduced to numerous people at the reception, all the while preoccupied with mentally rehearsing my talk. In the midst of a conversation with several people, I extended my hand and introduced myself to a woman who had just joined the group. She seemed familiar, and I thought I might know her from somewhere. As the woman grasped my hand, she looked vexed and reminded me that we had met just a few minutes before! I had registered enough about her to "know" that she was familiar, but not enough to "remember" the specific moment when I first met her.

The British psychologists John Gardiner and Alan Parkin have recently reported something similar in the laboratory. Some participants in their experiment paid full attention to faces that were presented for study; others divided their attention between studying the faces and carrying out another task. Dividing attention reduced the likelihood that people later "remembered" having seen a face, but it had no effect on the likelihood that they "knew" the face had been presented. Other evidence from the laboratory shows that when a word is flashed too quickly to see clearly, it can lead people to say that they "know" the word was presented earlier—even though they did not consciously perceive the word when it was first presented.[13] Such findings help explain why you sometimes have the experience of encountering someone who is familiar without remembering who they are: you may have been preoccupied with other concerns when you first met the person and not have made the associations and connections necessary to remember the person's identity.

It should be evident, then, that whether we "remember" a past incident or just "know" that it happened depends on how we attend to the event in the first place and what kinds of information we can bring to mind when recalling it. But, as with field and observer memories, subjective experiences of remembering and knowing can also be influenced by how we go about retrieving a past event. In one simple experiment, people recalled previously studied words and then indicated whether they actually remembered them or simply knew the words had been on the study list. When people recalled the target word on their own, without any external hints, they were likely to indicate that they remembered the word from the list. When given cues or hints to help trigger their memory, people were more likely to indicate that they knew that a word had been on the list. Once again, the recollective experience of the rememberer depends on the way in which a memory is retrieved.[14]

The experience of "just knowing" is related to another experience we are all acquainted with: the sense that a bit of information is on the "tip of our tongue" but we cannot retrieve it. In both experiences, we have a strong conviction that we know or remember something, but we are not quite sure exactly what it is. My own research and other studies suggest that the tip-of-the-tongue experience arises in part because the rememberer can retrieve *some* of the desired information but not enough to produce full recall.[15] For example, if I ask you who was standing next to Aunt Helen at that wedding, you may be unable to recall Bill's name. However, you might be able to remember what he looks like and that his name begins with "B." These tidbits may produce a strong sense that you will eventually recognize or retrieve the name.

But new research has shown that there is another important source of the tip-of-the-tongue experience: one's familiarity with the hint or cue that triggers the retrieval attempt in the first place. A sense of familiarity with a retrieval cue can induce a strong—and often spurious—feeling of knowing. For example, when I cue you for Bill's name by asking who was next to Aunt Helen, your familiarity with your aunt may make you almost certain that you will be able to retrieve Bill's name—even though you may not in fact be able to do so.[16] Here we have yet another example in which a feeling of memory depends as much on what is happening in the present as on what happened in the past.

As argued by the cognitive psychologist Larry Jacoby, our subjective sense of remembering sometimes depends on theories or attributions we generate about why something seems familiar or why an image or idea suddenly or easily pops to mind. If our goal is remembering a past event, we may be inclined to attribute feelings of familiarity to the past; if our goal is to make a judgment or solve a problem, we may attribute similar feelings to the relative ease of the task at hand. As we will see, this is one reason why subjective experiences of remembering can sometimes be mistaken.[17]

THE PULL OF THE PAST
Three Stories

To appreciate more fully the impact of subjective experience in memory, I now turn to three stories in which reexperiencing the personal past took on an unusual, even overwhelming, significance. Marcel Proust and Franco Magnani both developed an intense and unrelenting obsession with memory that they explored through art. An aging Italian artist known by the initials GR came to an unusual appreciation of what it means to have a personal past when he lost his memory and then, almost miraculously, regained it.

Marcel Proust: Involuntary Memory

No single work of literature is more closely associated with human memory than Marcel Proust's *À la recherche du temps perdu (In Search of Lost Time)*.[18] The depth of Proust's obsession with recapturing the past is difficult to overstate. The eight volumes that constitute *À la recherche* were written over a period of nearly fifteen years, beginning around 1908 and concluding several months before his death in November 1922. The entire treatise exceeds three thousand pages, most concerned in one way or another with personal recollections or meditations on the nature of memory. Proust may have become so single-minded because he had largely withdrawn from society by the time he began writing his opus. He confined himself to his room throughout much of the writing, suffering from illness and exhaustion, and in so doing substituted a world of time for the world of space. But his obsession with the past also reflects Proust's passionate conviction that the truth of human experience could be grasped only through an understanding of memory and time.

In the most dramatic memory-related incident of the novel, the narrator, Marcel, is visiting his mother, who serves him tea and pastries known as *petites madeleines*. After dipping a madeleine into the tea and imbibing the mixture, he is overcome by an unexpected, overwhelming, and entirely mysterious sense of well-being. "Whence could it have come to me, this all-powerful joy?" he asks. "I sensed that it was connected with the taste of the tea and the cake, but that it infinitely transcended those savours, could not, indeed, be of the same nature. Where did it come from? What did it mean? How could I seize and apprehend it?"[19] He tries to induce the experience again by tasting several more mouthfuls of the potent mixture, but each experience is weaker than the previous one, leading him to conclude that the basis of the effect "lies not in the cup but in myself." He surmises that the tea and cake have somehow activated a past experience, and wonders whether he will be able to recall it consciously.

Then comes the extraordinary instant when the mystery is resolved: "And suddenly the memory revealed itself. The taste was that of the little crumb of madeleine which on Sunday mornings at Combray [the fictional name of Proust's childhood town] when I went to say good morning to her in her bedroom, my aunt Leonie used to give me, dipping it first in her own cup of tea." Marcel notes that he had never elsewhere encountered the combination of smells and tastes that characterized the episode at his aunt's house, thus making them uniquely effective cues for an elusive but powerful memory: "But when from a long-distant past nothing subsists, after the people are dead, after the things are broken and scattered, taste and smell alone, more fragile but more enduring, more immaterial, more persistent, more faithful, remain poised for a long time, like souls, remembering, waiting and hoping, amid the ruins of all the rest; and bear unflinchingly, in the tiny and almost impalpable drop of their essence, the vast structure of recollection."

The moment when the madeleine memory revealed itself was the moment when the narrator saw that memory could be both fragile and powerful. Memories that can be elicited only by specific tastes and smells are fragile: they can easily disappear because there are few opportunities for them to surface. But those that survive are also exceptionally powerful: having remained dormant for long periods of time, the sudden appearance of seemingly lost experiences cued by tastes or smells is a startling event.

The madeleine episode also highlights that reexperiencing one's personal past sometimes depends on chance encounters with objects that contain the keys to unlocking memories that might otherwise be hidden forever. But Marcel's recognition that *involuntary* recollections are fleeting, lasting only several seconds, and depend on rare confrontations with particular smells or sights, leads him to alter the focus of his quest for the past. As the novel progresses, his quest for self-understanding depends increasingly on the active, *voluntary* retrieval of his past.[20] He explores the self-defining role of voluntary recollection in one of the key scenes from the final novel in the series, *Time Regained*. At a gathering of old friends whom Marcel has not seen for many years, he strains to recall their identities and to place them in the context of his remembered experiences. In so doing he achieves a synthesis of past and present that heightens his appreciation of his own identity.

Proust also draws on concepts and analogies from the science of optics to develop an analogy of time and memory, which he made explicit in a 1922 letter. "The image (imperfect as it is) which seems to me best suited to convey the nature of that special sense," Proust wrote, "is that of a telescope, a telescope pointed at time, for a telescope renders visible for us stars invisible to the naked eye, and I have tried to render visible to the consciousness unconscious phenomena, some of which, having been entirely forgotten, are situated in the past."[21]

Proust further develops his optical analogy. The experience of remembering a past episode, Proust contends, is not based merely on calling to mind a stored memory image. Instead, a feeling of remembering emerges from the comparison of two images: one in the present and one in the past. Just as visual perception of the three-dimensional world depends on combining information from the two eyes, perception in time—remembering—depends on combining information from the present and the past. The renowned Proust scholar Roger Shattuck explains: "Proust set about to make us *see time*. . . . Merely to remember something is meaningless unless the remembered image is combined with a moment in the present affording a view of the same object or objects. Like our eyes, our memories must see double; these two images then converge in our minds into a single heightened reality."[22] Foreshadowing scientific research by more than a half-century, Proust achieved the penetrating insight that feelings of remembering result from a subtle interplay between past and present.

Franco Magnani: Obsessive Memory

The raw psychological power of memory that is so evident in Proust's writings is also illustrated vividly by the story of Franco Magnani, an artist who has relentlessly attempted to recapture old memories by preserving them in paint.[23] The target of Magnani's obsession is his childhood village of Pontito, located in the Italian hills of Castelvecchio, about 40 miles west of Florence. Magnani was born there in 1934 and lived in the village on and off until 1958, when he left for good. He set out to see the world, settling seven years later in San Francisco. Shortly thereafter, he began suffering from a mysterious illness that left him feverish and delirious, throwing him into both physical and psychological turmoil. In the midst of the illness, Magnani began to experience, on a nightly basis, vivid dreams of Pontito that combined a hallucinatory intensity with a wealth of minute detail that far exceeded his waking recollections of the village. The force of the nocturnal visions inspired Magnani, who had never painted seriously before, to try to capture his images with brush and canvas. The extraordinary images then exploded into his waking life as involuntary, intrusive recollections.

Magnani completed his first canvas of Pontito in 1967. Soon, his entire life focused on painting his memories of the village. "He often feels a great urgency to get the scene down on paper immediately," observes an acquaintance, Michael Pearce, "and has been known to leave a bar in mid-drink in order to begin a sketch."[24] Magnani's finished works are exquisitely detailed paintings of the buildings, streets, and fields that he remembers from Pontito. They rarely include people and are typically characterized by a tranquil stillness that lends them a sort of timeless and magical quality. In 1988, a San Francisco science museum, The Exploratorium, mounted an exhibition of Magnani's work. Susan Schwartzenberg, a photographer at the museum, had journeyed to Pontito and photographed the scenes depicted in Magnani's paintings, attempting to capture each one from the exact perspective indicated in the work. The Exploratorium exhibited the paintings juxtaposed with the photographs, and the results revealed that Magnani's memories were impressively, sometimes astonishingly, accurate. On the other hand, it is equally evident that Magnani has painted highly idealized pictures of the village, a kind of paradise lost in which the remembered world is more beautiful, symmetrical, and whole than the inevitably blemished reality. (See figures 1.3a and 1.3b.)

These observations fit with the neurologist Oliver Sacks's observation that Magnani's painted memories, though often startling in their accuracy, are fundamentally imaginative reconstructions—not slavish reproductions.[25]

FIGURE 1.3

a: Franco Magnani, "Via Mozza, la casa del nonno di Franco," 1987. 14 x 10½". Oil on museum board. Courtesy of the artist.

b: Susan Schwartzenberg, Photograph of "Via Mozza, la casa del nonno di Franco." Courtesy of the artist.

In Magnani's painting of his grandfather's home the length and trajectory of the stone path, the structure that connects the two buildings and the statue that is part of it, and the placement of individual windows and doors all document remarkable memory for a place Magnani had not seen for nearly thirty years when he completed the work in 1987. But it is also apparent that the painting is highly romantic and contains distortions: the flowerbed could not have been seen from the perspective used in the painting, nor could the lovely rooftop above the statue; the curved doorway shown on the left wall of the photograph is omitted from the painting; and there is a general sense of order and even perfection in the painting that is not present in the photograph.

For Magnani, as for Proust, fixation on the past spills over from the making of art into just about every aspect of his life; he thinks or talks of little other than Pontito. His endless reminiscing has cost him many friends, and he rarely goes out or travels. In short, he has been reduced to what Sacks calls "a sort of half existence in the present."[26]

I experienced some of these qualities when I visited Magnani in the summer of 1993 at his home outside San Francisco. I had not yet reached the front door of his house before noting the first signs of his obsession: a personalized "Pontito" license plate, and brickwork reminiscent of the buildings depicted in his paintings. When Magnani emerged from his garage/studio, I saw a tall, thin man who looked to be in his mid to late forties, even though he was about to turn sixty. Magnani showed me how he was renovating his entire kitchen with cabinets, tiles, and closets to resemble those he remembers from Pontito. He was working on the time-consuming project by himself, found it difficult to locate funds to support the expensive renovations, and had lost the use of his kitchen indefinitely—yet he beamed as he talked about the noble task he had undertaken. He sought to create a three-dimensional environment in which Pontito was transported out of the past so that it became part of the functioning present.[27] Telling me about the paintings on the walls of his home, he virtually shouted out his recollections, finally easing back into the present once the memory had run its course. The aura of the past was so acute during these incidents that I had the sense that I was witnessing a kind of rupture in time, as if I had been there when Proust first tasted the madeleine.

Magnani has returned to Pontito on two occasions since the museum exhibit. He was surprised and disappointed by unpleasant changes (the village is now nearly uninhabited) and by deviations from his recollections. Yet he was also gratified and occasionally overwhelmed by the chance to see and touch the world that had for so long existed only in memory and dream. Franco is still devoted to the Pontito of old, an enterprise that has always been more than a purely personal indulgence of vivid recollections: he has sought to preserve the memory of Pontito for others, to capture his extraordinary recollections in a form that allows them to affect and enrich the lives and memories of many. "It is a project that has no end," concludes Sacks, "can never be brought to a conclusion or completion."[28]

"GR": Memory Lost and Regained

If Marcel Proust sought his memories in the objects of everyday life and Franco Magnani found them in dreams and visions that imposed themselves on him, a sixty-seven-year-old Italian man known in the medical literature by the initials GR was involuntarily plunged into a world that had no past. A poet, painter, and art reviewer, GR was deeply immersed in various cultural projects when he awoke on the morning of March 19, 1992, in a profoundly confused state of mind. He could not move his right arm and had difficulty speaking. Most frighteningly, GR had no specific memories of his past and was even uncertain about his identity. He was rushed to a hospital, where brain scans showed that he had suffered a stroke that damaged the left thalamus of his brain.

As days and weeks passed, GR still could not remember his occupation. He did not recognize his own paintings. He could not recall the subjects of the books he had been writing. Though able to recognize and name his wife and children, he could not remember anything about them. GR was shown photographs of himself at art exhibitions and other salient events, but he professed no memory for any of it. The city of Milan, which he had known well, seemed entirely unfamiliar to him. He could not recollect any specific incidents from his life. GR was suffering from what neuropsychologists call *retrograde amnesia,* in which people have problems remembering experiences that occurred prior to a stroke, head injury, or some other physiological or psychological trauma. GR also had poor memory for ongoing, day-to-day experiences, what neuropsychologists call *anterograde amnesia.*[29]

As his amnesia continued unabated for months, his sense of well-being evaporated. "GR felt deeply depressed, hopeless about his amnesia to the point that he could not find the inspiration to paint again," commented the neurologists who treated him, "because, as he said, he 'had no more self to express.'" GR spent most of his time sleeping or in an inert state of apathy. When he was told facts about who he was and what he had done in the past, GR could retain some of them. But this was secondhand autobiographical knowledge, not genuine memory. Though it enabled GR to make a few statements about his past, he disparagingly characterized his acquired knowledge of himself as "relearned," lacking entirely a sense of "true remembrance."

About a year after his stroke, GR showed signs of an irregular heartbeat, so his physicians decided to implant a pacemaker. He was given a local anesthetic, but remained alert throughout the procedure. As he was lying quietly on the operating table, GR felt some discomfort as the surgeon prepared his chest for the pacemaker. Then, in a stunning instant, GR clearly remembered that he had experienced a virtually identical situation some twenty-five years earlier when he had undergone an operation for a hernia. Within a few seconds, he remembered other aspects of the earlier operation. Soon his head was swimming in a roiling sea of memories, as his past life came back to him in a torrent of images and thoughts. Overwhelmed by what he termed a "catharsis" of remembering, GR could do little but talk about his past for the next several days. His memories, at first chaotic, soon rearranged themselves into a sensible chronology. As he sorted through and made sense of this vast array of incidents from different points in time, GR eventually came to feel like the self that had existed before his stroke.

GR's story is almost without precedent. Retrograde amnesia is a common consequence of brain damage, and sometimes old memories that are seemingly lost gradually return to patients as they recover from head injuries or other medical conditions. But it is extraordinary for someone to lose his entire personal past and then recover it all in an instant, as a result of a single cue that happens to match a specific memory. Not all of GR's memory problems evaporated—he continues to have great difficulty remembering ongoing events—but he has his past back, and with it a sense of self. Just as the madeleines triggered a torrent of childhood remembrances in Proust's novel, some aspect of what GR felt or thought as the surgeon worked on his chest reminded him of a distant event that opened the floodgates to the past. The neurologists who reported GR's memory recovery called it the "petites madeleines phenomenon."[30]

Nobody knows why recalling a single event in this way would restore GR's memory for the rest of his past. His neurologists suggest that brain damage might have temporarily distorted the neuronal networks in which personal memories were stored, offering the analogy of a compact disc that has become stretched into the shape of an egg and is thus unreadable by retrieval systems. Somehow, they suggest, the successful recall of a single event serves to "re-set" the distorted networks into their normal form. However it happened, it was only after he pieced together the bewildering assortment of memories that he experienced as his alone that GR once again felt that he had a self to express.[31]

With their telescopes pointed at time—Proust and Magnani for years, GR for several extraordinary days—all three men magnified the self-defining role of memory. They make visible what is perhaps less apparent in, but no less characteristic of, the rest of us: our sense of ourselves depends crucially on the subjective experience of remembering our pasts.

ARE COMPUTERS REMEMBERERS?

The stories of Proust, Magnani, and GR would be virtually incomprehensible without acknowledging the subjective side of remembering. The experience of remembering is what makes the everyday manifestations of episodic memory that we all know—the experience of mental time travel—a distinctly and perhaps uniquely human activity. Clearly, the ability merely to store and retrieve information is not a unique feature of the human mind, or even of living organisms. Every time we type on our personal computer, we interact with a formidable memory system.[32]

Cognitive scientists have pursued an analogy between human and computer memory at the level of software: the instructions, programs, and routines that are executed either by cells in our brains or silicon chips and wires in a computer. Many cognitive scientists see the human mind as a particular kind of computing device, and they assume that if they understood the rules by which the mind operates, they could program a computer to mimic it exactly. Could a computer engage in mental time travel, revisiting and reexperiencing the past, the way we do? Could a computer ever feel that a memory "belongs" to it, as Will McDonough feels that his recollections of the Boston Garden belong to him?

This question is closely related to a more elementary one: Are computers, in principle, capable of any form of conscious experience? This issue is typically broached with reference to the notion of a "Turing test," which stems from the work of the great British mathematician Alan Turing.[33] A Turing test is a hypothetical situation in which an observer asks questions of two respondents—one human and one computer, but disguised so that the observer does not know which is which. If the observer is unable to determine, by relentless probing, which is which, then the computer passes the Turing test. Many proponents of artificial intelligence (AI) have contended that when a computer passes a Turing test, it must be granted the ability to think like a human. For our purposes, let's grant this claim and ask a further question: Is a computer that passes a Turing test also consciously aware of its thoughts in a way that is similar to, or even remotely resembles, conscious awareness in a human being?

Proponents of "strong AI," who take the view that some day soon computers will exhibit all human mental abilities, answer the question with a resounding yes.[34] Some philosophers do, too. For instance, Daniel Dennett argues that human consciousness is produced by the operation of something like a computer program, what he calls a "virtual machine" that is installed and implemented in the parallel hardware of the human brain: "[If] all the phenomena of human consciousness are explicable as 'just' the activity of a virtual machine realized in the astronomically adjustable connections of the human brain, then, in principle, a suitably 'programmed' robot, a silicon-based computer brain, would be conscious, would have a self."[35] If Dennett's robot is granted consciousness and self, then it should probably also be granted full rights to subjective experiences of remembering and the ability to engage in mental time travel. Dennett's vision is reminiscent of the fictional worlds depicted by such writers as William Gibson in *Neuromancer* and *Johnny Mnemonic,* where humans and computers plug into a common cyberspace—a mental highway system in which information moves from mind to mind and the subjective experiences of humans and computers merge imperceptibly into each other.

The idea that human consciousness is a software package that just happens to be installed in brain cells is seductive, but this kind of analysis has also elicited incisive criticisms from philosophers and scientists who believe that it is naive.[36] If a computing robot cannot achieve rudimentary consciousness, then it is hard to see how it could ever engage in subjective experiences of remembering, or have the feeling that memories "belong" to it.

The debate over computer consciousness can help us to sharpen our ideas about exactly what kind of evidence we need before concluding that *any* act of memory involves a conscious experience of remembering. In experiments I have mentioned, for example, when a person says that she either "remembers" an item or simply "knows" it, the experimenter is willing to take these statements as reflections of the quality of her recollective experience. It would be simple to program a computer to make these two kinds of responses in a simulated memory experiment, but nobody would want to argue on that basis that the computer remembers some items and knows others in the same subjective sense that people do. What would it take to convince us that it does? Is there a Turing test for recollective experience?

In Ridley Scott's movie *Blade Runner,* computer technology and bioengineering conspire to produce a species of "replicants" that seem human in virtually all respects. Rachel is a newly developed experimental replicant that has been implanted with a rich set of memories that provide her with a personal past, a past so compelling that she is unaware of her nonhuman status. Deckard, whose job is to perform a kind of Turing test to weed out wayward replicants, awakens her to reality by reeling off a series of Rachel's most personal childhood memories and informing her that "those aren't your memories; they're somebody else's." But Rachel's emotional reactions to these memories, as indicated by her tears, facial expression, and tone of voice, are intense. Deckard is thus convinced that the memories do in some sense belong to her, and so concludes that she should be allowed to live as a human. Rachel has, in effect, passed a Turing test for recollective experience: Deckard cannot distinguish this replicant's subjective response to her memories from that of a person because Rachel shows the full subjective force of memory's power. The depth of subjective experience Rachel displays is the hallmark of explicit remembering in people. Because this is such an integral part of human remembering, compelling evidence of intense subjective experience is what it would take for most of us to be convinced that a computer does indeed remember in the same sense that we do.[37]

The neurobiologist Gerald Edelman has argued that the richness of human recollective experience "cannot be adequately represented by the impoverished language of computer science—'storage,' 'retrieval,' 'input,' 'output.'"[38] I agree with him. As Edelman emphasizes and we will see in later chapters, subjective experiences of remembering are closely linked with particular systems and networks in the brain. Consequently, I am skeptical that software that is not grounded in this biological substrate will ever have the experience of revisiting its past.(See figure 1.4.)

By looking at the end product of memory, the recollective experience of the rememberer, I have been attempting to bring to the foreground some of the key manifestations of memory's power in psychological life. But to fathom the nature and function of explicit remembering more deeply, we need to start at the beginning of the memory process and work our way through again to the end. The

FIGURE 1.4

Richard E. Schaffer, "The Color of Memory," 1988. 22 x 30". Mixed media on paper. Courtesy of the artist.

Richard Schaffer, an Arizona artist who employs visual symbols to express ideas about memory, provides a fitting summary reflection on the relationship between computer memory and human memory in his multimedia collage, "The Color of Memory." The left side of the piece contains an actual floppy disk along with various forms of computer code and digital readout; the right side consists of a series of fragmentary images, alluding to the visual information that is such an important part of human recollective experience. In the context of the preceding discussion, Schaffer's piece suggests—and I strongly concur—that the computer is a retriever of information but not a rememberer of experiences. Whether the gulf that separates the two is entirely and forever impassable remains to be seen.

subjective sense of pastness that makes our memories feel as though they belong to us, that drove Proust and Magnani to the brink of obsession, and that made GR feel that he once again had a self to express is a fundamental and perhaps singular feature of human memory. We need to understand more about the underlying processes that make the experience possible.

TWO

BUILDING MEMORIES
Encoding and Retrieving the
Present and the Past

ONE OF MY FAVORITE PLACES is the Museum of Modern Art in
midtown Manhattan. A native New Yorker, I have made regular pil-
grimages to this mecca of art since high school days, and have come
to regard many of the paintings there as wise and familiar old friends.
Like close friends, however, they cannot always be there when you
want them. More than once I have returned to a favorite spot, eagerly
anticipating another look at an esteemed painting by de Chirico,
Hopper, or Klee, only to learn that it was away on extended loan.
Although the painting's absence is disappointing, I sometimes attempt
to make up for it by conducting an informal study of my own memory for the piece: What objects and people does the painting include,
and how are they located relative to one another? How big is the
work? What are the dominant colors and important themes? I can
check the accuracy of my answers by locating a reproduction in the
museum shop.

The French artist Sophie Calle wondered what aspects of a painting linger in the memories of viewers who are familiar with it. To find
out, she conducted a kind of naturalistic memory experiment with an
artistic twist. Calle asked a cross section of museum personnel to
describe their recollections of several paintings that had been removed
from their usual locations at the Museum of Modern Art. She pro-

ceeded to create a "memory ghost" for each missing painting—
exhibiting the exact words used by the museum workers to describe
their recollections of the piece. The most striking outcome was the
sheer variety of recollections that her inquiry elicited. Some people
recalled only an isolated color or object; others remembered at length
subtle nuances of form, space, people, and things.

Calle's observations imply that different people retain and recollect
very different aspects of their everyday environments. Why would this
be so? Scientists agree that the brain does not operate like a camera or
a copying machine. Then what aspects of reality do remain in memory once an episode has concluded? These kinds of questions have
dogged every philosopher, psychologist, and neuroscientist who has
thought seriously about the nature of remembering and forgetting.
Throughout much of the history of scholarly thinking about memory, dating back to the Greeks, people have approached these questions by adopting a spatial metaphor of the mind. The Greek
philosophers held that memory is like a wax tablet on which experiences are imprinted, perhaps forever; centuries later, Sigmund Freud
and William James both conjectured that memories are like objects
placed in rooms of a house. One pundit compared memory to a
garbage can that contains a random assortment of objects.[1]

The cognitive psychologist Ulric Neisser called the idea that faithful copies of experience are kept in the mind, only to reappear again
at some later time pretty much in their original form, the "reappear-
ance hypothesis." Neisser proposed instead that only bits and pieces of
incoming data are represented in memory. These retained fragments of
experience in turn provide a basis for reconstructing a past event,
much as a paleontologist is able to reconstruct a dinosaur from fragments of bone. "Out of a few stored bone chips," reflected Neisser,
"we remember a dinosaur."[2]

A visual analogue of Neisser's reflections is found in the work of
the Israeli artist Eran Shakine. Shakine has explored his personal past
by making collaged paintings in which fragments of old photographs
and text are submerged in layers of milky white paint as exemplified
by his painting "Hadassah" (figure 2.1). Shakine struggles with the
seeming paradox that our sense of self, the foundation of our psychological existence, depends crucially on these fragmentary and often
elusive remnants of experience. What we believe about ourselves is
determined by what we remember about our pasts. If memory
worked like a video recorder, allowing us to replay the past in exact
detail, we could check our beliefs about ourselves against an objective

FIGURE 2.1

Eran Shakine, "Hadassah," 1992. 12 x 16". Collage, oil, and varnish on plywood. Courtesy of the artist.

Snippets of old buildings and a barely perceptible family photograph refer to different stages in the artist's personal history that now exist only as hazy bits and pieces of memory.

record of what happened in our lives. We must make do instead with the bits and pieces of the past that memory grants us.

The general idea that memories are built from fragments of experience can help us understand key aspects of the rememberer's recollective experience, as well as memory distortions and effects of implicit memory, to be discussed in the coming chapters. For now, it is important to understand something more about how the fragments are constructed and reconstructed.

BUBBLES P. AND THE NATURE OF ENCODING

Bubbles P., a professional gambler from Philadelphia, spends virtually all his time making bets: shooting craps at local gaming clubs, dealing cards in illegal poker games, attempting to come up with new systems to beat the numbers. He is not a highly educated man—Bubbles claims to have read only two books in his entire life—but he is capable of certain feats of memory that are well beyond the abilities of even the most erudite Ph.D.s. Most people have difficulty recalling in correct order a string of more than seven digits immediately after seeing or hearing them. When the task is to repeat them backward, most people remember even fewer digits. But Bubbles P.'s digit memory is equally spectacular in either direction.[3] To appreciate his ability, inspect each of the digits at the end of this sentence for one second each, then look away from the page and immediately try to recall them in reverse order: 43902641974935483256. I suspect that by the time you worked your way back to 8, 4, or 5, you were already having problems going any further, and I would be willing to place a bet that nobody made it to 0, much less all the way back to the beginning. Bubbles P., however, can rattle off in correct backward order every one of the twenty numbers in this sequence and similar ones. How does he do it? Has he simply been gifted with an extraordinary, perhaps photographic, memory?

The answer likely resides in the same process that contributes to constructing fragments of experience. Psychologists refer to it as an *encoding* process—a procedure for transforming something a person sees, hears, thinks, or feels into a memory. Encoding can be thought of as a special way of paying attention to ongoing events that has a major impact on subsequent memory for them.

Psychologists first recognized the importance of encoding processes during debates about short-term memory that raged in the 1960s.

Short-term memories last for only seconds. Nowadays, researchers believe that such temporary records depend on a specialized system, called *working memory,* that holds small amounts of information for brief time periods, as in the backward recall task you just performed. Everyone is familiar with the operation of working memory from experiences in day-to-day life. Imagine that you need to look up a friend's number in the phone book. You find the number, then walk across the room to make the call, all the while madly repeating the digits to yourself as rapidly as you can. If you are distracted for even a moment during your walk to the phone, you will need to consult the book again; if you punch in the number successfully, you will probably forget it almost immediately. Why are such memories so fleeting?

Part of the answer is that working memory depends on a different network of brain structures than long-term memory systems do. Some patients with damage to the inner part of the temporal lobes in the center of the brain have little or no difficulty retaining a string of digits for several seconds, yet they have great difficulty forming and explicitly remembering more enduring memories. Other patients who have suffered damage to a specific part of the parietal lobe on the cortical surface can form long-term memories but cannot hold and repeat back a string of digits. They lack a specific part of working memory, known as the *phonological loop,* that most of us rely on when we need to hold a small amount of linguistic information in mind for several seconds.[4]

This is where the concept of encoding comes in. By relying on your phonological loop to repeat a phone number madly to yourself, you encode it only superficially. To establish a durable memory, incoming information must be encoded much more thoroughly, or deeply, by associating it meaningfully with knowledge that already exists in memory. You must do more than simply recycle the information in the phonological loop. Suppose that instead of just repeating the phone number—555–6024—to yourself over and over, you attempt to make the number meaningful in some way. For example, if you play golf (as I do), you might encode the number by thinking that 555 is the yardage of a par–5 hole and that 6024 is the length of a relatively short 18-hole course. You have now carried out a deep encoding and should be able to remember the information much longer and more accurately than if you merely repeat it. This is known in the psychological literature as a "depth of processing" effect.[5]

The same sort of effect is probably at work in cases like that of

Bubbles P. Bubbles is knowledgeable about numbers and seems able to segregate effortlessly a long string of them into meaningful units or chunks. Rather than frantically recycling them, as most of us do, Bubbles uses the skill he has developed with numbers through years of gambling to link incoming digits to knowledge already in his memory. Bubbles does not have a generally extraordinary memory: his memory for words, faces, objects, and locations—anything other than numbers—is no better than average.

Elaborative Encoding

Memory researchers have tried to devise special techniques to gain control over the encoding operations that a person performs, and these operations have played a crucial role in the unfolding story of memory and amnesia research during the past twenty years.[6] Suppose I tell you that an hour from now, I will test your ability to recall the following words: floor, car, tree, cake, shirt, flower, cup, grass, dog, table. You might try to remember the words by conjuring up visual images, by simply repeating the words again and again, or by making up a story that connects the words to one another. As long as I leave you to your own devices, I cannot learn much about how encoding processes influence memory. I need to come up with some way of controlling how you think about the to-be-remembered items.

Memory researchers have solved this problem by using what is known as an orienting task. Instead of allowing people to memorize the target items in any manner they please, an orienting task guides encoding by requiring a person to answer a specific question about the target. For example, I could induce you to carry out a deep, semantic encoding of target words by asking for a yes or no answer to questions such as, "Is *shirt* a type of clothing?" You cannot answer this question accurately without thinking about the meaning of the word *shirt*. To induce you to engage in shallow, nonsemantic encoding of the word, I could ask you to answer a question such as, "Does *shirt* contain more vowels or more consonants?" You can answer this question easily without attending to the meaning of the word. If I later test your ability to recollect *shirt* and other words on the list, I can be fairly confident that you will be able to recall or recognize many of the words that you encoded semantically and few of the words that you encoded nonsemantically.

This finding may not seem particularly surprising; everyday experience suggests that something that is meaningful will be more easily remembered than something that is not. But it turns out that only a certain kind of semantic encoding promotes high levels of memory performance—an *elaborative* encoding operation that allows you to integrate new information with what you already know. For example, if I induce you to encode one of our study list words by posing the question, "Is *shirt* a type of insect?" you must pay attention to the meaning of the word in order to provide the correct answer. As you formulate a response to this question, however, you do not integrate the target word with your preexisting knowledge of shirts—that is, you do not carry out an effective elaboration of the word *shirt*. If I test you after you have answered this kind of orienting question, you will show surprisingly poor memory for whether the word *shirt* was on the list.[7]

In our everyday lives, memory is a natural, perhaps automatic, by-product of the manner in which we think about an unfolding episode. If we want to improve our chances of remembering an incident or learning a fact, we need to make sure that we carry out elaborative encoding by reflecting on the information and relating it to other things we already know. Laboratory studies have shown that simply intending to remember something is unlikely to be helpful, unless we translate that intention into an effective elaborative encoding. For example, when preparing for an exam, a good student may make a special effort to form meaningful mental associations among the study materials, whereas the same student may not bother engaging in such elaborative encoding if she is not going to be tested. In my earlier example, carrying out the orienting task—answering the question, "Is *shirt* a type of clothing?"—ensures that you have already made effective use of elaborative encoding processes; "trying to remember" adds nothing beyond that.

The issue can be turned around, too: most experiences that we recall effortlessly from our day-to-day existence—yesterday's important lunch date, the big party last weekend, last year's summer vacation—are not initially encoded with any particular intention to remember them. Occasionally, the apparent significance of an event may prompt us to make a special effort to encode it deeply. However, day-to-day existence would be precarious and probably unmanageable if we had to make an intentional effort to encode each and every episode from our daily lives in order to be able to recollect it later. Instead, a kind of natural selection drives us. What we already know shapes what we select and encode; things that are meaningful to us spontaneously elicit the kind of elaborations that promote later recall. Our memory systems are built so that we are likely to remember what is most important to us.

Carrying out a deep, elaborative encoding influences not only the quantity of what can be remembered but also the quality of our recollective experience. As I noted in chapter 1, when we meet a new person and encode information elaboratively, we are more likely later to "remember" the episode; if we do not elaborate, we are more likely to "just know" that the person seems familiar. Elaborative encoding is a critical and perhaps necessary ingredient of our ability to remember in rich and vivid detail what has happened to us in the past.[8]

But the dependence of explicit memory on elaboration has a downside, too: if we do not carry out elaborative encoding, we will be left with impoverished recollections. Experiments have shown that people are surprisingly poor at remembering what is on the front and back of a penny, despite seeing and handling pennies all the time.[9] It is likely, however, that we encode the features of a penny quite superficially, because using pennies in everyday life requires only that we notice the general shape and color of the coin. The encoding process can halt once we have extracted the necessary information; there is no need to carry out a more elaborate analysis of the coin. In this example, we are behaving like experimental volunteers who perform shallow or superficial orienting tasks, and later recall little or nothing of what they have seen. If we operate on automatic pilot much of the time and do not reflect on our environment and our experiences, we may pay a price by retaining only sketchy memories of where we have been and what we have done.

Encoding and Mnemonic Devices

Elaborative encoding is a critical component of virtually all popular memory-improvement techniques. The oldest example of a memory-improvement strategy is visual imagery mnemonics, first developed by the Greek orator Simonides in 477 B.C. As the story goes, Simonides, a poet, was called to recite verse at a large banquet. During the course of the evening, he was unexpectedly summoned outside to meet two young men; the moment he left, the roof of the banquet hall collapsed, crushing and mutilating beyond recognition all the guests. Simonides became a hero because he was able to reconstruct the guest list by imagining each location around the table, which brought to mind the person who had been sitting there.

He accomplished this feat by using a system of mnemonics he had developed known as the method of *loci,* which became famous in ancient Greece after this incident. The method involves encoding information into memory by conjuring up vivid mental images and mentally placing them in familiar locations. Later, at the time of attempted recall, one consults the locations, just as Simonides did.[10] If, for example, you wanted to remember to buy beer, potato chips, and toothpaste, you could use rooms in your home as locations, and imagine your bedroom afloat in beer, your kitchen stuffed from top to bottom with bags of potato chips, and your living room slathered with toothpaste. Upon arriving at the store, you could then take a mental walk around your house and "see" what is in each room.

Modern practitioners use the method of loci and other, related imagery techniques to perform such feats as remembering all the names and numbers listed in good-sized telephone books. These accomplishments are nothing new, however. Greek orators used mnemonics to memorize speeches of extraordinary length, and Roman generals used them to remember the names of tens of thousands of men in their command. During the Middle Ages, scholastics used mnemonics to aid in the learning of interminable religious tomes. In fact, throughout the Middle Ages, mnemonics played a major role in society, exerting a large influence on artistic and religious life.[11]

By the fifteenth and sixteenth centuries, Simonides' relatively simple method of loci had been superseded by increasingly baroque "memory theaters" that were conceived and drawn by some of Europe's most inventive minds. These intricate and sometimes beautiful structures consisted of hundreds of locations, each containing ideas and precepts that were frequently mystical. Learning all the locations and precepts in a memory theater—into which one could later mentally deposit new to-be-remembered information—was itself an arduous, sometimes impossible task. The excesses of mnemonic systems eventually created a backlash against them.[12]

My central point is that the core cognitive act of visual imagery mnemonics—creating an image and linking it to a mental location—is a form of deep, elaborative encoding. Mnemonic techniques produce rich and detailed encodings that are tightly linked to preexisting knowledge, yet are distinctively different from other items in memory. It also seems likely, in light of my earlier discussion about the importance of visual reexperiencing in conscious recollection, that the visual format of imagery mnemonics enhances its usefulness as an aid to explicit remembering.[13]

Elaborative encoding has also turned out to be important in cases of mnemonists like Bubbles P. Psychologists at Carnegie Mellon University wanted to determine whether ordinary people could be trained to remember more than seven or so digits after a single exposure. They invited two average undergraduates to the laboratory for daily sessions in which they were presented with, and attempted to recall, strings of digits. For the first several weeks of training, nothing much happened. One of the students then ceased training, but the other, known by the initials SF, persisted. Soon thereafter, his digit span began to rise systematically, and then spectacularly. After several months of training, SF could recall over eighty digits in correct order after being exposed to them only once.

Did the training strengthen a general-purpose memory muscle? Could anyone achieve a similar feat just by engaging in memory exercises? Clearly not. SF's remarkable accomplishments owe to his use of elaborative encoding. At about the time when his digit span began to improve, SF hit on a technique for carrying out elaborative analyses of incoming digit strings. He was a runner on the college track team, and called on his detailed knowledge of the meaning and significance of running times in order to encode the otherwise meaningless digits. For example, he might code the string 4125 as a "four minute, twelve and one half second mile, not bad for me on a windy day." The growth of his digit span tracked the increasing sophistication of his elaborative strategies. Yet SF's memory had not improved in any general sense. When asked at the end of training to recall strings of letters, SF could manage no more than about seven.[14]

Chess masters, too, can exhibit phenomenal memory for the locations of chess pieces on a board. After just a single five-second exposure to a board from an actual game, international masters in one study remembered the locations of nearly all twenty-five pieces, whereas novices could remember the locations of only about four pieces. Moreover, it did not matter whether the masters knew that their memory for the board would be tested later; they performed just as well when they glanced at the board with no intention to remember it. But when the masters were shown a board consisting of randomly arranged pieces that did not represent a meaningful game situation, they could remember no more than the novices. Later studies of high-level experts in bridge and electronics, among other fields, have revealed the same effect: experts' level of recall greatly exceeds that of novices for meaningful configurations of information within their domain of expertise, but it is no better than novices for random arrangements of the same information or for information outside their domain.[15]

Building up the extensive knowledge base that is required to support the supermemory of a skilled expert does not occur overnight. In a range of fields, it takes about ten years of extensive study, practice, and preparation to achieve an internationally recognized level of expertise. The knowledge base that is built during that decade provides the basis for a highly refined and powerful form of elaborative encoding that enables experts to pick out key information efficiently and to imbue it with meaning by integrating it with preexisting knowledge. This idea helps to explain how experienced actors memorize lengthy scripts. Recent studies have shown that rather than attempting rote memorization, actors analyze scripts for clues to the motivations and goals of their characters; memory is a natural by-product of this elaborative encoding. As one actor put it, "I don't really memorize. There is no effort involved . . . it just happens. One day early on, I know the lines." An actor's search for the deep meanings in a script often involves extended analyses of the exact words used by a character, which in turn promotes verbatim recall of precisely what was said, not just the general gist of it.[16]

The concept of elaborative encoding might even help explain some of the strange memory aberrations in people known as autistic savants. These individuals have low IQs and poor social skills that make it difficult for them to function in everyday life. Yet, as exemplified by Dustin Hoffman's character in the popular movie *Rain Man,* they may have spectacular memory capacities. One boy known by the initials JD received a diagnosis of autism when he was five years old. He had become socially withdrawn and started to make bizarre squawking noises and rocking movements by the age of three. His language development lagged behind other children of the same age.[17]

But JD's parents also noticed that he possessed isolated pockets of extraordinary visual memory. Without being able to read, four-year-old JD could spell out words with his play blocks that had appeared briefly on a TV screen. On family trips, JD remembered the exact route they had taken previously and became extremely upset if the driver deviated even slightly from it. His parents also noticed that JD had an uncanny ability to perform tasks that require complex visual analysis. While still young, he could assemble a five hundred-piece jigsaw puzzle in about two minutes!

The psychologist Lynn Waterhouse tested JD when he was eighteen years old. His vocabulary was still at the level of a six-year-old's, but on intelligence tests that require copying complex figures with a set of blocks or retaining visual memory for the location of an object, JD scored phenomenally high. Like Bubbles P. and SF, however, JD's exceptional memory is limited. For instance, he has a hard time remembering faces, not to mention words. He can effortlessly elaborate on and remember visual patterns, but cannot elaborate on or remember much else.

The Museum Test

The notion of elaboration also provides interesting perspectives on the recollections of the Museum of Modern Art personnel in the project I mentioned earlier. Several of them were asked to recall the Magritte painting, "The Menaced Assassin." (See figure 2.2.) Their memory reports are revealing:

1: There's a lot of pink flesh, red blood, guys in black. The background is blue with French ironwork on the balcony, the bedroom is beige, but the only striking color is that blood painted red that looks like ketchup.

2: It's a painting with a smooth surface, an easy one to spot check. It is approximately five feet high and seven feet long. It is framed in a plain, dark, walnut-stained molding, something austere. I never liked it. I don't like stories in painting. I don't like trying to figure them out. That's why I never gave it any time.

3: It has a film noir sort of feel, a mystery novel look to it. The puzzle is there. You have all those little clues that will probably lead you nowhere; there are men dressed in dark coats, and black bowler hats, the way Albert Finney was dressed in *Murder on the Orient Express,* placed in a room with a dead body. In the center, the one who seems to be the perpetrator is lifting the needle of a phonograph. Two weird-looking individuals are hiding to the side. There is a face looking from the balcony, almost like a sun on the horizon. And, when you look at her carefully, you realize that the towel probably conceals a decapitated head.

4: I think it's just a murder scene. Men in dark suits, a pale woman and dashes of red blood. That's all I remember.[18]

FIGURE 2.2

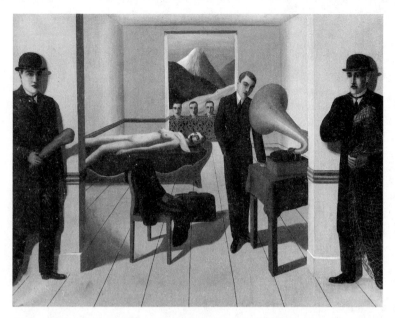

René Magritte, "The Menaced Assassin," 1926. 59¼" x 6' 4⅞". Oil on canvas. The Museum of Modern Art, New York. Kay Sage Tanguy Fund. Photograph © 1996 The Museum of Modern Art, New York.

Sophie Calle, an artist, queried museum personnel about their recollections of Magritte's painting, and elicited a wide variety of memories. (See page 50.)

Based on what they recollected, I feel I can make reasonably confident guesses about their identities: comment #4 probably belongs to a security guard or other nonprofessional staff, as does #1, which focuses solely on the physical features of the painting. Comment #2, which describes the work's exact measurements and properties of its frame, likely comes from someone charged with maintaining the painting. And the thematically rich set of memories in #3 no doubt belong to a curator or similar art professional. The rationale for these educated guesses is simple. What people remember about a painting is heavily influenced by how they think about or encode it, and exactly which aspects of a painting are elaborated depends on what kind of knowledge is already available in one's long-term memory.

Encoding and remembering are virtually inseparable. But the close relationship between the two can sometimes cause problems in our everyday lives. We remember only what we have encoded, and what we encode depends on who we are—our past experiences, knowledge, and needs all have a powerful influence on what we retain. This is one reason why two different people can sometimes have radically divergent recollections of the same event.(See figure 2.3.)

SCANNING THE MIND
Encoding Processes and the Brain

Memory is part of the brain's attempt to impose order on the environment.[19] In recent years, new insights into the brain substrates of elaborative encoding have emerged from studies that use powerful new functional neuroimaging techniques—tools that allow scientists to observe the activity of particular brain regions while people perform tasks designed to tap perception, language, memory, or other cognitive processes. The most advanced of these brain scanning techniques is known as positron emission tomography (PET). In a PET study, an experimental volunteer lies in a supine position, and the scanner forms a doughnut-shaped ring around the person's head. When the scanner is turned on, it provides a precise reading of blood flow in localized brain regions.[20] The general rationale underlying PET scanning experiments is that when a brain region is heavily involved in a cognitive task, it should become more active, and hence require more blood uptake, than a region that is little involved or uninvolved in the task. A related technique, known as functional magnetic resonance imaging (functional MRI), also

FIGURE 2.3

Jerry Coker, "The Memory Tree Man," 1993. 15 x 10¼ x 1". Mixed media on found metal. Marion Harris Gallery, Simsbury, Connecticut.

Coker is a self-taught maker of masks who uses scrap metal and other everyday materials to create expressive faces of people he remembers from his childhood. In "The Memory Tree Man" the metal face is that of a migrant worker traveling with his family in rural Arkansas. They came upon the young Jerry as he was playing near his grandfather's apple tree. The family stopped and stared at the tree with great interest. Sensing what they wanted, Jerry asked the migrants if they wished to pick some apples. They pulled out several bushels, filled them up, and happily chatted with Jerry about coming back the next day.

Jerry's grandfather was none too pleased, however, when the worker dutifully returned and demanded all the apples remaining on the tree. The migrant insisted that Jerry had told him he could pick all the apples he wished. But Jerry swore to his grandfather that he never promised anything. Was one of the two parties fibbing? Or had they remembered the event differently? Jerry's grandfather must have known something about how different people encode different aspects of the same event, because he came to the wise conclusion that only the apple tree knew what had actually happened. He worked out an equitable settlement between the boy and the worker, but he could not bridge the gulf between the two different versions of the past that each maintained.[21]

FIGURE 2.4

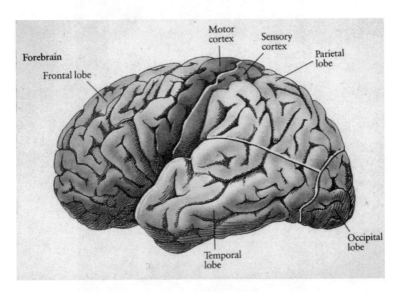

Each hemisphere of the cerebral cortex is divided into four major lobes, shown in this view of the surface of one hemisphere. The frontal lobes are a vast territory consisting of distinct subregions that play important roles in such processes as elaborative encoding, strategic retrieval, working memory, and recall of source information (see chapter 4). Specific regions within the parietal, occipital, and temporal lobes participate in the storage of different aspects or attributes of long-term memories (see chapter 3). These cortical areas cooperate closely with structures in the inner sectors of the brain, such as the hippocampus (see figure 5.1), to allow us to remember explicitly our ongoing experiences. Reprinted from F. E. Bloom and A. Lazerson, *Brain, Mind, and Behavior,* 2d ed. (New York: W. H. Freeman Co., 1988).

measures changes in regional blood flow across different task conditions.

A group of researchers at the University of Toronto that included Fergus Craik, a primary developer of the depth of processing framework, carried out PET scans while volunteers performed either a deep, elaborative encoding task or a shallow, nonelaborative one.[22] To determine which brain regions are specifically activated by the elaborative encoding task, the researchers subtracted the estimates of blood flow in the nonelaborative task from the estimates of blood flow in the elaborative task. They observed a strong region of activation (high blood flow) in the frontal lobes, the vast region of cortex that occupies the forepart of the brain. (See figure 2.4.) Blood flow increases associated with elaborative encoding were seen in a restricted area in the lower front part of the left frontal lobe (the left inferior prefrontal cortex), and the same or similar regions have been activated in other PET experiments that also require people to carry out deep or elaborative analyses. These results have been confirmed recently in a separate experiment using functional MRI. In addition, patients who have suffered damage to these frontal regions often have encoding problems: they fail to organize and categorize new information as it comes into memory. The left inferior prefrontal cortex plays an important role in "deep" or elaborative processing.[23]

Evidence showing frontal lobe involvement in encoding operations indicates that the cognitive processes identified by memory researchers can be related to specific regions of the brain. Further information concerning how the brain encodes incoming information comes from studies of event-related potentials, or ERPS—electrical waveforms in the brain that are elicited by specific sights, sounds, or other stimuli. Deep encoding processes are reflected in a specific part of the ERP known as the P300, a bump in the electrical waveform that occurs about one-third of a second after a person is exposed to a word or some other external stimulus. When something unusual or highly distinctive occurs—like a loud, jolting sound in a stream of quiet, soft tones—the brain emits an especially large P300. This heightened electrical activity reflects the extra processing that the brain devotes to novel, distinctive events. As you might expect, larger P300s during encoding tend to be associated with greater subsequent recall.[24]

Encoding of novel events also involves a structure familiar to memory researchers: the hippocampus. The hippocampus is a small, horseshoe-shaped structure tucked away deep in the inner or medial parts of the temporal lobes (see figure 5.1). Memory researchers have focused on the hippocampus for the past several decades because research on brain-injured patients suggested that damage to the hippocampus can produce a severe loss of memory for recent experiences. This conclusion has been modified somewhat because of newer evidence, but there is no doubt that the hippocampus is one of several anatomically related structures that play an important role in explicit remembering.

Some PET scanning studies have shown that the hippocampus becomes extremely active when people view pictures of certain scenes, like a rain forest in South America or a mountain range in Tibet. A PET experiment that I conducted with several colleagues revealed activity in the hippocampus when people saw "impossible" shapes and tried to classify them.[25] These neuroimaging studies suggest that part of the encoding process involves a hippocampal response to novelty. When the hippocampus becomes active during a novel event, our attention is drawn to it. Then another network may kick in, involving the left inferior frontal lobe, which makes available a wealth of semantic associations and knowledge—the stuff of elaborative encoding.

Taken together, the behavioral and physiological evidence I have marshaled highlights that memories of past experiences are natural and to some extent inevitable outcomes of the ways in which we think about and analyze the world. For better or worse, our recollections are largely at the mercy of our elaborations; only those aspects of experience that are targets of elaborative encoding processes have a high likelihood of being remembered subsequently. These targets of elaboration are the remains of experience that populate our minds—the bone chips of the dinosaur alluded to by Ulric Neisser, and the hazy bits and pieces of memory painted by Eran Shakine. More extensive elaborations leave more bone chips in their wake, thus promoting rich recollections of what we saw, felt, and thought during an episode. To a large extent, then, our memories are our elaborations. Or perhaps I should say that our memories are built on our elaborations, because, as I will show, the determinants of explicit remembering are not quite so simple.

HISTORICAL INTERLUDE
The Story of Richard Semon

The study of memory, like that of any scientific endeavor, has a history full of pioneering figures whose achievements are recognized and honored by researchers active in the field today. As a graduate student, I became intrigued by Richard Semon, who played an unappreciated role in the history of memory research. My curiosity was sparked by tantalizing comments from some of the twentieth-century's most towering intellects, such as the philosopher Bertrand Russell and the physicist Erwin Schrödinger, concerning the great value of his work. Hardly anyone working on memory in 1977 had heard of him, but I soon discovered that his ideas were both original and important.[26]

Semon was born in Berlin in 1859, the same year that Charles Darwin published *Origin of Species*. As a young man, Semon fell under the spell of this innovative approach to understanding evolution, and he went off to study at the University of Jena with the most famous German proponent of the new theory, the controversial biologist Ernst Haeckel. Semon received his Ph.D. and became a rising young professor at the University of Jena, a major European center for evolutionary research. Then, in 1897, he fell in love with the wife of an eminent colleague, Maria Krehl, who eventually left her husband to live with Semon. The two were vilified, Semon resigned his professorship, and the pair moved to Munich, where they were married. Semon, working on his own as private scholar, developed a theory of memory.

In 1904, he published a monograph, *Die Mneme,* that attempted to unite the biological analysis of heredity with the psychological and physiological analysis of memory. Semon argued that heredity and reproduction could be thought of as memory that preserves the effects of experience across generations. *Mneme,* a term Semon created in allusion to the Greek goddess of memory, Mnemosyne, refers to a fundamental process that he believed subserves both heredity and everyday memory. He conceived it as an elemental elasticity of biological tissue that allows the effects of experience to be preserved over time.

Semon distinguished three aspects or stages of Mneme that he deemed crucial to understanding both everyday memory and hereditary memory. Because he believed that ordinary language has too many potentially misleading connotations to be useful scientifically, Semon described the three stages with terms of his own invention: *engraphy* is Semon's term for encoding information into memory; *engram* refers to the enduring change in the nervous system (the "memory trace") that conserves the effects of experience across time; and *ecphory* is the process of activating or retrieving a memory.

Semon's unusual terminology and his emphasis on the memory/heredity analogy elicited a torrent of disapproval from prominent experts of the time. Yet precisely because of this controversy, his ideas about the operation of everyday memory tended to be overlooked. Only one reviewer of *Die Mneme,* the American psychologist Henry J. Watt, looked beyond the issues of heredity that so mesmerized biologists and picked out the single most important aspect of Semon's theory. "The most valuable part of the book is the concept of the ecphoric stimulus," reflected Watt. "However, Semon in his attempt to find something common in the reproduction of the organism and in the reproduction in the sense of memory, has lost sight of his own objective (the discovery of the nature of the ecphoric stimulus) and has gone astray."[27]

What exactly was Watt driving at? Psychologists at the time showed scant interest in memory-retrieval processes. Most of them believed that the likelihood of remembering an experience is determined entirely by the strength of associations that are formed when the information is initially encoded into memory. According to this view, if strong associations are formed—because the information is particularly vivid, or is repeated frequently enough—memory will later be good; if weak associations are formed, memory will later be poor. Semon, in contrast, argued that memory does not depend solely on the strength of associations. He contended that the likelihood of remembering also hinges on the ecphoric stimulus—the hint or cue that triggers recall—and how it is related to the engram, or memory trace, that was encoded initially. Watt realized that Semon had pinpointed a key aspect of memory that had been given short shrift, and wished that Semon had focused more extensively on it.

In 1909, Semon published a book that must have made Watt exceedingly happy. Entitled *Die Mnemischen Empfindungen* (*Mnemic Psychology*), it was entirely about everyday memory, leaving aside the contentious issues of heredity in *Die Mneme*. Semon elaborated his theory of ecphory (retrieval processes) and applied it to a host of critical issues. Sadly for Semon, however, the new book aroused slight interest among researchers and had no detectable impact on the study of memory. Psychologists had little use for Semon's iconoclastic views on retrieval processes; in fact, they misunderstood his ideas. In addition, Semon's status as a scientific isolate, without prestigious institutional affiliations, did not enhance his cause. He was accorded the same kind of treatment given to flat-earth theorists, believers in perpetual-motion machines, and other cranks who exist at the fringes of science: he was ignored.

In 1918, Semon's wife died of cancer. Later that year, he placed a German flag on his wife's bed and shot himself through the heart.

Despite his nagging despair over the neglect of his work, Semon believed that his ideas would soon achieve widespread recognition among researchers. His hopes went largely unrealized, with the exception of one of his terminological inventions: the engram. The great neuroscientist Karl Lashley wrote a paper in 1950 entitled "In Search of the Engram," which summarizes Lashley's unsuccessful attempts to find the engram (the representation of a memory in the brain) in any single, restricted location. Because the paper became a classic in the field and contains the first prominent invocation of the term *engram,* most scientists have assumed that Lashley invented the word—and he did not even cite, much less discuss, Semon's prior use of the term.

Engrams are the transient or enduring changes in our brains that result from encoding an experience. Neuroscientists believe that the brain records an event by strengthening the connections between groups of neurons that participate in encoding the experience. A typical incident in our everyday lives consists of numerous sights, sounds, actions, and words. Different areas of the brain analyze these varied aspects of an event. As a result, neurons in the different regions become more strongly connected to one another. The new pattern of connections constitutes the brain's record of the event: the engram. This idea was first suggested by the Canadian psychologist Donald Hebb, and has since been worked out in considerable detail.[28]

Engrams are important contributors to what we subjectively experience as a memory of something that has happened to us. But, as we have seen, they are not the only source of the subjective experience of remembering. As you read these words, there are thousands, maybe millions, of engrams in some form in your brain. These patterns of connections have the potential to enter awareness, to contribute to explicit remembering under the right circumstances, but at any one instant most of them lie dormant. If I cue you by asking you to remember the most exciting high school sports event you ever attended, a variety of engrams that only seconds ago were in a quiescent state become active as you sift through candidate experiences; if I ask you to remember what you ate the last time you had dinner at an Italian restaurant, a very different set of engrams enters into awareness. Had I not just posed these queries to you, the relevant engrams might have remained dormant for years.

Semon appreciated that, engrams being merely potential contributors to recollection, an adequate account of memory depends on understanding the influences that allow engrams to become manifest in conscious awareness: What properties of a cue allow it to "awaken" a dormant engram? Why are some cues effective in eliciting recollection whereas others are not? Semon argued that any given memory could be elicited by just a few select cues—parts of the original experience that a person focused on at the time the experience occurred. Thus, only a fraction of the original event need be present in order to trigger recall of the entire episode.

To recollect the most exciting high school sports event you ever attended, you need not reinstate all the cues that were present initially. Only a subset must be available, those that are closely related to your encoding of the event. Your original encoding and elaboration of the event—say, a football game in which the quarterback made a series of miraculous plays to pull off an unexpected victory—focused heavily on the role of the quarterback. Years later, the mere mention of the quarterback's name, or even a glance at his face, may bring to your mind the game, the participants, and how your team won. But if you do not encounter the critical cues, you will not recall the experience. A friend may ask if you recall the time your team beat the school with the young coach who went on to a career with a professional team. You may be puzzled about what game he is referring to, and have only a fuzzy recollection of the coach. But as soon as he says that it was the game in which your quarterback threw two long touchdown passes in the final minutes, you can retrieve the memory easily. Thus, if encoding conditions are not adequately reinstated at the time of attempted recall, retrieval will fail—even if an event has received extensive elaborative encoding.

Semon's Legacy: Cue-Dependent Memory

The contemporary researcher who has contributed most to understanding the relationship between encoding and retrieval is my former mentor, Endel Tulving. One of Tulving's most influential ideas is known as the *encoding specificity principle,* which is similar in many respects to Semon's theory. According to this principle, first advanced in the 1970s, the specific way a person thinks about, or encodes, an event determines what "gets into" the engram, and the likelihood of later recalling the event depends on the extent to which a retrieval cue reinstates or matches the original encoding. Explicit remembering always depends on the similarity or affinity between encoding and retrieval processes.[29]

A hypothetical study (what scientists refer to as a thought experiment) with some of the material from Sophie Calle's artistic investigation of memory will help illustrate the central notion at stake here. Consider two more recollections of Magritte's "The Menaced Assassin" that were reported by Museum of Modern Art personnel:

1: Large, awful. There's a pink boa around the neck of a naked woman lying on a table like a piece of lamb. That's all I remember.

2: I remember clothed men standing around a woman who is not only nude but dead, as if she was a sacrifice in the middle of the room. Your eyes go immediately to her. What I remember most is the blood coming out of her mouth and the assassin. He just looks evil.

In my imaginary experiment, I probe each person's memory by providing brief descriptive cues and asking him or her to try to remember a painting in the museum that matches the description. I would be willing to predict that the cue "snake around woman" is more likely to elicit a recollection of the Magritte painting from the first respondent than from the second, and that "wicked man shoots" is more likely to evoke a recollection from the second. The usefulness of the cue depends on the nature of the initial encoding, and vice versa.[30]

These considerations suggest that the way we perceive and think about an event plays a major role in determining what cues will later elicit recollection of the experience. But it is not the literal similarity between encoding and retrieval conditions that is the crucial determinant of explicit memory. Rather, what matters most is whether a retrieval cue reinstates a person's subjective perception of an event, including whatever thoughts, fantasies, or inferences occurred at the time of encoding. What do you think of when you read the following sentence?

The fish attacked the swimmer.

Most people infer that a shark is responsible for the attack. Experiments have shown that if I later give you "shark" as a retrieval cue, you will be more likely to remember this sentence than if I give you "fish," even though "fish" was part of the original sentence. "Shark" is an effective retrieval cue because it is more likely than "fish" to bring to mind what you thought about when you read the sentence.[31]

The close relationship between encoding and retrieval can help us understand instances of remembering and forgetting in our everyday lives. Recently I spent a pleasant week with my family in San Diego, enjoying a brief respite from the Boston winter. We passed a couple of happy afternoons, especially our two young daughters, at the San Diego Zoo and SeaWorld. But I had visited both places on earlier trips and wanted to see something new. So, on a misty Sunday morning, we trekked over to the historic nineteenth-century Coronado Hotel, located on a peninsula just off the San Diego coast. As we drove over the lengthy bridge that connects the peninsula to the mainland, my wife described the size and beauty of the hotel and noted that our guidebook said that it was the first hotel to use electric lights. I had no previous image of or knowledge about the Coronado, and eagerly anticipated seeing it.

When we pulled up in front of the hotel, I was not disappointed: it is an enormous and glorious example of Victorian architecture. The lobby is graced with magnificent, deep brown wood and elegant furniture. Behind the lobby there is a tranquil courtyard. As we entered it, I was suddenly gripped by an unexpected but compelling conviction: I had once stood in this very courtyard, conversing with participants at a scientific conference. I remembered clearly that several of us were discussing my impending move to Harvard University. In a matter of seconds, I recalled that I had stayed at the Coronado Hotel a little more than four years earlier. As I stood in the courtyard with my wife and children, I was able to remember which room I had stayed in and various other incidents from that earlier visit.

Why wasn't I reminded of the previous trip when we drove over the bridge, when my wife described the hotel, or when I saw the imposing structure and lovely lobby with my own eyes? Why did it take the sight of the courtyard to trigger the memory? I had encoded that trip to San Diego as the "conference before my move to Harvard." I was not particularly focused on the name of the hotel, its historic status, or the Victorian architecture. I was preoccupied with all that I had to accomplish in the two weeks before moving. During breaks between conference sessions, informal groups gathered in the courtyard, and everybody I spoke with seemed to want to hear about my move. The courtyard was an effective retrieval cue—it brought to mind my initial encoding of the trip—whereas the other features were not.

Our own states of mind can also serve as valuable cues for remembering. When people drink alcohol or smoke marijuana during the encoding phase of a memory experiment, they later have difficulty remembering what they encoded—but they recall more when they are later given similar doses of alcohol or marijuana. This is known as *state-dependent retrieval,* and it has been observed across a wide range of drugs, dosages, and experimental materials. Inducing the same intoxicated state helps to re-create more fully the state of mind that prevailed at the time of encoding; the improved match between encoding and retrieval conditions benefits memory.[32]

The exquisite interdependence between encoding and retrieval suggests some important qualifications to points I made earlier concerning elaborative encoding and explicit remembering. Recall the fundamental finding from depth of processing studies: when we engage in deep, elaborative encoding of an event, we are later likely to remember that event well; when we engage in shallow, superficial encoding, we will later remember the incident much less well. It turns out, however, that superficially encoded events can be remembered more accurately than deeply encoded events when people are given retrieval cues that match exactly a shallow encoding. Suppose I ask you to think of a word that rhymes with *brain*. You have carried out a shallow encoding, and you will have a hard time later remembering that I showed you the word *brain*. You would be much more likely to recall that I showed you *brain* if you had carried out a deep encoding (such as, think of three important functions that a brain performs). But if I ask you to remember a word that rhymes with *train,* you will be more likely to remember *brain* after shallow than deep encoding![33]

All else being equal, elaborative encoding yields higher levels of explicit memory than nonelaborative encoding, probably because a rich and elaborate encoding is accessible to a broad range of retrieval cues, whereas a shallow, more impoverished encoding can be elicited only by a few perfectly matched cues. Consider two bachelors who are seeking spouses. One of them, a doctor, has a broad range of cultural and recreational interests; he is potentially attractive to many different kinds of women. The other is entirely consumed by his work on high-energy particle physics, and would consider as a mate only another similarly devoted particle physicist. The second bachelor will have many fewer chances to locate a good match than the first, but if he is fortunate enough to find one, the physicist can be at least as happy as the doctor. Similarly, an elaborative encoding affords many more opportunities to "meet" the right retrieval cue than a shallow encoding, and thus increases the chances of successful retrieval; but if the right cue is encountered, a shallow encoding can yield comparable or even higher levels of recall.

One happy implication of this analysis is that when elaborative encoding has been carried out, and the right cue is available at the time of attempted retrieval, memory can achieve extremely high levels of accuracy. In one experiment, people were given the daunting load of 600 words to study. They were also induced to carry out extensive elaborative encodings, and were later given retrieval cues that reinstated those encodings. Shortly after seeing the 600 words, people recalled over 90 percent of them.[34]

Because our understanding of ourselves is so dependent on what we can remember of the past, it is troubling to realize that successful recall depends heavily on the availability of appropriate retrieval cues. Such dependence implies that we may be oblivious to parts of our pasts because we fail to encounter hints or cues that trigger dormant memories. This may be one reason why encountering acquaintances we have not seen for years is often such an affecting experience: our old friends provide us with cues and reminders that are difficult to generate on our own, and that allow us to recollect incidents we would ordinarily fail to remember.

In his relentless quest for self-understanding, the narrator in Marcel Proust's novel confronted the disturbing reality that his ability to recapture the past depended on finding retrieval cues that could unleash the torrents of memory that he sought. He ultimately came to realize that he could not allow his mental time travels to depend solely on chance encounters with smells and tastes, and so he instead pursued the past by actively seeking out cues and hints that would help him to remember. All of us share Proust's problem: to understand better who we are, we must somehow generate or find cues that allow us to remember things that might otherwise remain dormant or simply fade away. We saw how in the case of patient GR, encountering the right retrieval cue (a medical procedure similar to one he had had before) allowed him to regain his seemingly lost personal past.

We must not, however, confuse these ideas with the notion that all experiences are recorded somewhere in our brains, only awaiting the appropriate retrieval cue to be brought into awareness. While controlled research has demonstrated over and over that cues and reminders can lead to recall of experiences that have seemingly disappeared, it does not necessarily follow that all experiences are preserved and potentially recallable. Sometimes we forget because the right cues are not available, but it is also likely that sometimes we forget because the relevant engrams have weakened or become blurred.[35]

Retrieval cues are a bit like the portable metal detectors that scavengers sometimes use to try to recover coins on a beach. If coins are hidden somewhere beneath the sands, then the scavenger needs the detector to find them. But if no coins remain in the sand, then even the most powerful detector will turn up nothing. Our brains include some beaches with hidden coins and others that are barren. Like the scavenger seeking money, we do not know before searching which are which.

NEIL
Retrieval Processes and the Brain

In 1988, a fourteen-year-old English boy named Neil began radiation treatment for a tumor hidden deep within the recesses of his brain. Neil had been a normal child until the expanding tumor began to interfere with his vision and memory and to create a host of other medical problems. Chemotherapy was eventually successful, but Neil suffered heavy cognitive losses. He was virtually unable to read and could no longer name common objects on sight. Neil was able to recount most of his life prior to the operation, but he had great difficulty remembering his ongoing, day-to-day experiences.

Curiously, however, Neil performed reasonably well at school, especially in English and mathematics. The psychologists who tested his memory wondered how he managed to do so well. To find out, they asked him some questions about an audiotaped book he had been studying, *Cider with Rosie,* by Laurie Lee. He remembered nothing. Noting Neil's frustration, and realizing that his class performance was based on written responses, the examiner asked Neil to write down his answers, beginning with anything that he could recall from the book. After a while he wrote: "Bloodshot Geranium windows Cider with Rosie Dranium smell of damp pepper and mushroom-growth." "What have I written?" he then asked, unable to read his own handwriting but able to speak normally. The examiner, who was familiar with the book, immediately recognized that the phrases came directly from its pages.

Intrigued by Neil's ability to write down information that he could not express orally, the examiner asked whether Neil could write anything about incidents related to his hospitalization some two years earlier, which he had been unable to remember when asked to talk about them. "A man had Gangrene," he wrote, correctly recalling the ailment of another man in the ambulance that brought Neil to the hospital.

Neil's parents asked him to write down the names of the children in his class. He produced a long list, which turned out to be accurate. When his mother asked him what had happened at school that day, Neil wrote, "Mum I saw tulips on the way home." This was the first time in two years that Neil had been able to relate to his mother a memory of something that had happened to him in her absence.

Neil's parents equipped him with a small notebook, and he began to communicate regularly about incidents in his everyday life. Yet he remained unable to recount these episodes orally. When he wrote them down, Neil was unable to read them, and often expressed surprise when someone told him what he had written. After an afternoon's excursion to several familiar locations, Neil was unable to remember anything when asked. But when told to write down what had happened, he provided a succinct, and accurate, summary of the afternoon's activities: "We went to the museum, and we had some pizza. Then we came back, we went onto the Beach and we looked at the sea. Then we came home."

This case is unprecedented in the annals of psychology, psychiatry, or neurology.[36] Neil's tumor did damage his brain, including some structures that are known to be important for memory. But nothing about the condition of his brain provides specific clues to how or why he could retrieve recent episodic memories through writing but not speaking.

There are other indications that the brain uses different systems for retrieving written and spoken information. The neuropsychologist Alfonso Caramazza has described two patients who suffered strokes in different regions of the left hemisphere that are usually associated with language impairments. Both patients subsequently had special problems producing English verbs (they could produce nouns normally). One patient had problems writing verbs but not saying them, whereas the other had problems saying verbs but not writing them.[37]

Caramazza's findings still leave us a long way from understanding how Neil could recall his recent experiences through writing but not speaking. But these strange cases of disruptions of retrieval raise questions that are essential to understanding memory: Exactly how does the retrieval process work? What goes on in my mind/brain that allows the cue "What did you do during your summer vacation?" to evoke in me the subjective experience of remembering beautiful sunlit days of hiking and swimming at Lake Tahoe? We do not understand precisely how the retrieval process works, but some clues are beginning to emerge.[38]

One critically important idea is that the brain engages in an act of "construction" during the retrieval process. The idea is well illustrated by neurologist Antonio Damasio's theory of how the brain remembers. As I elaborate in the next chapter, Damasio and others have argued that there is no single location or area in the brain that contains the engram of a particular past experience. Posterior regions of the cortex that are concerned with perceptual analysis hold on to fragments of sensory experience—bits and pieces of sights and sounds from everyday episodes. Various other regions of the brain, which Damasio calls convergence zones, contain codes that bind sensory fragments to one another and to preexisting knowledge, thereby constituting complex records of past encodings. Damasio suggests that remembering occurs when signals from convergence zones trigger the simultaneous activation of sensory fragments that were once linked together. The retrieved memory is a temporary constellation of activity in several distinct brain regions—a construction with many contributors.[39]

New information regarding brain systems involved in memory retrieval has been provided by PET scanning studies. I noted earlier that regions of left inferior frontal cortex appear to be particularly active during encoding processes. In contrast, as Endel Tulving has shown, PET studies of memory for words, sentences, faces, and other materials consistently reveal that specific regions toward the front of the right frontal cortex are especially active during explicit retrieval of episodic memories—more active than the corresponding left frontal regions.[40] Of course, merely observing that a region is active during retrieval does not indicate exactly what role it plays in the retrieval process. For example, if the right frontal regions that have been activated during PET studies constitute a retrieval system that is necessary for recalling all episodic memories, then damage to right frontal regions should cause a devastating impairment of explicit retrieval; such patients should have grave difficulties recalling past events. However, studies that have included patients with right frontal damage typically fail to show generalized impairments of explicit remembering. But these patients can exhibit some memory difficulties, such as problems in remembering which of two events occurred more recently, and some are also susceptible to fascinating memory distortions. These impairments, which I consider later, may be caused by faulty retrieval processes.

In 1992, neuroscientist Larry Squire and colleagues reported a PET study of explicit retrieval that showed activation of the hippocampus, which we have already seen plays a role in encoding novel experiences.[41] Given that both the hippocampus and the frontal lobes can become active when people are instructed to remember recent events, it is natural to ask what role each structure plays in the retrieval process. A recent PET study I carried out with colleagues suggests that they play rather different roles. Think about what is involved when I ask you to recall what you did last Saturday night. Attempting to retrieve that memory involves a fair amount of mental work. You engage in search strategies and try to come up with cues, such as generating names of people you might have seen or where you might have gone. The mental effort that you expend is an important part of the retrieval process. But there is also the moment when you actually remember the event: you recall that you went to the movies and saw a thriller that kept you on the edge of your seat. This subjective recollective experience is, of course, an essential part of the retrieval process. When a brain area becomes active during a memory-retrieval task, it could reflect either the mental effort associated with trying to remember or the recollective experience associated with successful remembering. We designed our PET study to disentangle these two aspects of retrieval. Our results show that increased blood flow in the frontal lobes during explicit retrieval reflects primarily the mental effort involved in searching memory. However, simply trying to remember an event is not enough to activate the hippocampus. Increased blood flow in the hippocampus seems to reflect some aspect of the subjective experience associated with remembering the event.[42]

In line with these findings, the neuropsychologist Morris Moscovitch proposed that hippocampal and frontal systems may be involved in two different kinds of retrieval processes. One of them, referred to as *associative retrieval,* is an automatic reminding process that depends on the hippocampus and related medial temporal lobe structures. Associative retrieval occurs when a cue automatically triggers an experience of remembering. Everyone is familiar with this sort of experience: hearing a favorite song reminds you of where you were when you first heard it; you tell a new acquaintance that she reminds you of an old friend; seeing a cue word in a memory experiment easily brings to mind the word that was paired with it during the study episode. The other retrieval process, which is referred to as *effortful* or *strategic retrieval,* involves a slow, deliberate search of memory and depends on regions of prefrontal cortex—perhaps most critically, the right frontal regions that have been activated during explicit retrieval in PET studies.[43]

When I asked you to remember what you did last Saturday night, you relied on the strategic retrieval process to generate hints and cues, which you used in turn to "interrogate" the automatic retrieval process. If the frontal system generates a cue that has a match in memory, the medial temporal system will automatically "spit out" an engram that combines with the cue. Without the aid of the frontal system, the medial temporal system must simply "wait" for an appropriate cue to come along and make contact with a stored engram. As we will see in chapter 3, the medial temporal region works cooperatively with regions toward the rear of the brain where engrams are stored, including areas in the parietal and occipital cortices, forming distributed networks that allow us to encode and recall our recent experiences. Indeed, our PET study revealed blood flow increases in specific parts of the occipital and parietal lobes during recall, perhaps reflecting the dynamic interaction between medial temporal structures and cortical regions that results in the construction of a memory. But we will also see that the medial temporal region is not necessary for retrieving experiences from the distant past.

These ideas help to make sense of the fact that medial temporal system damage leads to severe memory loss for recent experiences, whereas frontal system damage typically does not. When the automatic retrieval system is dysfunctional, the interrogations of the strategic system will be fruitless, and it will be difficult to recall recent events. However, if the strategic retrieval process is impaired and the automatic retrieval process is intact, it should still be possible to remember reasonably well in the presence of appropriate reminders or cues. Deficits will be restricted largely to those situations in which effortful, strategic search is required—and this is a reasonably accurate description of what happens in many cases of frontal system damage.

The power of modern neuroimaging techniques raises the possibility that we may, in the not too distant future, learn enough about brain mechanisms of memory retrieval to be able to illuminate the disorder that rendered Neil mute about experiences that he could describe only when a pencil was placed in his hand.

CONSTRUCTING MEMORIES
The Role of the Retrieval Environment

Findings and ideas concerning brain mechanisms of retrieval are absolutely crucial to understanding memory's fragile power. But it is still important to develop an adequate conceptualization of retrieval at the psychological level. How are we to think about what is retrieved when we recall a past experience? Does the act of retrieval simply serve to activate, or bring into conscious awareness, a dormant memory?

Suppose, for example, that I provide a retrieval cue such as "tell me about last year's Thanksgiving dinner." It may take you a few seconds to recollect where it occurred and who was there, but by the time you reach the end of this sentence there is a good chance that you will recall some of the basic information. How did this subjective experience of remembering come about? The simplest account is that the cue somehow activated a dormant engram of the event, and that your subjective experience of remembering the event, however incomplete, is a straightforward reflection of the information that had been quiescent in your mind: a lightbulb that had been turned off is suddenly turned on.

But memory retrieval is not so simple. I have already suggested an alternative possibility, rooted in Neisser's analogy that retrieving a memory is like reconstructing a dinosaur from fragments of bone. For the paleontologist, the bone chips that are recovered on an archeological dig and the dinosaur that is ultimately reconstructed from them are not the same thing; the full-blown dinosaur is constructed by combining the bone chips with other available fragments, in accordance with general knowledge of how the complete dinosaur should appear. Similarly, for the rememberer, the engram (the stored fragments of an episode) and the memory (the subjective experience of recollecting a past event) are not the same thing. The stored fragments contribute to the conscious experience of remembering, but they are only part of it. Another important component is the retrieval cue itself. Although it is often assumed that a retrieval cue merely arouses or activates a memory that is slumbering in the recesses of the brain, I have hinted at an alternative: the cue combines with the engram to yield a new, emergent entity—the recollective experience of the rememberer—that differs from either of its constituents. This idea was intimated in some of Proust's writings, in which memories emerge from comparing and combining a present sensation with a past one, much as stereoscopic vision emerges from combining information from the two eyes.

If all a retrieval cue did was to activate a dormant memory, some findings I have considered would not make much sense: recalling an event from an "observer" perspective after recalling the same event from a "field" perspective leads people to say that the event seems less emotional than when they first recalled it; the feeling of knowing that an unrecalled bit of information is on the tip of the tongue is often an illusion produced by a familiar retrieval cue; and the experience of "remembering" a past event, as opposed to "just knowing" that it occurred, is lessened when memory is prompted with certain kinds of retrieval cues. Once we acknowledge that a retrieval cue combines with the engram in order to yield a subjective experience that we call a memory, we can begin to make sense of these apparent puzzles.

A recent study from my laboratory provides evidence that the properties of a retrieval cue can influence what we recall about the past. College students looked at photos of people and heard them speak in either a pleasant or an irritating tone of voice. Later, they saw the photos again and tried to recall the person's tone of voice. When students saw a face with a bit of a smile, they tended to say that the person had previously spoken in a pleasant tone of voice; when they saw a face with a slight scowl, they tended to say that the person had spoken in an unpleasant tone. In fact, there was no relationship between facial expression and tone of voice. Thus, the "memories" that people reported contained little information about the event they were trying to recall (the speaker's tone of voice) but were greatly influenced by the properties of the retrieval cue that we gave them (the positive or negative facial expression).[44]

There have been few other attempts to examine how the properties of a retrieval cue contribute to our subjective experiences of remembering. This is likely attributable to what Tulving has called the "overpowering influence" of the traditional theory that a memory is simply an activated engram of a past event.[45] The idea that there is a one-to-one correspondence between a bit of information stored away somewhere in our brain and the conscious experience of a memory that results from activating this bit of information is so intuitively compelling that it seems almost nonsensical to question it. Yet scientists who study memory and theorize about it are increasingly skeptical of this idea.

For example, one of the most influential approaches to thinking about memory in recent years, known as connectionism, has abandoned the idea that a memory is an activated picture of a past event. Connectionist or neural network models are based on the principle that the brain stores engrams by increasing the strength of connections between different neurons that participate in encoding an experience. When we encode an experience, connections between active neurons become stronger, and this specific pattern of brain activity constitutes the engram. Later, as we try to remember the experience, a retrieval cue will induce another pattern of activity in the brain. If this pattern is similar enough to a previously encoded pattern, remembering will occur. The "memory" in a neural network model is not simply an activated engram, however. It is a unique pattern that emerges from the pooled contributions of the cue and the engram. A neural network combines information in the present environment with patterns that have been stored in the past, and the resulting mixture of the two is what the network remembers. The same conclusion applies to people. When we remember, we complete a pattern with the best match available in memory; we do not shine a spotlight on a stored picture.[46]

The idea that a memory is an emergent property of the cue and the engram is difficult to accept. We must leave behind our familiar preconceptions if we are to understand how we convert the fragmentary remains of experience into the autobiographical narratives that endure over time and constitute the stories of our lives.

THREE

OF TIME AND AUTOBIOGRAPHY

THE ARTIST MILDRED HOWARD likes to relate visual stories about her family. Her parents moved their growing family from Texas to California at the beginning of World War II. Mildred, the youngest of ten children, was the only one born in California. Growing up, she listened intently to the stories of her parents, brothers, sisters, aunts, and uncles about their trials and adventures in the Texas countryside. She was especially moved by the tales of her elderly Aunt Mildred, a repository of family lore who mesmerized her young niece with colorful renditions of past events. In "Rose (Roosevelt)" (figure 3.1) the artist invites us to imagine one of Aunt Mildred's stories by reprinting a photograph from her family album on an old window frame and providing us with hints of the underlying narrative. Mildred Howard was enthralled by the oral history of her family but sometimes felt a twinge of jealousy that she had not been there herself to witness the escapades that she heard about. Perhaps this is one reason she has worked for years to capture in pictures the faded yet vital recollections of family stories that date back to before her birth. "The sepia-toned images of handsome men and women in their Sunday best," notes one observer about Howard's work, "speak of family pride dimmed through the passage of time and diminished memory."[1] The distant, almost translucent quality that characterizes some of the old memories is communicated effectively in "Caney Creek" (figure 3.2). Time and memory are inextricably interwoven; memories always refer to the past and often shape the future. Mildred Howard acknowledges this relationship by commemorating distant events with aged objects. She appreciates that our understanding of who we are and who we will become depends on memories that may fade, change, or even strengthen as time inexorably passes. And it is from this ongoing dynamic between time and memory that our autobiographies—the stories we tell about our lives—are born. We cannot hope to understand memory's fragile power without examining what happens to memory as time passes, and considering how we translate the residues of experience that persist across time into tales of who we are.

THE RECEDING PAST

In the first experimental analysis of remembering and forgetting ever reported, an epoch-making study by the German psychologist Hermann Ebbinghaus in 1885, lengthening the delay between encoding and retrieval produced dramatic increases in forgetting. Ebbinghaus, who served as his own and only subject, set about memorizing long lists of nonsense syllables. He then carefully tested himself at different times after learning. Ebbinghaus remembered progressively less at each of the six delays that he used, ranging from one hour to one month. The rate of forgetting was relatively rapid at the early delays and slowed down at later ones. Ebbinghaus forgot a great deal between a one-hour delay and a nine-hour delay, whereas he lost relatively little between a one-day delay and a two-day delay. Many later researchers have also found that the rate of forgetting is slowed down by the passage of time.[2]

Psychologists have more recently investigated how memory for everyday personal experiences is influenced by the passage of time. In the early 1970s the psychologist Herbert Crovitz rediscovered and refined a method for studying memories of real-life experiences that had been described by the nineteenth-century British scientist Sir Francis Galton. The method, now commonly referred to as the Crovitz procedure, is simple. Think of a specific memory from any-time in your life that comes to mind first when you are given the word *table*. Once you have retrieved a memory, do your best to assign a date to it. Now try the same procedure using the cue word *hurt*, and then do it one more time with the cue word *run*.

In Crovitz's experiments, people retrieved memories from many different points in their lives, ranging from a few minutes prior to the

FIGURE 3.1

Mildred Howard, "Rose (Roosevelt)," 1992. 28 x 18 x 2". Mixed media on window frame. Gallery Paule Anglim, San Francisco.

Two well-dressed young men surround a miniature window-within-a-window containing a photo of the artist's Aunt Mildred in her younger days. Are these two young suitors who vied for Aunt Mildred's affections? Relatives who participated with Aunt Mildred in some important or mysterious bit of family history? We don't know the particulars, but we can guess that it is an absorbing tale.

FIGURE 3.2

Mildred Howard, "Caney Creek," 1991. 21 x 24 x 6". Mixed media on window frame. Nielsen Gallery, Boston.

Three faint figures—members of the artist's family in rural Texas—fade like blurs into a receding background. A window frame scarred by peeling paint and cracked surfaces surrounds their image, further heightening the sense of an old memory ravaged by time. Six empty bottles of cream soda stand in front of the figures. For Howard, these empty vessels evoke images of a rousing family get-together or of conversations with brothers and sisters on a hot afternoon.

experiment to the early years of childhood. He found that the more recent time periods yielded the most memories, the more distant time periods the fewest. (When I tried the experiment myself, I remembered leaving some papers on a table for a colleague a week earlier; dislocating my finger playing baseball as a child; and running to catch a taxi in New York City several months earlier.) The drop-off in reported memories was steepest in the recent time periods and more gradual in the remote time periods.[3]

Despite a few deviations, the general rule that memories become gradually less accessible with the passage of time holds in many situations. It is sometimes surprising how much we may forget when a sufficient amount of time has passed. For example, survey researchers interviewed 590 people who were known to have been injured in an automobile accident during the preceding year. Almost everyone who was interviewed within three months of the accident remembered this disturbing event (fewer than 4 percent did not report it). But 27 percent of people interviewed between nine and twelve months after the accident failed to report it. "The obvious reason for this trend," the authors of the study comment, "is a decreased ability to recall the occurrence of a motor vehicle accident as the time between the date of the accident and the date of interview increases."[4]

Why is the passage of time associated with decreasing memory? As time passes, we encode and store new experiences that interfere with our ability to recall previous ones. I can remember what I had for breakfast today, but not what I had for breakfast on this day a year ago, because I have had many breakfasts since then that interfere with my ability to pick out any single one from the crowd. Interfering events of this kind may give rise to an increasingly fuzzy or blurred engram as time passes.[5] Many researchers would agree that blurring or even loss of information from the engram plays a role in the pervasive forgetting that afflicts us all. But some have contended that no information is ever lost from memory—that all experienced events exist somewhere in the mind, pretty much in their original form, simply awaiting the right cue to elicit them.

The memory researchers Elizabeth and Geoffrey Loftus asked psychologists to choose between two theories of forgetting. One theory holds that everything that happens is permanently stored in the mind, so that details we cannot remember at a particular time could eventually be recovered with the right technique. The other theory holds that some experiences may be permanently lost from memory, and would never be able to be recovered by special techniques. Eighty-four percent of psychologists chose the first option. This conclusion might appear to be justified by evidence I considered earlier concerning the importance of retrieval cues in remembering. It is likely, for instance, that many people who forgot about their motor vehicle accidents after a year could be induced to remember the event if given a specific retrieval cue, such as a detailed description of the circumstances surrounding the accident. But as I intimated in the previous chapter, there are problems with the idea that all experiences are kept forever in some dark corner of the brain.[6]

The idea received seemingly strong support from the oft-described brain-stimulation studies conducted by the Canadian neurosurgeon Wilder Penfield during the 1950s. In the Loftus and Loftus survey, psychologists frequently pointed to Penfield's work as crucial evidence favoring the idea that all experiences are permanently stored in the mind. Penfield's observations were certainly dramatic. Prior to operating on patients who required brain surgery, Penfield carefully placed an electrode on the surface of the exposed temporal lobe. The patient was fully conscious as Penfield turned on an electrical current. Sometimes he elicited surprising memories of seemingly long-forgotten events. "Yes, sir, I think I heard a mother calling her little boy somewhere," reported one patient. "It seemed to be something that happened years ago." Another patient exclaimed, "Yes, Doctor, yes, Doctor! Now I hear people laughing—my friends in South Africa." When asked if he could recognize them, the patient replied, "Yes, they are two cousins, Bessie and Ann Wheliaw."[7]

To Penfield, such examples revealed a lasting record of experiences in the brain: "It is clear that the neuronal action that accompanies each succeeding state of consciousness leaves its permanent imprint on the brain."[8] If we could just figure out a way to find the unchanging neural imprints that our brains preserve forever, Penfield thought, we could remember or even relive everything we have ever experienced. Maybe the passing of time does not, after all, erode or erase the brain's recordings of past events; it might merely wreak havoc with our ability to replay our dusty old records.

Although the idea has an undeniable appeal—it leaves open the possibility that we could all achieve Proust's and Magnani's dreams of recapturing the past fully—many psychologists and neuroscientists now concur that Penfield's results provide little support for this rather romantic proposition. Only 40 of the 520 patients who received temporal lobe stimulations reported any mental experiences that could be interpreted as memories. Even more important, Penfield failed to document whether his patients' experiences were memories of actual past incidents or mere fantasies or hallucinations.[9]

In a more recent investigation, French researchers described similar mental experiences in patients with temporal lobe epilepsy. What the researchers called the "dreamy state" was either evoked by electrical stimulation in the vicinity of the temporal lobes or occurred spontaneously during the aura that precedes a seizure. Patients sometimes reported the experience of remembering, but they tended to recall generic scenes rather than specific events. "I saw before my eyes the house of a friend in my grandmother's village," said one patient, "then it disappeared and I saw the house in Brittany where I spend my summer vacations." "I was in my kitchen, in front of the sink, dressed as usual," reported another. Still other patients described strange feelings of déjà vu, such as one who related "[t]he impression of having already done what I am in the process of doing; it seems to me that I have already lived through the entire situation; with a feeling of strangeness and often of fear."[10] It is important that these subjective feelings of remembering result from electrical activity in temporal lobe structures because this region of the brain plays a paramount role in memory. But, just as in Penfield's studies, the patients' reports provide no indication of a permanent record of specific memories that is impervious to the passage of time.

The idea that all experiences are recorded forever, requiring only a Proustian taste, sight, or smell to come dancing into consciousness, can never be disproved on purely psychological grounds. Even if we show that a person cannot remember an experience in response to a wide variety of retrieval cues, it is always possible that some other cue would result in sudden recall. And there is no question that providing cues, or reinstating the physical or mental context that prevailed during an experience, sometimes does lead to recall of seemingly lost experiences. However, neurobiological research with invertebrate organisms has shown that the neural changes that underlie some simple forms of memory can weaken and even disappear over time. Nobody has yet demonstrated that the same thing happens in mammals. But this kind of finding suggests that as time passes, there may be a diminution in the strength of connections among neurons that represent particular experiences. At a biological level, some engrams might literally fade away over time.[11]

The two extreme positions about the causes of forgetting—that it occurs either because an engram has disappeared from storage or because a fully intact engram is merely inaccessible at the moment owing to retrieval failure—are too simplistic. Rather than arguing about whether or not all experiences are preserved forever, we need to refine our ideas about why forgetting occurs. It seems likely that as time passes, interference from new experiences makes it progressively more difficult to find a retrieval cue that elicits an increasingly blurred engram. The cognitive psychologist Marigold Linton conducted a well-known study of her own memory that confirms this point. She wrote brief descriptions, every day, concerning at least two specific events in her life; she then tested her memory for random samples of these events at several points in time. The study had been under way for fourteen years when Linton reported on it in 1986. She notes that for about a year after the occurrence of an episode, it "can be accessed readily—with virtually any cue."[12] However, as more time elapses, and the engram becomes more blurry, the range of cues that elicits a specific episode progressively narrows. This means that when we suddenly and unexpectedly recover a seemingly forgotten memory, it may be because we have luckily stumbled upon a retrieval cue that matches up perfectly with a faded or blurred engram.

When I visited a summer camp where I worked as a waiter twenty-five years earlier, I drove by a spot on the lake that offers a lovely view back toward the camp. As I was looking out from my car, I suddenly remembered when several friends and I visited that exact spot—the only other time I had ever been to that part of the lake. I hadn't thought about the incident for a quarter-century, and I could not recall exactly what we had been doing or who else was there. But I am pretty certain there are few if any cues other than the sight of the camp across the lake that would have led me to recall this hazy memory.

These considerations also lead to another important implication for the relationship between the retrieval cue and the engram. All things being equal, when memory is probed soon after an event, the engram is a rich source of information and may even be the dominant contributor to recollective experience. Relatively little retrieval information is needed to elicit the appropriate engram, and the retrieval cue will play a more or less minor role in shaping the subjective experience of remembering. If I ask you to remember what you did just before you picked up this book, you probably will not have a problem recalling the incident. I need not provide you with extensive cues to elicit the memory, and your recollection of the event would probably be similar regardless of how I cue you. The same is often true of favorite past episodes that we have recounted frequently: we tell the same story over and over again, regardless of which particular cues elicit it.

However, the nature of the cue-engram relationship is likely to be quite different for episodes from the distant past that we have not recounted many times. Now that the engram of the event is a more impoverished source of information, considerable cueing may be needed to elicit memory for the episode, and the properties of the retrieval cue itself may figure quite prominently in shaping the rememberer's recollective experience. If, for example, I ask you to recollect events that transpired at your Thanksgiving dinner of six years ago, you will need a variety of retrieval cues in order to remember explicitly much of what happened. Now the quality of your recollective experience may indeed depend significantly on precisely which cues are used to trigger recollection. Suppose, for instance, you recall that six Thanksgivings ago, your old friend George flew in for the holiday; you attempt to cue additional recollections by thinking about him. Suppose further that in the intervening years, you and George had a serious disagreement and you no longer feel as warm toward him as you once did. These properties are now incorporated into your permanent knowledge of George, and they may play a role in shaping your memories of what happened at that Thanksgiving dinner. You may be inclined to recollect that he made a disparaging remark or that he behaved inappropriately, even though the engram of the event contains only vague information about what occurred. Because the engram is so impoverished, recollective experience may be determined more heavily by salient properties of the cue, which itself has stored associations and meanings in memory.

Weakening and blurring of engrams over time is, on the face of it, an unpleasant reality of memory. It is frustrating, even disturbing, to realize that past experiences are constantly slipping away from us, some rapidly and others imperceptibly. But we would be far worse off if we did not forget. In Jorge Luis Borges's jarring story "Funes, the Memorious," a young man remembers the tiniest details of all that has happened to him. He remembers every leaf of every tree he has ever seen and every separate occasion on which he has seen them: "I have more memories in myself alone than all men have had since the world was a world." But the price of perfect retention is high: Funes's mind is so cluttered with precise memories that he is incapable of generalizing from one experience to another. He has difficulty fathoming why a dog he encounters has the same name at one moment as it has a minute later. "To think is to forget a difference, to abstract," Borges reminds us. Years after Borges wrote this story, the Russian neuropsychologist Alexander Luria described a much-celebrated mnemonist, Shereshevskii, who was plagued by Funes's fictional problem: he was overwhelmed by detailed but useless recollections of trivial information and events. He could recount without error long lists of names, numbers, and just about anything else that Luria presented to him. This served him well in his job as a newspaper reporter, because he didn't have to write things down. Yet when he read a story or listened to other people, he recalled endless details without understanding much of what he read or heard. And like Funes, he had great difficulty grasping abstract concepts.[13]

Forgetting, though often frustrating, is an adaptive feature of our memories. We don't need to remember everything that has ever happened to us; engrams that we never use are probably best forgotten. The cognitive psychologist John Anderson has argued convincingly that forgetting memories over time is an economical response to the demands placed on memory by the environment in which we live. We are better off forgetting trivial experiences than clogging our minds with each and every ongoing event, just in case we might want to remember one of those incidents someday.[14] But we do need to form an accurate picture of the general features of our world, and it turns out that we are reasonably adept at doing so. Our recollections of the general contours of our pasts are often reasonably accurate. Perhaps paradoxically, if we, like Funes or Shereshevskii, were constantly overwhelmed by detailed memories of every page from our pasts, we would be left without a coherent story to tell.

HYPERMNESIA AND CONSOLIDATION
Do Memories Ever Strengthen over Time?

Though forgetting has adaptive features, time is still an enemy of memory. We forget our experiences—sometimes rapidly, sometimes slowly—as the delay between encoding and retrieval increases. But memory doesn't always fade over time. Consider a curious phenomenon that psychologists call *hypermnesia*. When people are shown a bunch of pictures, for example, and are later given a series of tests in which they try again and again to recall the pictures, the overall percentage of correct answers increases on each test, even though more and more time has passed since the original encoding episode. If one group of people had taken a single test at a short delay and another group had taken a single test at a long delay, there's no question that people tested at the long delay would remember less than people tested at the short delay. But when people are tested again and again, recalling the pictures on each test seems to minimize forgetting between one test and the next. This active rehearsal also promotes recovery of pictures that people failed to recall initially, perhaps because the rememberers generate new retrieval cues on later tests that dredge up previously inaccessible engrams. The net result is that memory seems to improve, not decay, over time. Likewise, psychologists and neurobiologists have discovered that some engrams appear to become more resistant to forgetting as time passes. Scientists use the term *consolidation* to refer to this seemingly paradoxical state of affairs.[15]

The concept of consolidation has had a long and somewhat controversial history in the psychology and neurobiology of memory. Many contemporary researchers distinguish between two quite different types of memory consolidation.

One type of consolidation operates over time periods of seconds or minutes; it converts immediate or short-term memories into more enduring long-term memories. The ability to perform this short-term consolidation is often interrupted when people sustain serious head injuries. Following such injuries, they are almost invariably unable to remember the accident itself or the few minutes preceding it, and they virtually never recover these memories. The events just prior to an accident may be registered and entered into short-term or working memory, but they never gain entry into the long-term system. Some years ago enterprising researchers accompanied a college football team to their weekly games, anticipating that players would occasionally suffer concussions. When there was a particularly hard hit— known in football as a "ding"—one of the researchers would rush out onto the field to interview the dazed player. One senior fullback carried the ball into the heart of the defensive line, was dinged, and then stumbled back to the huddle. When queried thirty seconds after the ding, the player thought he was in high school but still correctly recalled that his team had just executed a play called a "32-dive." Twenty minutes later, he regained his orientation, but had no memory of his injury or the 32-dive play. All of the dinged players responded similarly: they initially remembered the play that had just been run, but minutes later had no idea what had happened to them or what play had been run.[16]

Neurobiologists have studied this short-term consolidation process extensively in rats, mice, fruit flies, and even in simpler organisms such as the invertebrate sea slug Aplysia. This tiny organism has an extremely simple nervous system that consists of only about 20,000 neurons (compared to approximately 100 billion neurons in the human brain). When the experimenter applies an unpleasant stimulus to its tail, the tiny slug withdraws its gill. But it is quickly sensitized to the unwelcome stimulation, becoming increasingly adept at withdrawing its gill and making other defensive responses. Eric Kandel and colleagues have observed that following exposure to just one noxious event, Aplysia exhibits these enhanced withdrawal responses for several minutes—but then they disappear. Aplysia forms a short-term memory of the bothersome event, but not a more durable long-term memory. However, as the experimenter applies increasing numbers of unpleasant signals, Aplysia withdraws its gill across longer and longer periods of time. The short-term memory has been converted—consolidated—into a long-term memory.

Kandel and colleagues have provided persuasive evidence that Aplysia's short-term memory is based on an enhanced release of neurotransmitter at the junction or synapse between a neuron that receives the noxious stimulation (a sensory neuron) and a neuron that is involved in withdrawing the gill (a motor neuron). As a result of stimulation, a chemical messenger travels more easily across the gap that separates one neuron from another. The long-term memory involves a process known as protein synthesis and appears to be accompanied by the growth of new synapses. They conclude that "on the cellular level the switch from short-term to long-term facilitation is a switch from a process-based memory to a structural-based memory."[17]

Mounting evidence also points toward a second kind of consolidation that operates over time periods of months, years, and even decades. That is, some engrams appear to become more resistant to disruption by brain injury as the years pass. Patients with memory disorders from damage to structures hidden deep within the temporal lobes provide evidence for this kind of consolidation. These amnesic patients have problems remembering everyday experiences that take place after the onset of their brain damage (anterograde amnesia). Most of them also have problems remembering facts and events from periods of time prior to the brain damage (retrograde amnesia). In some cases, patients have great difficulty remembering experiences from relatively recent time periods and less difficulty, sometimes none at all, remembering experiences from the distant past. This temporal gradient was first noticed in the nineteenth century by the French psychologist Théodule Ribot, and is thus known today as Ribot's Law.[18]

Memory loss in head-injured survivors of accidents often obeys Ribot's Law. In addition to forgetting permanently the accident itself and the minutes preceding it, such people may temporarily lose memories of recent days, weeks, and months, while retaining memories of the distant past. This may be because some memories are subject to a long-term consolidation process that allows them to become more resistant to disruption over time.

During the 1970s and 1980s, researchers reached similar conclusions using carefully constructed tests. The neuropsychologists Marilyn Albert and Nelson Butters constructed a "famous faces test," in which patients identify pictures of people who became famous at different times during the past fifty years, such as Charles Lindbergh, Joseph McCarthy, and Oliver North. Some amnesic patients who took this test had great difficulty identifying faces from the recent past, but little trouble identifying faces from the distant past. But since many people who became famous in the distant past are still talked about today, the test may not provide a pure measure of memory for remote events. Larry Squire overcame this problem by developing a test that used television programs that remained on the air for only a single season, reasoning that people would not be likely to learn about such programs after they had been broadcast. He found that the amnesic patients had special problems remembering television programs from recent time periods. This finding was particularly clear-cut in studies of psychiatric patients who developed temporary retrograde amnesia after undergoing electroconvulsive therapy (ECT) for relief of intractable depression. Prior to ECT, these patients possessed more accurate memory for television programs from recent periods than from more remote periods—just like the normal control group. After ECT, however, they had trouble remembering programs that aired a year or two prior to ECT, even though they had no problems remembering programs from more remote time periods.[19]

Squire and others have also shown that patients with permanent memory problems that result from damage to structures in the inner parts of the temporal lobes, including the hippocampus, are better able to remember experiences from the distant past than from the recent past. On some tests, like recalling television programs, patients have problems remembering only the year or two preceding the onset of their amnesia; on other tests, their memory problems cover larger chunks of their pasts. For example, when Squire gave amnesic patients cue words and asked them to remember episodes from anytime in their lives, the patients recalled as many experiences from childhood as people who have no memory problems. But amnesics were less likely to remember experiences that occurred after childhood.[20] Thus, there is no single estimate of how long it takes for a memory to become fully consolidated.

One particularly fascinating, and sad, story of retrograde amnesia involves a famous scientist who became amnesic after years of prolonged alcohol abuse. Lengthy alcoholism sometimes results in thiamine deficiencies that wreak havoc with a part of the brain known as the diencephalon, which is closely connected with the medial temporal lobe. This condition is known as Korsakoff's syndrome, in recognition of Sergei Korsakoff, the nineteenth-century Russian psychiatrist who first described it. The amnesic scientist, now known in the literature by the initials PZ, was sufficiently famous that he had written an autobiography. Nelson Butters and Laird Cermak tested PZ's memory for some of the experiences described in his autobiography, with the certain knowledge that he once remembered them in rich detail. Results of the study were clear-cut: PZ remembered accurately most childhood events, but he could not remember any of the episodes in his autobiography from the last twenty years of his life; he showed gradually decreasing memory accuracy from the middle period of his life on.[21]

Studies of nonhuman animals have recently begun to provide important new information about retrograde amnesia. If a person who suffers a head injury in 1995 no longer recognizes the face of Oliver North, we do not know how well she would have recognized the face prior to the accident. But in animal studies, researchers can carefully control how well an animal encodes and retains a particular memory, and then make a brain lesion either days, weeks, or months after initial learning. If memories consolidate over time, and the medial temporal region plays an important role in the consolidation process, then a medial temporal lesion should have relatively little effect when it is made long after initial learning and a much more drastic effect when it is made soon after learning. This is exactly what has been observed in experiments using monkeys and rats.[22]

These observations all converge on the conclusion that it takes some time after initial encoding for a memory to become fully established or organized in the brain. At the level of brain systems, Squire and others have contended that the hippocampus and related structures in the medial temporal region play a role in memory consolidation, though for only a limited time after an event occurs. Long-term storage of memories appears to occur in cortical networks outside the medial temporal region, with different cortical networks representing different kinds of information. For instance, storage of visual memories depends on networks in the occipital lobes and the lower or inferior parts of the temporal lobes, which are essential for visual processing. (See figure 2.4.) Patients with lesions to a structure at the junction of the occipital and temporal lobes, known as the fusiform gyrus, have great difficulty recognizing faces of people who are familiar to them, and may also have problems recognizing other kinds of visual objects. Antonio Damasio and his colleagues described a sixty-five-year-old woman, EH, who suffered damage in the occipital/temporal region of both hemispheres as a result of a stroke. She could identify a face as a "face," but was unable to recognize the specific faces of her friends, relatives, husband, and daughter; she even failed to recognize her own face in a mirror, despite realizing that it must be hers. Yet EH had intact visual acuity, normal intelligence, full ability to use and understand language, and could identify people easily when she heard their voices. She also had difficulties recognizing her own house, car, and clothes, even though she could identify each generically as a house, a car, or clothes. EH's lesion prevented her from retrieving specific visual memories of unique objects.

In contrast, damage to other cortical regions impairs different kinds of knowledge. Patients with parietal damage forget once-familiar spatial layouts and have difficulty navigating routes that they used to travel with ease. Recent PET scanning studies have shown that parietal regions become especially active when people remember the location of objects. Long-term memory for the sound of a word depends on networks that involve a part of the temporal lobes in the left cerebral hemisphere known as Wernicke's area. After damage to this region of the brain, patients are unable to make much sense of spoken language and often speak a bewildering kind of gibberish.[23]

Explicit memories for past episodes typically include many different kinds of information: visual, auditory, spatial, verbal, and so forth. As I mentioned in the last chapter, Damasio has proposed that different kinds of information are linked together in "convergence zones" that bind together fragments of perceptual experience. Damasio envisages a series of convergence zones operating at different levels, binding visual features into representations of faces, for instance, or binding face representations to other kinds of information. The medial temporal region can be thought of as a critical convergence zone for assembling explicit memories. Many researchers believe that the medial temporal region contains a kind of index that "points to" the locations of different kinds of information that are stored in separate cortical regions. The index is needed to keep track of all of the sights, sounds, and thoughts that together comprise an episode, until the engram can be held together by direct connections between the cortical regions themselves. Then the index contained in the medial temporal region is no longer necessary in order to recall the episode. An important implication of this view of memory storage is that no single picture in the mind corresponds to a memory of last year's Thanksgiving dinner, or of seeing your dear old Aunt Helen at a family wedding. What comes to mind when you remember such events is something like a giant jigsaw puzzle, assembled from many constituents in response to a cue. The medial temporal region contains instructions that specify how to assemble the puzzle; eventually, the instructions are shifted over to cortical regions that contain all the component pieces of the puzzle.[24]

At the psychological level, long-term consolidation occurs in part because people talk about and think about their past experiences; the older a memory, the greater the opportunity for such post-event rehearsal. Perhaps thinking and talking about a past experience promote the direct connections between cortical storage areas that eventually allow them to assemble the jigsaw puzzle that constitutes an event. Once an experience has been repeatedly retrieved, it becomes consolidated and no longer depends on the integrity of the medial temporal structures. The idea that the medial temporal region works cooperatively with cortical storage areas to achieve a fully consolidated long-term memory has been formalized in a recent neural network model developed by James McClelland and colleagues. They developed a computer simulation that does a good job of mimicking the fact that retrograde amnesia tends to affect recent memories more than distant ones.[25]

Nobody knows exactly what changes in the brain correspond to long-term memory consolidation. We do know, however, that neurons in the brain are capable of rearranging themselves over time. In one particularly striking recent experiment, adult cats were partially blinded by lesions to retinas of both eyes. Specific visual areas in their brains no longer responded when lights or objects appeared in particular locations. Yet nine months later, some of these areas began to respond again to visual stimulation. A gradual reorganization had occurred, involving new connections among neurons. Perhaps something similar occurs in long-term consolidation, with the gradual development of new connections helping to make repeatedly rehearsed memories more resistant to forgetting.[26]

Recent research also points to another player in the consolidation process: sleep. Over a decade ago, the neuroscientist Jonathan Winson hypothesized that memories become consolidated during sleep, particularly during the rapid eye movement (REM) stage when we dream most frequently and intensely. Winson's idea was that during sleep, when the brain is not so preoccupied by the continual barrage of external stimulation that occurs during waking, it works through the experiences of the day, discarding the trivial and saving the significant.

Winson's ideas recently received support from electrophysiological recordings in rats suggesting that during sleep, the hippocampus "plays back" a recent experience to areas of the cortex where it will eventually be stored permanently. This could be an important part of the role that the hippocampus plays in consolidating new memories. Sleep researchers have long observed that dreams often contain remnants of recent experiences. It now seems likely that as we sleep, our brains are working hard to save the experiences that we will carry around with us for much of our lives. Memory consolidation during sleep is likely influenced by what we think about and talk about while awake. The important events in our lives that we often review during waking may be frequently "replayed" during sleep. Experiences that receive little attention during waking probably receive fewer nocturnal playbacks, paving the way for forgetting. Our conscious activities during waking probably conspire with unconscious happenings during sleep to shape and sculpt the stories that we tell about our lives.[27]

REMEMBERING THE EXPERIENCES OF A LIFETIME

In December 1991, the writer Isabel Allende attended a party in Madrid to launch her latest novel. As she was explaining to guests how she had come to write the book, Allende received disturbing news: her twenty-seven-year-old daughter Paula had been rushed to the hospital. Paula and her family had known for several years that she had inherited a rare metabolic disorder, porphyria, and now the disease caused her to lapse into a coma. Allende stayed at Paula's bedside for the year that she remained comatose before dying. Powerless to awaken her daughter, and unsure whether Paula would have any past of her own if she ever awoke again, Allende tried to infuse her with memories. "Listen, Paula," she wrote in the opening line of *Paula,* a memoir of the frightening illness, "I am going to tell you a story, so that when you wake up you will not feel so lost." She then relates experiences that she shared with Paula, divulges personal secrets that her daughter never knew about, and imparts family legends about ancestors from past generations. Allende attempted to break through the curtain of silence that isolated Paula by piecing fragments of her autobiography into a coherent whole for her lifeless daughter. "In the long silent hours," Allende reflected, "I am trampled by memories, all happening in one instant, as if my entire life were a single, unfathomable image. The child and girl I was, the woman I am, the old woman I shall be, are all water in the same rushing torrent. My memory is like a Mexican mural in which all times are simultaneous."[28]

Isabel Allende tells her story eloquently. And the fact that her own autobiography is so closely interleaved with her daughter's illness lends it a special poignancy. But in many respects, Allende's remembered autobiography is a lot like everybody else's recollections of their lives: a complex tapestry that includes memories of specific moments and more general recollections of larger chunks of time. She recollects what the stars looked like when she was a young girl in La Paz. She recalls a scary and confusing sexual encounter on a beach when she was eight years old. She remembers what it was like to live in Lebanon during the 1950s. And she recounts hundreds of other incidents, people, and lessons from her life as she sits at Paula's bedside.

Despite the complexity of personal memories, our autobiographical recollections also contain a good deal of underlying structure. Although memories of what has happened in the past may seem like a formless variety of snapshots and stories, many researchers distinguish among different levels of autobiographical knowledge. Various terms have been proposed to describe these levels, but I will adhere to the distinctions suggested by two pioneers in autobiographical memory research, Martin Conway and David Rubin.[29] They postulate three kinds of autobiographical knowledge that are arranged hierarchically. The highest level of the hierarchy contains lifetime periods: lengthy segments of life that are measured in years or decades, say, going to college, living in Arizona, or working at a particular place. The middle of the hierarchy includes general events: extended, composite episodes that are measured in days, weeks, or months, such as going to football games during freshman year, vacationing at the Grand Canyon, or the first professional stint you had. The bottom of the hierarchy is populated by event-specific knowledge: individual episodes that are measured in seconds, minutes, or hours, such as the big fight that ended the final football game of the season, the moment you first laid eyes on the Grand Canyon, or the time you arrived for a meeting unprepared.

When people tell the stories of their lives, all three kinds of knowledge are usually present and interleaved. Isabel Allende talks in global terms about the lifetime period when she resided in Lebanon. Embedded within this lifetime period, she imparts many recollections of what I have termed general events. She recalls, for instance, repeated trips to the *souks*—cramped and winding alleyways filled with shops that sell every kind of food imaginable. "I can still smell those markets!" she recalls. "All the aromas of the planet wafted through those twisting streets, a melange of exotic vapors." Allende recollects how "[m]erchants came out to meet their customers and nearly dragged them inside those Ali Baba caves glutted with treasures." Here Allende is not remembering a specific episode in a particular time and place; she is extracting features and themes that are common to many episodes, and hence is remembering a general event. But she can also proceed further down the hierarchy and recall event-specific knowledge. Thus, as she continues her recollection of markets in Lebanon, she remembers a particular shopping trip in which her mother prevailed upon her to buy cloth for a wedding dress at bargain prices, even though young Isabel had no marriage prospects in sight. "We left the bazaar with meters and meters of white, silk-embroidered organza," Allende remembers, "besides several tablecloths for my hope chest and a carved wooden screen that has survived three decades, countless moves, and exile."[30]

Controlled studies have revealed that each of the three kinds of autobiographical knowledge serves different functions, and may even be mediated by different underlying brain systems. General events appear to be the natural entry points into our autobiographical memories. When people are asked about experiences from their pasts, they prefer to describe their experiences at the level of the general event. People tend to say, "I really enjoyed going to basketball games during high school," rather than saying where they went to high school or recollecting a specific incident from a particular game.[31]

General events may enjoy this privileged status because they accrue the benefits of repetition. One reason it is easy for me to remember the first course I taught to Harvard undergraduates is that I taught many sessions of the class during the semester. I have a harder time recalling specific episodes from particular classes because they occurred only once. Remember that in Marigold Linton's study of her own experiences, she found that up to about a year after a specific event her memory was quite accurate, but beyond a year this event-specific knowledge began to lose individuating detail, and particular episodes began to merge into one another—they became general events. The fate of Linton's memories suggests that losses at the event-specific level can be turned into "gains" at the general-event level. This can help us to understand why we tend to "enter" our pasts at the level of the general event. General events capture a good deal of the distinctive flavor of our pasts, and are readily accessible because they have been strengthened through repetition.

The lifetime period serves a different function. If I asked you to recall experiences from anytime in your life, my guess is that you would not produce any lifetime periods, such as "when I went to high school." This information is so general that it does not convey much about your autobiography. However, you might have started your search by generating a lifetime period and then retrieving a general event from that time. Lifetime periods help us to find general-event knowledge and event-specific knowledge; they provide the skeletal structure of our autobiographical memories.[32]

These considerations led Conway and Rubin to an important proposal about the nature of autobiographical memories, one that echoes ideas I developed earlier. They contend that there is no single representation or engram stored in memory that has a one-to-one relationship with the mental experience of recollecting one's past. Instead, such experiences are always constructed by combining bits of information from each of the three levels of autobiographical knowledge. Just as memories for individual events resemble jigsaw puzzles that are assembled from many pieces, so do the stories of our lives.

This idea is illuminated by a bizarre variation of retrograde amnesia. In 1993, the British researchers John Hodges and Rosaleen McCarthy described a sixty-seven-year-old patient identified as PS who suffered a stroke in the thalamus, a structure that is often damaged in cases of amnesia. PS had great difficulty remembering ongoing events. He was also unable to remember just about everything that had happened to him before his stroke—except for one period in his life. PS insisted that he was temporarily on leave from the navy during World War II. He believed with great intensity that he was still in the midst of active navy service and that it would soon be time for him to return to his ship. The patient recalled a few scattered

fragments of knowledge about other parts of his life, but his understanding of himself was dominated by the delusional conviction that
he was living nearly a half-century in the past.

PS's bewildering fate illustrates what happens when different levels
of autobiographical knowledge are pulled apart from one another. PS
could recall a few general events but hardly any event-specific knowledge. It is unlikely that these memories were obliterated; nobody has
ever hypothesized that the thalamus is a seat of memory storage.
Remember that GR, who also developed amnesia as a result of damage to the thalamus, eventually recovered his past. Moreover, PS had
not sustained any damage to the cortical areas that I have suggested
are the repositories of our permanent (consolidated) engrams. But the
thalamus is a key switching station that connects systems in the front
and back of the brain. Hodges and McCarthy suggested that PS's
knowledge of past events had become disconnected from retrieval systems in the frontal lobes that ordinarily allow access to it.[33]

This disconnection hypothesis alone, however, does not explain
PS's persisting delusion. PS also suffered from a specific disruption at
the highest level of autobiographical knowledge—the lifetime period.
The knowledge that we all possess about specific past periods in our
lives is usually turned off, or inhibited, unless we engage in an act of
recollection that temporarily activates it. I know, for instance, that I
went to college in North Carolina during the 1970s, but this lifetime-
period knowledge normally rests in a quiescent state. The knowledge
becomes active when I turn my attention to that period of my life,
but it does not lead me to believe that I am now living in the North
Carolina of the 1970s, and it will surely settle back into a deactivated
state once I move on to thinking about other things. In PS, however,
the neural representation of the lifetime period "when I served in the
navy during World War II" seems to have become continuously and
irreversibly turned on. He is trapped in the world of navy service during the 1940s because damage to his thalamus somehow tripped a
switch that he is unable to shut off. Part of the reason PS actually
believes that he is living in the 1940s may be that his wartime service
constitutes an especially significant part of his life. I also suspect that
he has formed this pathological belief because the abnormally activated lifetime-period knowledge is cut off from other memories.
Unable to remember much of anything else about his past, PS cannot
escape the persistent conviction that he will soon be returning to his
ship.

When different components of autobiographical knowledge are

carved away from one another, we begin to appreciate that a great deal of structure and complexity lurk beneath the surface of our normally seamless recollections of the multitude of occurrences from our pasts. What we experience as an autobiographical memory is constructed from knowledge of lifetime periods, general events, and specific episodes. When we put all this information together, we start to tell the stories of our lives. Isabel Allende clearly appreciated the constructive nature of autobiographical remembering as she laid out the tale of her life to her gravely ill daughter. "My life is created as I narrate," she wrote, "and my memory grows stronger with writing." Looking ahead to a time when Paula would awaken—a time that never came—Allende imagined that the two of them could join together in the task of memory construction. "When you wake up we will have months, maybe years, to piece together the broken fragments of your past; better yet, we can invent memories that fit your fantasies."[34]

Psychologists have come to recognize that the complex mixtures of personal knowledge that we retain about the past are woven together to form life stories and personal myths. These are the biographies of self that provide narrative continuity between past and future—a set of memories that form the core of personal identity. The psychologist Dan McAdams, one of the most energetic developers of the hypothesis that life stories play a crucial role in cognition and behavior, emphasizes that these high-level memories, too, are constructions:

> The unfolding drama of life is revealed more by the telling than by the actual events told. Stories are not merely "chronicles," like a secretary's minutes of a meeting, written to report exactly what transpired and at what time. Stories are less about facts and more about meanings. In the subjective and embellished telling of the past, the past is constructed—history is made.[35]

If our memories are always constructed and occasionally distorted, might our most basic beliefs about our lives and our selves be fundamentally erroneous? If the construction of our autobiographies is like a jigsaw puzzle assembled from a multitude of contributors, and is influenced by large doses of our present needs and desires, then might we often be blind to the fundamental truths of our lives? The novelist Reynolds Price, reflecting back on his past, wished that his parents had taken more photographs and recorded more of what happened in order to help him overcome creeping uncertainties about the reliability of his own memories. "I think I recall the look and tone of many of those moments of laughter, pain, and bitter longing," muses Price, adding parenthetically that "the confidence that I do recall them, with a good deal of truthfulness, lies near the foot of my hold on sanity and on the work I do." But, Price continues, "an elementary understanding of the shaping force of memory requires me to grant that I may in fact be anything from fuzzy to lying to badly wrong on every such instance of what I think of as vital recall."[36]

Price is well aware that autobiographical memories are complex constructions. But this need not mean that we live in a world of wholly fabricated, self-serving fantasies. There are, in fact, good reasons to believe that our memories for the broad contours of our lives are fundamentally accurate. Sometimes specific events that are recalled by one member of a family are forgotten by others, and sometimes members of the same family remember specific incidents and general events differently. My younger brother, Ken, for example, has no memory of a hot June night when we went to a Yankees baseball game as kids and he cried when the Yankees lost. I recall the game clearly. He remembers incidents involving a pet dog that I don't remember. These discrepancies probably reflect differences in how deeply various family members encoded the events initially, what interpretations they gave them, and how often they later thought and talked about them. Ken had primary responsibility for the dog in our family, and thought and talked about incidents involving the dog much more frequently than I did. We went to the Yankee game for my birthday, which made it especially distinctive for me. Ken usually cried when the Yankees lost, so it was just one of many similar incidents for him.

In contrast, when adults retrospectively assess the general character of more extended time periods in their pasts, they are usually fairly accurate. My brother and I have similar recollections of how our parents got along with each other, the things we enjoyed doing as kids, and what our grandparents and other relatives were like. Our experience seems to be typical, because research has shown that siblings' memories of the general qualities of their family lives during childhood usually mesh.[37]

Interestingly, cognitive psychologists who have demonstrated distortions and inaccuracies in memories for single episodes have reached a similar conclusion. The cognitive psychologist Craig Barclay conducted a study of college students' memories for everyday events in which the students recorded in diaries brief descriptions of memorable things that happened in their lives just after they occurred. One student wrote: "I went shopping downtown looking for an anniversary present for my parents, but couldn't find a thing. I get so frustrated when I can't find what I want." Barclay later tested the students' memories for these events, at delays ranging from several months to two years. Sometimes he showed them a printed version of an actual diary entry and asked them to say whether this was exactly what they had written down. Other times descriptions had been changed in small respects, such as: "I went shopping downtown. I must have gone to ten stores before giving up and going home. I get so frustrated when I can't find what I want." As time passed, students were increasingly likely to say that these changed descriptions were exactly what they had written down months earlier. Less often, students falsely recognized descriptions that were taken from another student's diary. Overall, students retained the general meaning of their experiences, even though they were wrong about many particulars. "It is not the case," Barclay concluded, "that the meaning around which autobiographical memory is organized is a complete fabrication of life events. There is a fundamental integrity to one's autobiographical recollections."[38]

It is certainly troubling to confront the possibility that our life stories could be subject to profound distortion, because in the final analysis the memories that give rise to these stories are all that stay with us from cradle to grave. They tie us to the places we have been and the people we have known. There is even a sense in which one person's autobiographical memories allow other people to achieve a degree of immortality. The Argentina-born artist Diana Gonzalez Gandolfi conveys this important message in her painting "Memory Weaves the Echoes" (figure 3.3). Inspired by the poetry of Nobel laureate Pablo Neruda, she eventually came to terms with the death of close personal friends by appreciating that they continue to exist as echoes in her memory. Her painting juxtaposes images of these ghosts from the past with a solitary hanger and piece of cloth, physical reminders of an absent person.

Memory's echoes assumed enormous importance for Isabel Allende. Reflecting on her daughter's ordeal, Allende recalled what her grandfather once told her: "Death does not exist; people only die when we forget them." Allende recognizes that Paula continues to live on in her own autobiographical recollections of their shared past: "It is wonderful what memory does. You can remember how someone smelled, you can remember the tone of their voice, and re-create the person to carry inside you." Paula, too, appreciated this essential

FIGURE 3.3

Diana Gonzalez Gandolfi, "Memory Weaves the Echoes," 1990. 26½ x 33½". Oil, wax, and polymer. Randall Beck Gallery, Boston.

The ghostly figures in this painting refer to deceased friends of the artist, who now exist only as echoes in memory.

function of memory. Knowing that porphyria might claim her life prematurely, Paula wrote a sealed letter to her family. Her mother could not bear to open that letter for many months, but when she did, she found comforting words that recognized the power of memory: "I know you will remember me, and as long as you do, I will be with you."[39]

FOUR

REFLECTIONS IN
A CURVED MIRROR
Memory Distortion

ISABEL ALLENDE came to regard her memories as close friends, providing comfort and continuity during the course of Paula's illness. The psychologist Shlomo Breznitz, in reflecting on his terrifying wartime experiences of hiding from the Nazis, felt something similar: "The fields of memory are unbounded. Locations are their servants, and time is their playground. As we travel through life it is hard to find a truer friend."[1] Just as we can generally trust our close friends, we can usually rely on our memories. Yet even the best of friends may occasionally deceive us, and memory, too, can sometimes trick us at the very moment when we want to believe it most. When distortions and illusions of remembering do occur, these mistakes provide revealing clues about the nature of memory's fragile power, and also illustrate dramatically that our day-to-day lives can be turned upside down by what we believe about the past.

Frank Walus learned about memory distortion the hard way. In 1978, he was tried on charges that he had been a Nazi war criminal. Several witnesses identified him as a Gestapo monster who had terrorized civilians in the Polish towns of Częstochowa and Kielce between 1939 and 1943. One man recalled seeing Walus kill two children and their mother. Another told of a time that Walus entered his house and brutalized his father; the same man recalled seeing Walus shoot a Jewish lawyer. This witness easily picked out Walus's face from a series of photos. "I will never forget that face," he stated confidently. "This is the face [of a man] who killed an innocent man whose only crime was that he was a Jew." Based on such eyewitness identifications, Walus was convicted of war crimes and his U.S. citizenship was revoked.

When Walus's case was appealed, a different story emerged. Searches of German war records failed to turn up any record of a Frank Walus, or anyone with a similar name. A Polish war crimes commission had no record of any Walus. Perhaps most important, Walus was able to substantiate with documents and witnesses his wartime alibi: he had been sent to Bavaria, where he performed forced labor on farms. Wartime photographs of Walus on a Bavarian farm—which looked so different from his 1978 appearance that the judge in Walus's first trial suspected that it was somebody else in the photo—were matched to another, indisputable photograph of Walus as a civilian guard in the American occupation. The appeals court overturned the conviction, but left open the possibility that Walus could be retried. (He never was.) "The United States District Court admitted that a serious mistake had been made," observes the psychologist Willem Wagenaar, who has provided an informative summary of what happened to Walus; "that Frank Walus was not the criminal that witnesses knew from 35 years ago, and that Walus should receive compensation." Wagenaar suggests that the misidentifications occurred because Walus as an older man strongly resembled the true Nazi criminal at a younger age.

Wagenaar also points out similarities between the Walus story and the more widely known case of Cleveland auto worker John Demjanjuk. He was accused and convicted of being Ivan the Terrible, a heinous Nazi war criminal who terrorized Jews at the Treblinka concentration camp. Demjanjuk was sentenced to death and deported to Israel, where he served nearly eight years in prison before the Israeli Supreme Court overturned his conviction. The court found reason to believe that the true Ivan might have been one Ivan Marchenko, who had vanished once the war ended. Wagenaar served as a defense expert for Demjanjuk, and his detailed analysis of the case, published in 1988, after Demjanjuk had been convicted, raises serious questions about the kinds of questioning and identification procedures that led people to recognize Demjanjuk as Ivan. Leading questions were used, photo lineups were sometimes constructed improperly, and failures to positively identify Demjanjuk as Ivan were overlooked. There is no question that Ivan existed and perpetrated evil deeds, but the Israeli Supreme Court found many reasons to doubt the reliability of eye-witness identifications that portrayed Demjanjuk as the monster of Treblinka.[2]

Incidents such as these are frightening reminders of memory's fallibility. But they are hardly surprising to psychiatrists and psychologists, who have long been aware of the vulnerabilities of human memory. Much has been written about Sigmund Freud's ideas concerning his patients' recollections of childhood sexual trauma. He initially accepted such reports, often obtained with the use of hypnosis, as veridical recollections. But after 1897 he viewed them as fantasy-based confabulations, thereby exhibiting some of the same confusion concerning recovered memories of childhood sexual trauma that exists today. Some have contended that this change of view arose from careful analysis and rethinking of his clinical observations; others have suggested that Freud, shunned by his colleagues for accepting his patients' stories of sexual abuse, lacked the necessary courage to believe what he heard; and still others have argued that Freud initially coerced his patients into generating stories of abuse in order to confirm his own theories regarding the role of early sexual trauma in psychopathology.[3]

Whatever the reason for his change of view, Freud came to focus increasingly on the role of distortion in memory. In a classic 1899 paper titled "Screen Memories," Freud argued that the visual images that we bring to mind when recollecting early childhood experiences are not pictures of reality; they are distortions or screens that allow us to avoid facing what really happened. Freud's central idea here—that conscious recollections are inevitably distorted by a person's wishes, desires, and unconscious conflicts—became a core assumption of all psychoanalysis. A major goal of analysis, according to Freud, is to uncover the "true" reality hidden behind the screen memory. Freud likened the psychoanalyst to an archeologist, working back through ever more distant layers and strata in order to excavate the original traces and remains of remote events. But Freud never specified how to separate out the layers of distortion from the hidden core of truth.[4]

Freud's opinions were limited by the fact that he could not know what had actually happened during his patients' childhoods. To draw firm conclusions about the accuracy of a memory, we need to have an objective record of the remembered event. The British psychologist Sir Frederic Bartlett solved this problem by conducting controlled studies of how people recall complex events, which he described in his classic 1932 monograph, *Remembering*. Participants in Bartlett's experiments listened to an old Indian legend entitled "The War of the Ghosts," and later retold the story on several occasions. Bartlett found that people rarely recalled all the events in the story accurately; they often remembered occurrences that made general sense or fit their expectations of what should have happened, but were not part of the original story. Bartlett also observed that the recollections of his participants changed, sometimes substantially, across multiple retellings of the story. Bartlett concluded that memories are imaginative reconstructions of past events. He argued that the experience of remembering is shaped as much by the rememberer's "attitude"—expectations and general knowledge regarding what should have happened and what could have happened—as by the content of specific past events.[5]

While it is easy to agree that recollections are sometimes distorted, and even easier to see that this has enormous social implications and consequences, understanding the foibles of memory poses a formidable challenge. To unravel these mysteries, I will attempt to illuminate the murky twilight zone where memory and reality grope for each other, usually coupling nicely but sometimes yielding strange concoctions that have the power to change lives drastically and forever.

THE PERILS OF PRIOR KNOWLEDGE
Encoding and Distortion

We live in relativistic times, and the idea that people construct their own subjective realities finds ready acceptance among many people. Yet most of us are not easily willing to part with the assumption that there is a shared external reality that is at least partly knowable through memory. The assumption is fundamental to many of society's institutions, such as our legal and educational systems, and it also underlies our trust in autobiographical memory as a basis for self-understanding. Even when a person's memory for some aspect of external reality seems to be mistaken, he or she may be accurately remembering what was encoded into memory.

Eyewitness misidentifications sometimes arise because of limitations on what is encoded. More than two decades ago, eyewitness testimony led to the arrests of Lawrence Berson for several rapes and George Morales for robbery. Later, a man named Richard Carbone confessed to all of these crimes. It was the great misfortune of the unjustly arrested men that each shared several salient features in common with Carbone: all were about the same age, wore similar kinds of glasses, maintained small dark mustaches, wore dark curly hair of about the same length, and had similarly shaped faces. Suppose that an eyewitness had encoded those features of Carbone's appearance that were shared with Berson and Morales, but little or nothing else. By identifying a picture of Berson or Morales as the face of the person he saw commit a crime, the eyewitness would accurately reflect what he had originally encoded. But because distinguishing Carbone from Berson and Morales requires more specific information than he had encoded, the eyewitness would be tragically wrong.[6]

The encoding process can also add information to memory that later results in distorted recollection. For instance, verbally describing a face, a color, or even a taste of wine can impair subsequent recognition when an imprecise verbal description overrides a more precise nonverbal memory.[7] And knowledge about what we expect to happen can become incorporated into a new memory, even when the expected event did not occur. Our memories can be distorted by the same pool of preexisting knowledge that usually aids our ability to acquire and retrieve new information. As an example, imagine the following scenario. You are at a baseball game on a warm and sunny afternoon, comfortably watching the action from front-row seats. The home team has men on first base and third base, and there is one out. The pitcher throws the ball over the plate and the batter hits it on the ground to the shortstop, who fields the ball and attempts to execute a double-play. The runner from third scores.

If you do not know much about baseball, you probably imagined the events pretty much as described, perhaps filling in a stadium full of enthusiastic fans or creating hometown uniforms for the players. But if you are a true baseball aficionado, you may well have noticed something that was not stated in the passage: because the runner on third base scored, the batter must have been safe at first. If the batter had been out at first—that is, if the double-play had been successful—then the inning would have ended and the runner on third could not have scored. When baseball experts in an experiment were presented a story like this one, they often insisted that the passage contained the sentence "The batter was safe at first." People who knew little about baseball were not fooled into making this mistake. The experts were the victims of their own extensive knowledge about baseball, which infiltrated their encoding of the story.[8]

The fact that our general knowledge of the world is activated easily and effortlessly generally helps our cognitive lives run smoothly and efficiently. When we enter a restaurant, for example, we already know a great deal about the general sequence of events that will unfold, from being seated to leaving a tip; when we go to a concert, other knowledge structures become active that lead us to expect that quite a different series of events will occur. Yet precisely because our past knowledge of situations and event sequences is activated continually and effortlessly, we may be unaware that inferences based on this knowledge sometimes imperceptibly creep into our encodings—and our memories—of external events.[9]

There is a good chance that you can experience a memory distortion of this sort yourself by paying careful attention to the following series of words: candy, sour, sugar, bitter, good, taste, tooth, nice, honey, soda, chocolate, heart, cake, eat, and pie. Turn away from the page now and take a minute or so to write down all the words you can remember from this list.

Now take the following test. Consider the three words printed in italics at the end of this sentence and, without looking back to the previous paragraph, try to remember whether they appeared on the list that I just presented: *taste, point, sweet*. Think carefully about your answers, consider whether you actually remember seeing each word on the list, and assess how confident you are in your memory. Many people who study this set of words confidently recall that *sweet* was on the list—but it was not. The psychologists Henry L. Roediger and Kathleen McDermott have even shown that people not only believe that *sweet* was on the list but claim to remember it vividly.[10]

I have carried out demonstrations with audiences containing nearly a thousand people, and successfully induced 80–90 percent of them to claim erroneously that I had read the word *sweet* aloud a minute earlier. Why are people so easily fooled? Presentation of so many strong associates of *sweet* might activate the general category of "sweet things" in your mind. You may then remember this categorical knowledge on subsequent tests. A related possibility is that at the time of study, one or some of the presented words may trigger *sweet* as an associate. Later, on recall and recognition tests, people have difficulty remembering whether *sweet* was actually presented on the list or whether they merely thought of the word during list presentation.

In either of these scenarios, false recognition of *sweet* reflects generally accurate retention of the gist or meaning of the word list. Consistent with this idea, when I performed the "sweet" experiment with a group of amnesic patients, they had difficulty remembering the words that were actually on the list, as would be expected from patients with impairments of explicit memory. But they also made many fewer false recognitions of *sweet* than did people with intact memories. This is because the amnesic patients did not successfully encode and retain the gist of the studied words. False recognition of *sweet* requires accurate retention of the general meaning of the words on the target list, which in turn depends on the hippocampus and other medial temporal lobe structures that are damaged in amnesic patients. Consistent with this idea, in a PET study my colleagues and I found that many of the same brain regions were active during true recognition of previously studied words and false recognition of nonpresented associates, including an area within the left medial temporal lobe. In contrast, we observed trends for differences in brain activity during true and false recognition on the surface of the temporal lobe and in parts of the frontal lobe. A follow-up study that measured brain electrical responses also found mainly similar patterns of activity during true and false recognition, with differences observed under the specific testing conditions that had been used in the PET study.[11]

Clearly, then, encoding processes can introduce a degree of distortion into our memories. Preexisting knowledge, which often aids in the construction of elaborative encodings, can sometimes seep into and corrupt new memories. Such corrupting influences turn out to be a natural feature of many neural network models of memory. In such models, engrams are stored as patterns of activity that are superimposed upon one another. Some of the individual "units," or parts of a pattern, may be involved in the storage of several different engrams. This means that new memories are inevitably influenced by old memories, which opens the door to distortion as a relatively common occurrence. In a neural network, a memory for any single episode will necessarily be affected, and perhaps altered, by memories of other episodes.[12] We earlier saw the benefits of a memory system that relies on prior knowledge when building new memories; now we have seen the costs.

CUES THAT CONFUSE
Retrieval and Distortion

In the year 1030, a Bavarian monk named Arnold journeyed to Pannonia on behalf of his abbot. Years later, Arnold wrote about his trip and recounted a remarkable event: encountering a flying dragon. The huge beast hovered in the air and spanned an enormous distance, as much as a mile. Its head alone was the size of a mountain, Arnold remembered. Covered by a shield of scales, the frightening monster lingered in the sky for several hours before speeding away in a flash.

Arnold's memory of the giant dragon emerged gradually as he thought about his experience in the context of religious texts and precepts and as he related it to the widely held beliefs of his contemporaries about the meaning and significance of dragons. In other words, Arnold probably did encounter a large bird or creature of some sort on his trip, but his final memory took time to construct from an assortment of cues and beliefs that saturated his retrieval environment. Arnold's written recollection of the dragon is not merely an activated engram of what happened during the trip. It is an imaginative invention that incorporates information from the present as Arnold tries to make sense of what happened in the past. Eventually, Arnold generates a new interpretation of his original experience that fits with what current teaching says about the religious significance of dragons.[13]

Though few people nowadays remember seeing mile-long dragons floating in the sky, there are modern examples of memory distortion that are perhaps not so different from Arnold's. To understand Arnold's memory and the modern analogues of it, we will need to keep in mind the important lesson that a retrieval cue does not merely awaken a dormant engram, and that the subjective experience of a memory does not simply reflect the properties of an activated engram. As I have already suggested, the cue and the engram conspire to yield the subjective experience that we call remembering. This analysis implies that when a person produces a subjectively compelling, but demonstrably inaccurate, memory report, we must examine the environment in which retrieval occurs just as carefully as the past events to which the memory refers. Arnold's retrieval environment, full of texts and ideas about dragons, drove him to remember an appropriately formed monster.

In the twentieth-century psychology laboratory, distorted recollections sometimes result from the way memory is probed or cued. For instance, some experiments have shown that the exact way a question about the past is worded can influence what a person claims to remember.[14] Distorting effects of present circumstances on past events can also occur when people are asked to make retrospective judgments about attitudes and views they held in the past—what the psychologist Robyn Dawes has dubbed "biases of retrospection." For example, in a 1973 study, people were asked to rate their attitudes toward five salient social issues: guaranteed jobs, rights of accused people, aid to minorities, legalization of marijuana, and equality of women. In 1982, many of these people were asked to make the same ratings; in addition, they were asked to indicate what their attitudes had been back in 1973. Participants' recollections of their 1973 attitudes were much more closely related to their current views than to their past views. The views that people held in 1973 had little to do with how they remembered those views in 1982. Retrospective biases can occur over shorter time periods, too. In one experiment, for instance, people who heard a message extolling the virtues of toothbrushing remembered brushing their teeth more often during the preceding two weeks than people who heard a message that denigrated toothbrushing. Such recall biases may be one reason why people who take part in ineffective self-help programs often still believe they have made significant gains. For instance, students who participated in a study skills improvement program rated their skill level before beginning the program and then tried to recall their initial ratings after completing it. They remembered their initial skill ratings as being lower than they actually were, whereas students who were put on a waiting list showed no such bias. Having put much effort into the program, participants justified the investment by revising their recollections of the past in line with their present needs and beliefs.[15]

Clinicians and therapists have also recognized that the retrieval environment can influence how the past is reconstructed. In his trenchant monograph *Narrative Truth and Historical Truth,* the psychoanalyst Donald Spence rejects Freud's idea that the analyst is a kind of archeologist who attempts to excavate the patient's "true" memories from the scattered debris of the past. "More than we realized," Spence contends, "the past is continuously being reconstructed in the analytic process." Spence appreciates that the analyst is a critical component of the retrieval setting who helps determine—not merely uncover—the form and content of the patient's memories. The words and phrases used by the analyst do not merely "wake up" or "activate" a slumbering memory; they may shape what the patient recalls and influence the patient's subjective experience of remembering, as he seeks to unlock parts of the past that are most relevant to understanding the present. A therapist who responds with great interest to an isolated image or a vague feeling may lead a patient to construct a memory on the basis of what may or may not be the remains of a long past experience.[16]

These concerns are amplified when we consider that in psychoanalysis (and other forms of intensive psychotherapy), patients struggle to recover lost experiences that are typically not accessible to conscious recollection. The retrieval environment likely plays an especially important role in molding recollective experience when one is attempting to retrieve hazy or degraded engrams, and so it is particularly important in the therapeutic context. And therapists themselves are powerful figures for their patients; the intricate relationship between the two (the transference) is a fundamental principle of psychoanalysis. These are probably some of the reasons why, as we will see, people who have come to believe during therapy that they have recovered "real" memories of sexual abuse almost invariably point to the powerful influence of their therapists in generating and maintaining the distorted recollection. A therapist is a major part of a retrieval environment that helps to shape what a patient believes about the past.

The same sort of considerations apply to another interpersonal situation that often involves an attempt to recover degraded engrams of fleeting or distant experiences: hypnosis. Hypnosis is a social process in which the suggestions and cues provided by the hypnotist guide the hypnotized individual through an imaginative, role-playing activity. Not everyone is responsive to a hypnotist's suggestions. But those who are, referred to in the professional literature as "high-hypnotizable subjects," are vulnerable to creating illusory memories when given suggestions.[17] Nevertheless, the misbegotten image of a hypnotized person at the mercy of a kind of psychological truth serum, having no choice but to reveal past secrets that are hidden in the recesses of the unconscious mind, is a powerful and enduring one. A Florida jury convicted a man named Joseph Spaziano of the 1973 murder of an Orlando nurse. A judge sentenced Spaziano to death. The state's case against Spaziano was based almost entirely on the testimony of Anthony Dilisio, sixteen years old at the time, who recalled that Spaziano had shown him the dead body at a dump site. The jury did not know, however, that Dilisio failed to recall this incident until he was hypnotized. "All we are there for is to bring out the truth," said Joe B. McCawley, who hypnotized Dilisio and believes that reputable hypnotists do not create false memories: "When hypnosis is properly used, you just get the truth." Ironically, several years after Spaziano's conviction, and too late to influence it, the Florida Supreme Court ruled that hypnotically refreshed testimony is not reliable enough to admit in court. However, an impassioned June 1995 article by Spaziano's lawyer published in an Orlando newspaper motivated Florida governor Lawton Chiles to grant a temporary stay of execution. Anthony Dilisio now says that he never went to the dump with Spaziano and never saw the body.[18]

Despite the claims of practitioners, controlled studies suggest that hypnosis does nothing to enhance the accuracy of memory retrieval. Instead, hypnosis creates a retrieval environment that increases a person's willingness to call just about any mental experience a "memory." Sometimes hypnotized people do bring forth accurate memories, but they're just as likely to produce illusory ones—and there is no reliable way to tell the difference between the two. Experiments have also shown that hypnosis heightens a person's subjective confidence in the veracity of the memories produced, without a corresponding increase in accuracy. Importantly, hypnosis increases the vividness of visual imagery that people experience, and hypnotized subjects may sometimes misinterpret their vivid mental imagery as a sure sign that they are remembering a past event.[19]

The idea that hypnosis is associated with distorted memory can be traced back at least to Freud's work with hypnotically induced memory retrieval in the late nineteenth century. In his early work, Freud used hypnosis as a tool for uncovering his patients' traumatic experiences from childhood, which often involved sexual abuse by an adult. But as noted earlier, he later became convinced that the memories his patients reported under hypnosis were frequently confabulated, and soon abandoned the use of hypnosis in therapy.

Freud's skeptical view of hypnotic memories has been further supported by experiments showing that hypnotized individuals can be led to "remember" events that did not occur but were suggested to them by a hypnotist. In one study, for example, approximately half the hypnotized subjects later reported a false memory created by the hypnotist's suggestion that they had been awakened by loud noises several nights earlier. Many of them insisted that they had heard the noises even after being informed that the hypnotist had suggested them. "I'm pretty certain I heard them," said one. "As a matter of fact I'm pretty damned certain. I'm positive I heard these noises." More recent studies of hypnotic "pseudomemories" have shown that they occur frequently in highly hypnotizable people even when no formal hypnotic induction is used. The tendency to produce illusory memories in hypnotic contexts is closely related to a person's hypnotizability, and also to the quality of the retrieval environment. When experimental participants feel strong social pressure to produce memories, they tend to recall events that never occurred. Fewer illusory memories are reported when the rapport between hypnotist and subjects is poor, when people are provided incentives to distinguish carefully between real and imaginary events, or when they are led to believe that they will remain able to make such distinctions even when hypnotized.[20]

Other experiments have shown that hypnotized subjects can confidently remember past lives. The nation's attention was drawn to this curious phenomenon in April 1995, when a *Frontline* documentary concerning recovered memories of sexual abuse showed a hypnotized woman in the act of recalling her brutal death in a past life. The woman, referred to as Dawn, had experienced unexplained stomach problems all her life. As she drifted backward in time under hypnosis, Dawn, a therapist, remembered that she had been slashed to death by soldiers in the first century A.D. "When I was actually being killed, I had made this decision not to scream, to die with dignity. The screams were just trapped. The terror was trapped in my body. I think that's what the sick to my stomach has always been about." Another woman on the show recalled that a babysitter who molested her had been a mistreated servant in a past life. The sitter, she believed, had finally extracted revenge by abusing her centuries later.

These weird recollections probably result from the expectations of both hypnotist and therapist, and also reflect the demonstrated capability of hypnosis to lead people to believe that all manner of imaginative experiences are memories. In fact, experiments have shown that when people are regressed to "past lives," they tend to remember whatever the hypnotist suggests. The same kind of explanation applies to the recent rash of people who have claimed with great conviction that they remember being abducted and tortured by high-tech aliens. Not surprisingly, these claims almost invariably emerge under hypnosis.[21]

Although it sometimes elicits recollections of events that never happened, hypnosis is by no means necessary to create illusory memories. Recent research suggests that false recollections of relatively complex experiences can be created even without a formal hypnotic induction. In what has become a well-known study, Elizabeth Loftus asked pairs of siblings to "remember the time that . . ." The study focused on childhood experiences of being lost, with the critical twist that some of the events in question never occurred. One sibling (who had been briefed by the experimenter) described a relatively detailed but false recollection of a time when the other sibling had been lost; the latter sibling was asked to describe his recollection of the experience. In the best-known example from the study, fourteen-year-old Chris was told at length by his older brother Jim about the time the five-year-old Chris got lost in a shopping mall and was found, crying, by a kindly old man. Loftus probed Chris's memory of the experience for several days after Jim's recounting of it. Chris responded by providing a detailed memory of the experience. He related that he felt "so scared that I would never see my family again," recalled "the man asking me if I was lost," remembered that the old man wore a "flannel shirt," and recollected that his mother had told him "never to do that again."[22] Loftus found that four of the five people who participated in her experiment (three children and two adults) related memories of events that never occurred.

Do the participants really believe that these false events occurred, or are they merely complying with the social demands of the test situation? And how do we know for sure that Chris or others were not once actually lost in a shopping mall? These possibilities cannot be ruled out, but Loftus's basic findings have been confirmed in an independent study by Ira Hyman and his colleagues. They obtained information from college students' parents about various things that had happened to their children when they were young. The experimenters queried the students about actual as well as fabricated events: an overnight hospitalization for an ear infection; a birthday party with pizza and a clown; spilling punch at a wedding reception; evacuating a grocery store when sprinklers went off; and causing an accident by releasing a parking brake when left alone in a car. Although students tended not to remember any of these imagined events when first questioned, after several interviews approximately 20 to 30 percent of them generated false recollections. In follow-up studies, Hyman has confirmed these findings and discovered that instructions to imagine a fictitious event increase the likelihood that people will come up with a false memory. Hyman also reports that people who attain high test scores on scales that measure vividness of imagery, responsiveness to suggestions, and lapses in attention and memory are especially likely to create false memories.[23]

If we hold the traditional view that memories are simply activated engrams, these findings are puzzling: Why should people report experiences when there is no engram that corresponds to that experience? But when we consider that the retrieval environment contributes to the construction of a memory, these findings become comprehensible. In both the lost-in-the-shopping-mall study and Hyman's experiments, the retrieval environment consists of information from normally trustworthy sources who have provided specific information about a seemingly credible experience. Under these conditions, some rememberers may interpret any subjective sensations elicited by the cue—vague feelings of familiarity, fragments of other possibly relevant experiences, perhaps even dreams or fantasies that are not recognized as such—as signs of an awakening engram. Once the process is initiated, it is just a short step for these rememberers to do what I have suggested that all rememberers normally do: knit together the relevant fragments and feelings into a coherent narrative or story.

It is also noteworthy that false recollections emerged most clearly after several interviews and retrieval attempts, implying that repeatedly thinking about the event increased participants' confidence that it actually happened. Experiments have shown that simply repeating a false statement over and over leads people to believe that it is true. Likewise, when we repeatedly think or talk about a past experience, we tend to become increasingly confident that we are recalling it accurately. Sometimes we are accurate when we recount frequently discussed experiences. But we are also likely to feel more confident about frequently rehearsed experiences that we remember inaccurately. Retrieving an experience repeatedly can make us feel certain that we are correct when we are plainly wrong. The tenuous correlation between a person's accuracy and confidence is especially relevant to eyewitness testimony. Witnesses who rehearse their testimony again and again in interviews with police officers and attorneys may become extremely confident about what they say—even when they are incorrect. This consequence of rehearsal is especially important because numerous studies have shown that juries are powerfully influenced by confident eyewitnesses.[24]

All these effects of retrieving and rehearsing memories are illustrated in one of the most politically significant cases of memory-based testimony from recent decades: John Dean's recollections of conversations with Richard Nixon about the cover-up of the burglary at the Watergate Hotel, which led to the demise of Nixon's presidency. Dean's testimony concerning his conversations with Nixon, Robert Haldeman, and other principals contains highly detailed, seemingly verbatim memories of exactly who said what in particular conversations. The level of detail in Dean's recollections is so extraordinary that he came to be known as the human tape recorder. When Nixon's secret tapes of Oval Office conversations were made public, it became clear that Dean's memories were not terribly accurate. The psychologist Ulric Neisser, after comparing Dean's testimony and the actual record of the conversations, concluded that Dean rarely if ever recalled the verbatim content of a conversation. Despite his confident presentation, Dean often failed to recall correctly even the general gist of a conversation. In a crucial meeting with Nixon and Haldeman on September 15, 1973, for instance, Dean recalled that Nixon made comments indicating his full knowledge of the Watergate cover-up. Dean remembered many specific details from the beginning of that meeting:

> The President asked me to sit down. Both men appeared to be in very good spirits and my reception was very warm and cordial. The

President then told me that Bob—referring to Haldeman—had kept him posted on my handling of the Watergate case. The President told me I had done a good job and he appreciated how difficult a task it had been and the President was pleased that the case had stopped with Liddy. I responded that I could not take credit because others had done much more difficult things than I had done. As the President discussed the present status of the situation I told him that all I had been able to do was to contain the case and assist in keeping it out of the White House.

In reality, Nixon had not asked Dean to sit down, did not say that Haldeman had kept him posted, did not tell Dean that he had done a good job, and made no mention of Gordon Liddy. Nor did Dean say anything about not taking credit. Dean was correct, however, that Nixon revealed knowledge of the cover-up in this conversation; he recalled accurately general themes and points that were repeated again and again in different episodes and conversations. According to Neisser, "what seems to be specific in his memory actually depends on repeated episodes, rehearsed presentations, or overall impressions."[25]

The conflicting testimony of eyewitnesses in other high-profile cases reminds us that Dean is not an aberration. When Clarence Thomas and Anita Hill told radically different tales of what had happened between them years before Thomas's 1991 confirmation hearing for a seat on the Supreme Court, many people assumed that one of them had to be lying. Is it possible that both were remembering the past as accurately as they could, a past that had been shaped for each of them in different ways by how they thought about their interactions after they occurred?

In the O. J. Simpson case, many were left scratching their heads when Simpson's housekeeper testified that his infamous white Bronco had not moved from its spot all evening, yet Simpson's limousine driver testified that he had no memory of seeing the car when he arrived late that evening. Had each of them been so well rehearsed by defense and prosecution attorneys that both believed they were telling the truth?[26]

The act of retrieving selected memories by thinking about them to ourselves and talking about them with others helps to consolidate long-term engrams. But when we rehearse inaccurate information, which may have infiltrated our recollections during attempts to fill gaps in fragmentary engrams, we may unwittingly create mistaken—though strongly held—beliefs about the past. (See figure 4.1.)

FIGURE 4.1

Cheryl Calleri, "Fugitive Memory III," 1992. 15 x 12 x 5". Photographic construction. Ruth Bachofner Gallery, Los Angeles.

Calleri attempts to convey visually the idea that memories change over time by mounting a vintage photograph in front of a curved mirror. Reflected by the curved mirror, the single photograph is transformed into a double image that conveys the impression that memories are in a state of flux. "Fugitive Memory III" shows an ephemeral double image of a nineteenth-century tintype. Calleri's ambiguous images allude to the ongoing processes that serve to shape, sculpt—and distort—many of our recollections.

THE WOMAN WHO MISTOOK A PSYCHOLOGIST FOR A RAPIST
The Vagaries of Source Memory

Donald Thompson has devoted the better part of his life to the study of human memory. A native Australian, he emigrated to Canada in the late 1960s to study with Endel Tulving. Thompson collaborated with Tulving in a series of famous experiments that led to the *encoding specificity principle:* the influential idea that the specific manner in which we encode an event determines what retrieval cues will later help us remember it. After obtaining his Ph.D., Thompson returned to Australia and continued his studies, focusing most intensively on issues concerning memory distortion and eyewitness identification. He testified frequently as an expert witness in legal cases that involved eyewitness recollections.

One can imagine how Thompson must have felt, then, when authorities informed him that he was going to be questioned about a rape because he matched almost perfectly the victim's memory of the rapist. Although bewildered by the bizarre accusation, Thompson was fortunate because he had an airtight alibi. Just before the rape occurred, Thompson was doing an interview on live television—ironically, he was describing how people can improve their ability to remember faces—and he could not possibly have been at the scene of the crime when the rape occurred. When it came to light that the victim had been watching Thompson on television prior to the rape and had apparently confused her memory of him from the television screen with her memory of the rapist, Thompson was released immediately.

A number of similar cases have been reported. Each time, witnesses offered erroneous identifications of perpetrators because they had encountered the accused outside the context of the crime. They later failed to remember when and where they had seen the person, while retaining a strong sense of familiarity toward him.[27]

These dramatic instances of distorted remembering demonstrate that accurate recollection often depends critically on our ability to recall precisely when and where an event occurred, a process I will refer to as *source memory*. The rape victim correctly remembered that she had seen Thompson's face before, but was mistaken regarding the *source* of her recollection. Recent research shows clearly that source memory is extremely fallible, and that failures to remember the correct source of acquired information are responsible for various kinds of errors and distortions in eyewitness recollections and other aspects of everyday memory.

In classic studies on eyewitness memory by Elizabeth Loftus and her colleagues, people viewed slides in which a car is involved in an accident after coming to a halt at a stop sign. After witnessing the event, some people were asked, "What happened to the car after it stopped at the stop sign?" and others were asked a question containing a misleading suggestion: "What happened to the car after it stopped at the yield sign?" Later, everyone was asked whether the car had come to a halt at a stop sign or a yield sign. People who had been asked the misleading question tended to remember having seen a yield sign. Loftus argued that the misleading suggestion had effectively wiped out these individuals' memories of the stop sign.[28]

Important scientific results tend to generate a flurry of subsequent research that helps to refine and alter our understanding of the initial outcome, and Loftus's finding was no exception. Various studies have shown that misleading information does not eliminate the original memory; when people are given appropriate tests, it is possible to demonstrate that the original memory still exists. But there is mounting evidence that participants in such experiments often suffer serious source memory problems: they have difficulty recollecting whether they actually saw the yield sign or just heard about it later. In one particularly striking experiment, participants were specifically informed that all the information in the postevent narrative was bogus—yet when tested a week later, some of them insisted that this information had been part of the original event! Their source memories had failed: they no longer remembered what was in the postevent narrative and what was in the original scene.[29]

The cognitive psychologist Larry Jacoby devised a clever procedure that also illustrates how failures of source memory can lead to memory distortion. Consider the following names: Sebastian Weisdorf, Roger Bannister, Valerie Marsh, Minnie Pearl, and Adrian Marr. Do any of them belong to famous people? The track star Roger Bannister and the entertainer Minnie Pearl may ring a bell, but the others probably do not (they are not famous). In Jacoby's experiment, people hardly ever claimed that a nonfamous name such as Sebastian Weisdorf was famous when they were tested immediately after exposure to the nonfamous names. But when tested a day later, they often claimed that Sebastian Weisdorf was the name of a famous person. Once again, a failure of source memory is the likely culprit: with the delay, people forgot that they had encountered Sebastian Weisdorf in the study list, but still felt that they knew the name. Jacoby claimed—with tongue planted firmly in cheek—that he had shown that it is indeed possible to become famous overnight.[30]

The ability to recollect source information lies at the heart of our ability to distinguish memories from fantasies and other products of our imagination. Have you ever planned to carry out a simple activity, such as mailing a letter, and later had difficulty recollecting whether you had actually done it or simply thought about doing it? In an attempt to convince yourself that you indeed put the letter in the mail, you may desperately try to remember some aspect of the context in which you carried out the activity. If, for example, you can specifically recall that the mailbox was stuffed full of letters when you opened it, you can comfortably conclude that you did mail the letter. If, however, you are unable to recall any source information whatsoever, then you are likely to continue to fret over what you did or did not do.

Laboratory studies conducted by the cognitive psychologist Marcia Johnson and her colleagues have shown that our ability to distinguish memory from imagination hinges on the recall of source information. Memories of external occurrences typically contain perceptual details about the context or setting of an event, whereas memories of internal events (such as thoughts and fantasies) typically contain little contextual information. When we cannot recall anything specific about context or setting, we lose an important basis for determining whether a "real" external event occurred, and hence we are quite susceptible to memory distortions. Conversely, if an imagined or fantasized event does contain a wealth of details about the context and setting of an event, we will be inclined to believe that it is a real memory of an actual event. Later in the chapter, I will discuss how these considerations assumed paramount importance in the celebrated case of Paul Ingram, whose "memories" of unlikely events turned life upside-down for many members of a small Washington town.[31]

The relative fragility of source memory may have important social implications in everyday life. We live in a media-saturated environment in which we are constantly encountering news, gossip, and rumors from sources that vary widely in credibility. If, for instance, you are waiting in a checkout line in the supermarket and notice a tabloid containing an ugly story that impeaches the honesty or fidelity of a public figure, you may be inclined to dismiss it because you maintain little faith in the reliability of the source. But what if several months later you are engaged in conversation about the honesty of public figures, and you remember the negative story but no longer recall the exact source? You may be inclined to stake more belief in the story than is warranted because you fail to remember that your information was acquired from a dubious source.

Social psychologists have indeed documented that when people forget the source of their knowledge, beliefs can be unduly influenced by the statements of people who lack credibility. Suppose, for example, that Professor Jones, a self-professed memory expert, tells you that it is possible to remember events that occur during the first weeks of life. But you also learn that Jones's Ph.D. is a fake and that he has never had any formal training in memory research. You will be inclined to dismiss his claims about memories of infancy, but a week later you are more likely to accept them because you may have forgotten that he is a noncredible source. Such findings are particularly worrisome because social psychologists have also demonstrated convincingly that people are generally biased in the direction of believing new information. For example, Daniel Gilbert and his colleagues have shown people statements including made-up words—such as "A bilicar is a spear"—that are arbitrarily designated as either true or false. Gilbert finds that when people forget whether the statement was designated as true or false, they show a bias to call it true. It requires a good deal of effort, Gilbert reports, to muster the critical faculties to "unbelieve" new information. Failures of source memory, then, open the door to the formation of unwarranted and possibly dangerous beliefs.[32]

Remembering when something happened is also an important part of source memory. If I ask you to try to remember what you did on July 16, 1994, it is extremely unlikely that you can obtain direct access to the events of that day. At best, you may be able to narrow down the range of possibilities ("I was vacationing on Cape Cod in the middle of July that year, so I probably spent some of the day on the beach"), and you might be able to draw on other kinds of information to suggest further hypotheses ("The calendar says that July 16 was a Saturday that year, and I think that we spent one of our Saturday afternoons on the Cape visiting Provincetown"). Yet you almost surely cannot simply "look up" the date the way you could look it up in your appointment book for that year.

The reconstructive nature of memory for time is underscored by various illusions and distortions.[33] One common distortion is known as a *scale effect*. Try to remember a visit that you made to a museum during calendar year 1995. Can you recall the date and the time of day of the visit? You may remember correctly that you went to the museum in the evening, while at the same time recalling that the visit was in June when it was actually in August. If a literal record of time were recorded in memory, it would be impossible to misremember the date by several months but still remember the exact time of day.

The fact that such scale effects occur implies that people infer and reconstruct time of occurrence on the basis of other kinds of retrieved information, such as physical setting. For example, you may recollect that it was dark when you left the museum, which allows you to infer that you visited the museum in the evening. You may also recall that you were wearing light clothes because of the heat, but this tells you only that the visit occurred during summertime. Unless you can recall some other salient information that allows reconstruction of the date (for example, that the visit was part of an anniversary celebration), you are likely to make errors—perhaps large ones—when attempting to assign a date to the episode.

People also make systematic errors when trying to recall the dates of well-known public events, tending to estimate that extremely important and salient events occurred more recently than less important events that occurred at about the same time.[34]

The errors that people make when trying to remember the exact time of events, or other kinds of source information, highlight a major vulnerability of our explicit memories. The sights, sounds, and meanings of everyday experience are not always all bundled up together into a single package. When we lose source information but retain some aspect of an experience—like the face of an attacker or the sense of familiarity with a name—we cast about in our minds in an attempt to figure out why we have a feeling of knowing or remembering. If we are lucky, our erroneous guesses are benign; nobody suffers much if I come to believe that Sebastian Weisdorf is a famous person. But when the stakes are higher, the vagaries of source memory can lead to disaster.

MEMORY DISTORTION AND THE BRAIN
Source Amnesia and Confabulation

Some of the most dramatic failures of source memory are seen in brain-damaged patients. I had the chance to observe such failures when carrying out my own studies of memory and amnesia in the early 1980s. I sought to determine whether patients with explicit memory deficits could learn any new facts, and if so, whether they could remember when and where they acquired the facts. One of the first patients I tested was a young man who had been involved in a motorcycle accident several years earlier. The patient, whom I will refer to as Gene, had suffered a serious head injury that damaged the hippocampus and other medial temporal lobe areas that are implicated in explicit memory. In addition, the injury also caused extensive damage to his frontal lobes.

Gene was a polite, quiet, and cooperative young man who seemed entirely normal in most respects—except for his nearly total inability to remember his past experiences explicitly. To find out whether he could learn any new facts, a female assistant and I took turns telling him bits of trivia that we made up, such as "Bob Hope's father was a fireman," or "Jane Fonda's favorite breakfast food is oatmeal." A minute or two later, one of us would ask him, "What job did Bob Hope's father have?" or "What does Jane Fonda like to eat for breakfast?" Surprisingly, Gene could occasionally provide the correct answers to our questions. I was truly startled, however, when I asked him to tell me how he knew the facts. Gene consistently claimed either that he had just made a lucky guess or that he had come across the fact in a newspaper or heard it on the radio—he never remembered that my assistant or I had told him the specific facts just a minute or so earlier!

Gene exhibited a form of memory failure known as source amnesia: he could learn a new fact, but had no memory for the source of his knowledge.[35] He behaved much as you or I might if we were asked to indicate how we know that Paris is the capital of France. We do not remember exactly where or when we learned this fact, but we can infer that it was probably in elementary school or perhaps through reading an encyclopedia. Gene's case is striking because his source amnesia occurred almost immediately after he learned the fact; for normal adults, source amnesia is observed only with much longer delays.

We found that most of the other memory-impaired patients we tested also showed source amnesia to greater or lesser degrees. Patients who were particularly susceptible to source amnesia tended to have signs of damage to the frontal lobes, whereas patients who were less susceptible to source amnesia had few signs of frontal lobe damage. Subsequent research has confirmed that patients whose damage is restricted to specific regions of the frontal lobes, and are not globally amnesic, have great difficulty remembering source information. Patients with restricted frontal lobe damage also have problems remembering temporal information, such as which of two events came first, or the order in which a sequence of items was presented. These observations indicate that the frontal lobes play an important role in allowing us to remember when and where our past experiences occurred, and thus form a critical part of the episodic memory system.[36]

In certain cases of frontal lobe damage, failures of source memory are accompanied by extensive and even bizarre confabulations—false recollections of events that did not occur and, in some instances, could not have occurred. Confabulations frequently involve distortions in remembering the time of past events. The neuropsychologist Morris Moscovitch described a case in which a sixty-one-year-old man with widespread frontal lobe damage insisted that he had been married for just four months when he had been married to the same woman for over thirty years. He recalled correctly that he and his wife had four children, spontaneously adding—apparently with some laughter— "Not bad for four months." When asked about the ages of his children, he noted that the eldest was thirty-two and the youngest twenty-two. How could one produce these children in four months? The patient had a ready response: "They're adopted."[37]

Such confabulations are often subjectively compelling, as illustrated by a patient who was asked to say whether he actually "remembered" the personal experiences that he reported or he just "knew" that these experiences had happened to him. The patient consistently said that he remembered the experiences, both when his memories were accurate and when they were confabulations that contained gross errors in temporal dating.[38]

The fact that confabulations often contain elements of actual experience, divorced from their appropriate settings, suggests that source amnesia is a major contributor to them. Not all confabulations, however, are based on real events from the patient's past. In some instances of what is known as "fantastic" confabulation, patients invent implausible experiences that often have a grandiose quality. Such confabulations may be triggered by salient cues in the environment. For instance, one patient launched into an entirely fictional recounting of his "experiences" as a sailor, apparently stimulated by a painting of a seascape in his doctor's office. Even here, then, a kind of source amnesia is at work, in the sense that the patient is unaware that his subjective experience of recollecting a long past event is attributable to a present or recently encountered stimulus.[39]

Confabulation is also related to the distinction between associative retrieval and strategic retrieval that I discussed in chapter 2. *Associative retrieval* is an involuntary form of remembering that is triggered automatically by an object or what somebody says; it is epitomized by the kind of vivid recollections that imposed themselves on Marcel Proust. *Strategic retrieval* is more laborious and voluntary—the kind of retrieval that you would undertake if I asked you to try to remember what you did on a Thursday night six weeks ago. Associative retrieval is often operative in confabulating patients: all kinds of experiences automatically spring to mind in response to environmental cues. Strategic retrieval, on the other hand, may be totally incapacitated. This means that the patients do not make the efforts necessary to figure out exactly when or where their recalled experiences occurred. Their minds are filled with all kinds of mnemonic flotsam and jetsam—fragments of experience that are not anchored to a proper time and place, and thus enter into peculiar alliances and marriages with one another. The result is a jumbled life story that is confusing to friends and relatives, if not to the patients themselves. Confabulating patients tend to be unaware that their recollections are often distorted. For these patients, the truth of their recalled pasts is as compelling as it is for anybody else. Because they are often amnesic for recent experiences, however, attempts to implore them to stop confabulating are quickly forgotten and thus generally unsuccessful.[40]

REMEMBERING PHANTOMS
False Recognition and the Right Frontal Lobe

In the spring of 1994, I gave an informal presentation one morning to a weekly meeting of fellow memory researchers at the Veterans Administration Medical Center in Boston. I was trying out some ideas about the role of the right frontal lobe in memory retrieval, ideas that had been stimulated in part by PET scanning studies that suggested an important role for the right frontal lobe in explicit retrieval. One of my colleagues mentioned that he had just come across a patient who might be of interest to me. The patient, a man in his sixties whom I will call Frank, had suffered a serious stroke that produced extensive damage to his right frontal lobe, but spared all other parts of his brain. Frank had been a successful lawyer during his working life, and retained many of his cognitive skills. If you had no knowledge of his condition and spent several hours with Frank, chances are that you would not suspect that anything was amiss. He is a pleasant, cooperative man who behaves appropriately, can recall recent and distant past events, and converses easily. Yet large sectors of his right frontal lobe had been destroyed. What had this damage done to his memory?

To try to find out, my colleagues and I gave Frank a simple test of recognition memory.[41] Frank studied a list of familiar words, and a few minutes later saw old words from the list and new words that had not appeared on the list. We instructed Frank to indicate which words were old and which were new. In addition, we told Frank that he should say whether he actually had a specific recollection of having studied the word earlier ("remember"), or whether he thought that the word had appeared earlier because it just seemed familiar to him ("know"). We compared Frank's performance to a control group who were about his age and had a similar educational background.

Frank's responses to previously studied words were relatively normal; he made about the same number of "remember" and "know" judgments as people in the control group did. But when we examined Frank's responses to new, nonstudied words, we quickly noted something unusual: Frank claimed to "remember" that nearly 40 percent of the new words had appeared on the list! People in the control group rarely indicated that new words had appeared on the list, and when they did, they nearly always said that they "knew" that the word had been shown earlier; they hardly ever said that they "remembered" seeing a new word. In a series of similar experiments, we found that Frank frequently claimed that he "remembered" sounds, nonsense syllables, and pictures that had never been presented to him. People in the control group almost never said that they remembered items that had not been presented.

Frank's problem was also evident even in casual conversation. When I met Frank for the first time, at his downtown apartment, I asked him whether he had ever seen me before. Yes, he responded, he "recalled" that I had tested him at my office. Why did Frank claim to remember me? And why would he claim to remember that words, sounds, or nonsense syllables that had not been presented in an experiment had, in fact, been shown to him? There are a number of possibilities, but our research with Frank pointed in one direction.

We obtained an important lead from an experiment in which we figured out how to stop Frank's false recollections. We showed him some pictures of common objects, such as a chair or a shirt, and later asked him whether he recognized those objects; we also asked him about pictures of other inanimate objects that had not been presented earlier. The catch was that we also tested him on pictures of animals. Would Frank claim that he remembered seeing pictures of animals, even though no animals at all had appeared on the list? The answer was a resounding no. Frank almost never said that he remembered seeing a picture of an animal, yet he insisted that he remembered seeing many inanimate objects that had not been presented earlier.

We now had some insight into the basis of Frank's false recollections.

As long as a word or picture was generally similar to the items that had appeared in the study list, Frank was willing to claim he remembered it. When Frank saw common words during the study list, then seeing a common word during the recognition test—even one that had not been on the study list—was enough to make him feel that he had seen the word earlier in the experiment. When Frank saw nonsense words on the study list, then seeing a nonsense word on the test—old or new—elicited a feeling of remembering. However, Frank did not make false recognitions to pictures of animals because they were drastically different from anything he had seen during the study phase of the experiment.

These observations may remind you of the distinction that I drew between two different levels of knowledge that can be accessed when people attempt to remember past episodes: general-event knowledge and event-specific knowledge. Recall that general events refer to extended episodes, such as going to a movie, whereas event-specific knowledge refers to particular episodes that are nested within the general event, such as buying popcorn or being surprised by the end of a film. In a memory experiment of the kind that we conducted with Frank, the general event might be seeing a list of words or seeing some pictures of objects, whereas event-specific knowledge would refer to memory for the specific items that were presented during the experiment. Frank appeared to be inappropriately responding "remember" on the basis of general-event information, rather than event-specific knowledge.

Our findings and ideas provide clues regarding the functions that are ordinarily subserved by the frontal regions that are damaged in Frank. The hypothesis that frontal regions are specifically involved in effortful or strategic retrieval processes fits well with Frank's story. If strategic retrieval were disrupted in Frank, then he may have become "stuck" at the general-event level, failing to engage in the effortful search that is necessary to determine whether a specific word or picture had been shown to him. Frank seemed unwilling or unable to carry out the mental work necessary to determine whether a particular mental experience should be called a "memory."

This interpretation meshes well with the results of recent PET scanning studies. The frontal lobes become active when people engage in the mental work involved in trying to recall a past event. The damage that Frank suffered to his right frontal lobe made it difficult for him to put forth the same kind of effort during retrieval. The result was that Frank became too easily satisfied that he had "remembered" when there was only a family resemblance between a word or a picture and something he had seen earlier. Likewise, Frank's "memory" for having met me before was probably rooted in reality. An adult male psychologist had once tested him, but Frank mistakenly took this as evidence that the two of us were old acquaintances.

Frank's false recognitions are also illuminated by evidence from "split brain" patients, whose left and right cerebral hemispheres have been surgically disconnected from each other. The two hemispheres no longer communicate with each other, so researchers can present information separately to each one. Recent studies have demonstrated that the left hemisphere often falsely recognizes novel pictures or words that are similar to ones it has been shown recently. But the right hemisphere claims to remember only those pictures or words that match exactly the ones it was shown. The left hemisphere seems to make inferences and associations that render it susceptible to memory distortion, whereas the right hemisphere retains a less embellished and more veridical representation. Frank had sustained damage to his right hemisphere, so he probably relied heavily on the left hemisphere when making recognition decisions, thus making him vulnerable to remembering things that never happened.[42]

THE CONFABULATED MOUSETRAP
Source Amnesia and the Preschool

Some of the most striking and socially significant evidence for source amnesia and confabulation comes from recent studies of young children. The fallibility of children's memory has become a hot topic recently, largely because of the critical role that young children's testimony plays in cases of alleged sexual abuse. Public and media attention to such questions has been intense in episodes involving preschools, where teachers and professionals have been accused—and sometimes convicted—of carrying out lewd and often grotesque sexual acts.[43]

One poignant instance was broadcast by *Frontline* in July 1993. The show tracked the progress of a court case in the small North Carolina town of Edenton. Several members of the Little Rascals preschool staff, including young women who were mothers themselves, were accused of sexually abusing children at the preschool. The charges were based on the children's recollection of being abused and of witnessing sexual acts between staff members. But the children were subject to highly suggestive questioning, and their allegations included fantastic claims about preposterous events. One preschooler, for example, recalled diving into a lake to rescue a companion from the clutches of attacking sharks that had been released into the waters, and another child "remembered" an incident involving an alien spaceship. Nonetheless, the children's reports of abuse led to the conviction and imprisonment of Robert Kelly, Jr., who ran the preschool, and Kathryn Dawn Wilson, a young mother who worked there.[44]

In another case with many similar features, Margaret Kelly Michaels, a twenty-six-year-old teacher at the Wee Care Nursery School in New Jersey, was accused of various horrendous acts:

> Kelly Michaels was said to have licked peanut butter off children's genitals, played the piano while nude, made children drink her urine and eat her feces, and to have raped and assaulted these children with knives, forks, spoons, and Lego blocks. She was accused of performing these acts during school hours over a period of seven months. None of the alleged acts were noticed by staff or reported by children to their parents. No parent noticed signs of strange behavior or genital soreness in their children, or smelled urine or feces on them.[45]

Despite the absence of physical evidence and the curious circumstance that nobody at the preschool ever noticed or reported inappropriate behavior, the preschoolers' memories of abuse were convincing enough to lead to the conviction of Kelly Michaels on over one hundred counts of sexual abuse against twenty children. Although sentenced to a forty-seven-year prison term, Michaels's conviction was overturned on appeal after she spent five years in jail. As in the North Carolina case, the New Jersey preschoolers were subject to highly suggestive and relentless questioning by examiners who were convinced that abuse had occurred.

The accusations and convictions in the North Carolina and New Jersey cases were based on children's memories. Were the jurors correct to accept the preschoolers' recollections of abuse? To what extent are children's memories subject to distortion and even outright confabulation? When should their testimony be believed? These questions have vexed psychologists, social workers, lawyers—and parents—for decades. Professional opinions have tended to polarize toward one of two extreme views. Some have argued that "children do not lie," that they are capable of accurately recalling much of their pasts, and that they are no more susceptible to suggestive influences than are adults.

Others have claimed that young children are often unable to distinguish between fantasy and reality, are hypersuggestible, and are virtually incapable of offering credible testimony about past events. In a scholarly review of nearly a century's worth of research, Stephen Ceci and Maggie Bruck took an intermediate position: young children often are more suggestible and prone to distortion than older children and adults, but under the right circumstances they can accurately recall many aspects of their past experiences.[46]

Recent research has shown convincingly that young children often have great difficulty remembering source information, which in turn renders them vulnerable to false recollections. It has also been established that suggestive questioning can have devastating effects on the accuracy of some preschool children's memories. Ceci and his collaborators have provided some of the most dramatic findings.[47] In one experiment, for instance, they asked preschool children about some everyday events that had actually occurred. But they also inquired about other incidents that, according to the children's parents, had never happened. For instance, they asked children to recollect the time that they "[g]ot a finger caught in a mousetrap and had to go to the hospital to get the trap off." An interviewer asked the children to think hard about the events by attempting to visualize them; the procedure was carried out once a week for ten weeks. Finally, the interviewer probed the children's memories: "Tell me if this ever happened to you: Did you ever get your finger caught in a mousetrap and have to go to the hospital to get the trap off?"

Ceci and colleagues observed that over half the children produced "memories" of at least one of the made-up incidents. These false recollections were typically complex narratives that contained rich and detailed information about numerous aspects of the imaginary episodes. One little boy, for example, recalled that the trouble all began when his brother tried to wrestle a toy from him: "My brother Colin was trying to get Blowtorch [an action figure] from me, and I wouldn't let him take it from me, so he pushed me into the wood pile where the mousetrap was. And then my finger got caught in it. And then we went to the hospital, and my mommy, daddy, and Colin drove me there, to the hospital in our van, because it was far away. And the doctor put a bandage on this finger."[48]

This child and others appeared to be suffering from a type of source amnesia. The events in their narratives felt familiar because they had been thinking about them for weeks, but the children failed to remember that they had imagined these episodes. Unable to recollect the source of their knowledge, they behaved as though the events had actually occurred. These confabulated memories were, however, convincing to the children. Even when told that the mousetrap incident and other imaginary episodes never happened, some of the children insisted to their parents that these episodes must have occurred because they were so sure that they remembered them.

The psychologist Michelle Leichtman collaborated with Ceci on a study that showed how some children could be led to misremember an innocuous everyday event. A stranger named Sam Stone paid a two-minute visit to a preschool. Sam walked around the classroom, said hello to a teacher, who introduced him to the children, commented that the story being read to the children was a favorite of his, and left. In subsequent interviews concerning Sam's visit, some children were asked misleading questions about his behavior. "Remember the time that Sam Stone visited your classroom and spilled chocolate on that white teddy bear?" an interviewer asked these preschoolers; "did he do it on purpose or was it an accident?" The interviewer also asked whether Sam was being silly or angry when he ripped a book. Sam never spilled or ripped anything during his visit. But when probed ten weeks later about their memories for the episode, over 50 percent of three- and four-year-olds said that Sam had spilled chocolate on a teddy bear or ripped a book. About one-third of the three- and four-year-olds claimed that they actually remembered seeing Sam commit these acts. One three-year-old girl, for instance, recalled that "[h]e . . . he when my teacher said 'be careful with the dollies,' and he . . . he put it up. Then the dollies, some, some of them ripped off." The interviewer asked why some of the dollies ripped. "Because he was throwing them up and down," the little girl explained, "and he was trying to catch it." Did Sam Stone do anything else, the interviewer wondered? "Then he got a book and throwed it up," the girl answered, "and then one of the pages ripped off." "Really?" asked the interviewer. "How did he rip the page?" "When he was throwing it up," the little girl reported. The same youngster also recalled that "[h]e played with one of the toys, and said 'be careful!' But he didn't be careful with the toys. Then he went into Housekeeping to play with the toy. And he threw one of the toys in Housekeeping." Five- and six-year-old children fared somewhat better than the younger children: just under 40 percent said that Sam had done any misdeeds; only a few claimed that they saw him do these things.

In contrast to these children, other preschoolers did not receive any misleading suggestions at all. Hardly any of these three- and four-year-olds said that Sam had done anything to a teddy bear or a book, and none of the older children did. The boys and girls who had not been misled provided generally accurate accounts of what Sam had done.[49]

As in the mousetrap study, impaired source memory is a likely contributor to these instances of memory distortion: some misled children confused whether they had actually seen Sam spill chocolate all over a teddy bear or whether they had only been told about it. Then they built an inaccurate story around the fragments of information that had been "implanted" during suggestive questioning.

These observations suggest that when an examiner imparts misleading or erroneous suggestions to a young child, she may no longer be able to remember accurately what actually happened. Conversely, in the absence of heavy-handed suggestive questioning, the recollections of young children can be extremely accurate. These points are also borne out by Bruck and Ceci's observations of an everyday incident that is familiar to all preschoolers: visiting the doctor's office.[50] When a group of five-year-old children visited their pediatrician for a scheduled checkup, the pediatrician administered a physical exam, an inoculation, and an oral polio vaccine; an assistant gave the child some treats, read a story, and talked about a poster on the wall. A year later, children were questioned several times about the visit. Some children were given misleading suggestions that the assistant had conducted the exam and given the shots, whereas the pediatrician had given them treats, read to them, and talked about the poster. The other children received no misleading information. Over half of the children who received misleading questions incorporated the suggestions into their memories of what had happened. They now "remembered" that the assistant had given them a shot, and added in other false details. Some children, for instance, recalled that the assistant had checked their ears and noses. But children who received no misleading suggestions never generated false recollections.

Likewise, other studies have shown that children who are not subject to suggestive questioning can remember everyday events with impressive accuracy. For instance, the cognitive psychologist Robin Fivush and her colleagues found that three-year-old children recalled specific everyday events, such as a family outing to the circus or an airplane trip, with considerable accuracy; indeed, they showed impressive levels of retention when queried about the events a year later. Fivush also reports that preschool children do not routinely incorporate into their own memories information about a past event that is simply mentioned to them by their mothers.[51]

One worrisome aspect of the findings reported by Ceci and colleagues is that the false recollections of misled children are convincing to knowledgeable adults. In both the Sam Stone study and the mousetrap study, experts who viewed videotapes of children recounting their experiences failed to distinguish confabulated stories from accurate accounts of what actually did happen. Experienced memory researchers, therapists, and law enforcement professionals who all specialize in working with children were stumped by the task of separating out true and false memories—even though these experts were quite certain that they knew which children were remembering accurately and which were not. Clearly, adults who interview preschoolers must take careful precautions to avoid inadvertently creating distorted recollections of events whose existence they merely suspect. Bruck and Ceci have shown clearly that such precautions were sadly lacking in the Kelly Michaels preschool fiasco.

Research with young children is consistent with the links I have emphasized among source amnesia, memory distortion, and frontal lobe function. The evidence shows convincingly that preschool children can have problems with source memory, problems that appear to be closely linked with memory distortions. Intriguingly, studies of the developing brain indicate that frontal regions are especially slow to develop; they are probably not fully functional until near adolescence and are definitely immature in preschool children. Likewise, behavioral research has shown that preschool children often carry out cognitive tests in a manner similar to adults with frontal lobe lesions. I reviewed this evidence in detail with two of my Harvard colleagues, the developmental psychologists Jerome Kagan and Michelle Leichtman, and we concluded that preschoolers' false recollections are partly attributable to the relative immaturity of their frontal lobes.[52] Although it is too simplistic to attribute all the memory distortions exhibited by young children to immature frontal functions, the idea may help us to go some way toward understanding why some children stubbornly insisted that Sam Stone soiled a teddy bear and others remembered the pain caused by a mousetrap that never harmed them.

The confabulations of young children and patients with frontal lobe damage provide striking evidence that a subjective experience of remembering can be simultaneously compelling and dead wrong. But elaborate false recollections are not the sole province of preschoolers and frontal patients. They can sometimes turn up in the most unlikely settings.

REMINISCENCES OF A SHERIFF'S DEPUTY

In the spring of 1993, *The New Yorker* published an article about a case of memory retrieval so strange that it stimulated the intense curiosity of people who had never previously thought much about the workings of human memory. Provocatively titled "Remembering Satan," the article centered on the story of Paul Ingram, a forty-three-year-old deputy in a Washington county sheriff's office whose eighteen- and twenty-two-year-old daughters had accused him of sexually abusing them as children.[53] Ingram could not remember committing any abusive acts, and so initially denied the charges. Yet his daughters' memories were compelling enough to lead the local authorities to arrest him. Ingram continued to state that he did not remember any abuse, but the arresting officers—his own colleagues—assured him that if he confessed he would be able to remember the incidents. Ingram belonged to a fundamentalist Pentecostal church and was also encouraged by his pastor to remember the alleged events. After several hours of questioning and praying, he conceded that the allegations were true, that he had probably repressed the memories, and that he was willing to sign a confession.

As the questioning proceeded, the scope of the inquiry expanded, and the officers aggressively pursued their hunch that the abuse occurred in the context of a satanic cult involving several of Ingram's friends. Ingram again prayed with his pastor and began to recover the requested memories. He followed the officers' suggestions to visualize his coconspirators and the acts they had performed, and he was buoyed by assurances from his pastor that God would allow only true memories to enter his mind. When Ingram's daughters learned that their father had begun to describe satanic rituals in connection with the alleged abuse, they began to recover their own memories of ghastly cult activities, including mass orgies and murders of babies. Soon enough, Ingram had confessed to engaging in all manner of satanic rituals, including animal sacrifice and murder.

Ingram's recovered memories led to his own imprisonment and to the jailing of two alleged coconspirators. Both of these men vehemently denied all charges. There was no external evidence that Ingram's daughters had ever been abused, nor was there any physical evidence of murders and mutilations. And, to make matters even muddier, the memories reported by the two daughters frequently conflicted with one another. As he awaited a jury trial in prison, Ingram was interviewed by the social psychologist Richard Ofshe, who asked Ingram to remember the time he had forced his son and one of his daughters to have sex in front of him. This event was similar to others that Ingram had been queried about, but it differed in an important way: his daughter never claimed that it had occurred, and Ingram's son said that no such event had ever taken place. Yet Ingram's response to Ofshe's question followed a predictable pattern: he initially failed to recollect the episode, but after visualizing and praying on it, he recovered a vivid "memory" of the terrible act that he had ordered and witnessed.

This jarring observation does not show that all of Ingram's other "memories" are inaccurate, and there is no way to prove conclusively that Ofshe's made-up event never actually happened.[54] But assuming that this event never did occur, Ofshe's observations indicate that Ingram is susceptible to false recollections. Therefore, they also raise doubts about the validity of the other memories that Ingram recalled with his pastor's help. Eventually, the lack of external evidence for murders and sacrifices led to the dropping of cult-related charges against Ingram and his two friends.

Although Ingram's faith in his recollections had been shaken, he continued to believe that he had abused his daughters and that he owed it to them to plead guilty. Ultimately, however, after taking more time to carefully think through what had happened, Ingram concluded that none of his memories were real and proclaimed his innocence. He unsuccessfully attempted to change his guilty plea, was sentenced to a twenty-year prison term, and had two appeals denied during his first six years of imprisonment. With the widespread attention that followed the publication of the article and a book about the Ingram case, public sympathy for him increased. As of this writing, however, Ingram remains in jail.

The case of Paul Ingram is riveting because the magnitude of the apparent memory distortion seems so immense: How could anyone misremember ghastly murders and sacrifices that apparently never occurred? Nobody knows for sure exactly what did or did not happen to Paul Ingram and his daughters, but some features of Ingram's case become comprehensible when we consider the importance of the retrieval environment, the role of imagery in recollective experience, effects of rehearsal on memory, and the nature of source memory. The retrieval environment in which Ingram recovered his "memories" contained several crucial features: suggestive questioning by the arresting officers and assertions that he would remember his abusive acts if he confessed; their instructions to visualize the events he was trying to remember and to conjecture about what happened; and his pastor's assurance that God would allow only real memories to enter his mind. These factors, mutually reinforcing one another, freely encouraged Ingram to generate the kind of "raw materials" that are likely to give rise to a subjective sense of remembering—vivid visual images—and provided Ingram both legal and moral assurance that the resulting mental experiences would be accurate memories of horrendous events. Frequent repetition and retrieval probably increased Ingram's willingness to believe that these experiences were true memories.

Problems of source memory were largely "solved" for Ingram by the officers who asserted that confession would yield remembrance and by the pastor who offered assurances that God would let only genuine memories enter his mind. Ingram was thereby excused from grappling with the fundamental question that ought to have plagued him: Were the vivid images that came bursting into his consciousness recollections of events that had actually occurred, or were they merely products of current and past imaginings, thoughts, and fantasies? Unfettered by the need to analyze the sources of his subjectively compelling mental experiences, Ingram was free to create a complex network of evil acts, unspeakable rituals, and demonized individuals that confirmed the darkest suspicions of those who wished to expose—yet may have unwittingly helped to create—the hellish world that Ingram described.

Tragedies like the Paul Ingram story or the Kelly Michaels case teach us that fragility and power can coexist as salient attributes of memory because those aspects of memory that make it fragile—the role played by the retrieval environment in constructing subjective recollective experience, the susceptibility of remembering to postevent influences and change, and the evanescent nature of source memory—in no way diminish its power.

The fragility of memory is partly attributable to the fact that the seemingly straightforward task of remembering the what, where, and when of our past depends on subtle interactions among different processes of which we are only dimly aware, and over which we have little control. But, as I emphasized at the outset of this chapter, we must keep in mind that errors and distortions in remembering, though startling when they occur, are far from the norm in our mnemonic lives. Most of the time our memories reliably handle the staggering variety of demands that our day-to-day activities place on them. I have already touched on some of the brain systems and processes that allow us to remember the events and themes that constitute our lives. To understand more fully the brain substrates of memory's fragile power, we need to take a longer look at the foreign and bewildering world of the amnesic syndrome.

FIVE

VANISHING TRACES
Amnesia and the Brain

THE AMNESIA THAT RESULTS from brain damage provides an extraordinary window on many aspects of memory. It's also a fascinating human story. I recall that the first time I met an engaging man in his mid-fifties named Frederick, nothing suggested that he was in any way remarkable. Frederick came to the Unit for Memory Disorders, which my colleagues and I established at the University of Toronto in 1981. Its purpose was to evaluate, investigate, and rehabilitate memory problems that arise as a consequence of brain injury and disease.

It did not take long for us to see that there was indeed something wrong, terribly wrong, with Frederick's memory. When we showed him words and pictures, he remembered little or nothing of them. When I asked him how he had made his way to us for testing, he could not tell me. When I inquired about what he had done the day before, he looked at me with a blank stare. In view of these memory difficulties, I was not surprised to learn that Frederick had stopped working and that he led a quiet life with his wife. His physicians believed that he had entered the early stages of Alzheimer's disease, the devastating illness that often begins with memory loss and develops into a generalized deterioration of cognitive function.

Back in the early 1980s, I was starting to take seriously the idea that memory is not a single thing. Laboratory evidence pointed toward three different long-term memory systems: *episodic* memory, which allows us to recollect specific incidents from our pasts; *semantic* memory, the vast network of associations and concepts that underlies our general knowledge of the world; and *procedural* memory, which allows us to learn skills and know how to do things.

Spending time with Frederick, I started to see that he could help me study these memory systems in the everyday world. Golf became one of our favorite subjects. Frederick had been an avid golfer for thirty years. He still played from time to time, he said, although he could not remember any specific recent trips to the golf course. I, too, had long been an avid golfer, and always looked forward to talking with Frederick about our mutual passion.

What, I wondered, would a game of golf be like for someone with a severe memory disorder? Frederick would need episodic memory to remember where he hit the ball and how many strokes he took on each hole. Words like *par, birdie,* and *wedge* would be meaningless to him without semantic memory, as would the game's strategies and rules. And without procedural memory he couldn't make use of the skills he had acquired in the various facets of the game, such as driving and putting. Playing a couple of rounds of golf with Frederick, I realized, could be a revealing natural laboratory in which to study the effects of memory loss.

We played two rounds, one on a golf course that was familiar to Frederick and one on a course that was new to him.[1] Frederick had never been a highly skilled player but had always been able to hold his own, which he did during both of the rounds we played. As far as I could tell, his procedural memory for the golf skills he had acquired many years earlier was intact. Frederick's semantic memory, too, appeared to be relatively unscathed: I carried a tape recorder with me during both rounds, and every time Frederick used a term of golf jargon, I recorded what it was and whether it was being appropriately used. His golf vocabulary was perfect: he spoke easily about birdies, doglegs, and finesse shots. Frederick also exhibited excellent retention of the rules and strategies of golf: he knew that the player whose ball is farthest from the hole plays first; he regularly chose appropriate clubs; did his best when putting to assess the slope of the green. Frederick's access to semantic knowledge about the game was no different, at least in any obvious way, from that of any other experienced golfer.

But at one point Frederick's ball was between my ball and the hole, and he marked it with a coin—a standard item of golf etiquette—then began walking off the green after I had completed my putt. He had forgotten that he had marked his ball and not yet putted himself. To examine Frederick's episodic memory more systematically, I introduced a simple manipulation: on half of the holes, I hit first and he hit second, so that he could immediately search for his ball; on the other half, he hit first, thus creating a delay before he initiated his search. Frederick often found his ball in the first case, but almost never found it when the search was delayed. As long as he could hold his recollection of the tee shot in short-term or working memory, he generally remembered the location of his ball. But either the passage of time or the interference created by watching me hit was sufficient to eliminate his working memory of the ball's location, and he could not count on his long-term episodic memory. As we walked from each green to the next tee, I asked Frederick to recall his shots on the hole we had just completed, again testing his episodic memory. On most holes, he could not recall any shots.

A startling incident occurred on the 10th hole at the course Frederick had played many times before. This hole requires that the tee shot be hit over a creek, and Frederick was not sure whether he would be able to execute a good enough shot to avoid ending up in the water. But he hit one of his finest drives of the round, easily carrying the ball over the creek and setting up a relatively straightforward second shot to the green. Excited and impressed by his drive, Frederick immediately began to think about his next shot: Could he reach the green with an 8-iron or would he be safer to use a 7-iron? Could he manage to keep his approach shot out of the sand trap? Clearly, Frederick had carried out a deep, elaborative encoding of the tee-shot episode.

I then stepped up to the tee and hit my drive (carrying well over the creek, I am pleased to report). As I walked off the tee and headed down the fairway, I glanced back over my shoulder to an unexpected sight: Frederick was teeing up again and preparing to hit another drive. When I asked him what he was doing, he gave me a bemused look and said that he, too, would like to play the hole and so he would have to hit a tee shot. He had no memory of having teed off a minute earlier, and no idea that he had managed to hit his drive over the creek.

After each round, Frederick and I had drinks in the clubhouse, and I asked him to recall whatever he could about the game. Unable to recall a single stroke or episode from the entire round, he instead spoke in empty generalities, ruminating that "I hit some bad ones out there" or "Couldn't really putt today." No matter how much I prompted him, Frederick couldn't muster more than a perplexed look and an incredulous question, such as "Did I really do that?" or "Did that really happen?"

When I picked up Frederick at his home to play our second round, about a week later, he warned me that he was not a very good player, that he had not been out on a golf course for several months, and that he might be a bit nervous since this was the first time he had ever played with me. I did not have the heart to tell him the truth.

MAKING AMNESICS
The Machinery of Memory

Frederick's memory impairment, though unusually severe, is typical of one of the most extensively studied consequences of brain damage in all of neuropsychology: the amnesic syndrome. Modern research on the amnesic syndrome was stimulated by pathbreaking observations made by the neurosurgeon William Beecher Scoville and the neuropsychologist Brenda Milner of a young man now known widely throughout psychology and neuroscience by the initials HM— arguably the single most important patient ever studied in neuropsychology.[2] What makes him so special?

In 1953, Scoville operated on the twenty-seven-year-old HM to relieve serious, recurrent epileptic seizures. He removed a constellation of structures tucked deep within the medial (inner) sectors of the temporal lobes on both sides of the brain, including most of the hippocampus, the amygdala, and some adjacent areas of temporal cortex (see figure 5.1). HM's seizures diminished, leading to a general improvement in his medical condition. Prior to the operation, his IQ had measured 101 on the Wechsler Adult Intelligence Scale—nearly identical to the population mean of 100. When he was tested two years after the operation, HM scored 112. In just about all respects, he seemed exactly like the preoperative HM. The sad exception was that he appeared entirely incapable of remembering anything that happened to him after the operation.

HM's amnesia quickly became apparent when he could not recognize members of the hospital staff he used to see on a regular basis, and would frequently forget when he had recently eaten a meal. He performed disastrously on the Wechsler Memory Scale. When a person scores about 15 points lower on this test ("MQ") than on the IQ scale, most neuropsychologists classify that person as amnesic. After his

FIGURE 5.1

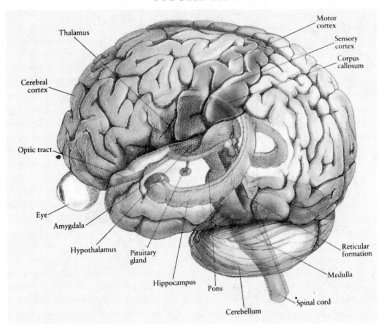

This figure allows us to look "through" the cerebral cortex and view some of the structures that occupy the inner regions of the brain. The hippocampus, part of the limbic system, and the thalamus, part of the diencephalon, both play important roles in explicit remembering. The amygdala, also part of the limbic system, is critical for emotional memories (see chapter 7). The cerebellum, part of the hindbrain, is prominently involved in procedural memory (see chapter 6). Reprinted from F. E. Bloom and A. Lazerson, *Brain, Mind, and Behavior*, 2d ed. (New York: W. H. Freeman Co., 1988).

operation, HM's MQ was 47 points lower than his IQ.[3]

The surgical removal of HM's medial temporal structures had demolished his explicit memory of recent experiences while leaving unscathed his general level of intelligence. Indeed, the key to understanding amnesic patients like HM is realizing that their disorders are highly selective. General intelligence, perceptual functions, language comprehension and production, and various kinds of knowledge and skills are all spared. Immediate or working memory is likewise unimpaired: when tested immediately, amnesic patients can remember just as many numbers as normal volunteers. But when required to remember information across a delay, amnesic patients' explicit memory for ongoing experiences is devastated.

HM provided the first direct evidence that structures in the medial temporal lobe play an important role in memory. In addition to his severe anterograde amnesia (that is, inability to remember events that occurred after the operation), HM also had some retrograde amnesia—he failed to recall events from several years preceding his operation. For instance, HM had forgotten about the death of a favorite uncle approximately three years earlier. Subsequent research suggests that the period of HM's retrograde amnesia covers more than just three years prior to the operation. When tested in the early 1980s, he did not remember any specific episodes that had taken place in the decade before his operation at age twenty-seven, but he remembered many episodes that occurred before his sixteenth birthday. This temporal gradient provided important early support for the consolidation hypothesis discussed in chapter 3, which holds that the medial temporal region is crucial to memory for a limited period of time after initial encoding of an experience. Because HM had no difficulty recalling childhood experiences, the engrams for such memories presumably had become fixed or consolidated in the extensive cortical networks outside the medial temporal region that subserve long-term storage. Accordingly, his retrieval of such experiences no longer depended on an intact medial temporal lobe.

In the years that followed the publication of Scoville and Milner's pioneering observations, HM's case was often cited to support the idea that memory for recent events depends on the hippocampus, the small seahorse-shaped structure that is a critical component of the medial temporal lobe system. During the 1970s, researchers who studied memory in rats and other animals reported that lesions to the hippocampus produce marked deficits in an animal's memory for recent experiences, particularly for spatial layouts.[4] These observations seemed to dovetail with HM's situation, but since the hippocampus was only one of several structures removed from his medial temporal lobe, his case could not determine whether damage restricted to the hippocampus causes severe amnesia.

In 1986, Stuart Zola-Morgan, Larry Squire, and David Amaral described RB, a patient with damage restricted to the hippocampus. When he was fifty-two years old, RB had undergone coronary artery bypass surgery and shortly afterward suffered an arterial tear that caused a temporary loss of blood flow to the brain. This is known as *ischemia,* and is often produced by temporary loss of oxygen to the brain as a result of cardiac arrest—a common cause of amnesic syndromes. A particular region in the hippocampus known as the CA1 field is especially sensitive to ischemia.

When RB died, in 1983, Zola-Morgan and colleagues carefully examined his brain and found damage only in the CA1 field of the hippocampus. Other structures within the medial temporal lobe, as well as elsewhere in the brain, were almost entirely unaffected. But RB's amnesia was not as severe as HM's memory loss, and RB had almost no retrograde amnesia. More recently, two patients have been described who also sustained significant damage only in the hippocampus; their memory impairments were generally similar to RB's, except that they had more extensive retrograde amnesias.[5] These observations indicate that damage to the hippocampus alone can produce a clinically significant memory loss. The kinds of profound amnesia observed in HM and Frederick may require damage to additional medial temporal lobe structures.

This idea is supported by observations concerning a rare but devastating neurological condition that often produces amnesia: herpes simplex encephalitis. Herpes simplex, a dangerous virus that is the primary cause of encephalitis in Western societies, produces symptoms of infection that include high fever, vomiting, and severe headaches. Unless treated quickly, encephalitic infection can produce serious brain damage. Structures throughout the medial temporal region are particularly vulnerable to herpes simplex, perhaps because the temporal lobe is close to the point at which the virus enters the brain, or because the virus has a special affinity for the specific neurochemical and neuroimmunological properties of the temporal lobe.[6] Sadly for those infected, herpes simplex encephalitis can produce the sort of full-scale annihilation of explicit memory for recent experiences seen in HM and Frederick. One patient known in the amnesia literature as SS used to be a physicist who worked on laser technology before contracting encephalitis. SS has maintained an IQ of 136, but he forgets most of his experiences after just a few minutes. Likewise, another well-studied patient known as Boswell seems to have no explicit memory for recent experiences despite generally intact cognitive functions.[7]

I recently encountered a particularly affecting case of encephalitis-induced amnesia involving a young British artist. David Jane, a respected painter in his mid-thirties, had exhibited his pictures of landscape forms and ancient Indian temples in small London galleries. In 1989, he and his family decided to take a Christmas vacation in

Brazil. Everything went well until New Year's Eve: "It was just before midnight," David relates. "The champagne was open and I thought 'thank God the eighties are nearly over.' Then I started getting this headache that got worse and worse."[8] As the headache became increasingly unbearable, David became confused and sick, then fell into a coma. He did not fully regain consciousness until after he had been flown back to England. He woke up in a London hospital remembering virtually nothing about his past. He possessed little or no memory for ongoing events, and was unable to speak or comprehend what others said. Written words were meaningless strings of letters to him.

David had contracted a herpes simplex virus in Brazil that spared his right hemisphere but destroyed much of his left temporal lobe and its connections to other regions of the left cerebral hemisphere. Consequently, his verbal memory and his ability to use and understand language had been obliterated. Neurologists and neuropsychologists have known for over a century that language and verbal abilities are heavily dependent on the left hemisphere, whereas nonverbal and spatial functions are more dependent on the right hemisphere. Memory is similarly lateralized. Patients with damage to the left hippocampus and medial temporal lobe tend to have difficulties explicitly remembering verbal information but have no problems remembering visual designs and spatial locations. Patients with damage to the right hippocampus and medial temporal lobe tend to show the opposite pattern.[9] In cases of global amnesia, like those of HM, SS, Boswell, and RB, damage to both the left and right medial temporal regions results in poor memory for both verbal and nonverbal information.

But David Jane's right hemisphere was perfectly fine and, during the earliest days of recovery, while his state of consciousness was still rather hazy, he tried to paint again and found that he could. When he returned home from the hospital and faced the excruciating task of learning to read, speak, and write again, he continued to paint with relative ease. His subject matter, however, had changed. Instead of painting landscapes and temples, David felt irresistibly drawn toward the high-tech images of his own brain that revealed clearly and dispassionately the damage that had radically altered his mental life. He embarked on a series of paintings of magnetic resonance image (MRI) scans that showed with pinpoint precision the areas of his left temporal lobe that had been destroyed by the herpes simplex virus. But these paintings are not merely slavish copies of the MRI images; the artist has succeeded in creating novel and highly personal interpretations of his brain scans. His paintings convey an eerie sense of how mind and memory are exquisitely, perhaps frighteningly, dependent on the integrity of the brain, as exemplified by "Reaffirmation II" (figure 5.2).

When I spoke with David Jane in early 1994, four years after the onset of his amnesia, his speech was still somewhat labored but he expressed unswerving determination to carry on with his art. David's new paintings had been shown publicly in 1993, and they received glowing reviews.[10] David remarked, only half-jokingly, that the destruction of his left hemisphere seemed to free up the right side to create more boldly than before his illness. But he is acutely aware of his memory problems, and still has difficulty reading and writing. David's memory impairments are much broader than those observed in classical cases of amnesic syndromes; he lost much of his semantic knowledge. Among encephalitic patients, however, David's case is not unique. When the virus spreads widely throughout the temporal lobe, and particularly when it damages the front of the temporal lobe, patients can have great difficulty accessing general knowledge about familiar objects, places, or words.[11]

Monkeys and Memory

With the relatively rare exception of cases like RB, brain damage in amnesic patients is not neatly restricted to the structures that are of interest to memory researchers. Studying amnesia in animals, though, enables scientists interested in the brain systems that subserve memory to make precise, experimentally controlled lesions to specific brain structures.

In 1978, the neuroscientist Mortimer Mishkin of the National Institute of Mental Health made a major contribution to the analysis of brain and memory by producing an analogue of human amnesia in monkeys. Mishkin used a simple task in which the animals are shown a small toy for several seconds. Shortly thereafter, the monkeys are shown the same object, plus a new one. Whenever they choose the new one, the monkeys are given a food reward. Once they learn the rules, monkeys can demonstrate recognition of what they were shown earlier by choosing the novel object. Mishkin observed that removing either the hippocampus or the neighboring amygdala had no effect on the monkeys' abilities to recognize which object had been presented earlier. But removing *both* structures led to a massive memory impair-

FIGURE 5.2

David Jane, "Reaffirmation II," 1992. 40 x 26". Oil on paper. Courtesy of the artist.

Here we see Jane's interpretation of a coronal section of an MRI scan. Imagine that you are looking at the front of the brain toward the back. A coronal section depicts a top-to-bottom slice of the brain at a particular location in the front-back plane. The standard radiological convention is to show the left side of the brain on the right and the right side on the left. This painting incorporates this convention: the small circular dark area in the middle of the right side of the painting represents the lesion that caused David's loss of memory (damaged areas of the brain show up as dark spots on an MRI scan). The large dark cavities in the middle of the painting are known as ventricles, which also show up as dark regions on an MRI. The brain as depicted in "Reaffirmation II" is a dangerous, foreboding place, full of ominous crevices and fissures. Looking at the painting, we can begin to appreciate the shadowy, foreign world of encephalitis-induced amnesia.

ment: the monkeys without a hippocampus and amygdala could learn the rules of the task and perceive the objects clearly, but they were just about as forgetful as patient HM.[12]

Since the publication of Mishkin's pioneering study, there has been a great deal of research on memory in brain-lesioned monkeys. It is now well established that damage to the amygdala alone does not produce a serious impairment of recognition memory (as I discuss in chapter 7, however, the amygdala does play a major role in memory for emotional experiences). But there has been a lengthy and often animated debate about whether damage to the hippocampus alone produces significant impairments of recognition. A number of psychologists and neurobiologists have argued that the hippocampus is a key structure—perhaps *the* key structure—underlying explicit memory for recent experiences in monkeys, humans, and other animals. In the early 1970s, neuroscientists exploring the cellular basis of memory discovered that electrical stimulation produces a long-lasting increase in the activity of synapses (the contact points between neurons) within the hippocampus. Called long-term potentiation, or LTP, this persisting effect of stimulation showed that hippocampal synapses can be altered by experience—a necessary property of any memory system in the brain. Although it has also been shown that other brain regions exhibit LTP, too, the initial discovery of LTP within the hippocampus led many neuroscientists to focus intensively, almost exclusively, on how this structure contributes to memory.[13]

While everyone agrees that the hippocampus plays a role in explicit memory, some have contended that it is not involved in all aspects of explicit recall and recognition. John O'Keefe and Lynn Nadel have argued that the hippocampus serves to create a mental map of the environment, and is crucial to memory only when people or animals must remember the spatial locations of objects and events. Recent experiments with monkeys indicate that when recall of spatial location is not specifically required, damage to the hippocampus alone produces a modest deficit of recognition memory that is most evident when monkeys are tested after relatively long delays.[14]

Something seems to be amiss here. If damage to the amygdala alone produces no memory deficit and damage to the hippocampus alone produces only a modest one, how can joint damage to the two structures yield profound amnesia? Using improved surgical techniques that allow researchers to make more precise lesions than was possible previously, Mishkin's group and a team headed by Zola-Morgan and Squire have shown that severe deficits of recognition memory result from damage to a cluster of cortical structures in the medial temporal lobe (the entorhinal, perirhinal, and parahippocampal cortices) that are adjacent to, and a major source of input for, the hippocampus and amygdala.[15] Mishkin's early finding that joint damage to the hippocampus and amygdala causes amnesia resulted from inadvertent damage to adjacent cortical areas during surgery. The newer findings are consistent with observations concerning human amnesia: some of the temporal cortex adjacent to the hippocampus and amygdala were removed in the severely amnesic patient HM, but such areas were not damaged in cases of milder amnesia such as RB.

Korsakoff's Syndrome

Taken together, studies of human patients and experiments with monkeys show convincingly that damage to the medial temporal lobe can cause amnesia. But the story of the brain and amnesia doesn't stop here, because brain damage in some amnesic patients is found primarily outside the medial temporal region. For example, patients with Korsakoff's syndrome, who have a long-term history of alcohol abuse, show a profound loss of memory for recent experiences that likely results from a thiamine deficiency sometimes linked to alcoholism. Alcoholism itself can lead to mild memory problems, but most alcoholics do not develop a full-blown Korsakoff's syndrome and associated amnesia.[16]

The onset of Korsakoff's syndrome is usually accompanied by a transient episode in which the patient suddenly becomes disoriented and confused. While in this acute stage of the illness, a person's behavior may change radically from one moment to the next. One Korsakoff patient interviewed in 1959, for example, knew the year he was born and correctly figured out that he was sixty years old. The next minute, he insisted that it was 1928 and that he was still a young man. Another conceded that he had been on a hospital ward for two weeks, but minutes later launched into a tale of having gone to church and dinner with his doctor the previous Sunday. One patient denied being married when a psychologist asked her about the wedding ring she wore. Then she proceeded to "recall" three fabricated husbands. The next day, everything she talked about involved her real husband.[17]

When this confusional state ends after several days or weeks, patients emerge with a chronic and debilitating memory impairment. In addition to memory loss, most patients with Korsakoff's syndrome have cognitive and motivational problems—they tend to be cognitively apathetic and to show little affect. The psychologist Howard Gardner relates a conversation from the early 1970s with a typical Korsakoff patient that illustrates these qualities. When he encountered Mr. O'Donnell on the ward of the Boston Veterans Administration Hospital, the patient was flipping through a magazine with a cover story on the explosive issue of the day: the Watergate cover-up. Asked what was in the magazine, Mr. O'Donnell responded, "Oh, politics and all that. I don't follow it much." When Gardner asked specifically about Watergate, the patient remained indifferent: "Oh, I don't pay it much mind. I've been busy lately and haven't been keeping up." But surely, Gardner continued, you must have heard of Watergate. "Oh, yeah if you say so, Doctor," O'Donnell conceded, "but I don't have any opinions about that sort of thing." Could the patient say anything at all about Watergate? "Oh, they got some stool pigeon, or something like that. It's all the same to me."[18]

Despite a generally bland state of mind, Korsakoff patients, like other amnesic patients, achieve IQ scores in the normal range and generally 20 to 40 points higher than their MQs. In other words, their motivational and cognitive deficits are not sufficient to explain their memory loss.

Amnesia and the Diencephalon

Postmortem studies of Korsakoff patients' brains have revealed the presence of extensive damage in a collection of subcortical structures known as the diencephalon. Two prominent components of the diencephalon are the thalamus (an important switching station in the brain through which virtually all sensory input passes) and the mammillary bodies (a nucleus of cells located just below the thalamus; see figure 5.1). The thalamus, you may recall, was damaged in patient GR, who lost and later recovered his entire past, and also in patient PS, who lived with the delusion that he would soon be sailing on a ship during World War II. Korsakoff patients usually have abnormalities in both the thalamus and the mammillary bodies. Studies of the brains of some Korsakoff patients, using either MRI to visualize damaged tissue in living patients or direct examination of pathology in postmortem cases, have revealed abnormalities in the hippocampus and other parts of the medial temporal lobe as well.[19]

The amnesic syndrome, then, can result from damage either to the medial temporal lobe or to the diencephalon. These two regions are connected by a structure known as the fornix, which is a major output pathway of the hippocampus. The interconnectedness of the two areas suggests that a brain network involving both the medial temporal and the diencephalic regions plays a key role in explicit memory, and that damage to structures in either the medial temporal or diencephalic components of the network may cause memory problems.[20]

This idea fits well with the recent work on brain-lesioned monkeys that has highlighted the importance of the entorhinal and adjacent cortices in memory function. These areas funnel inputs from earlier processing stations all over the brain that deal with different aspects of experiences—the sights, sounds, and smells that make up everyday episodes—to the hippocampus, amygdala, and their targets in the diencephalon. Here, the inputs are linked or bound together to form engrams that underlie explicit memories for day-to-day episodes. Damage to the entorhinal region, then, should have grave consequences. If the entorhinal cortex is dysfunctional, then the entire medial temporal-diencephalic network is sure to pay a heavy price, because little information can enter the system.

These considerations provide possibly important insights into the devastating memory loss I witnessed during my two rounds of golf with Frederick. Recall that he was in the early stages of Alzheimer's disease. Severe memory impairment is one of the most common early signs of the illness; in some cases, amnesia may be the only major sign of pathology until the disease runs its inevitable course and produces a global deterioration of intellectual function. There is now considerable evidence that the major pathological signs of Alzheimer's disease (known as neuritic or amyloid plaques and neurofibrillary tangles) are initially concentrated in the entorhinal cortex, as well as the hippocampus.[21] Frederick could perceive ongoing events during a round of golf, but those perceptions could not be transformed into explicit memories because the critical input pathway to hippocampal and diencephalic networks was probably ravaged by accumulating deposits of neural debris.

Studies of human amnesia and dementia, together with findings of memory impairment in monkeys, convey a profound message: a neural system within the medial temporal-diencephalic region carries out functions that are vital to establishing new explicit memories. This system allows us to link together the varied components of everyday episodes into integrated records of experiences: what we see and what we hear, what we think and how we feel. Medial temporal-diencephalic structures are thus essential to episodic memory, and they also contribute to the formation of new semantic memories. Amnesic patients generally have difficulty learning novel facts and vocabulary, although with enough repetition some of them can acquire new semantic knowledge. And in addition to failing to recollect episodes in rich detail, they feel little of the rudimentary sense of familiarity about recent events that most of us experience routinely. For instance, in experiments that required participants to say whether they actually "remember" specific details of a recent event or just "know" that it seems familiar, amnesic patients made fewer remember and fewer know responses than people with normal memory function.[22] Damage to medial temporal and diencephalic structures does not destroy all forms of memory: even amnesic and demented patients can be unconsciously influenced by ongoing experiences and can acquire new skills. But these implicit memories appear to be based on isolated slivers of information, rather than on the multimodal engrams that underlie explicit remembering. Our ability to form explicit memories of day-to-day experiences is inextricably intertwined with the normal flow of information into and out of the cluster of cells and synapses, hidden deep within the innermost regions of brain, that comprise the medial temporal-diencephalic circuit.

WHEN THE PAST DISAPPEARS
Retrograde Amnesia and the Structure of Memory

We have already seen that patients with damage restricted to the medial temporal lobes have retrograde amnesias that obey Ribot's Law: such patients can remember many experiences from the distant past but few from the recent past, just prior to their brain injuries. But when brain damage extends outside the medial temporal region, into areas of the cortex where engrams are actually stored or regions that are essential to retrieving memories, we see much more extensive retrograde amnesias that sometimes blanket nearly all of a patient's personal past. These retrograde amnesias underscore that our normally seamless awareness of episodes from our personal pasts and knowledge of the world masks a great deal of underlying complexity. Remembering one's wedding depends on a different brain network than knowing where a bar of soap can be found. Recognizing a submarine requires different neural machinery than recognizing a spider. Each of

these types of knowledge depends on the integrity of specific constellations of underlying brain structures and processes.

Gene helped teach me some of these lessons. He developed amnesia when he sustained a serious head injury during a 1981 motorcycle accident that damaged large sectors of his frontal and temporal
lobes, including his left hippocampus.[23] Thirty years old at the time of
the accident, Gene, like Frederick, is now unable to recall day-to-day
experiences except for a few isolated new facts (see chapter 4). In
addition to his anterograde amnesia, however, Gene also shows a
remarkable form of retrograde amnesia. Unlike amnesic patients who
obey Ribot's Law, Gene is unable to recall a single specific episode
from any time in his life.

Asking Gene about his personal past is an almost unnerving experience. He is a quiet, polite, and affable young man who always tries
his best to come up with answers to questions that are posed to him.
But no amount of prompting or cueing helps Gene recall specific past
events, whether happy or sad, at school or at work, or including family or friends. Even when detailed descriptions of dramatic events in
his life are given to him—the tragic drowning of his brother, the
derailment, near his house, of a train carrying lethal chemicals that
required 240,000 people to evacuate their homes for a week—Gene
does not generate any episodic memories. Though he had been an
avid motorcyclist prior to his injury, Gene no longer remembers any
of the numerous trips he had made with his cycling buddies. Nor can
he recall the frequent visits to bars he used to make with his friends.
Whereas other amnesic patients usually can dredge up some episodes
from the distant past, Gene remembers absolutely nothing. He looks
at me with a puzzled expression, as if he understood that he should be
able to provide a response to my questions. Gene appreciates that people are generally able to recall specific incidents from their pasts. Sitting quietly trying to come up with an episodic memory, he is apt to
emit a nervous laugh—a sort of recognition that it is strange, almost
silly, that he cannot come up with anything. Then there is usually a
sigh of resignation as Gene acknowledges that nothing is going to
come to him. Within a couple of minutes, this incident, too, vanishes
into the black hole of his episodic memory.

A life without any episodic memory is psychologically barren—the
mental equivalent of a bleak Siberian landscape. Nothing much happens in Gene's mind or in his life. He has few friends and lives quietly
at home with his parents. He performs many of the same routine
activities again and again. And just as his recollections of the past are

devastated, he thinks little about the future. It does not occur to him to make plans, and he has nothing to look forward to. If Gene were told today that he would soon be going on a trip around the world, he would forget this incident as quickly as any other.

But Gene knows some things about his past. He knows where he went to school and that he worked at a manufacturing plant for three years prior to his head injury. He knows that he owned two motor-cycles and a car, that his family owns a summer cottage where he has spent many weekends, and what the names are of the students in his class photograph. Gene has also retained a good deal of nonpersonal semantic knowledge that he acquired prior to his accident. He can describe accurately and in detail each step involved in changing a flat tire, even though he cannot recall ever having changed one himself. Gene can also name a number of former co-workers and correctly identify some photographs and drawings of equipment from the man-ufacturing plant where he used to work. Even more impressively, Gene easily and correctly defines technical terms he learned on the job, such as *keyway shank, spiral mandrel,* and *stellite.*

Gene's autobiographical knowledge is akin to the nonpersonal knowledge most of us have of other people's lives. I know, for instance, that my father served on a warship in Italy, and I know many things about the neighborhood where my mother grew up because my par-ents often talked to me about what happened to them in the past. But I have no episodic recollections of the settings and circumstances of their experiences. I can acquire all kinds of factual knowledge about another person's past without having any of the specific recollections that belong only to that person. So, too, with Gene: he knows things about parts of his autobiography but does not remember specific past episodes.

Interestingly, Gene can draw on this semantic knowledge when asked questions about his current personality and how it relates to what he was like before his head injury. Gene's friends and family agree that his personality has changed since his accident; he is now less active and outgoing than he once was. To investigate Gene's knowledge of these changes, Endel Tulving asked him and his mother to rate various aspects of his present and past personal traits. The two generally agreed about the characteristic features of Gene's previous and current per-sonalities. Despite an utter inability to remember a single episode of his own behavior, Gene has managed to learn something about his new traits. This is probably because he is still capable of gradually accumu-lating semantic knowledge on the basis of repeated experiences.[24]

Though Gene's total loss of episodic memory is rare among amnesic patients, a few other patients are almost as badly impaired. The encephalitic patient Boswell is unable to recall a single specific episode from any time in his life. SS, the ex–laser physicist who contracted herpes simplex encephalitis, cannot recount specific episodes from any time in his life. When SS is asked about his past he does not respond blankly, as Gene does. He can regale listeners with stories about his childhood and other times in his life. But SS's reminiscences are limited to oft-told tales about the general characteristics of jobs he held or people he knew. When asked to elaborate on one of his stories, or to provide information about the circumstances or settings of particular incidents, SS is at a loss: he cannot embellish his general descriptions with additional contextual details. SS has, however, also retained a considerable amount of the technical knowledge he acquired before becoming ill, and maintains a high level of vocabulary and general knowledge. He is able to recall and recognize some famous people from the past, albeit fewer than healthy people of his age.[25]

The kind of memory loss experienced by Gene and SS shows that semantic memory can be partially preserved even when episodic memory is entirely dysfunctional. Traditionally, psychologists have defined semantic memory as a network of associations and concepts that underlies our basic knowledge of the world—word meanings, categories, facts and propositions, and the like. But the retrograde amnesias I have just considered suggest that semantic memory also forms the basis for a good deal of personal, autobiographical knowledge. Even Gene can provide some autobiographical "facts" about general features of his pre-accident autobiography. Because he cannot recollect any particular episodes, it is likely that everything he knows about his past is contained in semantic memory; Gene has a past, but it is strangely impersonal.

This idea can be usefully linked to the distinction I discussed in previous chapters among lifetime periods ("when I went to college"), general events ("going to football games during freshman year"), and event-specific knowledge ("the big fight that ended the final football game of the season"). Gene and SS have no problem recalling lifetime period knowledge, and even show some knowledge of general events. But neither has any access to event-specific knowledge. Since Gene and SS have complete loss of episodic memory and partial loss of semantic memory, perhaps lifetime periods and general events are part of semantic memory, while event-specific knowledge is part of episodic memory and preserves the details of individual experiences.[26]

Neuropsychologists have described patients who are in some sense mirror images of Gene and SS: they can recall specific episodes from their lives, but have lost much general knowledge of the world. For instance, in a case of encephalitis described by the Italian neurologist Ennio De Renzi, damage was largely confined to the front portion of the temporal lobe, a part of the brain that is important for semantic memory. This patient no longer knew the meanings of common words, had forgotten virtually everything she once knew about historical events and famous people, and retained little knowledge of the basic attributes of animate and inanimate objects. She had difficulty indicating the color of a mouse, and had no idea where soap would ordinarily be found. Her semantic memory—the bedrock of our general knowledge of the world—was horribly impaired. However, when asked about her wedding and honeymoon, her father's illness and death, or other specific past episodes, she readily produced detailed and accurate recollections.[27]

A similar pattern has been seen in some elderly adults with a disorder called "semantic dementia." These patients have difficulty naming common objects, and have an impoverished vocabulary and poor comprehension of individual words. Over time, their semantic knowledge of words, objects, and facts gradually dissolves. Although they still have general categorical knowledge—they can distinguish between living and nonliving things, for example—they retain little or no knowledge about specific attributes of objects. One patient, for instance, was asked to identify a picture of a deer and responded, "Animal, gives milk, like sheep." Another was shown a picture of a violin and responded, "Is it an instrument? I think it's made of metal." These same patients can remember what they had for breakfast or where they went on a recent vacation; their episodic memories are preserved. The semantic impairments in such patients resemble similar deficits that have been documented in patients with Alzheimer's disease. But in Alzheimer's patients, disorders of semantic memory are generally accompanied by severe deficits in episodic memory. Patients with semantic dementias are important because they indicate that semantic memory can be seriously impaired even when episodic memory functions reasonably well.[28]

Semantic memory may sometimes break down in bizarre ways that provide important clues to how our general knowledge of the world is represented in the brain. In some particularly intriguing cases, patients lose only certain categories of knowledge. For example, in 1984 the British neuropsychologists Elizabeth Warrington and Tim

Shallice described four patients with encephalitis who had great difficulty identifying living things but easily identified most man-made objects. One patient, a forty-eight-year-old naval officer known by the initials SBY, defined a wheelbarrow as an "object used by people to take material about," a towel as "material used to dry people," and a submarine as a "ship that goes underneath the sea." This same man called a wasp a "bird that flies," a crocus "rubbish material," and a spider a "person looking for things; he was a spider for a nation or country." More recently, other patients have been described who exhibit the opposite pattern: greater difficulty identifying inanimate objects than living things. And even finer-grain distinctions between preserved and impaired categories have been observed. The neurologist Antonio Damasio has described a patient who can recognize tools but not clothes, and another who has little difficulty recognizing man-made objects except for a terrible problem with musical instruments.[29]

What accounts for these unusual impairments? Does the brain organize semantic knowledge along strictly categorical lines? Probably not. Damasio and others have suggested that apparent category-specific disorders are related to the kinds of information that are used to identify particular entities. We tend to distinguish among animals and plants based on details of their visual appearance, whereas we tend to distinguish among tools based on actions we perform when using them. Patients with problems recognizing objects on the basis of appearance would therefore also tend to have particular difficulties recognizing living things, whereas patients with problems recognizing objects on the basis of functions would tend to have particular difficulties recognizing such man-made objects as tools.

A recent PET scanning study by Alex Martin and colleagues at the National Institute of Mental Health provides some insight into these startling disorders. When healthy volunteers identified pictures of either animals or tools during separate brain scans, areas in the lower parts of the temporal lobes that participate in the perception of complex objects showed heightened activity (blood flow increases) compared to control conditions. But when they identified pictures of tools, there was also increased blood flow in the left premotor cortex—an area that becomes extremely active when people simply imagine moving their hands to grasp an object. Identifying tools was also associated with heightened activity in a part of the left hemisphere (the middle temporal gyrus) that is involved in producing action words (such as *write*). These results suggest that knowledge of tools, but not of animals, depends on brain regions that represent movements and actions: things people do when using tools. These areas of the brain are typically damaged in patients with problems naming man-made objects, whereas regions toward the rear of the brain that represent distinct visual features of complex stimuli tend to be damaged in patients with problems naming living things. The peculiar category-specific impairments seen in some brain-damaged patients arise because distinct brain networks are responsible for knowledge of different properties of objects.[30]

When functioning smoothly, the brain systems that support episodic and semantic memories allow us to recognize objects in the world, to travel in time, and to construct our life stories. But when they are disrupted by brain damage, we are afforded a glimpse of the building blocks from which we build the tales of our past that confer coherence and meaning on our day-to-day lives.

EXPERIENCING AMNESIA
Awareness and Unawareness of Memory Loss

We have all had the experience of forgetting a routine act we have just performed. In the midst of a long drive on the interstate, deeply immersed in our private reflections, we may suddenly realize that we can't remember any of the scenery for the past several miles. This kind of "amnesia" occurs because attention is required to form new episodic memories, and when our attentional resources are consumed by internal thoughts and feelings, there are few left over for dealing with the world outside. We can comfort ourselves by attributing such lapses of memory to being on "automatic pilot," but what if life were always like that?

When Frederick and I played golf, he sometimes failed to remember a shot he had hit minutes before; when I told him about it, he was amazed and bewildered. Frederick knew he had a problem with his memory, but he did not appreciate how far-reaching it was. Within minutes, however, he would invariably forget what he had forgotten—another testimony to the depths of his memory disorder—and resume the enjoyable business of striking the ball.

There is a kind of poetic justice at work for patients with amnesia: the impairment might mercifully serve a protective function by preventing patients from becoming aware of the catastrophic nature of their memory loss. In 1889, Sergei Korsakoff noted that his patients expressed little awareness of, or concern about, their memory difficulties. His observation has been confirmed by many subsequent descriptions of patients with Korsakoff's syndrome. When Howard Gardner spoke to Mr. O'Donnell, he gave him several words to remember and asked him to recall them several minutes later. Mr. O'Donnell could not remember any of them. "I guess I wasn't paying enough attention," reasoned Mr. O'Donnell. Gardner repeated the exercise, but the outcome was the same. "Sometimes I get preoccupied," the patient explained. "My memory's fine, I think."[31]

Korsakoff amnesics often overestimate how well they will perform on memory tests. Like Mr. O'Donnell, they believe their memory is just fine, so they think they will remember as much as anybody else. Simply telling the patients that they have a memory problem has little effect.[32] Patients who develop amnesia as a result of head injuries are also often unaware, or only partly aware, of their memory problems, as are patients who develop memory problems as a consequence of burst aneurysms in the anterior communicating artery. The anterior communicating artery supplies blood to the basal forebrain, a subcortical structure that provides the medial temporal lobes with a chemical messenger, acetylcholine, that is important for memory function. This artery also supplies blood to a lower sector of the frontal lobes known as the orbiofrontal region. Patients who have suffered ruptured anterior communicating artery aneurysms have great difficulty recalling recently presented information, but unlike other amnesic patients, seem to possess relatively intact feelings of familiarity: they can show normal recognition of recently acquired information when asked to choose between familiar and unfamiliar alternatives. Like patients with frontal lobe damage, they have problems generating useful retrieval strategies, and they also frequently engage in bizarre confabulations without any awareness of how implausible their concoctions are.[33]

A man I call Eric became amnesic after a ruptured anterior communicating artery aneurysm. Eric desperately wished to return to his job as an architect and insisted that his memory was as good as ever. Any occasional memory lapses on his part were insignificant, he claimed, and certainly not serious enough to prevent him from returning to work. In fact, however, Eric had little or no explicit memory for recent events. My colleagues and I asked him to predict how likely it would be for him to remember various everyday situations—such as a telephone conversation with a friend—either a few minutes or a few weeks later. Eric gave himself high marks. But when we asked Eric's wife to rate his memory, she thought he would be unable to remember any of the events we asked about after more than a few minutes. The data we gathered indicated that his wife's assessment was extremely accurate and that his was woefully wrong.[34]

Not all amnesic patients show such unawareness, however; some are acutely aware of their memory problems. One man who became amnesic after encephalitis commented: "There's nothing wrong with me physically, but mentally things as they happen don't seem to impress themselves on my mind." Another patient with extensive verbal memory loss as a result of damage to the diencephalon characterized his problem as "not knowing whether I will remember something when I need to remember it." Patient HM has some awareness of his memory loss, and has said that he feels as if he is constantly waking up from a dream. In his recent biography of HM, the writer Philip Hilts describes conversations in which HM confesses to being concerned about slipping up in front of others because of his amnesia. He once described his condition as "[t]he loss of memory, but not of reality."[35]

Patients who have been amnesic for a long time could, if told of their memory failures over and over, eventually learn that they have them. But awareness of memory loss also occurs in patients who suddenly develop a temporary amnesic syndrome known as transient global amnesia. This condition usually lasts for mere hours, is typically observed in otherwise healthy elderly adults, and is probably produced by temporary blood blockages in the hippocampus and related medial temporal lobe structures. These patients have problems remembering ongoing experiences and may also be afflicted by varying amounts of retrograde amnesia, ranging from the past couple of years to the past couple of decades.[36]

Why are some amnesic patients acutely aware of their memory problems while others vehemently deny them? Patients who are aware of their deficits might be better able than those who aren't to "remember that they forget." But this seems unlikely, because even severely amnesic patients are sometimes well aware of their problems. The key to solving this puzzle probably lies in the vast territory of the frontal lobes. Amnesic patients with impaired awareness are generally characterized by signs of frontal pathology, whereas amnesic patients with intact awareness typically show no signs of frontal impairment.[37]

We have already seen that brain damage restricted to the frontal lobes does not produce a full-blown amnesic syndrome. But it is often associated with source amnesia, false recognition, and confabulation.

These deficits arise because key functions subserved by frontal regions—strategic retrieval and monitoring—are impaired in patients with this damage. It seems likely that impairments of these same functions contribute to these patients' diminished awareness of deficit. Consider for a moment how an amnesic patient could become aware of his deficit. Suppose a patient attempts to recall some recent experience, such as what he had for breakfast this morning, and fails to remember anything—no memory of munching cornflakes in the kitchen, eating eggs Benedict in a restaurant, or anything else. If he realizes that a person with normal memory would have no difficulty remembering such an episode, then he should become aware that something is amiss with his memory.

Frontal lobe damage could interfere with this kind of on-line evaluation of memory in various ways. For example, a confabulating patient may produce erroneous memories when attempting to recall this morning's breakfast. Mistakenly remembering that he had eggs Benedict at a fancy restaurant when he ate cornflakes in the kitchen, he would have no reason to suspect that he is amnesic. In fact, clinical and experimental observations have revealed that patients who confabulate also tend to be unaware of their deficit.[38] However, this is not invariably true, and some patients who are unaware of their deficit do not confabulate. Frontal damage in these cases may disrupt patients' ability to integrate their observations of their own memory failures with their knowledge that normal people do not have such problems.

Damage to structures other than the frontal lobes can also lead patients to deny the existence of deficits that are readily apparent to others, such as paralysis of arms or legs. It has long been observed that patients who have suffered strokes in the parietal lobe of the right hemisphere maintain that their paralyzed limbs (on the left side) are functioning normally. The psychologist V. S. Ramachandran has reported some intriguing memory aberrations in an elderly woman who sustained a right parietal stroke. BM lost the use of her left arm, but denied that it was paralyzed. She rationalized her inability to move her arm by saying that she was tired that day or simply didn't feel like lifting it. Ramachandran performed an unusual experiment with her: he irrigated BM's left ear with cold water. For reasons that are not well understood, when this procedure is performed, some patients temporarily stop denying their paralysis. (It may be that the damaged right hemisphere is somehow stimulated into action by the cold water treatment; the right hemisphere is more strongly connected to the left side of the body than to the right—thus applying cold water treatment to the right ear generally has no effect.) After this procedure, BM acknowledged that her left arm was paralyzed and even stated correctly that it had been paralyzed for several days. Thirty minutes after the treatment, she said the same thing. Eight hours later, however, when the effects had worn off, BM once again stated with conviction that she could move her arm. When one of Ramachandran's colleagues asked what the two doctors had done to her that morning, BM remembered the irrigation. At first she didn't remember what she had said when the doctors asked about her arm, but then she asserted, "I said my arms were okay."

Ramachandran suggests that BM had selectively repressed the part of her memory that was inconsistent with her present beliefs: "it would have been very difficult for her to deny her present paralysis and yet admit the insight she had acquired 8 hours earlier, while at the same time maintaining an integrated self." In some amnesic patients, a similar kind of selective forgetting might help to maintain unawareness of deficit.[39]

Although the plight of BM and other patients suggests that impaired awareness of deficit is a mercy, it is often an obstacle to improving the quality of their lives. Amnesic patients who acknowledge their deficits may structure their environments so as to lessen the load on their memories, or they may use notebooks and other reminders to achieve some independence in daily living. But patients who deny or minimize their deficits often maintain unrealistic expectations about what they can accomplish, and so are less likely to benefit from intervention and training.[40]

But there is one circumstance in which impaired awareness of deficit can be a blessing: when the ravages of Alzheimer's disease destroy both episodic and semantic memory, thereby shattering a person's ability to comprehend the world. Early in the course of the disease, many Alzheimer's patients maintain acute insight into their problems, whereas others minimize or deny their symptoms. For those who retain insight, the awareness of their memory loss can be as crushing as forgetting itself. Diana Friel McGowin, a Florida legal secretary and mother of three, was diagnosed with Alzheimer's disease at the unusually young age of forty-five. She has written a harrowing account of her dawning awareness that something was terribly wrong with her memory. An intelligent woman who at one time possessed an IQ of 137, McGowin recounts the sheer terror of discovering that she could not remember where she lived. Unable to find her way

FIGURE 5.3

E. Stoepel-Peckham, "Alzheimer's I," 1983. 21 x 16". Mixed media collage. Courtesy of the artist.

Stoepel-Peckham's tribute to her father includes a handwritten excerpt from a newspaper article concerning memory loss in Alzheimer's patients; but her script quickly degenerates into gibberish, just as the disease destroys the mind. Pictures of people who are fragmented beyond recognition allude to loss of memory, and a cracked mirror highlights the eventual loss of self-awareness. Footsteps in the snow—traces of someone from the past—remind us that an intact person once inhabited the decimated world of the Alzheimer's patient. A veiled photo of the artist's father during his healthy years provides an image of that once-normal person.

home, she told a guard at a park entrance that she was lost and he asked where she lived: "A cold chill enveloped me as I realized I could not remember the name of my street. Tears began to flow down my cheeks." When he asked what part of town she lived in, "I felt panic wash over me anew as I searched my memory and found it blank."[41]

It is excruciating for family members to witness a patient's painful awareness of his own vanishing memory. "Alzheimer's is the cruelest of diseases," acknowledges the writer Glenn Collins, reflecting on his father's struggle with a ruthlessly advancing dementia. "What's bad is the meanness of it. The knowledge of forgetting. The frustration and confusion and shame of forgetting."[42]

As cognitive function deteriorates over a period of years, most Alzheimer's patients become progressively less aware of the extent, or even the existence, of their deficits. Recent evidence indicates that this dimming of awareness in Alzheimer's patients is accompanied by an increase in confabulations on memory tests and by a decline in frontal lobe function. However, signs of frontal dysfunction are probably not a necessary precondition for unawareness of deficit: some Alzheimer's patients who perform reasonably well on behavioral tests that are sensitive to frontal damage are largely unaware of their memory problems.[43]

In a moving visual memorial to her father's battle with Alzheimer's disease, the artist Ellen Stoepel-Peckham portrays the deterioration of memory, intellect, and awareness in her collage "Alzheimer's I" (figure 5.3).

The artist highlights that when the past vanishes as a result of amnesia and dementia, so does much of the person. Appreciating the present and anticipating the future hinge on an ability to communicate with the past. When we lose the capacity to travel in time, we are cut loose from much of what anchors our sense of who we are and where we are headed. Yet even in the most profound cases of amnesia, the past never fully relinquishes its grasp on the present. When explicit memory is destroyed, the past continues to affect the present through subtle influences that operate outside of awareness. To understand these influences, we must plunge into the world of implicit memory.

SIX

THE HIDDEN WORLD OF
IMPLICIT MEMORY

DECEMBER AFTERNOONS darken early in Boston. For most people, this is one of the more depressing features of the New England
winter. I don't mind it much, because the early evenings allow me to
enjoy the sunset from the windows of my office near the northern
fringe of the Harvard campus. The stunning view of the entire Boston
skyline is especially lovely in the fading light of dusk on a winter afternoon. At the close of one such afternoon in December 1993, I took a
much-needed break and gazed out the windows. But my pleasant
reverie was interrupted by the ring of a telephone.

The caller introduced himself as Rowan Wilson, an attorney with
the prestigious New York firm of Cravath, Swaine, and Moore. His
firm had been representing the computer giant IBM in a major lawsuit in which questions about memory seemed likely to play a role. I
agreed to hear about the case and to consider becoming involved in it.

Wilson's first question struck an immediate chord: Is it possible, he
wanted to know, for a person to retrieve information from a past
experience without being aware that he is relying on memory? Most
of my scientific efforts for the past decade had been directed toward
precisely that issue. I had been conducting experiments investigating
what my colleagues and I call *implicit memory:* when people are influenced by a past experience without any awareness that they are
remembering. Yes, I responded, a person most definitely can make use
of memory for a past experience without any awareness of remem-

bering. But why on earth would an attorney have any interest in knowing that?

This one had excellent reasons: parts of his case hinged on the viability of the idea that memory can be manifested without awareness of remembering. Wilson's case entailed a dispute over intellectual property: Who owns the rights to the ideas and knowledge that an employee develops in the course of performing his duties? Much depended on the status of technical knowledge residing in the head of an electrical engineer who had once worked at IBM, Peter Bonyhard. Beginning in 1984, Bonyhard played a key role in IBM's development of a revolutionary new technology for reading information from a computer disk. He had helped to develop what is known in the industry as an MR (magneto-resistive) head. This almost unimaginably tiny, paper-thin device uses a magnetically based method for decoding information stored on a disk that allows computer manufacturers to pack much more information onto the disk than they could with previous technology. The technical and financial implications of MR head technology are enormous, and Bonyhard was a valued IBM employee. But his services were also coveted by others. In 1991 Bonyhard left IBM to join a rival company, Seagate, that specializes in manufacturing disk drives and heads.

IBM objected to the fact that Bonyhard was allowed to work on MR heads at Seagate. While at IBM, he had been exposed to a large amount of confidential, trade-secret information about the manufacture and function of MR heads, information he had promised not to disclose. IBM contended that because he was deeply involved in Seagate's attempt to develop its own MR head, it would be virtually impossible—despite his best intentions—for Bonyhard not to disclose trade-secret information. This was the heart of Rowan Wilson's case and the reason he was consulting me: he suspected that Bonyhard might unknowingly divulge trade-secret information in his new job.

Although I never had the opportunity to address the issues—IBM and Seagate settled their dispute and Bonyhard could no longer work directly on the development of MR heads—the case raises questions that are central to understanding memory's fragile power: To what extent can people show memory for previous experiences even when they are not aware of remembering them? What is the evidence for such implicit memories, and how do they influence what we do and what we think in our day-to-day lives? What does the existence of implicit memory tell us about the nature and organization of memory in mind and brain?

During the past fifteen years, psychology and neuroscience have made immense progress toward answering those questions. It is no exaggeration to say that research on implicit memory has revolutionized how we measure the effects of past experiences and how we think about the nature of memory.[1] The path that led to implicit memory—both for me personally and for the field as a whole—can be traced back to events that unfolded some two decades earlier in the ancient town of Oxford.

WHY DO AMNESIC PATIENTS LEARN?

When I arrived in Oxford just after the New Year in 1978, it was the first time I had ever been to England. I was captivated immediately by the impressive towers and intricate spires of All Soul's College, the golden brown stones of the magnificent Bodleian library, and the narrow stone paths that lead to centuries-old stores and pubs. Enrolled as a graduate student at the University of Toronto, I had been blessed with a stroke of good fortune: my supervisor, Endel Tulving, had been awarded a visiting chair at Oxford for a year and I would be spending most of that year with him.

Tulving had arranged for me to meet weekly with Professor Lawrence Weiskrantz, one of the world's authorities on how the brain accomplishes perception and memory. Weiskrantz and his colleague, the London neuropsychologist Elizabeth Warrington, had recently published several articles about amnesic patients that intrigued and puzzled memory researchers. In their experiments, amnesics and a group of normal volunteers studied a list of common words, such as *table* or *garden*. When shown some of these words several minutes later, together with words that were not on the list, amnesic patients had great difficulty remembering which had been on the list and which hadn't. No surprise here: previous studies had already shown that amnesics have problems recognizing words from a recently presented study list. But Warrington and Weiskrantz gave another kind of memory test. They provided the first three letters of a word, such as tab—— or gar——, and asked people to supply the remaining letters. On this test, amnesic patients wrote down more words from the study list than would be expected if they were guessing randomly. Even more impressively, in some experiments they wrote down as many words as did people who had no memory problems.[2] How is it possible to explain such a curious pattern?

Warrington and Weiskrantz suggested one reason why the three-letter cues might have been especially useful to amnesic patients: they help patients avoid being confused by irrelevant memories that ordinarily spring to mind and interfere with their recall of the correct answer. But something else was noteworthy about the amnesic patients' performance: they did not appear to be aware that they were recalling words from the study list when they provided them in response to the three-letter test cues. Instead, they often behaved as if they were in a guessing game. They were showing memory for the studied words, but they were not "remembering" in the ordinary sense of the term.

Weiskrantz noticed something even more extraordinary about a different type of brain-damaged patient. He started to study a man who had lost much of his vision as a result of damage to the occipital lobes, the structures in the rear of our brains that are necessary to perceive the external world around us. When a light was flashed in the part of visual space affected by his brain damage, the patient typically claimed to see nothing. But when asked to "guess" the location of the flash, he performed extremely accurately! The patient seemed capable of some form of unconscious perception. Weiskrantz called this remarkable ability *blindsight,* and suggested that it might be related in some way to memory without awareness in amnesic patients.[3]

I was excited by these observations, which dovetailed with pioneering studies in the 1960s by Brenda Milner and her colleagues showing that the profoundly amnesic patient HM could learn new motor skills. When HM practiced tracking a moving target, his performance—just like that of people with intact memories—became increasingly accurate. HM, however, was not aware that he had ever performed the task before.[4]

When first confronted with this surprising finding, memory researchers did not show much interest in it. The standard interpretation held that HM could learn new motor skills because motor learning is a special kind of memory that does not depend on the hippocampus and the other medial temporal lobe structures that were removed from HM's brain. Most memory researchers conceded that motor learning is different from other kinds of memory and pursued the matter no further. Yet Warrington and Weiskrantz's findings with amnesic patients, together with the demonstration of blindsight in vision, suggested that preserved motor learning in HM might have much broader implications. To me, these counterintuitive observations intimated the existence of a subterranean world of nonconscious memory and perception, normally concealed from the conscious mind.

Philosophers, physicians, and psychiatrists had already made sporadic observations about this intriguing hidden world. I was well aware that Freud and other psychoanalysts had theorized for decades about an unconscious mind that is a repository of repressed wishes, fantasies, and fears. But, as far as I could tell, retention without awareness in amnesic patients or perception without awareness in blindsight had nothing to do with repressed urges and desires. And there had been scant scientific progress in investigating or understanding the Freudian notion of the unconscious. Even before Freud, the British physician Robert Dunn reported in 1845 that a woman who had been rescued from a near-drowning incident seemed incapable of remembering anything (probably because of oxygen loss to the brain). Dunn wrote with some amazement how she learned to be a skilled dressmaker—even though she couldn't remember making any of the dresses! In 1911, the great French philosopher Henri Bergson distinguished conscious remembering of the past from learned habits that influence our behavior unconsciously. Bergson argued with great eloquence that the past survives in two fundamentally different forms, conscious and unconscious. It was exciting for me to contemplate using scientific techniques to study what Bergson and others had theorized about or observed in the clinic.[5]

After returning to Toronto, I witnessed firsthand the peculiar kind of memory that others had described in amnesic patients. During the summer of 1980, Dr. Paul Wang, a clinical psychologist, invited me to test a patient who had sustained a serious head injury in an accident. The patient, whom I refer to as Mickey, remembered little or nothing of his recent experiences. I sat across a testing table from him and told him that I was going to try to teach him some interesting bits of trivia. I asked him about obscure facts that I had dredged up by rummaging through encyclopedias and similar sources, such as "Where was the first game of baseball played?" (Hoboken) and "Who holds the world's record for shaking hands?" (Theodore Roosevelt). When Mickey did not know the correct answer—and he almost never did—I told it to him. He was intrigued by these tidbits and enjoyed our trivia game. After I left the testing room and returned twenty minutes later, Mickey maintained only a dim memory that I had tested him. He did not recollect that I had mentioned any items of trivia. But when I asked him where the first game of baseball was played, he confidently answered "Hoboken," and when I inquired about the world's record for shaking hands, he felt certain that it was Theodore Roosevelt. He generally said that he had no idea how he had acquired this knowledge—the answer just "seemed reasonable"—although sometimes he proffered that he might have heard about it from his sister.[6]

My encounter with Mickey dramatically confirmed what I had discussed with Professor Weiskrantz and read about in medical journals: amnesic patients could indeed be influenced by recent experiences that they fail to recollect consciously. At the same time, Tulving and I continued to mull over the Warrington and Weiskrantz experiments. Why did amnesic patients do so well when given letter cues as hints for recently studied words? If these cues tapped into some sort of nonconscious memory that is preserved in amnesic patients, shouldn't it be possible to uncover something similar in people without amnesia?

We designed an experiment to find out. Our reasoning was simple: if letter cues tap into a form of memory that is spared in amnesic patients, then we might be able to elicit such memory in healthy volunteers by giving them letters from a previously studied word and asking them to try to guess the answer. Weiskrantz had observed that amnesic patients treat the letter cue test as a guessing game. If young adults could also be induced to treat the test as a guessing game, we reasoned, then they might rely on the same kind of memory that Warrington and Weiskrantz had observed in amnesics.

We carried out our experiment in the summer of 1980. For you to get a feel for our procedure, you should study each of the following words carefully for five seconds: *assassin, octopus, avocado, mystery, sheriff,* and *climate.* Now imagine that you go about your business for an hour and then return to take a couple of tests. First I show you a series of words and ask whether you remember seeing any of them on the earlier list: *twilight, assassin, dinosaur,* and *mystery.* Presumably you had little difficulty here. Next I tell you that I am going to show you some words with missing letters. Your job is to fill in the blanks as best you can: ch----nk, o-t--us, -og-y---, -l-m-te. You probably had a hard time coming up with a correct answer for two of the word fragments (*chipmunk* and *bogeyman*). But with the other two fragments, the correct answers probably jumped out at you. The reason these fragments are so easy to complete, of course, is that you just saw the words *octopus* and *climate* in our study list. This kind of memory is called *priming*: seeing the words on the list seems to prime your ability to come up with the correct solution when you try to complete a word fragment.

We tested people either one hour or one week after they studied the list. Conscious memory was, of course, much less accurate after a week than after an hour, but there was just as much priming on the word fragment–completion test after a week as there was after an hour. The implication of this finding is fascinating: something other than a conscious memory of seeing the word is responsible for priming on the word fragment–completion test. Equally intriguing, priming occurred even when people said they did not remember seeing a word during the study phase; in fact, the priming effect was just as strong for words that people did not remember seeing earlier as for words they did remember seeing. The results pushed us toward a strong, seemingly unavoidable conclusion: priming occurs independent of conscious memory.[7]

These findings hit us with the force of an avalanche. We believed that we had been able to get a handle on the peculiar kind of memory that Warrington and Weiskrantz had documented in amnesic patients with the letter cueing task. This "other" kind of memory seemed to be lurking in the minds of healthy adults, and could be tapped by giving the word fragment–completion test. We felt a bit like astronomers must feel when discovering a new star or an entire galaxy whose existence had been only suspected: a whole new world of possibilities is suddenly open for exploration.

I also started to notice manifestations of priming in everyday life. It is likely involved in instances of unintentional plagiarism. Probably the best-known case in recent decades involved the former Beatle George Harrison and his 1970s hit "My Sweet Lord." Unfortunately for Harrison, his melody nearly duplicated the tune of a 1962 classic by The Chiffons, "He's So Fine." When a lawsuit was brought against him, Harrison conceded that he had heard "He's So Fine" prior to writing "My Sweet Lord," but denied that he had intentionally borrowed from the earlier song. Reasoning that the resemblance between the two was simply too strong to be the product of coincidence, the trial judge "held that Harrison's work did infringe through what the courts felt must have been unintentional copying of what was in Harrison's subconscious memory."[8]

You may have encountered instances of this kind of priming, too. You propose an idea to a fellow employee or a friend, who seems unimpressed by it or even rejects it altogether. Weeks or months later, that person excitedly relates your idea as if he had just come up with it. When you draw this inconvenient fact to his attention—with an edge in your voice betraying exasperation—you may be faced with either heated denial or a sheepish apology born of a sudden dose of explicit memory. An incident from Sigmund Freud's life clearly illustrates this. Freud had maintained for years an intense and tumultuous friendship with the Berlin physician Wilhelm Fliess. He frequently confided his latest ideas and insights to Fliess, and was emotionally dependent on his approval of them. When Freud announced to Fliess a momentous new insight—that every person is fundamentally bisexual—he fully expected Fliess to be amazed by the idea. Instead, Fliess responded by reminding Freud that he himself had made exactly the same discovery two years earlier and told Freud all about it, and that Freud had rejected the idea. Freud eventually explicitly remembered the earlier incident, commenting that "[i]t is painful to have to surrender one's originality this way." Inspired by such observations, psychologists have recently been able to demonstrate a kind of unintentional plagiarism in the laboratory and tie it directly to priming.[9]

Research into priming exploded during the early 1980s, as provocative new articles appeared in scientific journals. Priming occurred on a variety of tests in which people were instructed to identify a briefly flashed word or object, or guess an answer, rather than try explicitly to remember a word or an object from a list they had studied earlier. For example, Larry Jacoby and Mark Dallas found similar amounts of priming after deep encoding (focusing on a word's meanings and associations) and shallow encoding (focusing on the individual letters in the word)—a remarkable result, since deep encoding yields much higher levels of explicit memory than shallow encoding. Yet the priming effect could be easily eliminated. If people heard the target words on an audiotape during the study task but did not see a printed version of them, little or no priming was observed on a later visual test. Something about perceiving the actual word form was crucial for priming to occur.[10]

Considered together with the results of our word fragment–completion experiment, these findings indicated that the new and mysterious phenomenon of priming obeys different rules than the kind of memory that researchers had been investigating for years. It became increasingly clear that part of the mystery could be traced to the instructions people are given when their memories are tested. For example, when amnesic patients are given word beginnings or other cues, and are instructed to think back to the study list to try to remember target words, they perform quite poorly. But when given the same test cues with instructions to guess or to provide the first word that pops to mind, they do just as well as people without memory problems. Likewise, depth of encoding influences later retention when normal volunteers try to remember the target items, yet has little effect when they respond with the first word that comes to mind.[11]

Scientists love a good mystery, and many researchers tried to figure out what priming effects might mean. Tulving and I had already staked out a position: because priming seemed unrelated to conscious recollection, we reasoned that it does not depend on the episodic memory system that allows us to recollect specific incidents from the past. That system plays a key role in much of what I have discussed in the book so far: remembering what happened at last year's Thanksgiving dinner, remembering where you hit a tee shot during a round of golf, or remembering that you saw the word *octopus* in a study list. Amnesic patients have little or no episodic memory, but they often show normal priming. We concluded that the source of priming must lie outside the episodic system. But where?

Semantic memory—the intricate network of concepts, associations, and facts that constitutes our general knowledge of the world—seemed a reasonable place to look. When an amnesic patient such as Mickey learns that the first game of baseball was played in Hoboken but does not remember the episode in which he acquired that fact, semantic memory may be responsible. Likewise, in a priming experiment, exposure to a word such as *octopus* might result in a jolt to semantic memory, a kind of power surge that excites or activates the semantic representation of *octopus*. Perhaps amnesic patients benefit from such a jolt to semantic memory, even though their defective episodic memory prevents them from consciously recalling that they saw the word *octopus* during a recent study episode. The idea is reasonable enough, but we could see that it had problems. If priming depends on semantic memory, why doesn't deep, semantic processing of a word during the study task lead to more priming than shallow, nonsemantic processing? Why does priming depend on actually seeing the word during the study task? And since priming can be quite long-lasting, and we are constantly encountering words in our everyday lives, shouldn't just about all entries in semantic memory be chronically primed? We speculated that priming reflects "the operation of some other, as yet little understood, memory system."[12]

We had postulated the existence of a new memory system, even though we didn't yet know what it was. The idea that the mind contains more than a single memory system had been around for a while. Bergson had come to this conclusion in 1911 when he distinguished conscious memory from habit, and other philosophers had made similar distinctions. In fact, during the early nineteenth century, a little-known French philosopher, Maine de Biran, had argued that memory can be subdivided into three different systems for ideas, feelings, and habits. But many experimental psychologists were reluctant to part with the idea of one all-purpose memory system. It is simpler and more parsimonious to assume a single memory system until and unless the evidence forces one to postulate multiple memory systems. During the 1960s and 1970s, they had fought a great battle about whether short-term memory (now called working memory) depends on a different system than long-term memory. I earlier mentioned evidence that it does, but not everyone was convinced. Tulving introduced the distinction between episodic and semantic memory in 1972, and some psychologists resisted this division of long-term memory into two further systems. Now we were proposing the addition of a third system—and this was simply unacceptable to some. Priming, these researchers believed, occurs within a single, undifferentiated memory system that can be investigated in different ways. Appealing to the operation of different memory systems seemed unparsimonious and just plain wrong.[13]

A lively debate surrounded these questions. To fuel the fires, new evidence showed that amnesic patients could learn perceptual skills without remembering when and where they learned them. Neal Cohen and Larry Squire studied amnesic patients and healthy volunteers who read mirror-image versions of common words. Everyone has difficulty reading such images at first, but with practice people typically read them faster and faster. Amnesic patients showed a normal benefit of practice, yet they had problems consciously remembering which words they had read.[14] The researchers suggested that such skill learning depends on a "procedural" memory system that is spared in amnesia. This system is selectively involved in "knowing how" to do things: ride a bicycle, type words on a keyboard, solve a jigsaw puzzle, or read words in mirror-image form. Could the procedural memory system also be involved in priming? Or does procedural memory constitute a fourth memory system, in addition to episodic memory, semantic memory, and the memory system Tulving and I had alluded to?

By the mid–1980s, the controversy over multiple memory systems had become so intense that it was difficult to talk about priming and skill learning without committing to one side of the quarrel or the other. The field needed terms that allowed researchers to talk about the exhilarating new phenomena of priming and learning without remembering, yet did not force them to side with one or the other warring faction in the memory systems debate. I decided to face this problem squarely in 1984, when my colleague Peter Graf and I were writing up the results of some new priming experiments. We recognized that new vocabulary was needed to talk about what we and others had been observing in our experiments.

We worked through several possibilities before settling on the contrast that seemed best to capture the distinction we wished to draw: *implicit* memory versus *explicit* memory.[15] When amnesic patients showed priming or learned a skill, they were implicitly remembering some aspect of a recent experience, even though they had no explicit recollection of it. When a college student completed the fragment o-t--us with *octopus*, yet said that she did not remember seeing *octopus* on the list, she was showing the implicit influence of an experience she did not explicitly remember.

Soon I began to see that implicit memory might play a more prominent role in our everyday lives than anyone had suspected. For example, social psychologists who sought to understand why people prefer some things more than others had shown that a brief glimpse of a drawing—so brief that it was hardly possible to see it—led participants in an experiment later to say that they liked the flashed drawing more than one they had not seen. Yet people could not explicitly remember which drawings had been presented. These findings smacked of subliminal perception, illustrated by the apocryphal story about a sinister 1950s advertising ploy in which the words *Coca-Cola* and *popcorn* were flashed on a movie screen so briefly that nobody in the theater could see them. Supposedly, there would be a sudden mad dash to the concession stand to purchase these products. Although the effect turned out to be part of a publicity hoax, implicit memory was held to be reflected by an unexplained desire to drink Coke and eat popcorn.[16]

By the mid–1980s a number of well-controlled studies had shown that preferences and feelings can be shaped by specific encounters and experiences that people do not remember explicitly. For instance, exposure to negative words that were flashed too quickly to register in conscious perception caused people later to feel hostility toward a fictional person. Some form of memory was responsible for their hostility, but participants had no idea that they were "remembering" any negative information. Likewise, studies of amnesic patients revealed implicit memory for emotional experiences they could not remember explicitly. For instance, the encephalitic patient Boswell, whose severe amnesia I mentioned in the previous chapter, took part in an experiment in which one researcher was designated a "good guy" (he gave Boswell special treats), another was designated a "bad guy" (he denied requests for treats), and a third behaved neutrally. Later, Boswell had no explicit memory for, or any sense of familiarity with, any of these people. Yet when pictures of them were each paired with pictures of unfamiliar people, and Boswell was asked to choose which one of the two he liked best, he selected the "good guy" most often and the "bad guy" least often.[17]

There were also intriguing reports about people who had been given general anesthesia during surgical procedures. Received wisdom holds that patients cannot perceive or attend to anything that is said or done when they are unconscious during an operation. But in an experiment conducted during the 1960s, surgeons staged a mock crisis during surgery that included dire statements to the effect that the operation was in trouble and the patient might not pull through. Some of the patients who had been exposed to the mock crisis subsequently became extremely agitated when asked about it later, suggesting that they formed some sort of implicit memory while lying unconscious on the operating table.[18]

On a more positive note, later studies showed that anesthetized patients who were given suggestions that they would make a quick recovery spent less time in the hospital postoperatively than patients who were not given any such suggestions. Yet none of the patients explicitly remembered the suggestions. My colleagues and I later demonstrated that patients who heard a list of spoken words during surgery showed priming for those words when tested during postoperative recovery. Not surprisingly, they had no explicit memory for the words.[19]

Implicit memory may also be related to some of the memory distortions I considered earlier. When we forget the source of retrieved information—who said what, whether an incident actually occurred or was merely imagined—we may generate an inaccurate source and hence become prone to false recollections. Implicit memory, by definition, does not involve recollection of source information. Thus, we may generate plausible but incorrect sources in attempting to make sense of why a particular idea pops to mind or why we feel a certain emotion.[20]

For instance, implicit memory might play a role in the perplexing experience of déjà vu. Most people have on some occasion suddenly been possessed by a feeling of already having lived through an event that is occurring ostensibly for the first time. This unexplained feeling of familiarity was first called *déjà vu* in the late nineteenth century, and it became the subject of spirited debate among psychologists and psychiatrists. According to one theory, déjà vu reflects the influence of a fragment of experience that is activated by the present situation, but cannot be recollected explicitly. For instance, if you are talking with an associate at work and suddenly feel that you have had the same conversation before—but don't remember it—it might be because a phrase or an idea has triggered an implicit memory of something that was said in a previous conversation. You are left with the task of trying to make sense of the anomalous sensation.[21]

Implicit memory research has also provided a fresh perspective on another important facet of memory: how infants and young children learn from experience. Developmental psychologists have shown that prelinguistic infants—even newborn babies—are capable of a surprising amount of learning. Using a procedure in which newborns can control the sounds they hear by sucking on a non-nutritive nipple, researchers have shown that a three-day-old infant will suck more frequently when hearing the sound of its mother's voice than when hearing the sound of an unfamiliar voice. This preference shows that an infant has retained in memory information about the mother's voice. In another study, women repeatedly read aloud a Dr. Seuss story during the final six weeks of pregnancy. Newborns showed through sucking that they preferred to listen to their mothers telling this story, rather than one they had never heard before. These infants encoded and retained something about their mothers' recitation of the Dr. Seuss story that later influenced their sucking behavior.[22]

Do such demonstrations show that an infant explicitly remembers encounters in the womb? No. Amnesic patients with medial temporal lobe damage and patients undergoing surgical anesthesia can be influenced by past experiences that they do not explicitly remember, and the same may be true of many manifestations of early infant memory.

Other research has shown, however, that young infants can retain specific details of particular episodes. For instance, Carolyn Rovee-Collier and her colleagues observed that babies as young as two to five months old can learn to move a colorful mobile that is attached to one of their legs by a string. As soon as the infants kick, the mobile moves around and starts to play music, which the babies enjoy greatly. When they are brought back to the lab a day or two later, even two-month-olds will spontaneously kick a lot, indicating that they have retained in memory some information related to the mobile. Three-month-old infants still show elevated kick levels after a week, and six-month-olds do so even after two weeks have passed.

Rovee-Collier has also shown that infants do not kick frequently when brought back to the lab a day later and shown a mobile that physically differs from the one they learned to move. Even more amazing, when a cloth liner behind the mobile is decorated with squares during an infant's first encounter, but with circles one day later, six-month-old infants "merely gape" at the mobile. But if the liner is decorated with squares during the second encounter, the babies kick frequently.[23]

These findings show that young infants can retain in memory details of an object and some information about the context in which it was encountered. Are the infants "remembering" their past encounters with the mobile when they kick spontaneously? Or are they merely showing some form of implicit memory, perhaps a procedural or motor response? Infants obviously cannot tell us what they remember, but some examples of infant memory seem more implicit than explicit. In one study, five-month-old infants were conditioned to turn their heads when a tone sounded to receive a squirt of milk. Even after the infants were full and refused to drink more milk, they kept turning their heads when they heard the tone! If the infants actually remembered what transpired when the tone sounded, why would they continue to turn their heads when they were too full to drink?[24]

Over a decade ago, my colleague Morris Moscovitch and I published a paper suggesting that the brain structures that support implicit memory are in place before the systems needed for explicit memory. And, indeed, we have already seen that the frontal lobes, which play an important role in elaborative encoding, strategic retrieval, and source memory, mature late in development. However, recent work with one-month-old infant monkeys shows that lesions to structures in the medial temporal lobe, including the hippocampus, disrupt memory.[25] If the same applies to human infants, then even some relatively early manifestations of retention may depend on brain systems involving the hippocampus, which are linked with explicit remembering in adults. The kinds of retention seen in Rovee-Collier's experiments, for example, might signal the rudimentary beginnings of some primitive form of explicit memory.

Nonetheless, it is only toward the end of the first year, around eight or nine months, that infants show strong signs of explicit recall. Then they begin to search for and find hidden toys, even when they must wait several seconds before looking for the object. More impressively, studies by the psychologist Andrew Meltzoff show that nine-month-old infants can recall specific actions after a week's delay. For example, infants who saw an experimenter bang the top of a plastic box with his forehead often carried out the same action when they saw the box a week later. Infants who saw the box, but not the action, hardly ever repeated that behavior. This behavior doesn't necessarily show that the infants actually recollect that the experimenter banged his head against the box, but they clearly know something about the episode. Other recent studies with thirteen-month-old infants using a related type of imitation procedure have shown clear evidence for knowledge of specific event sequences after a one-week delay and even after an eight-month delay. For example, children who watched an experimenter put together a gong from several props later knew how to assemble it when given the props. But when adult amnesic patients were given a similar task they showed little memory, suggesting that the youngsters are not merely demonstrating priming or procedural learning. This is the beginning of a steady age-related increase in explicit recall and recognition; eventually, children develop language skills and learn to impose narrative structure on their experiences. In contrast, a growing number of studies have shown that priming and related kinds of implicit memory show little change during childhood. Three-year-old children, for instance, show just as much priming as do five-year-olds, even though the older children remember much more than the younger ones. Likewise, sixth-graders recall more words from a list than first-graders do, but the two groups of children show nearly identical levels of priming.[26]

In addition to these implications for memory development, it also became clear that implicit memory provides important clues concerning the nature of neurological deficits in various patient populations. Several researchers discovered that prosopagnosic patients, who have difficulties explicitly recognizing familiar faces (see chapter 3), nonetheless possess implicit knowledge of them. For example, Daniel Tranel and Antonio Damasio showed pictures of well-known and unknown faces to a prosopagnosic patient and recorded an index of physiological arousal, the skin conductance response. The patient showed a larger skin conductance response to familiar than to unfamiliar faces, even though she did not consciously recognize any of them! Subsequent studies using priming techniques have also shown that prosopagnosic patients possess implicit knowledge about unrecognized faces.[27]

As these fascinating studies were beginning to appear, I was drawn toward another implication of implicit memory research for everyday life. Working with amnesic patients, I became acutely aware that memory loss wreaked havoc in their day-to-day lives. Most amnesics could not hold down jobs or be trusted with elementary responsibilities. The daily existence of an amnesic patient is impoverished and dull. Yet studies of implicit memory indicated that these people undeniably possessed some preserved learning abilities. Could they be put to work for the patients? Was there some way for amnesics to draw on memory capacities that they were unaware they possessed?

PUTTING PRIMING TO WORK
The Story of Barbara

When the woman I call Barbara turned twenty-six years old, in 1980, her life seemed full and secure. She was happily married and held an office job in a large company. Then, suddenly and unaccountably, Barbara became dreadfully ill: she had contracted encephalitis. As she recovered from the dangerous disease, it became evident that Barbara was little more than a shadow of the woman she had been. She had forgotten large chunks of her personal past and much of her general knowledge of facts, concepts, and the routine activities of everyday life. And she had little or no memory for the ongoing incidents of her life.

Like the British artist David Jane (see chapter 5), Barbara was able to relearn many of the facts and skills that the devastating virus had taken from her. She eventually was able to read and write again. But the disease left many permanent scars, the most prominent of which was a profound amnesic syndrome. Barbara could no longer handle the demands of her job. Fortunately, she worked for a supportive company that managed to find simple clerical work that Barbara could perform adequately.

Six years later, Barbara received some unexpected news. The simple clerical job she had been performing would soon be carried out entirely by machines. Losing this job would be a shattering blow to the relatively stable life Barbara and her husband had managed to build in the wake of her encephalitic infection. The company was fully aware of this, and did not want to turn her loose without exploring all options. Because Barbara had been taking part in the research that my colleagues and I were conducting at the Unit for Memory Disorders, the company turned to us for advice and possible help. Was Barbara capable of any learning? Was it even reasonable, they wondered, to try to teach her a new job?

We had reason to be optimistic about Barbara's chances. Although her explicit memory was poor, Barbara showed normal priming effects. Even more important, we already knew that Barbara could acquire a surprising amount of new knowledge. Fellow psychologist Elizabeth Glisky and I had set out three years earlier to determine whether amnesic patients could acquire new knowledge and skills that would be helpful to them in their everyday lives. Previous attempts at memory rehabilitation with amnesics had not been terribly successful, all failing to restore an amnesic patient's damaged explicit memory.[28] Glisky and I believed that a radically different approach was needed.

We reasoned that if we could tap into amnesic patients' preserved implicit memory abilities, we could teach them knowledge and skills to help them deal with specific problems in their day-to-day lives. Here we returned to the basic insight from Warrington and Weiskrantz's early studies: when amnesic patients are given letter cues, they show normal priming for previously studied words. Based on this insight, we developed a procedure we called the "method of vanishing cues." For example, to teach an amnesic patient some basic vocabulary involved in interacting with a computer, we would show her a definition such as "a repeated portion of a program" on a computer monitor. If she does not know the answer, letter cues start appearing one by one until she correctly states *loop*. The computer records how many letter hints the patient requires. Later, that definition is presented with one fewer letter than the patient had required to come up with *loop*. Eventually, letter cues are withdrawn entirely and the patient generates the correct word on her own.

We were encouraged by the results of our first study: amnesic patients learned computer definitions more rapidly when we used the vanishing-cues procedure than when we simply repeated the words and definitions.[29] And Barbara was one of our star pupils: she picked up the computer vocabulary relatively quickly and retained it well. She was also a star pupil in another study, in which we used the vanishing-cues procedure to teach her and other amnesic patients to create and store their own programs, edit documents, use directories, and so forth. Surprisingly, the amnesics showed essentially no forgetting when we retested them approximately a year after training—even though several patients had no explicit recollection that they had ever worked on a computer before![30]

So when Barbara's company approached us, we knew she could learn complex new tasks in the laboratory and felt she could do the same in a work environment if a suitable task could be found. After visiting the company, we settled on a promising possibility: a job that required learning how to enter data from company records into a computer file. To perform the job, Barbara would have to learn a great deal of new information—the records contained various kinds of codes and symbols, and some of the rules for entering them into the computer were complicated—but we felt she could master it. We set up a mock version of the task in our laboratory, and proceeded to use the vanishing-cues procedure to train Barbara. If we were successful, the company agreed, Barbara could try to perform the actual job in the work environment.

When we began training, we feared we had taken on too much. Barbara needed lots of letter hints to perform just about every part of the job, and she initially performed the task far too slowly to meet the job demands. A skilled performer was expected to enter data at a rate of about fifteen seconds per record. Barbara required nearly an hour! Nevertheless, each time she carried out the task, she performed it more quickly and with fewer hints. Eventually she required no hints and consistently entered the data even faster than fifteen seconds per record. Next came the acid test: Could Barbara perform the job adequately in the work environment? She passed with flying colors. Our mission had succeeded—but it was not quite finished.

Performing this single task was sufficient to employ Barbara for only a few hours per week. To perform a full-time job, she would have to learn how to enter data from many different kinds of company records: invoices, purchase orders, shipping documents, and the like. Learning to enter information from each one of these documents is a complicated task by itself, but if we were to train Barbara for full-time employment, she had to learn to enter data from eleven different documents! All told, there were over 250 different rules, symbols, and codes that she had to master. As far as we knew, nobody had ever attempted to teach an amnesic patient anything on this order of magnitude. However, following the same procedures that we used in the earlier phases of our research, we obtained the same outcome. After six months of training, Barbara was able to perform this complicated task flawlessly in the work environment. She had earned a full-time job.[31]

At the conclusion of all this learning and practice, Barbara's explicit memory was no better. She still had great difficulty recollecting day-to-day events. But by allowing her to draw on her preserved capacities for priming and skill learning, our training procedure made a major difference in her life. And it had implications for other amnesic patients. If Barbara could learn a relatively complicated job, there was no reason why other patients couldn't do so also. And, indeed, follow-up studies indicated that patients who had developed memory disorders as a result of head injuries could learn the jobs we had taught Barbara. Other researchers attempted to refine and improve our vanishing-cues procedure, and they reported new successes in teaching amnesic patients knowledge and skills that could be used in their daily lives.[32]

But the fact that amnesic patients like Barbara rely heavily on implicit memory to learn complex tasks carries some costs. In all our training studies, the knowledge that amnesic patients acquired was quite inflexible. When we made relatively small changes in the wording of a computer command that patients had already learned, they had great difficulty coming up with the correct answer. For example, in our computer vocabulary study, patients who learned to respond "loop" when given the definition "a repeated portion of a program" often could not come up with the answer when given the reworded definition "If you want a program to perform the same operation repeatedly, you put the instructions in a . . ." Changes of this kind had little effect on people without memory problems.[33]

Amnesic patients were responding on the basis of a relatively primitive connection between the definition and the target word. Their learning was driven more by simply seeing the words in a sentence than by any deep understanding of the underlying concepts. The priming that allowed amnesic patients to learn seemed to be rooted more in perception than in comprehension. I started to wonder whether the perceptual quality of priming could provide clues concerning the nature of the memory system that Tulving and I had speculated about in the early days of implicit memory research.

OBJECTS OF THE MIND

Cheryl Warrick is an abstract painter who has always been fascinated by the fleeting shapes and objects that spontaneously pop into her mind. Images of circles, spheres, ovals, and other basic forms provide the raw materials for her elegant, often mysterious paintings. Warrick treats the canvas as a metaphor for memory itself, building up layers of paint that visually represent the layers of everyday experience that accumulate in our minds. She then scratches, erases, and scrapes back the layers of paint to reveal the hidden "past" of her painting, analogous to the way in which we attempt to work back through layers of our personal pasts when seeking to understand ourselves. "My paintings are unique to me," comments Warrick, "but about human experience, the emotional space that you travel through to understand

yourself and the painting. You have to understand the past to understand how we are now."[34]

In 1991, Cheryl noticed that new kinds of shapes kept intruding
into her mind: knobby, fistlike structures attached to thin tubes. What
were these peculiar forms, so different from the circles and ovals that
usually populated her paintings, and why did they keep imposing
themselves on her? One day, while playing with her new baby, Cheryl
spotted the intruding shapes right in front of her: baby rattles. Cheryl's
life had been full of these rattles for months. She had been "remembering" them in her intrusive images, but wasn't aware that she was
doing so. Warrick's painting "Visible Past" (figure 6.1) shows the
intruding forms, at once unusual yet also vaguely familiar. The title
reflects Cheryl's insight that the images in the painting allow her
unusual "memories" to become visible to all of us.[35]

Writing about Cheryl Warrick's paintings, one observer commented: "Like memories or dreams, the images are hazy and illogical,
but penetrating in their emotional force."[36] Part of their "hazy and
illogical" quality stems from the fact that Warrick's painted images are
not explicit recollections of people and places. They are implicit memories of shapes and forms, perceptual fragments of experience that
materialize in awareness unattached to recognizable settings or stories.

During the late 1980s, I began to think a lot about perceptual
memories of shapes, forms, and objects. Our work with amnesic
patients indicated that priming is intimately related to perception. And
others had shown that when people are given a word fragment–completion test, having seen a word during the study task produces a
stronger priming effect than having heard the word. In fact, some
experiments indicated that priming is stronger when a word is studied and tested in the exact same typefont or typecase than when these
details of the word's visual appearance are changed between study and
test.[37] This implied to me that priming likely depends on brain systems that are especially involved in perceptual analysis.

I also began to see links to some intriguing cases that had been
reported a number of years earlier. Several neuropsychologists had
described brain-damaged patients who could read familiar words
aloud reasonably well, but had little or no idea what the words meant.
One patient, known by the initials WLP, could even say words with
irregular spellings, such as *blood* and *cough,* even though she could not
appreciate their meaning. To pronounce such words correctly, you
must be able to retrieve a stored visual memory of the word, which
in turn leads you to the correct pronunciation (to pronounce more

FIGURE 6.1

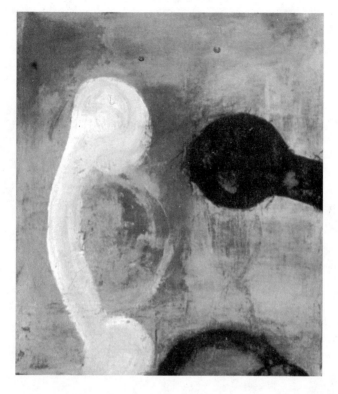

Cheryl Warrick, "Visible Past," 1991. 12 x 10". Acrylic on canvas. Gallery NAGA, Boston.

Baby rattle shapes kept popping into Warrick's mind after playing with her infant daughter, but the artist was unaware that she was remembering.

regularly spelled words correctly, you need only sound them out). By reading aloud a word such as *blood,* WLP was showing that she could retrieve a stored visual memory of the word's form and a link to the word's phonology. But her failure to understand its meaning showed that she could not retrieve a semantic memory of the word. The case of WLP and similar patients implied that visual information about words is stored separately from semantic or conceptual information.[38]

At around the same time that I was thinking about the implications of these intriguing patients for understanding priming, new studies using PET scanning techniques showed that different areas of the brain become active during visual and semantic analyses of familiar words. Merely seeing a familiar word activates a specific part of the occipital lobes, the brain region that is essential for visual perception. Thinking about the meaning of a word activates other areas in the temporal and frontal lobes.[39] Putting together the observations from patients like WLP with these PET results, we saw that a distinct brain system is responsible for storing visual information about a word. Could this be the memory system to which Tulving and I had alluded?

Because experiments had already shown that seeing a word enhances visual priming, I felt confident in theorizing that it depends on a perceptually based memory system. This idea also fit well with the studies of Warrington and Weiskrantz, and of many others, showing that priming is spared in amnesic patients. Amnesics have suffered damage to the hippocampal and diencephalic brain regions that are necessary for explicit memory, but not to occipital areas that are involved in visual encoding of words. If these occipital areas play an important role in priming, the results from amnesic patients could be explained easily. This idea could even help to understand why patients like Barbara learn new information in such a rigid and inflexible way. Barbara relied heavily on priming to acquire new knowledge. Perhaps she performed poorly when we changed the exact wording of questions because she was highly dependent on a perceptually based memory system. She might have learned the rules and commands as a literal sequence of visual forms.

All this evidence seemed to fit together nicely, yet everything I have said so far about priming and perception relies on studies that used verbal materials—familiar words. If priming is closely linked with perception, then it should occur with nonverbal shapes and forms. The baby rattle shapes that kept popping into Cheryl Warrick's mind, for example, probably reflect the influence of priming. But I needed to figure out how to investigate this sort of process in the laboratory. Experiments had already shown that seeing pictures of familiar objects such as a chair or a house produces priming when people later attempt to identify fragmented pictures of chairs or houses.[40] Familiar objects, however, all have names; I wanted to determine whether priming occurs for novel forms that cannot be coded easily with a verbal label. So I embarked on a series of experiments with Lynn Cooper, a psychologist who has made pioneering contributions to our understanding of object perception. We found a way to demonstrate and explore implicit memory for novel visual shapes.

We used unfamiliar objects like those in figure 6.2. Some are "possible" objects—you could build them out of wood or clay—but others

FIGURE 6.2

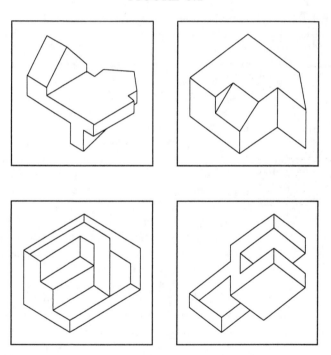

Sample of objects used in Schacter and Cooper's experiments on implicit and explicit memory for novel objects. The drawings in the upper row show possible objects that could exist in three-dimensional form. The drawings in the lower row depict impossible objects that contain structural violations that would prohibit them from actually existing in three-dimensional form. See text for further explanation.

are impossible structures. Like the drawings of M. C. Escher, they could not exist in three dimensions. We flashed each object briefly on a computer screen and asked college students to make a decision about whether it was possible or impossible. Decisions about possible objects were primed by exposure to the object several minutes earlier. Surprisingly, there was no priming effect for impossible objects. We found similar results in amnesic patients. Because amnesic patients had difficulty explicitly remembering which objects they had seen, we could be confident that the priming effect for possible objects reflects implicit memory.[41]

We were excited by these results, because they showed that priming occurs even for novel shapes with no verbal labels. Why wasn't there any priming for impossible objects? The brain cannot create a unified image of an impossible object. We theorized that priming depends on a perceptually based memory system that stores information about the overall structure of objects. Perhaps the system does not store the overall structure of an impossible object because there is no consistent overall structure to store.[42]

The results of our object priming studies fit nicely with the results on visual word priming: both lines of research showed that a perceptual system plays a key role in priming. I now had a firm basis to theorize about the memory system that Tulving and I had been groping to characterize. In several articles, including a paper I co-authored with Tulving, I called this system the *perceptual representation system,* or PRS. The PRS allows us to identify objects in our everyday environment and to recognize familiar words on a printed page. The PRS is specialized to deal with the form and structure of words and objects, but it does not "know" anything about what words mean or what objects are used for. Meaningful associations and concepts are handled by semantic memory, which cooperates closely with PRS.[43]

The two systems normally operate in seamless cooperation, so that when we recognize familiar words we are immediately aware of what they mean, and when we see familiar objects we can easily recall how to use them. But in some cases of brain damage, semantic memory can be seriously disrupted while PRS functions relatively well. WLP, who could read words without understanding them, is a good example. Other patients can recognize everyday objects, but have difficulty recalling their names, remembering what they are used for, or saying where you would be most likely to find them. One such patient, JB, was shown a fork and called it a toothbrush. When presented with a cherry, he called it an apple. And when shown a shopping bag, he said it was an umbrella. His ability to retrieve concepts and associations from visual inputs had been horribly disrupted, yet he could easily tell pictures of real everyday objects from pictures of nonsense objects.[44]

If my view is correct and priming depends on the PRS, then patients such as WLP and JB should show intact priming effects. In the early 1990s, I had a chance to test this idea. I encountered a patient, JP, who had a serious problem understanding spoken words. He could hear them and even repeat them accurately, but he had difficulty comprehending what they meant. This made it difficult to converse with him, especially over the telephone. As it happened, I had just embarked on a new series of experiments concerning auditory priming, showing that hearing a word helps college students identify the word several minutes later when it is played on a noise-filled audiotape (having *seen* the word earlier provides little or no benefit). The auditory priming effect, like the visual priming effects I described earlier, was nearly identical after deep encoding and shallow encoding, even though explicit memory for spoken words was much higher after deep than shallow encoding. Amnesic patients, too, showed this auditory priming effect, despite the fact that they had almost no explicit memory for having heard the words. Because auditory priming closely resembles visual priming, these results led us to suggest that priming of spoken words depends on an auditory PRS—a cousin of the visual PRS we had already theorized about. If so, then JP should show auditory priming, even though he has little understanding of what words he is hearing and identifying. This is exactly what we found.[45]

PET scanning studies provided another way to test my ideas about priming and the PRS. PET studies of visual word priming, for example, have revealed evidence to back up my theory that priming is associated with blood flow changes in the occipital lobes. In studies by colleagues and me, the hippocampus was not active during priming, but became very active when people consciously recollected words they had recently studied. Consistent with these findings, studies of patients with damaged occipital lobes have shown impaired priming for words they have just seen, just as you would expect if this part of the brain plays an important role in visual priming.[46]

PET scanning has also helped reveal the physiological basis for some of the differences we observed between possible and impossible objects. We found that when people made decisions about briefly flashed possible objects, there was extensive activity in two adjacent regions at the interface of the temporal and occipital lobes known as the inferior temporal gyrus and the fusiform gyrus. But there was little or no activity in these areas when people made decisions about impossible objects. Cooper and I had theorized that priming of possible objects depends on inferior temporal regions. Our theory was based largely on studies with monkeys that showed that cells in the inferior temporal lobe respond selectively to the general shape of an object, as opposed to its size or isolated parts of the object. And other studies had shown that the fusiform gyrus is involved in perceiving and recognizing faces, which we tend to see as unified wholes. The new PET data provide strong evidence that these two areas are specifically involved in encoding the overall shape of an object, and suggest that they play a role in priming. The hippocampus was silent during priming, but became active when people explicitly remembered seeing possible objects.[47]

These results, encouraging for the PRS theory, allow me to speculate about what might have been happening to Barbara when she learned so well on the vanishing cues task, and to Cheryl Warrick when the baby rattle shapes kept inexplicably popping to mind. I would hazard a guess that as Barbara required progressively fewer letter hints to complete target words, changes were taking place in the occipital regions of the PRS. And I would conjecture that when the baby rattle shapes kept intruding into Cheryl's mind, the inferior temporal and fusiform regions of the PRS were strongly engaged. The hippocampus, however, was probably inactive in both cases, because neither Barbara nor Cheryl felt they were remembering their past experiences.

These suggestions are highly simplistic, of course. No complex task or mental activity involves only a single region of the brain. Multiple brain areas involving distributed networks are active during the performance of just about any task, and we are only at the very beginning of understanding what they do and how they communicate with one another. The PRS plays a role in our ability to recognize words and objects. Priming reflects the fact that this system changes in response to encounters with words and objects. Reading words on a page, hearing words and voices, or seeing objects that populate the world around us may sometimes produce subtle alterations in our brains, alterations that later influence the way we respond to the environment or that make it more likely for a particular idea or image to spring to mind, seemingly out of nowhere. We are for the most part entirely unaware that any of these changes are taking place. Priming, like other kinds of implicit memory, operates invisibly. It is a silent part of our mental lives, but an important source of memory's fragile power.

BEYOND PERCEPTUAL PRIMING
The Many Manifestations of Implicit Memory

When I was poring over the stack of legal documents concerning Peter Bonyhard's knowledge of MR heads, I realized that any testimony I might offer about his case would have to go well beyond citing experiments on priming of words and objects or theories about the PRS. The exceedingly complicated knowledge he possesses is far more complex and meaningful than the primitive fragments of perceptual experiences that have been studied in laboratory priming experiments. If all of implicit memory could be explained as perceptual priming, then it would be difficult to invoke implicit memory as a factor in Bonyhard's case. The key issue here concerned the possible unconscious influence of complex conceptual knowledge. But there is indeed far more to implicit memory than perceptual priming of words and objects.

I have already mentioned that amnesic patients can learn new perceptual and motor skills. Nelson Butters and his colleagues have shown that skill learning depends on a different brain system—procedural memory—than priming does. Butters's group studied patients with Alzheimer's disease, who have damage to the medial temporal lobes and other regions of the cortex. They compared the Alzheimer's group to patients suffering from Huntington's disease, the devastating, genetically transmitted illness that destroys the brain's motor system. In Huntington's disease, damage is largely restricted to a subcortical collection of structures known as the basal ganglia, which are critical to executing learned movements. Butters and collaborators found that patients with Huntington's disease show normal priming on a word completion test, but have great difficulty acquiring new motor skills. Alzheimer's patients, in contrast, have no difficulty acquiring motor skills but show impaired priming. These results demonstrated convincingly that priming and skill learning depend on separate memory systems in the brain.

More recent work on procedural learning has shown that in addition to the basal ganglia, the cerebellum (see figure 5.1), a structure long known to be involved in motor performance, is also crucial for motor skill learning. Patients with damage to the cerebellum have grave difficulty learning tasks that require mastering sequences of events, such as learning how to play the piano. Such patients also have difficulties planning out sequences of actions that are required to solve problems. After reviewing the relevant evidence, Butters and co-author

David Salmon concluded that the cerebellum plays a key role in carrying out the timing operations that allow us to arrange motor movements in their proper sequence. The basal ganglia, in turn, are responsible for refining the sequence and storing it as an organized motor program. Because the basal ganglia and cerebellum are typically not damaged in amnesic patients, we should not be surprised to find out that a severely amnesic patient was able to play familiar tunes on the piano and even learn some new ones. Likewise, Mary Jo Nissen and her colleagues have shown that amnesic patients can learn novel sequences implicitly on a task in which they respond as quickly as possible to asterisks that appear one after another in different locations on a screen. When the asterisks appear in a recurring sequence, amnesic patients respond more quickly than when no pattern is present—yet they show no explicit knowledge of the sequence. Recent evidence from PET scans has shown directly that the basal ganglia and a part of the motor cortex play an important role in this kind of procedural memory. In a particularly striking experiment, people practiced making a sequence of finger movements outside the scanner, and were scanned (using functional MRI) at weekly intervals. At first, when people performed the sequence there were isolated patches of increased blood flow in the motor cortex (see figure 2.4); but with practice, they gradually expanded. One aspect of learning a new motor sequence, such as playing the piano, appears to involve the increasing participation of neurons in the motor cortex.[48]

Procedural memory is also involved in the development of habits—those well-practiced and largely unconscious behavioral routines we all carry out in everyday life. Pioneering studies by Mortimer Mishkin and colleagues have shown that monkeys with lesions to the medial temporal lobes, who show poor memory for their recent experiences, can nonetheless form new habits at a normal rate. When given hundreds of practice trials, these amnesic monkeys can gradually learn what to do in order to obtain a food reward, even though they have little memory for what happened on any particular trial. Human amnesic patients, too, can show analogous forms of habit learning. With extensive practice, amnesics can gradually learn to classify visual patterns into categories at the same rate as people without explicit memory problems, and can even learn the rules of a made-up grammar at a normal rate. Yet amnesic patients, like the animals in Mishkin's studies, have little ability to remember what happened on any particular trial. Conversely, damage to the basal ganglia disrupts habit learning, just as it disrupts motor skill learning.[49]

Skill and habit learning, however, were not the issue in Bonyhard's case. The central question involved the possible unconscious influences of semantic knowledge on his job performance. Here, too, we have evidence of the operation of implicit memory. Consider the following sentence: "The haystack was important because the cloth ripped." Does it make any sense to you? Probably not. But I can provide a single word that should make this peculiar statement suddenly comprehensible: *parachute*. You can now imagine a scene in which the unfortunate person whose parachute has ripped is saved by landing on a cushioning mound of hay. Likewise, the sentence "The notes were sour because the seams split" probably makes no sense until I give you the clue *bagpipes*. When my colleagues and I showed these sentences to amnesic patients, they, like you, could not figure out what the sentences meant until we gave them the critical clue. Interestingly, when we showed them the sentences again minutes, hours, or days later, they easily came up with the clue word on their own. Clearly, the amnesic patients benefited from their earlier encounter with the sentence and the clue. Yet they frequently said that they had never encountered these sentences or clue words before, typically stating that the sentences were just easy to figure out. This is not a perceptual priming effect that depends on the PRS: patients must understand how the critical word relates to the full sentence in order to show a memory benefit. It is, instead, a conceptual priming effect that probably depends on a modification of the semantic memory system. Other experiments with both amnesic patients and college students have shown that conceptual priming occurs, and they suggest that it depends on semantic memory, not on the PRS.[50]

These experiments show that implicit memory operates in the conceptual domain as well as the perceptual domain, and thus bring us closer to seeing how implicit memory could be influential in a real-world situation involving access to conceptual knowledge. Indeed, the cases of unconscious plagiarism that I cited earlier probably illustrate the influence of conceptual priming. Ideas pop to mind unattached to any setting or context, and we believe that we have come up with them ourselves, even though they derive from a specific experience. This is exactly the kind of conceptual priming that might have been operating in the case of Peter Bonyhard.

The occurrence of conceptual priming and other semantic forms of implicit memory may have far-reaching implications for many aspects of our everyday lives. Recent research in social psychology, for example, has implicated implicit memory as a contributor to gender and racial biases that people are not aware they possess. We maintain stereotypes about groups of people, including women and minorities, that may be automatically and unconsciously activated when we interact with, or are asked about, members of the group. Even though we are unaware that we hold such stereotypes, once they are turned on they can exert a powerful influence on our judgments about group members. For instance, in studies by the social psychologist Patricia Devine, white American students were exposed to a list of words, most of which suggest a stereotyped black American—welfare, basketball, ghetto, jazz, slavery, busing, Harlem, and so forth. The words were flashed so quickly that they were difficult to perceive and remember consciously. Nonetheless, when these students later read about the ambiguous behaviors of an imaginary male (whose race was not specified), they rated him as more hostile than students who had been exposed to mostly neutral words. This biasing effect was just as pronounced in students who expressed little racial prejudice on a questionnaire as in those who expressed higher levels of prejudice. Exposure to the racially loaded words may have automatically activated black stereotypes that some students were not aware they possessed.[51]

Implicit influences on our judgments and behaviors may be especially pernicious because they operate outside our awareness. Commercial advertising provides a good example. You may think that because you pay little attention to commercials on television or in newspapers, your judgments about products are unaffected by them. But a recent experiment showed that people tend to prefer products featured in ads they barely glanced at several minutes earlier—even when they have no explicit memory for having seen the ad. Such implicit effects make us vulnerable to what social psychologists call "mental contamination": when our thoughts and judgments are biased by unwanted but unconscious influences. None of us like to think that our purchasing decisions are swayed by advertising we barely notice, that our judgments are affected by racial stereotypes, or that our ideas are unintentionally plagiarized from somebody else. Yet it is precisely because we are oblivious to the source of these influences that we are prone to mental contamination. Studies have shown that making people aware of a biasing influence can counteract some kinds of mental contamination, but it is difficult to become aware of implicit memories whose existence one does not suspect.[52]

The nonconscious world of implicit memory revealed by cognitive neuroscience differs markedly from the Freudian unconscious. In Freud's vision, unconscious memories are dynamic entities embroiled in a fight against the forces of repression; they result from special experiences that relate to our deepest conflicts and desires. The implicit memories I have been considering are far more mundane. They arise as a natural consequence of such everyday activities as perceiving, understanding, and acting. The systems that perform these functions often change, perhaps only slightly, as they go about their business. Our brains are constantly adjusting and adapting to the world, and when these changes persist, they can affect our thoughts, judgments, and behaviors in surprising ways that scientists are just beginning to understand. Yet because priming generally reflects small changes in the PRS or semantic memory, and acquiring skills and habits involves slow procedural learning that builds up over time, we require additional machinery that allows rapid association and recall of the sights, sounds, places, and thoughts that come together in single episodes. As I have emphasized, networks of structures within the medial temporal lobes appear to do just that.[53]

Appreciating the pervasiveness of implicit influences on our thoughts, feelings, and behaviors provides an essential insight into the fragile power of human memory. If we are unaware that something is influencing our behavior, there is little we can do to understand or counteract it. The subtle, virtually undetectable nature of implicit memory is one reason it can have powerful effects on our mental lives. But we must resist the temptation to attribute every strange thought, unusual feeling, or odd action to the implicit effect of some experience that we have consciously forgotten. Attempting to interpret feelings and behaviors as signs of implicit memory for a particular forgotten experience is potentially dangerous because there are many possible determinants of what we think and feel.

These pitfalls notwithstanding, the invisible influence of implicit memory is an important part of the story of memory's fragile power. The past does not always shape us so subtly and indirectly, however. I now turn to those times when memory's power is expressed with a force so overwhelming that it can shake the very foundations on which our lives are built.

SEVEN

EMOTIONAL MEMORIES
When the Past Persists

IN 1987, MELINDA STICKNEY-GIBSON was a promising young artist whose colorful abstract paintings had attracted attention in and around Chicago, where she lived and worked. One warm June night Melinda was awakened by the smell of smoke. She lived in a converted loft in an industrial sector of Chicago, close to inner-city neighborhoods where fires were common. She saw smoke from her bedroom window, then emerged from the bedroom and saw ominous black plumes seeping up through cracks in the floor and through the hinges of the front door. She tried to call the fire department, but the phone lines had been burned out. The thick smoke expanded rapidly, seeming to double in volume every few seconds, until it encompassed the entire living space. Soon, Melinda found it nearly impossible to breathe.

All her possessions were in the apartment, as well as her beloved dog, but there was no time to search for them. The third-story apartment had no fire escape, so she first attempted to flee down the stairs. But the blistering heat on the steps forced her to turn back. There was only one option: she would have to jump onto a concrete landing dock three stories below. Walking out on a metal ledge, Melinda tried to cut the distance between herself and the ground by hanging from the ledge by her fingers. She let go and went crashing onto the concrete. Shortly thereafter, the entire building exploded in a spectacular fireball. The loft where she had been sleeping peacefully a few minutes earlier was reduced to a charcoal-seared rubble, her dog was killed, and all the possessions of a lifetime, including valued family heirlooms and photographs, were destroyed.

Melinda's life and art changed immediately and radically as a result of the fire. She was fortunate to survive her three-story fall with only a few broken bones, but found herself unable to evade a persistent, throbbing memory of the incident. She left Chicago and moved to a new home in the California desert. In place of her bold, expressive canvases, highlighted by beautiful mauves and blues, she began painting darkly introspective works on lead, steel, and concrete. Now she used only the colors of the fire: orange, black, and okra. Her new artwork became a vehicle for repetitively and exhaustively exploring her traumatic memory. The exploration has been almost entirely involuntary. Melinda describes how the memory simply imposes itself on her as she begins to paint:

> Sometimes I will be sitting thinking, I will be in a thoughtful place, and I will just be thinking and the images will come, but I don't ask for them. It's not like I say, I am going to work on this painting and I need to get this feeling or I need to get this image. I am just thinking about the painting, and this image, this event, will come. . . . Then after I make the painting it will connect. I will recognize it as part of the memory. Like the way the black smoke looked. The lights were still on, you know, the electricity was not off. So the light would be on and there would be this thick black smoke.[1]

These reflections are illustrated in her painting "Story II" (figure 7.1). Melinda surrounds a photograph of herself asleep in bed, suggestive of her last few moments prior to being awakened by the conflagration, with eerie black blotches and milky yellow-white blobs that capture her memory of the black smoke filtered by the apartment lights.

The power of Melinda's memory for what she saw and felt that night is remarkable. Even when I spoke with her in 1993, six years after the fire, Melinda pointed out that her memories of those few awful minutes were every bit as intense and real as in the days and weeks following the fire; fortunately, they came to mind much less often. Only recently, Melinda reflected, had she felt less controlled by the memory and "kind of complete" again. Happily, the new approach to her art that was brought about by the fire turned out to be aesthetically compelling, and in the years since she has achieved widespread recognition.

FIGURE 7.1

Melinda Stickney-Gibson, "Story II," 1993. 11¼ x 12¾". Oil, wax, gold leaf, and collage on paper. Littlejohn-Sternau Gallery, New York.

This painting recalls the terrible fire that woke the artist one night and dominated her memory for years.

Melinda Stickney-Gibson's memories of black fumes and filtered light illustrate how an emotionally traumatic incident can be vividly, intrusively, and repeatedly recollected. Her experience represents only one of the ways the power of the past can be expressed. For now I will explore a type of vivid recollection that provides some hints about the sources of memory's power. Then I turn to far more potent experiences, where emotional traumas leave behind the kind of intense, seemingly indelible, marks that haunted Melinda Stickney-Gibson with a searing force that matched the energy of the smoke and flames that changed her life forever.

FLASHBULB MEMORIES
Where Were You Then?

It was a school day like any other, and I sat in my usual seat toward the rear of my sixth-grade classroom. I was not the world's most attentive student in those days, often preferring to work out the batting averages of my favorite baseball players rather than closely follow the day's lesson. But I paid rapt attention when the school's principal unexpectedly entered the classroom and pulled our teacher aside. He brought with him the terrible news that President Kennedy had been shot.

I do not remember much of what happened just before or after the stunning announcement, but an image of the moment when I first learned the news has remained fixed in my mind for over thirty years. For many of us, the memory of that November afternoon in 1963 feels as though it has been frozen forever in photographic form, unaffected by the ravages of time that erode and degrade most other memories.

In 1977, the psychologists Roger Brown and James Kulick picked up on just this feature of people's recollections of the Kennedy assassination when they referred to them as *flashbulb memories*. They suggested that a novel and shocking event activates a special brain mechanism, which they referred to as *Now Print*. Much like a camera's flashbulb, Brown and Kulick hypothesized, the Now Print mechanism preserves or "freezes" whatever happens at the moment when we learn of the shocking event.

Brown and Kulick interviewed eighty adults in 1976, forty white and forty black, about their recollections of the Kennedy assassination and other shocking public events, including the assassination of Martin

Luther King, Jr., and Robert F. Kennedy. People were given credit for a flashbulb memory when they answered yes to the question, "Do you remember the circumstances in which you first heard . . . ?" and when they could provide details about where they learned the news, who told them, or how they or others felt at the time. All but one of the interviewees possessed flashbulb memories of the JFK assassination, which Brown and Kulick contended reflects the unusual significance of this event for the entire population. In contrast, only about half of both whites and blacks had flashbulb memories of Robert F. Kennedy's assassination, which was rather less cataclysmic than his brother's. Thirty of the forty blacks but only thirteen of the forty whites possessed flashbulb memories of King's assassination. Brown and Kulick hypothesized that the "consequentiality" of an event determines whether the Now Print mechanism is triggered and the brain's flashbulb pops.[2]

The Now Print account of flashbulbs is intuitively compelling, and it fits well with the subjective experiences of people who feel that their memories of the JFK assassination are among the most vivid of their lives. This hypothesis inspired the photographer Anne Turyn to create an extended series of works that visually depict flashbulb experiences for shocking news events of the twentieth century. For each work in her series, Turyn paired a newspaper headline of a jarring news event—the crash of the Hindenburg, the end of World War II, and the moon landing are just a few examples—with a photograph of the physical context in which a person might have learned of the event. The photographs are characterized by a kind of hyperclarity, preserving precise nuances of light and shading as well as the exact arrangement of objects—the kinds of details that a Now Print memory mechanism might preserve, as in "5/10/1926 (Flashbulb Memories)," shown in figure 7.2.[3]

Turyn's visual rendition of flashbulb memories that result from a Now Print mechanism captures their salient features. But is there good scientific evidence for the Now Print theory? Are flashbulb memories different in kind from ordinary memories? Is the event somehow etched indelibly in the mind, perhaps forever, in its pristine original form?

Brown and Kulick did not query participants in their study about the JFK assassination until years after the event. To evaluate the accuracy of a flashbulb memory, we need some way to check the veracity of a person's recollection. Subsequent researchers have investigated memories for flashbulb events—the attempted assassination of Ronald

FIGURE 7.2

BYRD FLIES TO NORTH POLE AND BACK;
ROUND TRIP FROM KINGS BAY IN 15 HRS.51 MIN.;
CIRCLES TOP OF THE WORLD SEVERAL TIMES

**Anne Turyn, "5/10/1926 (Flashbulb Memories)," 1986. 11 x 14".
Ektacolor print. Copyright © Anne Turyn.**

A headline proclaiming that Admiral Byrd has flown to the North Pole and back is paired with an image of a dimly lit desk in a study. One can imagine a person sitting at the desk reading the headline or being told about the event by someone entering the study. The internal flashbulb pops, and the exact scene is recorded forever—or is it? For more modern incidents, Turyn frequently includes radio and television as part of the frozen memory.

Reagan in 1981, the explosion of the space shuttle *Challenger* in 1986, the Gulf War in 1991—by obtaining recollections from people within a few days or weeks after the event. Assuming that these very recent memories are accurate, they can be compared with recollections from the same people obtained months or years later.

Some flashbulb memories are indeed accurate and persistent. In a recent multinational study, the British psychologist Martin Conway and his colleagues examined what they believe constitutes a flashbulb event for British but not American adults: Margaret Thatcher's unexpected resignation as prime minister in 1990. The researchers collected memories from over three hundred British and American college students within two weeks of the resignation, and then again a year later. They found that British students showed extremely accurate retention of how they learned of the news, whereas American students showed a good deal more forgetting. Consistent with Conway's findings, Ulric Neisser and his colleagues have recently reported that Californians who were affected by the 1989 earthquake in Loma Prieta (near San Francisco) showed highly accurate memories when tested several years later, far more accurate than a control group from Atlanta who had only heard about the event on the news. These results support Brown and Kulick's idea that consequentiality—the personal significance of a flashbulb event—plays a key role in the durability of memory for that event.

Yet even some highly consequential flashbulb events are not wholly unaffected by the passage of time that weakens other memories. The Swedish researcher Sven-Ake Christianson explored memories of his country's equivalent of the JFK assassination: the 1986 assassination of Prime Minister Olof Palme as he was walking home from a movie theater. Christianson probed young adults' memories for the tumultuous event six weeks after it happened and then again one year later, and found that the accuracy of their memories had declined after a year.[4]

Even if flashbulb memories are prone to fading and decaying over time, they still might be better retained than memories for more ordinary events. I can remember relatively little about what happened in November 1963 other than the JFK assassination; even if my JFK flashbulb memory has lost some information over the years, it is surely richer and more reliable than memories of mundane events from that time period. (And Christianson found that people remembered the Palme assassination more accurately than they remembered an unremarkable event from around the same time.)

The Danish psychologist Steen Larsen was conducting a study of his own memories when he heard about the Palme assassination, and immediately entered into his computer a detailed account of how he learned the news. When the computer queried Larsen about this event several months later, as part of his ongoing study, he remembered correctly that he had heard it on the radio while having breakfast. He also noted that the sheer vividness of this memory contrasted with his impoverished recollections of how he learned about less important news events, which generally faded away within a month or so. But Larsen's flashbulb memory was not entirely accurate. When he checked his clear memory that his wife had been with him when he heard the news against his written record, Larsen discovered that he had heard the news alone. He also discovered, much to his surprise, that his recollections of what he did immediately after learning the news were inaccurate. Larsen's erroneous flashbulb memory was subjectively compelling, however; he commented that he could still "see" the scene of his wife and him hearing the news together.[5]

Other evidence, too, indicates that some flashbulb memories are far from photographic preservations of the original scene. In a study of memory for the *Challenger* explosion by Ulric Neisser and Nicole Harsch, college students were interviewed less than twenty-four hours after the event and then again two and a half years later. Over this long interval, students showed substantial forgetting of the circumstances in which they learned of the event, and the recollections of a number of them differed substantially from their earlier reports. Nevertheless, many students expressed high confidence that their false recollections were accurate. Indeed, Neisser and Harsch observed little relationship between the accuracy of a flashbulb memory and a person's subjective confidence that it was correct.[6]

Some have suggested that high confidence is the hallmark of a flashbulb memory. Charles Weaver, a psychologist, wanted to know whether people could form something like a flashbulb memory for an everyday event. At the first meeting of his undergraduate memory laboratory, he instructed students that the next time they encountered their roommates (or a close friend if they lived alone), they should try to remember as much as possible about the event. He gave students a questionnaire that probed various aspects of their memories for the personal encounter, and told them to fill it out as soon as possible after the key event occurred.

Weaver's timing turned out to be fortuitous. The first meeting of his laboratory class was January 16, 1991—the day President Bush announced the bombing of Iraq. Moving quickly, Weaver put together another questionnaire to assess memory for this flashbulb event, and administered it to his class when they next met, two days later. He then assessed memory for both the personal event and the public event three months later, and again a year later. Weaver's results were clear: students' memories were no more accurate for the Iraq bombing than for the personal encounter, and there was evidence of forgetting over time for both kinds of memories. But the students were generally more confident about their memories of the bombing than about their memories of the personal encounter. As in Neisser and Harsch's study of the *Challenger* disaster, a person's subjective confidence in a flashbulb memory was not matched by its objective accuracy.[7]

Why should flashbulb events sometimes give rise to confidence in a mistaken recollection? Part of the answer lies in the fact that people are prone to forgetting or confusing the source of a memory when long periods of time have elapsed after an event. Neisser and Harsch relate an example of a student who, when queried the day after the *Challenger* disaster, said she had learned of it during her religion class when she heard some friends talking about it. After class, she went to her room and found out more about it from television. Three years later, this young woman insisted that she had first learned about it from TV: "When I first heard about the explosion I was sitting in my freshman dorm room with my roommate and we were watching TV," she remembered clearly. "It came on a news flash and we were both totally shocked."[8] The student was probably so certain because she was indeed remembering an actual event, although she didn't realize she was confusing two sources of her knowledge of the event. Neisser and Harsch note that such "time slice errors," as they call them, occur frequently when people are queried years after an event. The psychologist William Brewer has observed that these errors constitute a form of source amnesia, and I agree.[9]

Likewise, Larsen's illusory memory of hearing about Palme's assassination while listening to the radio with his wife probably seemed convincing because he had recollections of similar scenes from prior occasions. This made it easy for Larsen to "insert" his wife into this particular memory. We have already seen that general knowledge and expectations can sometimes creep into memories for specific events— during encoding, retrieval, or both—which in turn can produce significant distortions. Recollections of flashbulb events are not immune to the kinds of reconstructive errors that occur when we attempt to remember any distant episode.

We may also hold unusually high confidence in the accuracy of our flashbulb memories because we believe that they have been imprinted forever on our brains in some immutable form. But the evidence shows that they have not; some flashbulb memories decay and change over time. It is doubtful whether such memories are preserved by the Now Print mechanism that Brown and Kulick envisaged. Yet it is equally certain that flashbulb memories are, on balance, more durable and accurate than most memories of day-to-day events. One reason for their strength is that they are likely to be discussed and thought about frequently in the days, weeks, and even years following the event. Certainly this "rehearsal" was the case with JFK's death.

The evidence also suggests that rehearsal alone cannot explain why flashbulb events tend to be better remembered than more mundane events. The emotions elicited by a flashbulb event also increase its memorability. For instance, in Conway's study of memory for Thatcher's resignation, the degree of emotional arousal that people experienced when hearing the news, as well as the amount of later rehearsal, contributed to the high levels of recollection that British students maintained even a year after the event.[10] Both rehearsal and emotion are relevant to understanding why certain memories stay with us for much of our lives. I can remember what happened on November 22, 1963—but not on November 21 or 23—because of the emotional arousal I felt at the exact moment of hearing the news and because I have talked about and strengthened the memory many times since.

PERSONAL TRAUMA
The Persistence of Memory

Flashbulb memories are fascinating phenomena. But when people in a 1984 study were asked to produce their three most vivid memories, hardly any of the recollections involved events of national importance; they tended to be highly personal events with great emotional signif-icance.[11] Perhaps memories of episodes that induce emotional trauma are fundamentally different from ordinary memories. Might it be these memories are unusually accurate, depend on special brain mech-anisms, and even involve something like the Now Print process?

"An experience may be so exciting emotionally as almost to leave a scar on the cerebral tissue," observed the great Harvard psychologist and philosopher William James in 1890. More recently, the child psychiatrist Lenore Terr stated that after experiencing a traumatic event, children retain "'burned-in' visual impressions" that may last a lifetime.[12] I can readily think of several experiences that feel as though they have left permanent scars in my brain. I remember all too well exactly where I was and how I felt when I received a telephone call from my mother informing me of the unexpected death of my father. On the positive side, I am grateful that I possess a "burned-in" memory of the exact moments when my two daughters, Hannah and Emily, entered the world.

One way to gain insight into the nature of memory for emotionally arousing events is to probe the recollections of people who have experienced extreme or unusual traumas. In the great majority of such individuals (as with Melinda Stickney-Gibson), the most commonly observed symptom is a repetitive, intrusive recollection of the traumatic event. Consider, for instance, the memories of people who witnessed the horrific collapse of two skywalks at the Hyatt Regency Hotel in Kansas City on July 17, 1981. Nearly 2,000 diners, dancers, and observers were in the hotel lobby or on the skywalks when the bridges connecting the second- and fourth-floor levels came crashing down—a thundering collapse that dumped some 65 tons of concrete and steel into a lobby packed with unsuspecting victims. The disaster produced 114 deaths and over 200 injuries.

The psychiatrist Charles Wilkinson probed the reactions of 102 of the victims, observers, and rescuers in the weeks following the tragic event. Nearly 90 percent of these people said they kept remembering the disaster repeatedly. The intrusive recollections were potent enough to disrupt the daily functioning of one in five of those who had witnessed the scene. Nearly half said they actively attempted to avoid situations that were likely to elicit recall of the incident. But try as they might, these attempts to avoid remembering the catastrophic collapse were not terribly successful. The memories kept coming back, bringing with them feelings of sadness, anxiety, depression, and even detachment. Nearly one in three people reported experiencing "memory difficulties" after the traumatic event, probably because they were so upset and distracted that they did not encode ongoing events normally.[13]

These intense reactions and recollections are not unique. A number of other studies of real-life traumas—including the Loma Prieta earthquake, the 1976 Chowchilla school bus kidnapping, a devastating

1984 tornado in rural North Carolina, and combat experience in Vietnam and other wars—have yielded similar profiles. The most common post-traumatic symptom is unbidden recollection of the trauma, which occurs in the context of emotional disturbances and spotty memory problems. In a few instances in which follow-up studies have been done months or years after the trauma, available evidence suggests that the frequency of intrusive recollections tends to diminish but not disappear.[14]

Some of the most poignant evidence for the persistence of emotionally traumatic memories comes from the recollections of Holocaust survivors. Lawrence Langer has described and analyzed many such memories in his eloquent and moving book *Holocaust Testimonies: The Ruins of Memory.* "I have children . . . I have my family," reflected one survivor, "but I can't take full satisfaction in the achievements of my children today because part of my present life is my remembrance, my memory of what happened then, and it casts a shadow over my life today." Another commented: "You sort of don't feel at home in this world any more, because this experience—you can live with it, it's like constant pain: you never forget, you never get rid of it, but you learn to live with it."[15]

Similar themes are evident in the story of Jadzia Strykowska, a Polish woman who survived the Nazi concentration camp at Bergen-Belsen and later settled in the Chicago area. Jadzia related her memories of the concentration camp to Jeffrey Wolin, a well-known photographer who has produced a series of works examining the recollections of Holocaust survivors. In "Jadzia Strykowska, b. 1924, Tomaszow-Maz, Poland, 1993–94" (figure 7.3), Wolin juxtaposes his handwritten transcription of Jadzia's memories with an image of her holding precious family photos that helped her to survive the inhumanity of Bergen-Belsen.

The inescapable power of traumatic memories is also exemplified in the wartime recollections of soldiers who have experienced the terrors of battle. *Regeneration,* Pat Barker's moving novel about hospitalized British soldiers coping with the traumas of World War I, provides a fictionalized account of efforts made by a real psychiatrist, William Rivers, to help soldiers who wish to hide from their demons:

> The typical patient, arriving at Craiglockhart, had usually been devoting considerable energy to the task of forgetting whatever traumatic events had precipitated his neurosis. Even if the patient recognized that the attempt was hopeless, he had usually been

FIGURE 7.3

Jeffrey Wolin, "Jadzia Strykowska, b. 1924, Tomaszow-Maz, Poland, 1993–94." 16 x 20". Toned Silver Print. Courtesy Catherine Edelman Gallery, Chicago.

Jadzia Strykowska, a survivor of the Bergen-Belsen concentration camp, describes how she smuggled her family pictures into the camp in a little celluloid tube, which she had to hide in her rectum. But the risks Jadzia took to hold on to these pictures were worth it: "My solace were my pictures," she reflects. "I used to unroll them and look at them and say, 'My goodness, I am not from stone. I am from people. I am from a family.'"

Reflecting on her later life in the United States, Jadzia recalls how difficult it was to heed the advice of those who urged her to leave the past behind and begin anew: "We didn't talk [about Bergen-Belsen] for a few reasons. People did not want to listen. They told us to forget about it, to start a new life, to live here for today, not for yesterday. It's not a question of forgetting—we never, ever forgot." When a group of Nazis attempted to march in Skokie, Illinois, in the late 1970s, "it kind of woke us up and we decided not to let it happen . . . when it was over we started speaking, started telling our stories."

encouraged to persist in it by friends, relatives, even by his previous medical advisors. The horrors he'd experienced, only partially repressed even by day, returned with redoubled force to haunt the nights, giving rise to that most characteristic symptom of war neurosis: the battle nightmare.[16]

Rivers encouraged his patients to spend parts of each day remembering what had happened to them. Like many other survivors of horrifying experiences, the soldiers under his care learned to live with memory's power by telling their stories, trying to fit these aberrant incidents with the rest of their lives, and waiting for the relief that only the passing of time can bring.

TRAUMATIC MEMORIES
How Accurate Are They?

Some researchers have adopted the view that memory for emotionally traumatic events is accurately preserved—perhaps forever—in great detail, and therefore differs fundamentally from memory for nonemotional events, which is subject to decay and distortion.[17] There is a good deal of merit to this view: memory for emotional trauma *is* frequently more accurate than memory for ordinary events. But even traumatic memories are sometimes subject to distortion. Consider, for example, Lenore Terr's studies of the children who had been kidnapped at gunpoint on a school bus in Chowchilla, California, and then buried underground for some sixteen hours before escaping to safety. The children possessed the classic signs of traumatic memory—vivid and detailed recollections—but when Terr interviewed twenty-three of the twenty-six children four to five years after the terrifying episode, she noted the occurrence of rather striking errors and distortions in about half of them. Terr posed the key question: "One might ask: 'How can a particular memory be precise, detailed, and at the same time wrong?' "[18] She believes that the memory distortions are largely attributable to perceptual errors that occur at the time of the event, caused by the stress of the shocking episode. But Terr also observed that seven of eight children whose memories were accurate when they were questioned in an interview conducted shortly after the trauma—implying that initial perception of the event was adequate—exhibited distortions when tested four to five years later. For example, one mistakenly remembered a man who had pillows stuffed in his pants and another recalled a pair of girl kidnappers in addition to the men who were actually there. These observations suggest that even "burned-in" traumatic memories are not immune to change over time.

Some evidence for distortion was also observed in a study of children's memory for a sniper attack at an elementary school in 1984 that killed one child and a passerby. Based on interviews conducted between six and sixteen weeks after the violent episode, the researchers noted that children who were at school during the attack tended to remember themselves as being in a situation of greater safety than they actually were. More remarkably, some children who were not present during the attack remembered that they were! One boy who had been away on vacation the day of the attack recalled that he "had been on his way to the school, had seen someone lying on the ground, had heard the shots, and then turned back."[19]

A variety of influences could be at work here. The tendency of some to recall themselves as being safer than they were may represent a kind of emotionally driven retrospective bias: in attempting to reduce their anxiety about what had happened, some children may have reconstructed the event in a way that fit more closely with their current emotional needs than with the true details. Likewise, children who were not at the shooting may have felt a need to participate in the event. They probably discussed the episode frequently with their friends. Because children are often vulnerable to confusing the sources of their knowledge when they are tested long after an event—and the participants in this study were not interviewed until at least six weeks after the shooting—it is likely that some children mistakenly incorporated bits and pieces of incidents from other children's recollections into their own memories. I would bet, for example, that the child who had been on vacation would not have falsely remembered being near the scene had he been tested the day after he returned home.

Compelling but inaccurate memories of traumatic events are not restricted to children. In 1988, a woman entered a suburban Chicago school and carried out a daylong reign of terror, killing a child and wounding five others. At five months and eighteen months after the tragedy, psychologists asked school personnel questions about where they had been during the shooting and how they had felt about it; most had been at the school, but some had been miles away. Two of three who initially said they had been in the building claimed later to have been close by outside; two of six who initially said they had been more than 25 miles away later claimed to have been within a mile. On the second interview, people whose symptoms of post-traumatic stress had worsened since the first interview tended to amplify the personal threat they had felt at the time of the shooting. But those whose post-traumatic stress symptoms had declined since the first interview tended to remember the shooting as less threatening during the second interview. People appeared to be remembering the event through the filter of their later emotional states.

A related kind of emotional filtering seems to occur with combat "flashbacks" of war veterans, which are often so intense that veterans feel as though they are reliving an actual experience. Flashbacks sometimes contain elements of both real and feared or imagined events. In his pioneering study of trauma and World War I veterans, John Mac-Curdy observed that these overwhelming moments of "reliving" prior experiences often involved veterans' "worst fears," rather than actual combat episodes. He referred to such incidents as *visions* in order to reflect the mixture of fantasy and reality that they often contain. This characterization is less laden with assumptions about the historical accuracy of these experiences than is the commonly used term *flashback* and hence may be a more appropriate descriptor.[20]

The psychiatrist Fred Frankel notes that the term *flashback* did not appear until the late 1960s, in reference to the experiences reported by LSD users. Sometime after the major effects of the drug had worn off, users reported flashbacks, in which they suddenly reexperienced aspects of their drug-induced imagery or hallucinations. Those most likely to report flashbacks were highly hypnotizable people who easily engaged in imaginative, fantasy-based activities. Frankel notes that flashbacks in such people are more akin to dreams than to real memories. The term *flashback* was later applied to the involuntary, compelling recollections of Vietnam war veterans. Echoing MacCurdy's observations, Frankel urges that we remain skeptical about the truthfulness of flashbacks unless they are accompanied by corroborating evidence. He describes a veteran plagued by a flashback in which he killed a villager who kept getting up again and again. This is a worst-fear vision, not a playback of something that happened.[21]

A clinical case that also appears to involve a worst-fear fantasy was reported by the psychoanalyst Michael Good. He describes an adult patient who was plagued by a traumatic memory of having had her clitoris removed when she was five years old. The patient also described repetitive dreams involving this incident. When Good suggested that she visit a gynecologist in order to explore the matter further, an examination revealed that she was anatomically normal—her clitoris had never been removed. Good points out that the patient may have indeed feared such an act as a child. The patient remembered that when she was between the ages of three and five, her mother, a highly religious woman, had made her wear a device that made it physically impossible for her to masturbate. As an adult, unfortunately, she may have been the victim of a kind of source amnesia—she could no longer distinguish between an imagined and an actual event.[22]

Even traumatic experiences that extend over long periods of time are subject to a degree of distorted recall. The psychologists Willem Wagenaar and Jop Groeneweg examined various recollections of inmates in Camp Erika, a Dutch prison that was converted into a concentration camp when it came under German rule during 1942–43.[23] Much of the maltreatment, torture, and even murder of camp inmates was perpetrated by Martinus De Rijke, a prisoner who was promoted by the Germans to the role of *kapo*, which involved terrorizing and intimidating other inmates. When the camp was disbanded, Dutch police interviewed many of the survivors. Fifteen of those survivors were then interviewed again between 1984 and 1988, when the case against De Rijke was reopened (leading to his capture in 1987). Wagenaar and Groeneweg were able to check some of the memories obtained from survivors during the first and second interviews against objective records, and to assess the extent to which survivors' recollections agreed with one another.

Even forty years after their imprisonment, the camp survivors held recollections that were generally accurate. Most of them agreed about the torture methods employed in the camp, about the horrific treatment of Jewish prisoners, and about the fact that De Rijke was a *kapo*. Everybody recalled the general features of the camp and the gist of what went on. But when it came to specific events and facts, some forgetting and distortion occurred. For example, when interviewed between 1943 and 1948, nearly all survivors recalled their date of entry to the camp within one month; forty years later, less than half of them did. In some cases, people remembered entering the camp during the wrong season of the year. During the forty years between the two interviews, a number of survivors had forgotten specific episodes in which they had been brutalized or had witnessed others being brutalized. A photo of De Rijke was shown to survivors between 1984 and 1988, the same photo that had been shown on national television. Among those who had not seen the show, 58 percent claimed to recognize De Rijke, whereas 80 percent of those who had seen the show said they recognized De Rijke—raising the possibility that exposure to the photo on television and not their wartime experiences was the source of recognition.

Studies of real-life traumas, then, indicate that memories of emotionally traumatic events are generally persistent and often impressively accurate, but also that they are sometimes subject to decay and distortion. When a person has actually experienced a trauma, the central core of the experience is almost always well remembered; if distortion does occur, it is most likely to involve specific details. When a person has not endured a trauma but believes to have, chances are that he or she feared it, imagined it, or heard about it. The general principle I developed in earlier chapters—that memories are not simply activated pictures in the mind but complex constructions built from multiple contributors—also applies to emotionally traumatic memories.

EXPERIMENTING WITH EMOTION
What Do We Remember from Emotional Experiences?

Recollections of real-life traumas provide important insights into memory and emotion. But to understand more fully the basis of these rich and affecting experiences, we also need controlled studies. Despite the limitations of experimental research—it is obviously difficult to induce profound emotions in the laboratory—the benefits of enhanced control and precision make this approach to memory and emotion well worth pursuing.

Some recent laboratory studies have begun to tease apart different factors that render emotional events especially memorable. In one, people looked at some slides that were highly pleasant, such as pictures of attractive men and women, and other slides that were terribly unpleasant, such as mutilated bodies. In addition to these highly arousing materials, participants in the experiment also saw neutral, low-arousal slides, including pictures of household objects. People recalled many more high-arousal than low-arousal slides, but recalled pleasant and unpleasant slides equally well. This finding and similar ones suggest that the accuracy of memory is often directly related to the emotional arousal elicited by an experience, independent of whether it is positive or negative.[24]

Arousal may also influence what is remembered from an emotional experience by focusing our attention on specific aspects of an experience. For instance, people who were exposed to a traumatic sequence of slides (depicting a bloody car accident) remembered more of the central, important themes from the sequence and fewer of the specific, peripheral details than did people who were exposed to a nontraumatic sequence. This outcome suggests that in the traumatic condition, participants' attention was captured by the salient, emotionally arousing parts of the episode; consequently, less attention was "left over" for the details.[25]

This laboratory finding is reminiscent of a real-world phenomenon known as *weapon focusing*. Witnesses to a crime that involves the visible use of a weapon, such as a bank robbery at gunpoint, typically retain accurate memories of the weapon. But they often have rather poor memories of other aspects of the event, including the criminal's face. The emotionally salient information (the gun) appears to capture attention so that other aspects of the scene are not well encoded into memory. The weapon focusing effect is most pronounced in people who report feeling anxious when they see the weapon. This finding is consistent with other research showing that high levels of anxiety can lead to a narrowing of attentional focus.[26]

Some of the difficulties experienced by Vietnam veterans who suffer from post-traumatic stress disorders also reflect the attention-driving effects of past emotional trauma. Traumatized veterans may be chronically vigilant and hyperaroused, and thus prone to treating harmless signals in the environment as serious threats. Their attention may be easily captured by stimuli that remind them of past traumas, which can create an overwhelming sense of anxiety and panic. This is clearly illustrated in a terrifying incident experienced by one Vietnam veteran, which the psychologist Richard McNally related to me:

> He was driving his jeep on a Fourth of July holiday years after having returned from Vietnam, when several children tossed firecrackers under the wheels of his vehicle. The sudden noise initiated a terrifying flashback wherein he felt and acted as if he were once again being ambushed. Ducking behind the wheel, he slammed on the gas in a frantic attempt to flee the "enemy" and, moments later, crashed. Although on one level he realized that he was in Colorado, not Vietnam, the emotional and behavioral reaction triggered by the firecrackers was the same he had exhibited years before during ambushes while in Vietnam.[27]

Some veterans become fixated on remembering their war experiences, to the point where it is difficult for them to remember much about other times in their lives. McNally and his colleagues report that some traumatized veterans are so consumed by their Vietnam experiences that they continue to wear war regalia—fatigues, combat medals, POW buttons—twenty-five to thirty years after having left Vietnam. One veteran arrived in the laboratory with a loaded gun. When asked to remember events from anytime in their pasts, these regalia-wearing veterans retrieved far more memories from their time in Vietnam than did well-adjusted veterans. They also had difficulties coming up with specific memories of pleasant events from any period in their lives. They are so emotionally tied to their Vietnam experiences that they attend to and care about little else.[28]

Emotions can bias attention and memory in similar ways with other kinds of patients. Mark Williams and his colleagues in Wales were the first to report what are known as "overgeneral" autobiographical memories in their studies of suicidally depressed patients.[29] These patients remember the general emotional gist of past experiences, but do not recollect as many specific details as nondepressed people do. The overgeneral memories may result from biased encoding. Patients' depressed moods focus their attention on the general negative themes in everyday incidents that fit with their previous negative experiences. They tend to encode (and therefore retrieve) everyday episodes through a negative filter that confers a kind of repetitive and pervasive drabness on all their experiences. At the same time, they tend not to elaboratively encode the distinctive particulars of individual experiences. Consistent with this idea, PET scanning studies have shown reduced activity in the left frontal lobe of depressed patients. We saw earlier that left frontal regions play an important role in elaborative encoding.

Even nondepressed people report that sad moods tend to feed on themselves: when you feel sad, it somehow seems all too easy to think negative thoughts and remember painful experiences. Psychologists have a name for this common experience: *mood-congruent retrieval.* Experiments have shown that sad moods make it easier to remember negative experiences, like failure and rejection, whereas happy moods make it easier to remember pleasant experiences, like success and acceptance.[30] This means that when we are in a blue mood, and have a relatively easy time recalling painful past experiences, we may unwittingly perpetuate and intensify our sadness. This kind of a negative feedback cycle can have serious consequences for people who are clinically depressed. Depressed patients, in contrast to nondepressed people, more easily recall their negative experiences than their positive experiences—which can serve to maintain the depression. Patients who are suffering from depression also acquire new information more readily when it is negative than when it is positive.

When asked to study a series of pleasant words (such as *smile*) and unpleasant words (such as *despair*), depressed patients show unusually accurate memory for the unpleasant words, especially when they think about these words in relation to themselves.[31]

Mood-congruent retrieval has other important clinical implications. Mood-congruent biases might distort a depressed patient's ability to remember accurately early childhood experiences that are important in a therapeutic context. Some evidence consistent with this possibility was provided in a study that examined the childhood recollections of depressed and nondepressed adult women regarding various qualities of their parents. Women who were depressed when they completed a questionnaire concerning childhood experiences remembered their parents as being more unloving or rejecting than women who had never been depressed. Could it be that the depressed women were remembering their parents accurately? Possibly. However, these women remembered their parents as being more rejecting than women who had been depressed in the past but were not depressed when completing the questionnaire. Being in a depressed mood while completing the questionnaire seemed to contribute to the women's negative recollections of their parents. Something similar occurs in patients with chronic pain: their recollections of how much pain they experienced in past episodes depend on their current pain levels.[32]

These findings are reminiscent of the retrospective biases I considered earlier. But remember also that people are generally accurate when reflecting on the broad outlines of their past lives. In fact, mood-congruent biases are sometimes difficult to observe when people are asked general questions about qualities of their childhood, whereas they are observed more consistently when questions are asked about specific episodes and events. Effects of mood on memory may be most pronounced at the level of event-specific knowledge, and less pronounced at higher levels of autobiographical knowledge.[33]

THE BRAIN'S ALMOND
Amygdala, Emotion, and Memory

In 1937, a paper in the *American Journal of Physiology* summarized the results of behavioral experiments with monkeys that had received an operation to remove both temporal lobes. The authors reported that such monkeys suffer from a kind of "psychic blindness": they failed to recognize many familiar objects that were easily recognized by normal monkeys. Even more striking were bizarre aberrations of emotional behavior: the lesioned monkeys lost their fear of previously threatening objects that frightened normal monkeys; tried to eat unusual objects such as rocks and feces; and, uncharacteristically, attempted to copulate with members of other species. This constellation of abnormal behaviors came to be known as the Kluver-Bucy syndrome, after the authors of the article. Some two decades later, a young neuropsychologist, Lawrence Weiskrantz, showed convincingly that the specifically emotional aberrations associated with temporal lobe removal were caused by damage to a single small structure hidden deep within the innermost regions of the temporal lobe: the amygdala.[34]

The amygdala is a tiny almond-shaped formation located next to the hippocampus. (See figure 5.1.) The hippocampus, as we have seen, plays a key role in our ability to remember the ongoing incidents in our day-to-day lives; when the hippocampus is damaged, people have difficulty remembering what has happened to them recently. The amygdala is a critical structure in the brain network that regulates emotions—including emotional aspects of memory. It has become increasingly apparent that the amygdala plays a vital role in the emotionally charged memories that wield such a potent influence in our mental lives.

I pointed out in chapter 5 that monkeys (or rats) that have had only the amygdala removed are not generally amnesic. When given simple laboratory tests that require them to remember where food was placed, or which toy object they were shown a few seconds earlier, animals without an amygdala do just fine.[35] But these same animals can show the kinds of aberrant emotional behaviors that were observed by Kluver and Bucy, and they can also have problems with specifically emotional forms of memory. Fear learning is a good example. It is essential for animals to learn to fear dangerous situations, and they are generally able to do so rapidly. In the laboratory, for example, rats that are given electrical shocks at the same time they hear the innocuous sound of a tone soon begin to show signs of fear when they hear the tone. The animals may "freeze" when they hear it—a sure sign that they are afraid of it. Or their hearts may begin to race when the tone is played, another indication that they are in a fearful state. When the amygdala has been removed, however, animals do not learn to fear the sound of the tone, even when given many electrical shocks at the same time that they hear it. As already noted, these animals are not generally or globally amnesic; rather, they have a specific problem learning and remembering fear. A series of important studies by Joseph LeDoux and his colleagues has shown that this impairment can be produced by damaging a single structure within the amygdala, known as the lateral nucleus.[36]

A recent study by Antonio Damasio and his colleagues has specifically linked the amygdala with emotional conditioning in people. They examined several different patients: one had suffered damage restricted to the amygdala as a consequence of a rare hereditary disorder known as Urbach-Wiethe disease; another had selective damage to the hippocampus after temporary loss of oxygen during a cardiac arrest; and in a third patient, both the hippocampus and amygdala were damaged as a result of encephalitis. Damasio's team showed each of these patients a series of different colored slides—red, green, blue, or yellow. The blue slide was sometimes accompanied by the startling sound of a loud horn. This jarring noise produces an easily detectable physiological reaction, known as the skin-conductance response, which reflects a person's emotional arousal. All three patients showed large skin-conductance responses when they heard the blaring horn. After the blue slide had appeared several times with the sound, people without brain damage showed skin-conductance responses to the blue slide alone—emotional conditioning had taken place. The patient with selective hippocampal damage showed normal emotional conditioning to the blue slide, yet remembered little of what had occurred during the conditioning episode. In striking contrast, the patient with amygdala damage had no problem remembering what had happened during the conditioning episode, but failed to show any effects of conditioning. And the patient with damage to both the hippocampus and amygdala neither recollected what had occurred during the episode nor showed any evidence of conditioning. These results show clearly that the effects of emotional conditioning depend on the amygdala, and are processed separately from explicit knowledge about what happened during the conditioning episode, which depends on the hippocampus.[37]

As both Damasio and Joseph LeDoux point out, the amygdala is well placed to play an important role in emotional memory because it receives inputs from many other structures in the brain. The amygdala has access to relatively primitive sensory information from early perceptual processing stations, and it could use this information to determine quickly whether a situation is threatening enough to merit a "flight or fight" response. The amygdala also has access to more refined and elaborated information from later processing stages, so that it can evaluate a current situation in light of previous experience and help to guide an appropriate behavior. In short, the amygdala is per-

fectly positioned to evaluate the significance of incoming information, which is an essential function of emotion. Events of high significance require immediate attention and action; events of low
significance can be safely ignored. A normally functioning amygdala
helps a rat—or a person—determine the significance of an event,
behave accordingly, and retain the emotional event. As shown by the
work of LeDoux and Damasio, some kinds of emotional conditioning
are retained independent of explicit memory for the conditioning
episode. However, an activated amygdala can also drive the system to
attend to and elaborate on emotionally significant events, thereby promoting accurate explicit memory for such events. The amygdala can
help to influence or modulate explicit memory for emotionally significant events.

This modulatory role of the amygdala is linked to its role in determining how various hormones affect memory. Studies of rats and
other animals have shown that injecting a stress-related hormone such
as epinephrine (which produces high arousal) immediately after an
animal learns a task enhances subsequent memory for that task. This
strongly implies that some of the beneficial effects of emotional
arousal on memory are due to the release of stress-related hormones
by a highly emotional experience. The amygdala plays a key role in
this process. When the amygdala is damaged, injecting stress-related
hormones no longer enhances memory. The amygdala, then, helps to
regulate release of the stress-related hormones that underlie the mem-
ory-enhancing effects of emotional arousal.[38]

Do these findings imply that the intrusive recollections of trauma
survivors are associated with stress-related hormones? Are Melinda
Stickney-Gibson's persistent memories of the fire she barely escaped
attributable to changes in brain chemistry that occurred in response
to signals from the amygdala as she jumped from a third-story window? Recent evidence from brain-damaged patients and traumatized
people suggests an affirmative answer to these questions. One patient
whose amygdala had been virtually destroyed by Urbach-Wiethe disease remembered emotionally neutral pictures normally. But unlike
people without amygdala damage, her memory was not enhanced by
emotionally arousing pictures. Damasio's group has described another
Urbach-Wiethe patient who was specifically unable to recall or recognize facial expressions of fear, even though she had no problem
remembering the identity of familiar faces. Electrical stimulation of
the amygdala in patients with temporal lobe epilepsy frequently produces an intense experience of fear, and can also lead to a general

"feeling of remembering," even though patients do not report any specific remembered contents. In a recent PET study conducted by the psychiatrists Scott Rauch and Roger Pitman and their colleagues, war veterans and others with symptoms of post-traumatic stress disorder remembered personal traumas while they were scanned. Compared to a nontraumatic control condition, the right amygdala was one of several structures that showed heightened activity during traumatic recall. Interestingly, there was increased activity in areas of visual cortex during traumatic recall along with decreased activity in Broca's area, a key region for language production. These results and other PET data are consistent with the idea that traumatic recollections are characterized by intense and absorbing visual imagery.[39]

Studies of Vietnam veterans who suffer from intrusive recollections and other symptoms of post-traumatic stress disorder have revealed abnormalities in the levels of chemical messengers known as catecholamines, whose release can be stimulated by stress-related hormones in response to arousing experiences. One study revealed a specific association between intrusive symptoms, such as flashbacks, and the levels of two catecholamines (norepinephrine and dopamine) that were excreted in the urine samples of traumatized Vietnam veterans. Other studies have revealed that a drug named yohimbine, which activates neurons that respond to stress-related hormones, can induce flashbacks and panic attacks in combat veterans. These induced memories often involve an intense reliving of a war experience that has a here-and-now quality. One traumatized Vietnam veteran, for example, looked at a shadow made by a sink in the testing room and perceived it to be a shadow created by a tank turret. He was not just remembering a past encounter with a tank; he was living through it again as if it were happening in the present.[40]

Stress-related hormones can also influence specifically emotional aspects of memory in nontraumatized people. In an experiment carried out by Larry Cahill and colleagues in the laboratory of James McGaugh (whose work with rats has helped to establish and clarify hormonal influences on memory), college students were shown a series of slides accompanied by a story line. Some participants were exposed to a relatively uneventful, neutral story. For others, the beginning and end of the story were relatively uneventful, but in the middle there was an emotionally arousing section involving a victim of a bloody car accident. Prior to seeing the slides, half of the experimental volunteers were administered a placebo pill. The other half were given a drug (propranolol) that blocks the usual effects of stress-related hormones. After exposure to the slides and story, all participants were asked to recall the story as best they could. The drug and placebo groups remembered the nonemotional story equally well. However, whereas the placebo group remembered the emotionally arousing story more accurately than the neutral one, there was no such arousal benefit for the drug group—they remembered about the same amount of emotional and nonemotional information. This outcome indicates that administration of a drug that interferes with the production of stress-related hormones eliminates the usual benefit of emotional arousal on memory performance. Cahill and McGaugh found something similar when they studied a patient with amygdala damage. He remembered nonemotional aspects of a story normally but, in contrast to healthy volunteers, failed to show enhanced memory for emotional parts of the story.[41]

The release of stress-related hormones, signaled by the brain's emotional computer, the amygdala, probably accounts for some of the extraordinary power and persistence that characterize many highly emotional or traumatic experiences. Just like our more mundane memories, recollections of emotional traumas are constructions, not literal recordings. The amygdala works cooperatively with many other brain structures in order to assemble emotional memories. But unlike our more routine rememberings, Melinda Stickney-Gibson's memories of the terrible fire, the unyielding recollections of those who witnessed the collapse of the skywalks in Kansas City, the flashbacks of traumatized war veterans—and maybe even my own recollections of November 22, 1963—all reflect to greater or lesser degrees the workings of the brain's almond. In the next chapter, I examine a darker side of emotional trauma and memory by exploring the twilight world of psychogenic amnesia.

EIGHT

ISLANDS IN THE FOG
Psychogenic Amnesia

THE INTRUSIVE recollections that plagued Melinda Stickney-Gibson, Jadzia Strykowska, and numerous other people who have experienced profound traumas underscore that emotionally overwhelming events are frequently our best-remembered experiences. And the research I considered in the last chapter is beginning to uncover the reasons why this is so. But under special circumstances, trauma is associated with far-reaching amnesias. What accounts for such a seemingly paradoxical state of affairs? This question has assumed paramount importance during the past few years because of the controversies concerning recovered memories of childhood sexual abuse (which I examine in the next chapter).

Heated debates have raged about whether or not people can temporarily forget terrible traumas. Students of memory, mostly clinicians, have reported instances of trauma-related forgetting for more than a century. Unlike the material I have considered in previous chapters, these examples of traumatic amnesia have not played a major role in shaping the new conceptions of memory that have unfolded in recent years. When we enter the world of trauma and amnesia, we encounter exotic cases of fugues and multiple personalities that populate the edges of memory research. We do not yet understand such cases very well. But some of the techniques and ideas I have considered are beginning to illuminate these strange manifestations of memory's fragile power. Given the urgency surrounding questions of trauma and amnesia in our society, we must examine carefully some of the peculiar instances in which a person's past seems to vanish without a trace.

I became involved in such a case back in September 1980. I was then a graduate student at the University of Toronto when a call arrived from Dr. Paul Wang, the clinical psychologist who just months earlier had arranged for me to test a fascinating head-injured patient who gave me a firsthand glimpse of implicit memory. Dr. Wang informed me that a most remarkable new patient had just been admitted: a young man who did not know his name, where he lived, or just about anything else about his personal past. About all he could say about himself was that he had once been called by the nickname Lumberjack.[1] Lumberjack, Dr. Wang continued, had approached a policeman in downtown Toronto two days earlier complaining of excruciating back pains. He was taken to the hospital, but when he arrived the young man was not able to identify himself, nor was he carrying any identifying information. A local newspaper printed his photo the next day in an effort to locate family members. Dr. Wang wondered whether I might be interested in testing Lumberjack's memory.

As a graduate student with interests in both normal and abnormal memory, I found such an invitation irresistible. Lumberjack appeared to be suffering from *psychogenic,* or functional, amnesia: a temporary loss of memory that is precipitated by a psychological trauma. Psychogenic amnesias involving loss of personal identity have been reported in the psychiatric literature for at least a century, and they are often depicted on television and in movies. But in reality they are quite rare. Psychiatrists have estimated that extensive functional amnesias that cover large sectors of the personal past occur in less than 1 percent of psychiatric patients. The incidence rate may be somewhat higher during wartime, when combat-related stress can produce temporary amnesic episodes in traumatized soldiers. One study of soldiers who were hospitalized during World War II, for example, reported a 14 percent incidence of various forms of psychogenic amnesia. Soldiers who had been subject to heavy fire were more likely to present with amnesia than those who had no combat exposure.[2]

Motivated by pure fascination with the subject, I had spent hours hunting through remote library stacks of musty, turn-of-the-century journals in which Pierre Janet, Morton Prince, and other psychiatrists had described their impressions of patients who responded to overwhelming stress or unbearable disappointments by blotting out much of the past. Some wandered for days in what psychiatrists call a *fugue state,* in which a person is totally unaware of having lost all knowledge of personal identity. Patients in fugue states often focus their attention exclusively on achieving a specific goal, such as finding their way to a particular destination. In one case of a wartime fugue, an Australian soldier serving in Africa during World War II became traumatized when a German fighter plane came swooping down at him. He remembered trying to fire at an approaching dive bomber, then he "blacked out." Thirty-two days later he "came to" in a Syrian hospital, hundreds of miles away. After the bombing incident, he had become totally focused on seeking refuge near a camp he had heard about in Syria. He wandered in a fugue for over a month, not knowing who he was or what he was fleeing, until he became aware of his memory loss in the hospital.[3]

Patients in fugue states are generally oblivious to their disconnection from the past until a situation arises that requires them to identify themselves or to provide information about their background and experiences. Lumberjack was in just such a state prior to entering the hospital. He had been wandering the streets of downtown Toronto for more than a day. It was only when hospital personnel asked him to identify himself that he realized, much to his surprise, that he could not.

Back in 1980, there was not a single controlled investigation of memory retrieval during an amnesic episode of the sort that Lumberjack was experiencing. Here was an opportunity to break new ground by carefully studying Lumberjack with scientific procedures. But I would have to move quickly, since psychogenic amnesias frequently clear up within a few days, and Lumberjack had already been in the hospital for more than two days by the time I learned about him.

When I met Lumberjack the next day in his hospital room, I encountered a quiet young man with stringy blond hair who appeared mildly embarrassed by his inability to recall his past. His IQ was in the normal range. He had some difficulty recalling stories and pictures that were presented to him, but his memory for ongoing experiences did not seem to be seriously disrupted. Lumberjack could recognize faces of famous people and use vocabulary normally, showing intact semantic memory.

To find out more about his ability to recall episodic memories, I used the Crovitz technique described earlier: I read out to Lumberjack a series of common words, such as *table, hurt,* and *run,* and asked him to try to think of a particular experience from a specific time and place that was triggered by the cue word. Normal young adults retrieve memories ranging from the immediate past to the early years of childhood, but over 90 percent of Lumberjack's memories came from the two days since he had been admitted to the hospital. He could remember little else.

I noticed one intriguing feature of the few memories that Lumberjack was able to recall from his prehospital life: they were largely restricted to a time period about a year earlier, when he worked for a courier service. When I probed, Lumberjack provided detailed recollections of specific incidents that had occurred during his time there, and he remembered a great deal about his fellow employees and what they did. I had apparently managed to stumble upon a preserved island of memory in a vast sea of amnesia.

This memory island turned out to be a key feature of Lumberjack's amnesia. I contacted the courier service to confirm Lumberjack's memories and learned that employees there had come up with the name "Lumberjack"—and that this had been the only time in his life he had been called by that nickname.

Why was Lumberjack able to remember this particular period and no others? His time at the courier service, he said, was one of the happiest in an otherwise difficult and sad life. It emerged later that Lumberjack had been abandoned by his parents as a young child and had been raised almost singlehandedly by his grandfather. Lumberjack's life appeared to consist of a series of disappointments, rejections, and failures. At the courier service, however, he was liked, accepted, and successful. The one happy period in his life seemed somehow immune from the amnesia that had hidden just about everything else.

Lumberjack's amnesia cleared up the evening after I tested him. While watching the television rendition of the novel *Shōgun*, Lumberjack began to recall during an elaborate funeral and cremation scene that he, too, had recently been at a funeral: his grandfather had died a week earlier. He then remembered his real name and, during the next several hours, managed to recover and piece together the rest of his past.

The death of Lumberjack's grandfather—the single most important person in his life—had apparently triggered the amnesia. Lumberjack eventually recalled going to his grandfather's funeral, and leaving it in a state of shock and grief. He recalled nothing else after that until twenty-four hours later, when he approached the policeman. Even after the amnesia cleared up, Lumberjack did not recollect anything that had transpired during the day or so when he walked the streets of Toronto in a fugue state—and it is unlikely that he ever will. In most cases of psychogenic amnesia, patients eventually recover their entire personal past with the exception of what happened during the fugue state.

When I saw Lumberjack again several weeks later, he said he had felt "stupid" about being unable to remember his name and so much else about his past that day. Now that I could compare Lumberjack's performance in his normal state with his performance during the amnesic period, the results were clear-cut. His IQ and recognition of famous faces remained unchanged, but he was now able to recollect episodes and experiences from many parts of his life. He could barely contain his happiness as he showed me that he, like everybody else, could travel in time and tell the story of his life.

WHEN THE MIND FORGETS ITS SELF
Beyond Lumberjack

Because there have been so few controlled studies of memory during episodes of psychogenic amnesia, it is difficult to say whether the constellation of features that characterized Lumberjack—loss of explicit memory for individual episodes and other personal information, a preserved island of autobiographical recall involving a specific lifetime period, and excellent retention of nonpersonal, semantic memory—is typical of other patients. The neurologist Marc Kritchevsky and colleagues recently reported that ten patients with psychogenic amnesias involving loss of personal identity performed just like Lumberjack on the Crovitz task, recalling many episodes since the onset of their amnesias and virtually none from before. But only half of these patients recognized famous faces normally; the other half, in contrast to Lumberjack, performed poorly on this test of semantic memory. All of them had problems recalling specific public events (for example, Who killed John Lennon?), a task that probably draws on both episodic and semantic memory. In contrast to Lumberjack, some of the patients remained amnesic for weeks and months. These findings indicate that no single profile characterizes all patients with psychogenic amnesia and loss of personal identity. This should not be surprising, because such amnesias are no doubt influenced by idiosyncratic features of each patient's psychological history and present conflicts.[4] (See figure 8.1.)

FIGURE 8.1

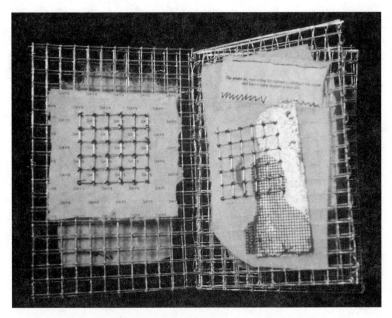

Martha McCollough, "Amnesia," 1992. 9 x 26 x 6". Mixed media construction. Clark Gallery, Lincoln, Massachusetts.

Psychogenic amnesias often serve the purpose of temporary escape from an intolerable situation, as highlighted in this evocative wire-mesh sculpture. We see part of the piece, which consists of seven interconnected "pages" of wire. The work centers around the printed phrase: "The amnesiac, recovering his memory, changes his name and leaves home to start a new life." This is an enigmatic offering: in classical cases of fugue and functional amnesia, patients adopt new identities and leave home upon losing their memories. But the phrase does imply that intolerable life events caused amnesia in the first place. Below this phrase is a shadow figure, perhaps symbolic of lost identity. On the facing page we see an empty grid overlaid on the repeated word *days,* suggesting lost periods of time. Other pages contain empty grids overlaid on the words *years* and *ages;* ladders leading to and from nowhere; and a sinking ship. With this piece, McCollough manages to convey a sense of the bewildering state of mind that characterizes patients with psychogenic amnesias.

These points are illustrated by one of the most bizarre cases of amnesia ever reported. I first learned about K. in April 1986, when I received a letter from one of his physicians. This fifty-three-year-old married man had been found sitting on his kitchen floor, silent and dazed. He held in his hands a defective electrical element from a 220-volt oven, but his body was neither scarred nor burned. In an ambulance on the way to the hospital, K. began to speak. He was confused and said that he had a terrible headache from being hit on the head with a baseball bat. It was later revealed that he had indeed been hit on the head with a bat—in a Little League game when he was fourteen years old. K., however, believed he was still fourteen years old and had no memory for anything that had happened to him after that age. He failed to recognize his wife and children. He believed he was still living in his childhood town, felt shock and dismay when he learned that his father had died, and was taken aback by how old his mother looked in photographs. He was equally surprised by the sight of his own face in the mirror and was amazed that he needed to shave every day. "It was as if," wrote his physician, "Rip Van Winkle had awakened."[5]

This extraordinary amnesia was unlike anything I had ever heard about before. A team of researchers at Johns Hopkins University who tested K.'s memory found that his amnesia was not confined to autobiographical recollections.[6] He showed no memory for famous people or public events after 1945, although he easily remembered those before 1945. He was unfamiliar with, and amazed by, electronic devices such as televisions and VCRs. Incredibly, K. had lost the ability to execute skills he had acquired after 1945, including such basic ones as driving and shaving. Yet he had no difficulty remembering ongoing, day-to-day events. Extensive neurological examination failed to reveal direct damage to the brain. It turned out, however, that K. had been under severe job-related stress. He had been experiencing breathing difficulties and chest pains, and was on a disability leave for these psychosomatic problems at the time his amnesia occurred.

Why did the amnesia affect the lifetime period beginning abruptly in 1945? K. experienced several salient life changes shortly after that year, including a family move, change of schools, death of a close grandparent, and a fire that destroyed his family's uninsured house. Moreover, World War II ended in August 1945, signaling the end of one lifetime period and the beginning of another. K.'s amnesia provides further evidence that lifetime periods serve as organizing structures in memory, helping to separate different constellations of experiences from one another. Although K. differs from Lumberjack in many respects, in both patients some lifetime periods were resistant to amnesia.

The prospect of faking must be taken seriously in certain cases of psychogenic amnesia; indeed, some warning signs often point toward a simulated amnesia. If a patient has been charged with a criminal offense, is attempting to escape financial difficulties or some other legal obligation, or stands to benefit in some material way from the amnesia, then there is certainly cause for suspicion.[7]

In genuine cases, psychogenic amnesias may result from the combined effects of brain damage and emotional trauma. A considerable proportion of patients have a history of prior head injury or some other kind of brain abnormality. Lumberjack, for example, was involved in a car accident when he was four years old that damaged his right temporal lobe. This damage was serious enough that a brain scan administered during his hospital stay clearly revealed it. K. was hit over the head with a baseball bat at age fourteen. Several other cases of functional amnesia reported during the 1980s also include a history of head injury or brain damage.[8] In fact, nearly all early psychiatric studies of psychogenic amnesias and fugues published from the 1930s through the 1950s indicate that many patients had once suffered brain trauma or disease.[9]

Knowing that does not tell us much about why psychogenic amnesias present in the way they do. Psychogenic amnesias are rare, and it is safe to assume that most people who once suffered brain damage do not end up like Lumberjack or K. And we have already seen that memory is affected in specific ways by damage to different regions of the brain; the general notion of "brain damage" is too coarse to be helpful in illuminating psychogenic amnesias. But further on in the chapter, I will discuss how damage to specific parts of the brain could alter a person's response to psychological trauma occurring later in life to produce a highly unusual outcome: extensive amnesia.

HOLES IN THE PAST
Limited Amnesia

Psychogenic amnesias are not always as extensive as in the cases of Lumberjack and K. Stress and trauma are sometimes associated with loss of memory for single events or a small number of experiences—a condition I call *limited* amnesia. Some cases of memory loss in combat involve temporary amnesia for a specific traumatic experience. Limited amnesias have also been reported in victims of brutal rapes and other violent crimes, who are sometimes unable to recall the occurrence of the crime and the events leading up to it.[10]

In North American and European societies, claims of limited amnesia are frequently seen in perpetrators of violent crimes. One study revealed that 26 percent of men who had been convicted of murder or manslaughter stated that they could not remember committing the crime; in other studies, between 25 percent and 65 percent report some kind of amnesia. Because claims of amnesia could lead to a reduction in the severity of criminal charges, the prospect of faked amnesia in such cases looms large. Most experts agree that numerous alleged amnesias for violent crimes are feigned, but there is no general agreement about how to tell the genuine cases of limited amnesia from the simulated ones.[11] In the studies just referred to, defendants who claimed amnesia had higher levels of alcohol intoxication during the crime than those who said they remembered their violent acts. Numerous studies have shown that excessive alcohol intake can impair explicit memory, sometimes producing a blackout in which people can recall nothing that occurred during the period of intoxication.[12] In many cases of legitimate amnesia for violent crime, it may be intoxication, not emotional trauma, that produces limited amnesia.

These issues have also arisen in the most infamous case of a forgotten violent offense: Sirhan Sirhan's assassination of Robert F. Kennedy. Although Sirhan claimed no memory for the murder, the defense psychiatrist Bernard Diamond used hypnosis to re-create the frenzied emotional state in which he committed the crime. We have already seen that hypnosis is not a reliable means for recovering accurate memories, but hypnotized people do occasionally recall actual experiences they might not otherwise remember. As his mood approximated his earlier agitated state, Sirhan apparently remembered the assassination episode and reenacted parts of it. After the hypnosis, when he returned to a more placid mood, however, Sirhan once again claimed amnesia. In the journalist Dan Moldea's recent reexamination of the assassination, he quotes a 1972 declaration by Sirhan's lawyer, Grant Cooper: "Sirhan at all times stated he could not remember firing the shots." After he received the death sentence, Moldea points out, "all Sirhan could say to his beloved mother, Mary Sirhan, was 'Mom, I'm sorry. I don't remember anything.'"[13]

The coming and going of memory in Sirhan's case appears to resemble the state-dependent retrieval effects I mentioned in chapter 2.

When people encode new information in a state of drug or alcohol intoxication, they recall that information more accurately when they are intoxicated again than when they are sober. It turns out that emotional states can produce a similar effect. When experimental volunteers learn new information in a sad mood, they sometimes remember it more accurately when a sad mood prevails during attempted retrieval than when a happy mood prevails. Could such state-dependent retrieval account for Sirhan's memory loss, and possibly other instances of amnesia for traumatic episodes? Possibly, but I am skeptical.[14]

More important, Sirhan's amnesia for the assassination is probably not attributable to trauma-induced forgetting. Moldea considers the possibility that Sirhan was intoxicated on the night of the murder. He ultimately rejects that idea and presents evidence that Sirhan has been faking memory loss for much or possibly all of the time since the shooting. When Moldea interviewed Sirhan in September 1993, he held firm to his story. "I don't remember being in the kitchen pantry," Sirhan stated. "I don't remember seeing Robert Kennedy. And I don't remember shooting him. All I remember is being choked and getting my ass kicked." But Moldea concludes his book with a dramatic incident in which Michael McCown, a member of Sirhan's defense team, attempts to reconstruct the crime during a prison visit:

Suddenly, in the midst of their conversation, Sirhan started to explain the moment when his eyes met Kennedy's just before he shot him.

Shocked by what Sirhan had just admitted, McCown asked, "Then why, Sirhan, didn't you shoot him between the eyes?"

With no hesitation and no apparent remorse, Sirhan replied, "Because that son of a bitch turned his head at the last second."

Was Sirhan merely engaging in empty bravado? Or does this single incident mean that he has always remembered his crime? We don't know for sure, but Moldea believes that Sirhan's amnesia fits a general pattern of attempting to evade personal responsibility for the crime. This would be consistent with the emergence of memories when Sirhan was hypnotized. Sirhan might have felt that remembering under hypnosis allowed him to profess no conscious knowledge of the crime. "Perhaps, over the years, Sirhan has somehow managed to convince himself that he does not remember the events of that terrible night," reflects Moldea. "But I doubt it. I believe he relives that moment every day."[15]

Another case of forgotten-and-recovered memory for a violent crime cannot be easily explained in terms of faking, alcohol intoxication, or state-dependent retrieval. Marvin Bains, a fifty-year-old machinist who was upset with his wife for suspected infidelity, turned up on a neighbor's doorstep with the lower right side of his jaw blown away. Police were summoned to the scene and discovered the man's wife in the kitchen of their home, dead from a shotgun blast. Bains, eventually charged with murder, claimed amnesia for the episode; he could provide no information about how his jaw had been damaged or how his wife had been killed. A member of his defense team who was a psychiatrist hypnotized Bains and elicited an account of the incident. According to Bains's recollection while hypnotized, he had intended to shoot himself and had killed his wife by accident. After the hypnosis, Bains continued to claim no memory for the murder. But his account of the event under hypnosis suggested a possible solution to an unsolved puzzle in the case: the fate of a missing bullet that nobody could explain. Following up on what Bains said under hypnosis, the defense attorney and a prosecution expert returned to the scene of the murder and searched above the kitchen ceiling, where Bains had indicated the missing bullet had passed. They found a buckled beam, apparently damaged by a bullet, in just the right location. Based on this evidence, the charge of murder was dropped to manslaughter. After serving three years in prison, Bains was released. Shortly thereafter, he shot himself to death.[16]

The kind of profound amnesia for an overwhelming emotional trauma that appears to have occurred in the case of Marvin Bains is exceedingly rare. Most cases that involve amnesia for a single traumatic event can be attributed to such factors as intoxication, head injury, or loss of consciousness during the trauma. Even in Bains's case, we must remember that his jaw was severely damaged by a gun blast, which might have caused temporary loss of consciousness or a concussion that contributed to his loss of memory. We do have some evidence of limited amnesia for an overwhelming emotional trauma—examples from war veterans, criminal cases in which complicating factors are frequently involved, and scattered case reports of traumatized people, many dating from the turn of the century. But the evidence is not strong enough to allow firm conclusions about the role of emotional trauma (as opposed to intoxication, brain injury, or loss of consciousness) in amnesia for a specific event that would normally be well remembered, a point I will return to when I consider forgetting of sexual abuse in the next chapter.[17]

These caveats apply to memory for recent traumas. But traumatic episodes from the more distant past are sometimes subject to a kind of limited amnesia: trauma-related fears and stresses that lay dormant for years are sometimes suddenly reactivated when people are exposed to a new traumatic stress. To take just one example, fears acquired during early childhood, which had seemingly disappeared during adulthood, can reemerge unexpectedly, with blazing force, in a stressful situation. People may have no memory for how they initially acquired the fear, reflecting the normal amnesia that we all have for the first years of life. In research studies, infant rats who learned to fear a particular sound through a conditioning procedure seemingly "forgot" the fear several weeks later, no longer behaving fearfully when they heard it. But when they were later subjected to stress—either by injection with stress-related hormones or electric shock—they once again were paralyzed with fear by the sound.[18]

Although normal processes of infantile or childhood amnesia may be responsible for this kind of memory loss, fear reactions acquired during adulthood can also fade with the passing of time and then return under stress. Several cases have been described in the context of combat. One Israeli soldier who took part in the 1973 Yom Kippur war became traumatized when a grenade was thrown into an armored carrier and he was the only one to escape alive. With treatment, he eventually recovered from this post-traumatic stress disorder, and after the war he resumed military activity. In 1982, when Israel entered into a war with Lebanon, the soldier was called to active duty. He performed well until he encountered a situation that was in some respects similar to the original trauma: he was riding in an armored carrier that was hit by enemy fire. The soldier became virtually incapacitated by the same problems that had plagued him previously.[19]

This soldier might have been able to remember the initial trauma all along but simply ceased to become upset by it as time passed. In a related case of a World War II veteran, dormant memories associated with combat traumas suddenly resurfaced over thirty years after the conclusion of the war. Mr. A. was an American machine gunner who fought many battles in Germany, killing numerous enemy soldiers at close range. In the Battle of the Bulge, he became disoriented and confused after an artillery shell killed his assistant gunner and a sergeant. In a later, even more disturbing episode, Mr. A. and some fellow soldiers mistakenly shot and killed several adolescent German boys who had been playing in uniform.

After the war, Mr. A. adjusted well and showed no signs of post-traumatic stress disorder. He did, however, suffer various medical problems that worsened during the 1970s. Mr. A. was a fiercely independent man who found it distressing when, in 1976, he was forced by his health problems to retire and seek a medical disability. At around the same time that he was attempting to grapple with this new stress, he began to suffer—for the first time—repetitive, terrifying nightmares of the war. These unwelcome dreams made him totally preoccupied with his memories of what had happened in Germany three decades earlier. The psychiatrists who described his case said that "[f]rightening memories of events that had, for the most part, been out of his awareness for over 30 years were remembered in exquisite detail and with affects that were more intense than he had allowed himself on the battlefield."[20]

We have no way to assess the accuracy of the war memories that resurfaced during Mr. A.'s retirement. And it is difficult to determine whether Mr. A. was ever truly unable to recall these experiences prior to the onset of his nightmares. For example, his psychiatrists note that after his assistant gunner and sergeant died during the Battle of the Bulge, Mr. A. had thought about writing to their families, which shows that he was not amnesic for the event. Indeed, in 1964 he returned to the battlefield where they died. Nonetheless, for thirty years, Mr. A. was free of the intrusive, charged recollections of trauma that are so starkly evident in other survivors of traumatic experiences. This kind of forgetting is not quite the same thing as becoming amnesic for a violent crime or other traumatic event that occurred only hours or days earlier, but it does show that the full force of memory's power may sometimes remain unexpressed for years.

LEAKS FROM THE PAST
Implicit Memory for Traumatic Events

Can psychogenic amnesia patients, who have temporarily lost explicit memory for parts or all of their past, show any implicit memory for these missing pages of their life stories? Unfamiliar images that suddenly pop to mind, an aversion to a particular food, or an irrational fear or phobia—are these implicit memories of past events that are no longer remembered consciously? The specter of a hidden traumatic memory unconsciously influencing the emotions and behaviors of an unsuspecting victim possesses undeniable elements of high drama.

Alfred Hitchcock made effective use of this compelling theme in such films as *Marnie* and *Spellbound,* which were probably inspired by the reports of Sigmund Freud, Pierre Janet, and other turn-of-the-century psychiatrists who described clinical cases in which childhood traumas not available to the conscious mind nevertheless influenced patients' ongoing experience and behavior.

A classic example was reported in 1907 by the Boston psychiatrist Isador Coriat. He tells the tale of a woman who was found wandering the countryside without any knowledge of her personal past. After relatives identified her, Coriat took her on a trip to the house in which she had lived as a child. She said the house was "strange and unfamiliar" to her but also pointed out with surprise that she had recently dreamed of exactly that house—a possible indication of implicit memory. Coriat also reported that when he instructed the patient to relax and tell him whatever came to mind, she would occasionally report isolated images and flashes that depicted aspects of her past. But these disconnected fragments did not feel like personal memories. The patient had no idea where they came from and referred to them as "wonderments."[21]

More recent case reports of psychogenic amnesia occasionally include similar kinds of observations, although the evidence remains largely anecdotal. In one particularly striking example, a man was found in the desert after enduring a violent homosexual rape. He had no memory for the incident and had lost access to much of his personal past. Nonetheless, after seeing an ambiguous drawing that people often interpret as an attack, the patient became distressed and even attempted suicide—but he still had no explicit memory for what happened. In another case of extensive amnesia, investigators were unable to establish the identity of a patient who could not recollect even a sliver of her personal past. Exasperated, they handed her a telephone and instructed her to dial the first number that came to mind. Happily, she dialed her mother and was identified immediately![22]

Similar observations have been made in a few cases of limited amnesia for specific incidents. Again, turn-of-the-century pioneers, most notably French psychiatrist Pierre Janet, provided the most compelling material. For much of this century, Janet's contributions were lost in the seemingly infinite shadow cast by Freud's work over much of psychology and psychiatry, but his work on amnesia, trauma, and memory has been increasingly recognized.[23] In a case report published in 1904, for instance, Janet told the story of Madame D., who was traumatized by the death of her mother. Even though she had cared for her mother throughout her illness, Madame D. could not explicitly remember the occurrence of, or the circumstances surrounding, her mother's demise. Yet throughout the period of amnesia (which eventually cleared up), Madame D. was haunted by isolated mental images related to the illness that she experienced as "hallucinations." In these powerful images, details of her mother's appearance were preserved, yet the patient expressed no familiarity with any of them. Janet described other cases in which patients were plagued by overwhelming emotions that seemed to be caused by traumas they did not recollect explicitly. Based on such observations, Janet concluded that in functional amnesia, the patient's "inability to consciously and voluntarily evoke certain memories" is accompanied by "the automatic, irresistible, and inopportune [implicit] reproduction of these same memories." Joseph Breuer and Sigmund Freud reported similar observations and ideas, which led to their famous statement that "hysterics suffer mainly from reminiscences." Translated into contemporary vocabulary, Breuer and Freud observed that psychogenic amnesia patients are plagued by implicit memories of events they cannot remember explicitly.[24]

Modern investigators have also reported case studies suggesting preserved implicit memory for specific events that are not consciously recollected. In a Swedish case, for instance, a woman who was amnesic for a brutal rape that occurred on a brick pathway reported that the words *brick* and *path* kept popping to mind, even though she had no idea why. This woman became extremely upset when taken back to the scene of the rape, yet she did not remember that the rape had occurred there.[25]

Some of these implicit effects of traumatic experiences might be related to the operation of the amygdala. As we saw in chapters 6 and 7, the amygdala plays a specific role in fear conditioning, and amnesic patients with hippocampal damage can be affected implicitly by emotionally arousing experiences that they do not remember explicitly.[26] We don't yet know whether differences between the hippocampus and the amygdala are implicated in the peculiar kinds of implicit emotional memory that have been observed in some psychogenic amnesia patients. But the work of LeDoux, Damasio, and others, discussed in the previous chapter, has begun to provide a biological basis for understanding why someone might experience emotions and affects that result from incidents that are not recollected explicitly. Though the clinical observations I considered earlier are largely anecdotal, they remind us that implicit effects of past experiences may shape our emotional reactions, preferences, and dispositions—key elements of what we call personality. Freud, of course, realized something similar when he postulated a dynamic unconscious and emphasized the important role of early experience. With the tools available to modern cognitive neuroscience, we can now explore the memory processes and systems that contribute to our likes and dislikes and our habitual ways of responding to the world. While our sense of self and identity is highly dependent on explicit memory for past episodes and autobiographical facts, our personalities may be more closely tied to implicit memory processes. Leaks from the past in cases of psychogenic and organic amnesia could turn out to be clues that can help us to think about the relationship between personality and memory.

HOW THE PAST IS LOST
Dissociation, Repression, and Inhibition

Functional amnesias are often characterized as dissociative disorders. Dissociation, according to some psychologists and psychiatrists, causes the mind to become split into streams. Thoughts, feelings, and memories splinter into separate worlds of their own: memory systems and subsystems that ordinarily communicate closely, passing information back and forth, lose touch with each other and go about their business separately. Dissociation does not erase a person's memories. Instead, stress or trauma somehow severs the links among memory systems, so that large sectors of the past, or periods of ongoing experience, become detached from a patient's conscious awareness. Evidence of implicit memory for forgotten experiences in functional amnesias could thus indicate "leakage" of information across dissociative barriers that are strong enough to prevent explicit recall.

The idea of dissociated memories dates to Pierre Janet, who believed that some people are genetically unprepared to handle the overwhelming stress of emotional trauma. Instead, they automatically, and pathologically, react to it by splitting off memories and feelings into a nonconscious stream that parallels the conscious mind. Trauma, according to Janet, can dissolve the mental glue that ordinarily links together separate streams of ideas, emotions, and memories.[27]

Modern proponents of the dissociation hypothesis, including the psychologists Ernest Hilgard and John Kihlstrom, view dissociation as a natural consequence of the basic architecture of normal cognition. For these and other proponents of dissociation, the idea that memory is composed of parallel, interacting systems provides potentially fertile ground for the operation of dissociative processes. If our brains normally engage in extensive parallel processing, then there may be conditions—including traumatic stress—that disrupt the normal lines of communication among parallel processes.[28]

Dissociation, then, creates a kind of "horizontal" split in mental life. Another way to think about functional amnesias centers on Sigmund Freud's idea of repression. Repression involves a "vertical" pushing down of affectively charged and unwanted mental contents. Repression is a defensive process whose main function is to protect the ego from threatening material. Like dissociation, repression does not erase a memory; it merely makes an experience difficult to recall consciously. Repressed memories, according to some theorists, fester in the unconscious and make their presence felt through peculiar images or inexplicable behaviors that relate to a forgotten trauma, which we might now call implicit memories. Breuer and Freud conceptualized psychogenic amnesia as a product of intense or extreme repression, a view that has been widely accepted in psychoanalysis and other sectors of psychiatry. Some contemporary psychiatrists, however, believe that repression operates on particular experiences, not on whole sectors of the personal past. For example, the psychiatrist David Spiegel contends that repression is not a powerful enough mechanism to account for extensive fugues and functional amnesias. He argues instead that dissociative processes must be invoked.[29]

The concepts of repression and dissociation enjoy wide currency in some sectors of clinical psychology and psychiatry. Yet both ideas are difficult to test and neither of them provide terribly convincing explanations of psychogenic amnesias. But there must be some internal mechanism that prevents or inhibits retrieval from taking place. Something in the brain shuts down recall processes that ordinarily allow a person to remember who she is and what she has done. For the most part, memory researchers have paid little attention to inhibitory processes, except for the enduring fascination of some with the concept of repression. Yet there is mounting evidence that inhibitory mechanisms play a significant role in memory. Inhibition is a fundamental process in the nervous system. Neurons communicate by sending excitatory signals that increase each other's activity. They also send inhibitory signals that cause other neurons to decrease or "turn off" their activity. Without such inhibitory processes, our mental lives would be unbearably chaotic: we would be constantly overwhelmed by a dizzying array of external objects and internal thoughts, sensations, and feelings. Our brains must constantly inhibit a good deal of neural activity in order for us to function effectively. Recent experiments have shown that the process of focusing attention on one object and ignoring another involves inhibition of the brain's response to the object that we ignore.[30]

Inhibitory processes also operate in memory. Recent PET scanning studies have shown that whereas some brain regions increase their activity during explicit retrieval of episodic memories, other networks of structures decrease their activity, reflecting the operation of inhibitory processes. And just as some cognitive studies have shown that recollecting an experience makes it more likely that we will be able to remember that experience again at some later time, recent research indicates that the act of recalling one experience may actually make it more difficult to remember other, nonrecalled experiences later. Suppose, for example, that you study the following list of words, each one paired together with the category label "fruit": *apple, pear, grape, peach, strawberry, orange, grapefruit,* and *plum.* Then I let you practice recalling a few of the words from the list. For example, I give you a cue such as "Fruit-Or———" and ask you to write down the appropriate word from the list. The act of recalling *orange* during the practice phase will make it even easier for you to remember *orange* when I probe your memory on a later test. Surprisingly, however, practicing *orange* will make it harder for you later to remember other words from the category that you did not practice. Recalling some words from the list causes others to become inhibited.[31]

Along the same lines, if I instruct you to forget about a set of materials that you have recently studied, you may later have difficulty remembering those materials when you desire to do so. Suppose that after you finished studying the fruit names, I told you that you need not remember them; you should do your best to forget about them. If I later inform you that I would like you to try to remember the words after all, you will have problems recalling them in comparison to someone who was not told to forget them. Your recall of the targeted items has been inhibited by the instructions to forget. The common experience of not recalling something that feels like it is on the tip of your tongue also involves inhibition. Research on tip-of-the-tongue states has shown that recall of the sought-after information is actively inhibited by retrieving other kinds of information about it.[32]

Nobody knows exactly how such inhibitory processes are related to the spectacular kinds of memory loss seen in some cases of psychogenic amnesia. In attempting to explain Lumberjack's amnesia, my colleagues and I suggested that in order to recall specific incidents from our lives, we must first be able to remember higher-level autobiographical knowledge, such as our names and general lifetime periods. Such knowledge might serve as an "access code" that provides entry into our episodic memories. We speculated that an inhibitory process "turned off" some of Lumberjack's high-level autobiographical knowledge (such as knowledge of his real name). With this access code inhibited, he could not recall any of the particular experiences that were associated with it. But he could recall experiences linked to the access code "Lumberjack," which was not inhibited.[33] These ideas, though suggestive, still beg the question of why a psychological trauma would produce such extraordinary inhibition of memory in the first place. I will return to this puzzle later, when I talk more about the brain and functional amnesia. But first let us enter into an even more mysterious realm of psychogenic amnesia, one that has recently become a bloody battleground for competing views of memory, the mind, and the practice of psychology itself.

MULTIPLE PERSONALITIES
Dissociation or Invention?

In the mid–1980s, a collaborator of mine, the cognitive psychologist Mary Jo Nissen, came across a remarkable patient: a middle-aged woman who apparently harbored multiple personalities. In fact, Dr. Nissen said, she appeared to have twenty-two such personalities, ranging from a five-year-old girl to an abrasive forty-five-year-old male. One personality, thirty-nine-year-old Alice, was studying to be a counselor, spent a good deal of time reading the Bible, and enjoyed painting religious subjects. Bonnie, aged thirty-six, was interested mostly in the theater. Charles, the forty-five-year-old, drank heavily, liked to watch televised wrestling matches, and painted wild animals. Thirty-two-year-old Gloria was one of several left-handed personalities. She also painted, but more abstractly than the other personalities. Gloria adopted a different last name from the others so that she could obtain her own social security number. Each of these and other personalities came forward to deal with the external world at different moments in the patient's life. Some of the personalities knew about each other, but many had no memory for the others' experiences and were unaware that any other personalities existed. Dr. Nissen wanted to know whether I would be interested in collaborating with her on a study of the patient's memory.

I knew that amnesias could present in unusual ways, and I was also aware that experts consider amnesia to be a hallmark of multiple-personality disorder. Although at least one of the personalities usually has some memory for experiences of the others, most personalities can remember only those events that occur when they are center stage, guiding the person's behavior and action. In a series of one hundred carefully studied patients, ninety-eight of them displayed amnesia between personalities. Such patients often complain of "losing time": suddenly finding themselves in strange places or unexpected situations without any memory of how they arrived there.[34] The patient Dr. Nissen described seemed to fit this mold.

Yet I had just finished writing a series of articles about simulated amnesia, and immediately developed serious concerns that a patient with twenty-two personalities could well be faking the disorder. I was also aware that diagnoses of multiple personalities had been rising rapidly in recent years. Many critics believe that the condition is the product of suggestible patients, misinformed diagnoses, and incompetent therapy involving suggestive techniques such as hypnosis. Public curiosity regarding multiple personalities had been around at least since the appearance of the popular book and film *The Three Faces of Eve* in the late 1950s. But mass interest skyrocketed with the spectacular success of the 1973 best-seller *Sybil,* which told the story of a child who had been severely abused by a sadistic mother and went on to develop sixteen separate personalities, or "alters."[35] Some of the alters were children; two were men. Before the appearance of this book and television miniseries, patients tended to have two or three different personalities of the same gender and age as the primary personality, but cases diagnosed in the "post-Sybil" era typically have many more, including child alters and opposite gender personalities. I worried that Dr. Nissen's patient might have been seen by a clinician who was too eager to diagnose this exotic condition.

But Dr. Nissen could find no motive for the patient to fake the disorder, nor any evidence that she was doing so. Besides, the woman had a relatively low IQ and did not seem capable of the enormous mental effort that would be involved in keeping straight twenty-two feigned personalities. Dr. Nissen felt confident that the clinical diagnosis of multiple personality had been arrived at carefully and cautiously. Hypnosis had not been used to elicit personalities. The patient had numerous gaps in her memory and often failed to remember where she had been or what she had done. And her history contained signs and symptoms of a disturbed identity that dated back to childhood. Beginning at around the age of five or six, the patient had displayed unpredictable bursts of aggressive, violent behavior. Family members noted that she referred to herself by different names during these outbursts. Her attendance at school was irregular and her behavior erratic. These problems are similar to those typically observed in children with dissociative disorders. They have severe behavior problems that are noted by family members, teachers, and others; they are frequently in trouble; they receive a variety of psychiatric diagnoses from professionals; and they are often referred to as pathological liars or persistent daydreamers. A person with a true dissociative disorder leaves behind a trail of serious pathology, a trail that was easy to follow in Dr. Nissen's patient.[36]

Although multiple personalities had been known to psychology and psychiatry since the first reports of the condition appeared in the nineteenth century,[37] the idea of separate personalities inhabiting a single body was—and still is—difficult to accept. But when looked at from a slightly different perspective, this strange disorder may be somewhat more comprehensible. All of us experience different moods and act out many different roles in our everyday lives. As I noted earlier, experiments have shown that memories established in one mood state are often more readily recalled in that same mood state than in a different one. Perhaps in a case of multiple personality, different moods and roles come to be labeled with separate names. Somehow—nobody understands exactly how—these clusters of experience become dissociated from one another. When one identity and an associated set of memories is "turned on," some or all of the others are "turned off." Some multiple-personality patients may use dissociation to a pathological extent, but the term *multiple personality* may not be the best way to describe this process. Indeed, the recognized standard bearer in clinical psychiatry and psychology (the fourth edition of *The Diagnostic and Statistical Manual of Mental Disorders,* or DSM-IV) has recently changed the term *multiple personality disorder* to *dissociative identity disorder.*[38]

Persuaded that the patient Dr. Nissen described was neither a fake nor a product of shoddy diagnosis and treatment, I agreed to collaborate on a memory study. We wanted to find out whether a personality with no explicit memory for another personality's experiences could show some implicit memory for them. There was already evidence suggesting that cross-personality implicit memory might occur. In a classic case from the early twentieth century, Morton Prince described a patient referred to as Miss Beauchamp, who possessed four personalities, some totally amnesic for the others' experiences. For instance, the personality named B IV had no recollection of anything that happened to B I, yet occasionally experienced sudden "visions" that pictured incidents from B I's life. "When seeing a vision," Prince wrote, "she did not recognize the pictorial experience as her own, even though it was of B I's life; there was no sense of memory connected with it."[39]

If Prince's observations are generally characteristic of dissociative patients, then modern techniques should reveal hard evidence of implicit memory. We set up an experiment that included only personalities who professed no explicit memory for each other's experiences. For instance, the patient's psychiatrist elicited a personality named Alice, who viewed a list of words from one of my early priming experiments: *octopus, assassin,* and so forth (see chapter 6). Later, the psychiatrist elicited the personality called Bonnie, who had no explicit memory for having seen any of the words. Nevertheless, Bonnie came up with more correct answers when she was provided fragments of words that Alice had seen than when she was provided fragments of words that Alice had not seen. We also observed evidence of priming on other tests that are thought to engage the perceptual representation system (PRS) I considered earlier.

Interestingly, we observed little evidence of cross-personality implicit memory when tasks involved semantically richer materials, such as sentences and stories. Showing Alice the phrase "The haystack was important because the cloth ripped" along with the clue word "parachute" didn't help Bonnie come up with the clue word later when she saw the sentence. Yet, as we have seen, even severely amnesic patients show priming on this task. Why didn't this type of priming transfer from Alice to Bonnie? Alice might encode the sentence one way, but Bonnie might interpret it differently. When a memory contains a large dose of an individual personality's unique thoughts and associations, even implicit tests may not breach the amnesic barrier.

It is impossible to know from this single case whether our results generalize to other patients.[40] I was therefore excited when an opportunity arose in 1987 to study another patient with dissociated identities. IC had a history of amnesic gaps, sometimes turning up in unfamiliar cities without any idea how she had arrived there. She was brought to a hospital emergency room by local law enforcement in early 1987 after walking across a crowded highway and attempting to injure herself. It was then learned that IC's husband had contacted the police several times in the preceding month when she had also tried to injure herself. Her behavior, he said, had become increasingly bizarre. She regularly acted like distinctly different people, her voice and temperament changing suddenly and dramatically, yet later had no recollection of the changes and denied that they occurred. Over the course of several weeks in the hospital, several distinct personalities emerged. All showed varying degrees of awareness of each other, but IC was totally amnesic for all of the alters and actively resisted the idea that she harbored dissociated identities.

Unlike with Dr. Nissen's patient, we could not elicit IC's alters during a testing session. When these alternate personalities emerged, IC's psychological condition usually deteriorated, so it was best to avoid situations that caused her to dissociate into another identity. This meant that we could not conduct studies on transfer of implicit memory across personalities. But IC knew that she had memory problems and was curious about the missing pages of her personal past. We were, too, because the professional literature contained no hard information on the autobiographical memories of patients with dissociated identities. So we began to explore IC's ability to recollect incidents from her past, using a variety of cueing techniques and protocols for assessing autobiographical memories. One particularly striking finding emerged: IC was unable to recollect a single incident from her life that occurred prior to the age of ten, and she recalled only a few scattered episodes from between the ages of ten and twelve.

All of us are subject to childhood amnesia: we remember nothing prior to the ages of two or three, and little prior to the ages of five or six. But nobody in our study except IC had difficulty recollecting childhood experiences prior to age ten. We could not say conclusively why, but one possibility centers on evidence that IC had been sexually abused by her father during adolescence.[41]

At the time we were studying IC, in late 1987 and early 1988, many clinicians and researchers involved with multiple-personality patients believed that childhood sexual abuse is closely associated with the development of dissociated identities. Several papers had been published linking dissociative disorders with reports of childhood sexual abuse, and we had no reason to doubt them. In the years since then, however, this issue has become considerably more contentious. With the emergence in the early 1990s of the controversy over recovered memories of forgotten childhood sexual abuse, critics have claimed that memories of sexual abuse in patients with dissociated identities may be the product of the same flawed therapy that helps to create the multiple personalities in the first place. The early papers associating multiple personalities with childhood sexual abuse, the critics charge, are based on patients' uncorroborated recollections of abuse. If these memories are recovered during therapy that uses suggestive techniques, then it is possible that they are illusory.

Cases have been described in which something along these lines appears to have occurred. In *Making Monsters,* a scalding attack on therapists who aggressively pursue hidden memories of sexual abuse, the social psychologist Richard Ofshe and the writer Ethan Watters describe the wrenching story of a woman they call Anne Stone. Anne entered therapy because she was having emotional difficulties adjusting to her new baby. When she addressed her husband one morning as a childlike character, Anne's therapist became convinced that she harbored multiple personalities, and proceeded to pursue and find them. Anne was later treated by specialists in dissociative disorders who believed that patients with multiple personalities are nearly always victims of sexual abuse. Anne initially denied any such abuse, but as therapy progressed she recovered increasingly weird recollections of years of sexual abuse at the hands of a satanic cult. She came to believe that she had been a high priestess in the cult and had committed despicable acts, including sacrificing children and eating her own aborted fetuses. The allegations became so outlandish that the cult eventually evolved into a conspiracy that included "AT&T, Hallmark Greeting Cards, the CIA, and FTD florists."[42] Even the Federal Bureau of Investigation was brought in to look into the charges. Perhaps not surprisingly, the FBI failed to substantiate the incredible stories. Eventually, Anne abandoned her memories and her multiple personalities and filed a lawsuit against the psychiatrist who treated her.[43]

An October 1995 *Frontline* documentary presented two women who were strikingly similar to Anne Stone, with a diagnosis of multiple-personality disorder leading to recovered memories of satanic cult abuse during therapy, ultimately followed by the patients' rejections of the personalities and satanic cult memories after withdrawing from the therapeutic setting. I suspect that there are many such patients, and believe that we should heed the critics' warnings that suggestive therapies can help to create both multiple personalities and illusory memories of sexual abuse. If ill-conceived ideas about the widespread incidence of multiple personality are leading some therapists unwittingly to elicit dissociated identities during therapy, this is a tragedy for both the patients and the therapists.

As a memory researcher, I would have grave concerns about studying a patient whose personalities emerged for the first time in therapy, especially if suggestive techniques like hypnosis had been used. But it seems unlikely that all instances of dissociated identities come about this way. In cases such as the two I studied, dissociation was evident prior to any therapy and hypnosis was not used to elicit personalities. And recent research has provided external corroboration of sexual abuse in several patients with multiple personalities.[44]

When dissociated identities do not arise in direct response to questionable diagnosis and treatment, the character of the disorder may still be influenced by the contemporary social and cultural milieu. The extensive media exposure received by such cases as Sybil means that potential multiple-personality patients are likely to know about the disorder and perhaps have preconceptions about how it should look. The psychiatrist Harold Merskey has gone so far as to suggest that no case of multiple personality has ever been reported "without any shaping by or preparation by external factors such as physicians or the media."[45] Social and cultural factors no doubt do play a role in shaping the kinds of memory loss that are seen in patients with dissociated identities (or fugues and psychogenic amnesias), even when blatantly suggestive therapy has not occurred. The disorder may constitute a specific idiom of distress for some deeply troubled people who have been suitably prepared by the cultural environment. But unless one wants to argue that all of these amnesias are consciously faked—and neither Merskey nor other critics do—some of these cases may still provide important clues concerning memory's fragile power.[46]

STRESSFUL EXPERIENCE AND THE BRAIN
Clues to Psychogenic Amnesias?

Science cannot yet provide convincing explanations of all the aberrations of memory I have considered in this chapter. But something has gone terribly wrong with the process of remembering in many cases of fugue, psychogenic amnesia, and dissociated identity. To better understand them, we need to figure out how and why some people respond to stress and trauma by "losing time" or forgetting chapters from their life stories.

This is the fundamental question of trauma and memory, and so far no one has a definitive answer to it. But recent discoveries in neuroscience do suggest intriguing speculations. Some of the most promising leads reside in a class of steroid hormones that are secreted by the adrenal glands and are known by the rather forbidding name of glucocorticoids.

When we are affected by either a physical stressor, such as a brain injury, or a psychological stressor, such as an emotional trauma, our brains initiate a cascade of responses that culminates with the release of glucocorticoids. They are an essential part of the body's response to stress: they help us mobilize energy where needed, increase cardiovascular activity, and dampen down processes that need to be inhibited during a physiological crisis. Yet as necessary as they are for us to respond effectively to stress, glucocorticoids also pose a danger. As argued convincingly by the neuroscientist Robert Sapolsky and his colleagues, excessive exposure to glucocorticoids can seriously damage neurons. The region of the brain that appears most susceptible to harm from glucocorticoids is a familiar one to memory researchers: the hippocampus. Endocrinologists and stress researchers are well acquainted with the hippocampus because it contains an unusually high concentration of glucocorticoid receptors.[47]

Sapolsky and colleagues have found that injecting glucocorticoids in rats for several months produces a permanent loss of glucocorticoid receptors in the hippocampus as well as significant damage to hippocampal neurons; indeed, signs of degeneration are evident after just a few weeks. Other experiments have revealed that exposing rats to sustained stress (for example, foot shock that causes anxiety), which stimulates the brain to release glucocorticoids, creates many of the same destructive effects.

These researchers have also shown that administration of glucocorticoids to prenatal rhesus monkeys produces neuron loss throughout much of the hippocampus. Sapolsky has studied primates in their African habitats and reports that animals who occupy a low position in a social hierarchy are exposed throughout their lives to various stressors—harassment, attacks, difficulty hiding from predators—that are not encountered by dominant animals. These "stressed-out" monkeys show abnormally elevated levels of glucocorticoids. Sapolsky examined the brains of several subordinate monkeys who died as a result of prolonged social stress, and found that they contained pronounced hippocampal degeneration. (No such degeneration was observed in the brains of nonstressed control monkeys.) Another experiment revealed that hippocampal damage in stressed monkeys can emerge within a matter of weeks after the onset of social stress.[48]

Do these linkages among stress, glucocorticoids, and hippocampal damage apply to human beings? I considered evidence in the last chapter that prolonged stress results in elevation of glucocorticoids (cortisol) in some Vietnam veterans. Other experiments show that drugs that cause temporary elevations in glucocorticoid levels can produce explicit memory impairments in healthy volunteers. Longer-term effects have also been observed. Patients treated with glucocorticoids for at least one year had problems explicitly remembering a paragraph across a delay. But they showed normal priming effects on an implicit memory test (word completion), suggesting an impairment of brain regions specifically associated with explicit memory—perhaps including the hippocampal formation. Remarkably, two recent studies that examined the brain with magnetic resonance imaging have found that the hippocampus is smaller in traumatized veterans than in nontraumatized veterans. One possible interpretation of these findings is that high levels of glucocorticoid exposure in the veterans who found the war most stressful resulted in damage to the hippocampus. But it could also be that veterans who entered the war with an unusually small hippocampal formation were for some reason more vulnerable to traumatic stress than other veterans.[49]

Traumatized Vietnam veterans are not generally amnesic, yet they are susceptible to various abnormalities of memory that might reflect altered hippocampal functioning. I have already discussed the intrusive, uncontrollable "flashbacks" of combat experiences that can plague traumatized veterans, and have noted that some of these men have problems remembering specific episodes from parts of their past. They can also have a hard time recalling a list of words presented to them in the laboratory. Studies of World War II concentration camp survivors and prisoners of war likewise show impaired explicit memory for recent experiences.[50]

This collection of findings raises the possibility that prolonged stress, resulting in excess exposure to glucocorticoids, could damage the hippocampus and thereby contribute to memory-related abnormalities. The same line of reasoning may apply to people who have suffered extensive childhood abuse. Frank Putnam and his colleagues have reported that sexually abused girls and adolescents have difficulty regulating cortisol levels. A recent study used magnetic resonance imaging to examine the brains of women who had suffered severe sexual and physical abuse when they were young. The volume of the left hippocampus in the abused women was significantly reduced compared to a control group. Abused women with large reductions in hippocampal volume tended to have more severe psychiatric problems than abused women with lesser reductions in hippocampal volume. But none of these abused women showed any memory problems on a standard laboratory test of explicit memory for recently studied words, and all of them had always remembered their abuse. Yet a separate sample of women who reported an abuse history and showed normal explicit memory for recently studied materials nonetheless had problems, compared to a control group, coming up with autobiographical episodes from childhood and adolescence in response to cue words (much like our patient IC). Consistent with the latter finding, another study has revealed that depressed women who report a history of childhood sexual abuse, compared to depressed women who do not report such a history, have a more difficult time remembering specific autobiographical memories in response to either positive cue words (such as *successful*) or negative cue words (*sorry*).[51]

Could reduced hippocampal volume, perhaps brought about by excessive exposure to glucocorticoids, contribute to memory problems in cases of dissociative identity disorders with a documented history of sexual abuse? Possibly, but as of now there are no direct links between reduced hippocampal volume and between-personality amnesias. Before any conclusions can be drawn, we need data from patients with dissociative disorders that directly and specifically link memory problems, reduced hippocampal volume, physical or sexual abuse, and glucocorticoid exposure.

What about fugue and psychogenic amnesia patients, like Lumberjack and K.? These people became amnesic after a specific trauma or period of stress, but typically do not possess histories of lengthy abuse or prolonged psychological stress that would be likely to damage the hippocampus through excessive glucocorticoid exposure. Remember, however, that many functional amnesia patients have a history of head injury or related brain insult that predates the onset of their memory loss. It is possible that these insults directly damaged the hippocampus or other structures important to explicit memory. Interestingly, neuropsychologists have described a growing number of brain-damaged patients who, like psychogenic amnesia patients, have extensive retrograde amnesias that cover much of their personal pasts, yet also have relatively mild problems recalling recent events. The right temporal cortex (the general area where Lumberjack had sustained brain damage as a child) is often damaged in such patients. Antonio Damasio has proposed that parts of the temporal cortex contain high-level knowledge, which he calls "binding codes," that allow us to piece together bits and pieces of episodic memories that are stored elsewhere in the cortex (see chapters 2 and 3). Damasio's binding codes might be the neural equivalents of the access codes that my colleagues and I suggested had been inhibited in Lumberjack's case. If so, then we can see how this early brain damage might have combined with a new stress to yield extensive amnesia.[52]

Yet even if a blow to the head does not directly damage the hippocampus or related structures, brain injuries are powerful elicitors of the body's own glucocorticoids. Sapolsky suggested that the brain's own protective response to a brain injury, such as a head trauma, might result in damage to the hippocampus because of its vulnerability to the tidal wave of glucocorticoids released in response to the damage.[53]

Could the unusual responses to trauma that culminate in fugue and psychogenic amnesia reflect, in part, the confused response of a once-damaged hippocampus to a new and powerful stress? A new psychological trauma could suppress the hippocampus through overexposure to glucocorticoids, and the effect might be magnified in people who have sustained prior hippocampal damage. However, damage to the hippocampus alone does not result in loss of personal identity and childhood memories, but does yield significant problems remembering recent events. This is a very different profile than what we see in patients like Lumberjack.[54] It therefore seems unlikely that extensive psychogenic amnesias are attributable to a malfunctioning hippocampus. The character of psychogenic amnesias is no doubt shaped by emotional and social forces that are irrelevant to organic amnesias, so it should not be surprising that they differ in important respects. Nonetheless, the frequent presence of prior brain trauma in cases of functional amnesia, paired with the data on glucocorticoids and the hippocampus, are tantalizing enough to factor into our thinking about elements that contribute to psychogenic amnesias.

A similar kind of thinking may apply to people who are plagued by the return of long-dormant childhood fears as a result of new stresses in their lives. In a provocative paper, the neuroscientists W. J. Jacobs and Lynn Nadel noted that many fears develop in very early childhood but the hippocampus does not mature fully until somewhat later. A childhood fear might be stored as implicit memory in brain circuits outside the hippocampal system. As the hippocampal system develops, the fear may recede into the background. But when a new stress releases a bombardment of glucocorticoids that temporarily suppresses the hippocampus, nonhippocampal systems may become more active. As a result, hidden implicit memories, such as long latent childhood fears, may suddenly resurface.[55]

As promising as these brain-based ideas are, psychogenic amnesias are still puzzling to scientists. As we will see, our limited scientific knowledge about amnesia for emotionally traumatic events has important implications for the most charged and divisive mental health crisis of our time.

NINE

THE MEMORY WARS
Seeking Truth in the Line of Fire

LATE ONE SUNDAY night, I was sifting through the electronic mail messages that had accumulated on my computer. I subscribe to an Internet discussion group on memory and psychotherapy, and there was a large backlog of messages to check. I dwelled over several posts from an unfamiliar sender named Diana Halbrooks who described how, during psychotherapy that had begun ten years earlier, she came to believe that her mother had tried to kill her. Then she remembered that her father had sexually abused her as a child. As she delved deeper into her past, listening to the "little girl" inside, as her therapist advised, Diana grew to believe that she had been raised in, and ritually abused by, a satanic cult that included some of her family. She recalled horrendous acts of torture and child sacrifice and concluded that a baby sister who had lived only one day—supposedly because of a rare and untreatable respiratory disorder—had been sacrificed by the cult. Diana believed that she, too, had participated in the ritual sacrifice of a baby.

I had heard and read about similar stories, but I was particularly intrigued by Diana's story because she no longer believed that any of these memories were true. She spoke eloquently about how she had reunited with her family and turned her life around. What, I wondered, could lead someone to abandon such vivid and strange memories? When I answered Diana on the Internet, she told me that, try as she might, she could find no evidence that anyone in her family had ever taken part in any satanic rituals. She obtained a hospital death certificate, signed by a physician, stating that her infant sister had died of a respiratory disorder. Yet her therapist said that this merely confirmed that the doctor was part of the cult.[1] One day, when Diana arrived fifteen minutes late for a therapy appointment to discover her therapist had not waited for her—and would not return her repeated phone calls—she had a sudden crisis of confidence about her six years of therapy. She decided to give her family the benefit of the doubt and never went back to the therapist.

Diana Halbrooks's memories of sexual and ritual abuse at the hands of her parents were illusory, but there are stories about people who suddenly recover memories of long-past abuse that turn out to be accurate. Ross Cheit, a college professor of public policy, entered therapy because of a general uneasiness about his life. "I felt somehow adrift, as if some anchor in my life had been raised," he reflected. "I had doubts about my marriage, my job, everything."[2] Several months later he awoke from a dream with a strong feeling about a camp counselor named Bill Farmer whom Cheit had known as a youth in the 1960s. Within a few hours, that feeling turned into a recollection that Farmer had molested him at camp. With the help of a private detective, Cheit tracked down his assailant in a small town in Oregon nearly a year later. After thirty-two unsuccessful attempts to reach him by telephone, Cheit finally contacted him and taped their phone conversation. Farmer admitted that he had molested various boys and that he had lost jobs as a result of his problem. He remembered Cheit, but did not recall abusing him at first. The initial sexual experience had not been horribly traumatic—"I didn't dread it," Cheit said; "I wasn't thinking, 'Oh my God, he's going to come in again' "—and he had never thought about the abuse in the intervening years. He recovered his memories of it decades later.

The stories of Diana Halbrooks and Ross Cheit are part of a social epidemic that has affected thousands of American families during the 1990s. In the typical scenario, an adult, usually a young woman, recalls during the course of psychotherapy long-forgotten memories of sexual abuse at the hands of a parent or other close family member, or an authority figure such as a teacher or a priest. When confronted with the allegations, the accused typically deny them. Families often split at the seams as members align on different sides of the dispute. In many instances, the matter extends beyond the personal into the public domain of the courtroom. The psychological toll on those involved is massive and often irreversible.[3]

The first widely publicized case of a recovered traumatic memory involved a murder in northern California. In 1990, George Franklin was convicted of the 1969 homicide of nine-year-old Susan Nason. The conviction (overturned on appeal) was based entirely on memories of the murder that were recovered and reported to authorities by Franklin's daughter Eileen. Eileen Franklin was eight years old when, according to her testimony, she witnessed her father rape and murder her friend. She claimed to have repressed her memories of the awful event until 1989, when a glimpse of her own daughter in a certain pose brought Susan's death instantly to mind. Soon, celebrity cases involving recovered memories of sexual abuse came to the fore, including ones by a former Miss America and the comedian Roseanne. By 1992 allegations of abuse based on recovered memories were so pervasive among ordinary American families that a group of accused parents joined with concerned professionals to form the False Memory Syndrome Foundation, which established a professional advisory board that included some highly respected names in psychology and psychiatry. As of this writing, over 4,000 people are either members of the Foundation or subscribe to its newsletter. Approximately 17,000 people have contacted the organization regarding repressed memory cases.[4]

As heightened media attention began to foster a public perception that false memory is a possible, even likely, explanation for many alleged recovered memories of sexual abuse, some clinicians and therapists who treat abuse survivors wrote angrily about an unjustified backlash against genuine victims. They pointed to the lack of any systematic evidence for a false memory syndrome. Instead, they suggested, the label of "false memory syndrome" may serve as a politically convenient but fundamentally inaccurate way of denying a reality that accused parties cannot accept.[5]

With the formation of the FMS Foundation and the opposing cries of backlash, a bitter debate erupted among professionals in the fields of mental health, medicine, and law.[6] I found myself drawn into this arena after an article by Daniel Goleman appeared in the *New York Times* on May 31, 1994.

Titled "Miscoding Is Seen as the Root of False Memories," it highlighted a recent conference on memory distortion that I had helped organize and quoted me several times. The conference brought into sharp focus the important role of source amnesia—forgetting how a memory was acquired—in generating false recollections, and Goleman built his excellent article around that theme. The article was reprinted in newspapers around the world.[7]

I was soon inundated with phone calls and letters. Some of these communications were from accused parents of children who had recovered, in therapy, memories of sexual abuse that, according to the shaken parents, had never occurred. Their calls and letters gave me a glimpse of the emotional devastation experienced by some people caught in the maelstrom of recovered memories. Yet I had no way of knowing what had actually occurred in any of these families, nor did I have the clinical training or expertise to offer professional advice.

The recovered memories controversy, though a complex affair that touches on issues of incest, family, social mores, and even religious beliefs, is fundamentally a debate about accuracy, distortion, and suggestibility in memory. This is why scientists such as I feel professionally obligated to try to uncover the truth about aspects of memory that are relevant to the raging disputes. Searching for truth in this charged atmosphere is not easy. When I participated in a December 1994 memory symposium in Boston, I spoke to some incest survivors who picketed to protest the participation of Elizabeth Loftus, a vocal critic of therapists who aggressively hunt for recovered memories. The protesters felt that those who questioned the validity of any recovered memory were in effect questioning, or at least undermining, the validity of their memories. The anguish of these people was palpable. I gave another talk the following week at an FMS Foundation conference in Baltimore, where I spoke with parents who said they had been falsely accused of sexual abuse by their children. I listened to women who had recently disavowed the memories they recovered in therapy. Their anguish, too, was deep and affecting.

Having devoted a good deal of my career to the study of amnesia, I am naturally intrigued by the possibility that a person could exhibit amnesia for traumatic events over a period of many years and subsequently recover them. I have studied instances of traumatic amnesia, such as the case of Lumberjack, and I know that some traumatic events can be associated with temporary forgetting and subsequent memory recovery. I am convinced that child abuse is a major problem in our society. I have no reason to question the memories of people who have always remembered their abuse, or who have spontaneously recalled previously forgotten abuse on their own.

Yet I am deeply concerned by some of the suggestive techniques that have been recommended to recover repressed memories. I am aware that people undergoing certain kinds of therapy have claimed with great confidence to remember episodes that occurred in past lives, and that some have recalled abuse on spaceships at the hands of alien abductors.[8] In short, I think I know enough about memory's fragile power to appreciate that extreme views on either side of this issue are likely to be wrong.

I believe that the depiction of the recovered memories debate as a winner-take-all battle between advocates of recovered memory and proponents of false memory is overly simplistic and needlessly divisive.[9] We need instead to distinguish among several intertwined questions, each of which should be considered carefully on its own. One question is whether sexual abuse can be forgotten. If some episodes of abuse can be forgotten—I believe that they can—it is also important to ask whether a special mechanism of repression must be invoked to explain the forgetting that does occur. Here much depends on exactly what is meant by the term *repression*. A related but distinct question concerns whether forgotten episodes of abuse are ever recovered; I believe that they are. This still leaves a separate question of whether people ever develop false recollections of traumatic events that never occurred; I believe that they do. If recovered memories of actual abuse and false memories of implanted abuse both exist, it becomes crucial to consider whether there are reliable ways to distinguish between them. To address this question, we must revisit the hidden world of implicit memory, which has come to play a peculiar role in the memory wars that have damaged so many people in our society.

FORGETTING ABUSE
How Often Does It Happen and Why?

Recall from chapter 7 that Melinda Stickney-Gibson, haunted for years by memories of the destructive fire that nearly took her life, described trying hard to avoid thinking about the incident; sometimes she succeeded and sometimes she did not. And Jadzia Strykowska, who lived through terrifying years as a child in the Bergen-Belsen concentration camp, tried not to talk about the horrors of the Holocaust, attempting instead to get on with her new life in America. Yet Jadzia never forgot her experiences and began speaking about them again after the neo-Nazis marched near her home during the 1970s.

Melinda and Jadzia both used a cognitive strategy that is probably familiar to everyone: when something painful happens to us, we try not to think about it. Rehearsal facilitates recall of past experiences, so it makes sense that not rehearsing painful experiences (or any experiences) would lessen the likelihood of their springing to mind in the future. Indeed, I have already alluded to experiments in which participants are instructed to forget about a subset of information that was presented to them. Such "directed forgetting" instructions usually produce a modest decrease in volunteers' recollection of target information.

It is hardly controversial, then, to state that people sometimes attempt to avoid or suppress painful experiences. And since sexual abuse, most would agree, is typically not discussed, victims may be robbed of opportunities to talk about and reflect on their traumatic experiences, which in turn could weaken their memories for those experiences. This kind of explanation could well apply to a case like Ross Cheit's, where the initial experience was not highly traumatic but may have been disturbing or confusing enough to make him avoid thinking about it. It may also apply to a case shown in Ofra Bikel's documentary on the recovered memory controversy, "Divided Memories," which aired in April 1995 on PBS's *Frontline* series. "Jane Sanders" was sexually abused by her father in a hotel room when she was five years old. He admitted his misconduct to Jane's mother, who reasoned that if she did not talk about the incident with Jane, it might fade from her memory—and it did. Jane first learned of the abuse as a young woman when her mother finally told her what had happened. Results of a recent survey of rape experiences in adult women are consistent with these observations. Women who had been raped rated their rape memories as less often thought about or talked about, and less clear and vivid, than women who recalled other bad experiences.[10]

Conscious suppression of childhood trauma also played a role in the sad and strange case of former American University president Richard Berendzen, who came to the attention of psychiatrists in April 1991 when he was caught making obscene phone calls from his university office. In treatment, Berendzen revealed something he had never told anyone: his mother, who had a history of mental illness, had sexually abused him at ages eight and eleven. After pleading guilty to misdemeanor charges, Berendzen discussed his memories of the abuse with Ted Koppel on *Nightline*. Reflecting on the various strategies he had used over the years to try to keep the abuse out of his mind, he said: "I pretended it had never happened. And that worked for a year or two. And then I decided I would just forget it. And that worked for a few months. Then I decided that I would work terribly hard. And if you're working very hard, you somehow don't remember it anymore." Berendzen's interview and his moving memoir about his abuse indicate that he always maintained some sort of general knowledge about what had occurred; he conceded to Koppel that his suppressive strategies ultimately failed. As he relates in his book: "When I would think of the abuse and remember the confusion and pain, I would say to myself, 'That was then; this is now.'" He managed to suppress details of the abuse, and the intense feelings associated with it, for significant periods of time. But when he returned home upon the death of his father in the late 1980s, Berendzen experienced vivid memories of what had happened there years earlier. Shortly thereafter, he began his campaign of sexually explicit phone calls.[11]

Richard Berendzen's attempts to suppress his memories of sexual abuse were only partly successful; he never banished all knowledge of what had happened. His story is similar to that of Mr. A., the war veteran I described in chapter 8 who became overwhelmed by wartime traumas some thirty years after they occurred, although he never forgot having participated in the war. But in some cases of recovered memories, people seem to have become totally amnesic for years, never suspecting they had been abused until going into therapy.[12] If Diana Halbrooks's memories of satanic ritual abuse were real, then she must have repressed them completely for long periods of time. Before therapy, Diana never had even an inkling that she had been abused by her parents or had participated in cult activities, much less murdered an infant. Could someone manage to forget about such ghastly activities merely by avoiding talking about them or mentally rehearsing them?

There is no evidence that intentional forgetting in laboratory experiments produces serious amnesia.[13] Analogously, Jadzia Strykowska comments that she and other Holocaust survivors did not talk about their experiences for years, yet they never developed amnesia for them. It seems far more probable that intentional avoidance of unpleasant memories reduces the likelihood that the suppressed experiences spontaneously spring to mind with the kind of vigor that plagues so many survivors of psychological traumas. And, as stated earlier, it might even make some individual episodes extremely difficult to retrieve. But this is a far cry from developing a total amnesia for years of violent abuse.

Remember also that when people are asked to assess retrospectively the general qualities of their childhoods, they are usually fairly accurate.[14] If Diana Halbrooks had been raised in a vicious cult and lost all memory of it for years, it would signal the presence of an extraordinary distortion in her recollection of the general contours of childhood. If her post-therapy memories were accurate, it follows that her pre-therapy childhood memories must have been entirely illusory. Because this degree of distortion is highly abnormal, a much more formidable mechanism than simple lack of rehearsal would be needed to produce it. This is where the concept of repression, a cornerstone of Freud's psychoanalytic edifice, comes in.

The mechanism of repression has been portrayed as a protective device used by the brain to fend off the emotional ravages of experiences that are simply too overwhelming to be borne by the conscious mind. According to some therapists, repression is powerful enough to block out horrifying months and years of sexual abuse, rape, even ritualistic torture; some terrible events are thought to be inaccessible to the conscious mind virtually immediately after they occur.[15] Yet, consistent with Freud's early formulations, the repressed memories are not lost forever; they are thought to percolate in a remote corner of the unconscious, causing various problems and symptoms, until they are recovered through therapy or some other favorable circumstance. This kind of massive repression is, evidently, a far more potent means of suppressing unpleasant experiences than the intentional avoidance strategies that most of us are familiar with in day-to-day life.

It is perhaps ironic that Freud's initial conception of repression was much closer to the mundane, everyday form of intentional suppression than to the massive repression mechanism that has been invoked by some therapists. Freud's early writings state specifically that repression involves intentional rejection of distressing thoughts and memories from conscious awareness. But the idea subtly changed over time. Freud began to use the term *repression* in a much more general sense, to refer to a variety of defense mechanisms that operate outside a person's awareness and automatically exclude threatening material from consciousness. Freud thus created a good deal of confusion regarding the distinction between *unconscious* defenses and *intentional* repression.[16]

The strength of the scientific evidence for repression depends on exactly how the term is defined. When defined narrowly as intentional suppression of an experience, there is little reason to doubt that it exists. But when we talk about a repression mechanism that operates unconsciously and defensively to block out traumatic experiences, the picture becomes considerably murkier.

Some people may be more apt than others to engage in a defensive form of repression. In several studies, people who say they feel little anxiety but nonetheless behave defensively have been defined as "repressors." This type of person will insist that nothing is wrong even though his face is beet red or he strenuously resists advice offered by others. Repressors tend to remember fewer negative experiences from their lives than nonrepressors. Defensive repression has also been reported in brain-damaged patients. The psychologist V. S. Ramachandran has made some fascinating observations of selective forgetting in patients with paralyzed limbs who are unaware of their paralysis. Patient BM, you may recall, was specifically unable to remember experiences that were inconsistent with her delusional beliefs about her paralyzed arm.[17]

Even if some form of defensive repression occurs, this still does not speak to the question of whether non–brain damaged people are capable of the kind of repression that would block out overwhelming traumas. Evidence concerning memory for real-life traumas in children and adults indicates that these events—such as the Chowchilla kidnappings, the sniper killing at an elementary school, or the collapse of skywalks at a Kansas City hotel—are generally well remembered. Some forgetting and distortion occur, but complete amnesia for these terrifying episodes is virtually nonexistent. Many limited amnesias, in which people fail to remember a traumatic event such as committing a murder or being raped, are due to alcohol intoxication, brain injury, loss of consciousness, or even deliberate faking. There are only a few dramatic examples, like Marvin Bains's apparent amnesia for shooting his wife, in which forgetting is not easily attributable to these factors.

For these and other reasons, some therapists have argued that extensive repression is observed only for repeated traumatic events. Lenore Terr contends that single traumatic experiences ("Type I" traumas) are generally well remembered, whereas repeated or multiple traumatic experiences ("Type II" traumas) are repressed. The repeatedly abused child, for example, becomes more practiced at using repression in order to banish overwhelming experiences from conscious awareness. If the abuse is perpetrated by someone the child looks to for nourishment and support, like a parent, it is easy to see how forgetting might aid the child's survival.

Terr's ideas are provocative, but hundreds of studies have shown that repetition of information leads to improved memory, not loss of memory, for that information. To produce profound amnesia, the repression mechanism would have to be so effective as to succeed despite the normal tendency for repeated experiences to enhance memory. People who have lived through repeated traumas in war generally remember these terrifying experiences all too well. An individual experience or trauma may be set aside, especially when much time has passed, but with rare exceptions such as fugue states—which are generally of short duration—people do not forget an entire set of repeated traumas.

This point is well illustrated by the story of Erika Marquardt, an artist who grew up in Germany during World War II and remembers clearly the repeated traumatic experiences that shaped her childhood in ways she could not comprehend:

> The early years of my life I spent in bunkers, bombs falling, destruction, ruins. And strong political repression, first under the Nazis and then under the Communist regime—being scared of being overheard. You always felt submerged into a world of fright; at the mercy of outside forces—not being in control of what you would like to do.
>
> I grew up in the company of women and kids, trying to survive. In a way I couldn't understand because I was too young. But only felt how scared I always was. The sound of the sirens and you really have to run for your life to find shelter. And at night the . . . beautiful designs in the sky were of the areas to be bombed, and the fantastic flash and detonation of houses being hit. The fright of uniforms and the sounds of boots marching at night.[18]

Marquardt's painting "Miniature View from the Berlin Wall (#3)" (figure 9.1) captures some of this terror.

Erika Marquardt and many other survivors of extended terror always remembered that these repeated traumas happened. This may also apply to traumas that are associated with sexual abuse, as illustrated by the memories of people who said they were abused by Father James Porter, a Massachusetts priest. Porter admitted his guilt to one victim, Frank Fitzpatrick, and there is no reason to doubt the testimony of the others who have since come forward. The great majority of these people always remembered their abuse. But approximately 20 percent of them said that they never thought about it until decades after it occurred, when the case achieved sudden prominence in the media. It is important that those who said they were repeatedly abused were less likely to forget than those who said they were abused only once.[19] This finding is exactly the opposite of what Terr's ideas about Type II traumas seem to predict.

We can make sense of these ideas, however, by recasting them in light of the distinction between general-event knowledge and event-specific knowledge that I have discussed. Nobody doubts that having repeated experiences of a similar type can make it difficult to remember the details of a specific event, even though the repeated features of the general event are remembered well. For example, I spend a good

FIGURE 9.1

**Erika Marquardt, "Miniature View from the Berlin Wall (#3)," 1991.
11 x 13½". Oil/mixed media on canvas. Courtesy of the artist.**

On the left are graphic renditions of the traumatic events that marked the artist's early years: bombers, explosions, and bright lights. On the right are a skull and slices of brain, perhaps indicating that the memories exist only in her head. Bits and pieces of the Berlin Wall (which Marquardt chipped when it was destroyed in 1989) are stuck between the rememberer and her memories.

deal of time on airplanes, and I have considerable difficulty recalling the details of many of the specific events that occurred during particular flights. But I do not have amnesia for ever having flown before; I can tell you just about everything that ordinarily happens on a typical flight. I have excellent memory for the general event of flying in airplanes and poor memory for most specific flying episodes.

Obviously, flying on numerous airplane trips is not traumatizing abuse, yet a person who experiences repeated sexual trauma could have considerable difficulty remembering the details of a particular episode of abuse for many of the same reasons that I cannot recall the particulars of an individual airline flight: the specific events become blurred in memory and are difficult to separate from one another. If this is the kind of forgetting that characterizes Terr's Type II trauma, then it seems entirely plausible that such forgetting would occur. It need not have anything to do with repression, however. Nor would it lead to total amnesia for all the relevant experiences—the abused person would still recall the general event of being abused. But blurring and merging of details from repeated episodes might help explain why the memories of sexual-abuse survivors are sometimes patchy and incomplete.[20]

Remember also that in Lumberjack's case and in other examples of psychogenic amnesia, trauma is associated with a severe though temporary memory loss. These cases demonstrate that emotionally devastating events can be associated with substantial forgetting. But they differ from the kind of forgetting that seemed to have engulfed Diana Halbrooks, whose repeated traumas were supposedly blocked out again and again. For Lumberjack, a single traumatic event produced amnesia, and virtually all his past experiences were subject to amnesia, not just a narrow band of traumatic events. Lumberjack's amnesia lasted only a few days, and it disrupted his entire life. Repression is only one of several possible explanations for this kind of amnesia.

Ultimately, the best way to shed light on the possible operation of massive repression in cases of sexual abuse is to examine evidence concerning the memory of sexual-abuse survivors. A few such studies have been reported, all indicating that anywhere from 20 percent to nearly 60 percent of people who now remember their abuse say there was a period of time in the past when they did not recall it. But a major drawback is that many of the participants in such studies are people who recovered uncorroborated memories of abuse in therapy. Critics have pointed out some participants in these studies might have recovered illusory recollections of abuse that never occurred. In a more recent study, trauma researchers Diana Elliott and John Briere sent a questionnaire survey to people selected at random from the general population; of the 505 who responded, only a small percentage were involved in any form of psychological treatment. Just over one in five reported they had been sexually abused. Among them, 20 percent indicated there was a period of time when they had no memory for the abuse. While less problematic than some earlier studies, without corroborating evidence that the abuse occurred, it is difficult to make much sense of estimates of forgetting and amnesia.[21]

This problem was addressed in an important study by Linda Meyer Williams. She interviewed 129 women who were admitted to a hospital emergency room in the mid–1970s because of abuse ranging from inappropriate touching to sexual intercourse. The age of the women at the time ranged from ten months to twelve years. Seventeen years later, forty-nine of these women, or 38 percent of the sample, failed to remember this particular hospital admission. Several critics have enumerated reasons why this figure might overestimate amnesia for the admission episode.[22] Even if it does, the study shows convincingly that a significant proportion of women forgot about it. This is still a long way from repressing years' worth of abuse, however. The women might have forgotten the episode because they engaged in conscious suppression, or because it was one of many similar episodes that occurred at the time, or because they were too young to remember it. Indeed, among the women who did not remember the specific hospital admission that Williams inquired about, roughly two-thirds did remember other sexual assaults.

Another finding from Williams's study that is also important is that sixteen of the women (12 percent) reported no history of abuse. This finding comes closer to supporting claims of massive repression. However, some of the women in Williams's study were infants or toddlers when the abuse occurred, and probably forgot the hospital admission for reasons having to do with normal infantile and childhood amnesia. Williams does not provide the ages of the women who were among the 12 percent, but reports that those who had endured repeated abuse tended to recall it at least as often as those who were abused only once, contrary to Terr's idea that extensive repression occurs in victims of repeated, Type II traumas.

Williams's findings show beyond doubt that some abuse survivors fail to recall single abusive incidents, and are consistent with the possibility that some may forget repeated incidents of abuse. Consistent with this latter observation, the psychologist Jonathan Schooler describes a thirty-year-old man called JR who had forgotten about several incidents of abuse by a priest that occurred during the years of early adolescence. However, there is no evidence that JR massively repressed the abuse at the time that it occurred. All we know is that years later, he had forgotten about these painful incidents, perhaps because he did not think or talk about them until encountering reminders of what had happened.[23]

Williams has recently reported new observations concerning women with documented abuse histories that speak to this issue. She asked those women who remembered the abusive incident that led to their hospital admission whether "there was ever a time when you did not remember that this had happened to you."[24] Twelve of seventy-five women (16 percent) responded affirmatively. Some of them provided information about how they came to forget the abuse. In most cases, the women said they began to forget years after the abusive incident. A woman called Kim, for instance, was molested at age seven. She said she forgot the abuse at age 12 and remembered it again at age 22. Tanya, sexually assaulted at age eight, said she forgot about the incident when she was 16 or 17 before remembering at age 24. Two other women, in contrast, said they forgot about the abuse immediately after it occurred. "I blocked it out right away, the first time it happened," commented one of them.[25]

The delayed onset of forgetting in most cases suggests that lack of rehearsal or other relatively benign processes were responsible for it. But a more potent process of repression might have played a role in the two women who reported immediate forgetting. However, it is difficult to know exactly what mental processes occurred years earlier when someone says in retrospect that she blocked out the abuse right away: Was she truly unable to remember the incident immediately after it occurred? Was the "blocking out" an automatic, unconscious act of repression or a conscious attempt to avoid thinking about a distressing event? Some women in Williams's study misremembered when the actual abuse occurred, and it may have been difficult for them to recall exact details of when and how they forgot about it. For example, a woman called Joyce commented that "I don't know how old I was, I used to think about it for the first two years, then I just blocked it out. I may not have completely forgot, I just didn't think about it."[26]

I have already pointed out that excessive exposure to stress-related hormones (glucocorticoids) can damage the hippocampus. I also cited evidence that some abused women have problems regulating stress-related hormones, may show some deficits in autobiographical memory, and may even have a smaller left hippocampus than do nonabused controls. All these findings fit with Williams's results, inasmuch as they imply that some survivors of sexual abuse may have difficulty recalling some aspects of their abuse. As I pointed out in the last chapter, however, abused women with reduced hippocampal volumes always remembered their abuse and failed to exhibit memory deficits on laboratory tests. And no direct cause-and-effect relationship between sexual abuse and reduced hippocampal volume has been shown. Yet even if reduced hippocampal volume is linked to some sort of memory problem in abused women, none of these findings proves or implies the existence of a special repression mechanism that allows people to blot out repeated, horrendous abuse immediately or soon after it happens (nor do they explain how memories could be recovered). Cases such as the one reported by Schooler indicate that some people forget multiple incidents of abuse, but the evidence is not strong enough to warrant any definitive claims about massive repression, as opposed to more benign forms of conscious suppression and lack of rehearsal.

Dissociation, rather than repression, might be responsible for extensive amnesia in abuse survivors. Dissociation refers to a failure to integrate different aspects of an experience, with the result that it is difficult to explicitly remember the experience. I have discussed evidence that people suffering from dissociative disorders, including multiple-personality patients, can forget large chunks of their pasts. Williams suggests that the women in her study who reported forgetting immediately about their abuse may have dissociated the episode. It seems plausible to me that some survivors of sexual abuse might repeatedly dissociate during recurring incidents of abuse, perhaps even creating imaginary identities to handle the abuse. However, recent evidence suggests that traumatized survivors of sexual abuse may have great difficulty forgetting about abuse-related information, at least when it is presented to them in the laboratory. Moreover, if people become skilled enough at dissociation to develop total amnesia for traumatic experiences, it would imply the existence of a dissociative disorder—a serious matter. If they have engaged in extensive dissociation, then patients who recover previously forgotten memories involving years of horrific abuse should also have a documented history of severe pathology that indicates a long-standing dissociative disorder.[27]

A particularly affecting case that illustrates the point was shown in Ofra Bikel's "Divided Memories." A young woman named Ann described how she recovered in therapy memories of terrible satanic ritual abuse at the hands of her parents, and also discovered that she

harbored multiple personalities. Family videotapes and photos showe
Ann, prior to therapy, as a vibrant young woman and a budding young
singer. But the documentary revealed serious problems in Ann's family
life: her mother admitted that she had withdrawn from Ann emotionally during a separation from her husband when Ann was young. "It
was a traditional family," said the film's narrator. "Every Christmas was
celebrated. No birthday was ever forgotten and there were always gifts.
But Ann remembers only anger and a yearning for her mother." Both
parents seemed bewildered by the accusations of sexual and ritualistic
abuse, which included allegations that Ann's mother had attached elec-
trodes to Ann's genitals and that her father had abused her with tools
from a hardware store. Her father, on the verge of tears as he described
"the enormity of the absurdity" of Ann's abuse memories, related how
her medical records showed no effects of the vicious ritual abuse that
she recalled, and her school records revealed perfect attendance despite
the torture that had supposedly been inflicted on the young girl.

If Ann had been dissociating throughout childhood to cope with
nightmarish ritual abuse—thus explaining her amnesia for the abuse
prior to therapy—there should have been telltale signs of a dissociative disorder, such as spotty attendance at school, serious childhood
behavior problems, and the like. "I don't care if it's true," asserted Ann's
therapist, Douglas Sawin. "What's important to me is that I hear the
child's truth, the patient's truth. That's what's important. What actually
happened is irrelevant to me." Asked about the possibility that a
client's report is a delusion, Sawin did not flinch: "We all live in a delusion, just more or less delusionary." If these chilling beliefs are shared
by other therapists, then it is hardly surprising that there are so few
well-corroborated cases of recovered memories and so little direct
evidence for the operation of dissociation in therapy patients who
remember previously forgotten abuse.[28]

In the Eileen Franklin case, the prosecution apparently wished to
avoid applying the term *dissociation* to Eileen, probably because it
implied the existence of a severe dissociative disorder that could not
be demonstrated.[29] I suspect that dissociation may indeed occur in
some cases of genuine forgetting of extensive sexual abuse. But when
it does, there should be a long and well-marked trail of associated
problems and pathologies.

My reading of the evidence concerning memory for sexual trauma
points toward three conclusions. First, there is no question that some
survivors of childhood sexual abuse forget about single abusive incidents, and some evidence that they may forget multiple episodes of

abuse. This forgetting is most likely attributable to some combination of normal processes of memory decay and interference, conscious suppression and lack of rehearsal, and perhaps physiological changes caused by sexual abuse. Second, there is as yet little or no scientifically credible evidence that people who have suffered years of violent or horrific abuse after the years of infancy and early childhood can immediately and indefinitely forget about the abuse. If convincing evidence of this kind does surface, I believe it will occur in the context of a dissociative disorder. Third, the idea that forgetting in abuse survivors is caused by a special repression mechanism—something more powerful than conscious suppression—is still without a scientific basis.

RECOVERED MEMORIES
How Accurate Are They?

Forgetting about abuse need not necessarily mean that it can be remembered again years or decades later. There are countless banal episodes in our lives that we are now unable to remember, and may never remember. Some may come back to us when we encounter cues that trigger what we felt or thought during the experience, but some engrams may have faded away to the point where no cue can elicit them, perhaps because much time has passed and we have not thought or talked about the incident since it happened.

Probably the best-known recent example of a recovered traumatic memory is that of Eileen Franklin. Eileen's memory was compelling enough to convince a jury that her father was guilty of murder and to convince a psychiatrist as experienced as Lenore Terr that it is genuine. But there was no independent corroboration of Eileen's memory. As the attorney Harry MacLean describes clearly in his authoritative account of the Franklin trial, there are reasons to doubt the veracity of Eileen Franklin's recollection of what happened on that tragic day. The recent reversal of George Franklin's conviction may provide another opportunity to examine the credibility of Eileen's memory in the courtroom.[30]

Although the Franklin trial received enormous publicity because it was the first time a recovered memory had ever been the basis for a criminal prosecution, the idea that a forgotten traumatic memory can be later recovered has a long history. Standard Freudian lore had it that repressed traumatic memories can subsequently be recalled, usually after much work and searching in psychoanalysis. For more than fifty years there has been a large clinical literature on psychogenic amnesias indicating that events that could not be recalled during the amnesic episode are subsequently recovered.

Because therapists who seek out forgotten memories of sexual trauma believe that accurate recovery can and does occur, it seems only reasonable to expect that studies have provided solid evidence that recovered memories are generally accurate. Unfortunately, little such evidence exists. This may be because actual abuse often occurs in secrecy, making it difficult to find witnesses or other corroborating evidence, and also because perpetrators typically deny abuse when it has occurred.

In addition to the cases of Ross Cheit, Frank Fitzpatrick, and JR, all of whom recovered memories that were corroborated, another case with solid documentation has been reported by the clinical psychologist Michael Nash. He describes a forty-year-old man who entered therapy in part because he was bothered by an intrusive and unwanted mental image of himself at age ten, surrounded by a group of threatening young boys. The patient suspected that the image alluded to a sexual experience and eventually proceeded to recover a traumatic sexual memory involving the boys. He then contacted a cousin whom, he believed, had been present during the episode. The cousin recalled the incident quite clearly and with considerable embarrassment: he had never forgotten that the patient had been unwillingly drawn into the group's sexual activities.[31]

Additional examples of corroborated cases are found among the twelve women in Linda Meyer Williams's recent study who had temporarily forgotten and later recovered memories of documented abuse. Interestingly, none of the women that Williams describes recovered their memories in therapy or used special techniques such as hypnosis to hunt for them. Most were spontaneously reminded of the abuse by cues: Mary remembered when she encountered a man who looked like her perpetrator and then started having nightmares; Kim began to remember when someone asked her whether she had been sexually abused; Tanya suddenly recalled her molestation as she watched a movie about childhood sexual abuse.[32]

But if recovered memories are sometimes accurate, we don't yet know how accurate they are. The psychiatrist Bessel van der Kolk has speculated that memories of temporarily forgotten traumas might be exceptionally accurate. Ordinary experiences that we mull over and

discuss with others can be changed by the retelling; repressed memories of trauma may remain frozen in their original form: "Conceivably,
traumatic memories then could emerge, not in the distorted form of
ordinary recall but as affect states, somatic sensations, or visual images
(for example, nightmares or flashbacks) that are timeless and unmod-
ified by further experiences." And, indeed, van der Kolk and his colleagues report that people who have experienced severe traumas
reexperience them as isolated pictures or bodily sensations accompanied by intense feeling, whereas the same people recall personally significant (but nontraumatic) experiences in a more storylike narrative
form.[33]

We have already seen that the amygdala and stress-related hormones play a special role in emotional memories, so it makes sense
that memory for trauma does differ in important ways from ordinary
memory. But these differences between traumatic and nontraumatic
recollections do not demonstrate or imply that traumatic memories
that have been repressed and later recovered are also especially accurate. The idea of an unchanging imprint of exactly what happened at
the time of a trauma brings us perilously close to the dubious notion
that memory (or at least traumatic memory) is like a camcorder, preserving all aspects of an episode.[34] We have seen that this idea is fundamentally misguided when applied to ordinary experiences, and I
pointed out in chapter 7 that it does not work well for traumatic
memories that people always remember. It would be surprising, even
extraordinary, if it were to apply to traumatic experiences that are
buried and then recovered years later. There is currently no scientifically credible evidence to support the idea.

The flashbacks of war veterans and others suffering from post-
traumatic stress disorders are sometimes cited as evidence for the
accuracy of recovered traumatic memories. But we saw in chapter 7
that flashback memories often involve a mixture of memory and
fantasy. Flashbacks are heavily influenced by expectations, beliefs,
and fears. The contents of a flashback may say more about what a
person believes or fears about the past than about what actually happened.

Flashbacks are especially relevant to recovered memories of sexual
abuse because some trauma therapists say that memories of abuse
often return as isolated flashback images.[35] A recent report by the psychiatrists Joseph Lipinski and Harrison Pope dramatically illustrates
that such flashbacks must be viewed with a great deal of caution. They

describe three patients who developed vivid, intrusive images of highly disturbing incidents. One patient "saw herself as a child with her father about to stab her, and then herself sitting in a pool of blood."[36] In all three cases, the images were interpreted as flashbacks of repressed childhood trauma, and the patients were referred for appropriate psychotherapy. Something was amiss with these patients, however. All three of them compulsively engaged in unusual rituals, such as cleaning or washing over and over again. These disturbed behaviors are characteristic of the psychiatric disturbance known as obsessive-compulsive disorder. When the patients were given drugs that are ordinarily used to treat this debilitating condition, the intrusive imagery disappeared completely. It turned out that the images were not flashbacks of actual events; they were symptoms of the patients' obsessive-compulsive disorder. This in turn suggests that the diagnosis of repressed childhood trauma was incorrect. Yet had it not been for the dramatic effects of the drug, the patients would have been engaged in a needless—and possibly disastrous—search for repressed traumatic memories.

The current state of scientific evidence concerning the accuracy of recovered memories of childhood sexual abuse can be summarized easily: there are a few well-documented cases, but little scientifically credible information is available. The courts have recently started to grapple with this point. In May 1995, a judge in New Hampshire, faced with two cases in which recovered memories formed the basis of sexual assault charges, brought in experts on both sides of the issue. "The Court finds," wrote Judge William J. Groff in the opening sentence of his opinion, "that the testimony of the victims as to their memory of the assaults shall not be admitted at trial because the phenomenon of memory repression, and the process of therapy used in these cases to recover the memories, have not gained acceptance in the field of psychology, and are not scientifically reliable." In a more recent New Hampshire case, Judge Linda Dalianas cited the same expert testimony as Groff, but ruled in favor of allowing the alleged victim to testify and allowing experts to testify concerning the general phenomenon of traumatic amnesia. Nonetheless, she also concluded that "[t]he Court will not allow expert evidence regarding either the process or the plausibility of 'recovering' an allegedly repressed memory, because the experts have not offered any data either supporting or refuting any theory of how or whether a 'lost' memory might be recovered."[37]

ILLUSORY MEMORIES OF SEXUAL ABUSE
What Is the Evidence?

We have already seen that some recovered memories are accurate. That still leaves a separate and crucial question: Is there any evidence that people can come to believe that they were sexually abused when they weren't? In the summer of 1987, Diana Halbrooks's therapist suggested terminating treatment. "I panicked, became very anxious and increasingly depressed," Diana remembered. "I felt it was due to thinking about not seeing him regularly any longer, but he informed me that it was not that at all, that it was due to abandonment pain related to my father." She became increasingly depressed, but despite her best efforts, "I couldn't come up with anything that my father had done to cause such pain." In a last effort to find out what her father had done, her therapist asked Diana to write down whatever came to mind while she was in a hypnotic trance, telling her that "writing in a trance with my eyes closed would allow my unconscious to speak freely." Diana had become adept at entering hypnotic trance states in therapy. When she opened her eyes this time, she was met with a shocking sight: "I had written that my father molested me."

With a door to her unconscious seemingly opened, Diana continued this exercise. At the same time, she entered a weekly support group that her therapist had initiated, consisting of women who were also exploring recovered traumatic memories. The atmosphere of the group was highly charged, as women discussed and sometimes acted out their memories and dreams of terrible events that had come back to them in therapy. Diana recalls: "The memories that others were sharing in the group were getting more and more bizarre: satanic ritual abuse, babies being sacrificed, group sex and horrible tortures." It was not long before the same kinds of horrific incidents began showing up in Diana's own trance writings. "In November of 1988, I wrote in a trance and 'recalled' the first memory of satanic ritual abuse. Everything just seemed to go downhill from there." By 1989 Diana had remembered killing a baby.

A surprisingly large number of recovered-memory cases involve satanic ritual abuse, including reports of child sacrifice, cannibalism, and various gory rituals. A survey of members of the American Psychological Association revealed that 12 percent reported having treated ritual abuse cases. Memories of satanic ritual abuse nearly always emerge during therapy; clinicians who treat these patients acknowledge that it is rare for them to enter therapy with any memory of ritual abuse. But even though thousands of patients have "remembered" ritual acts, not a single such case has ever been documented in the United States despite extensive investigative efforts by state and federal law enforcement. FBI agent Ken Lanning has investigated over 300 cases of satanic cult abuse, for example, without finding corroborating evidence for a single one. A recent report from the National Center for Child Abuse surveyed several thousand professionals about satanic ritual abuse and failed to turn up conclusive evidence for this kind of abuse or for the organized, intergenerational cults that have been implicated in recovered-memory cases.[38]

These failures to document cult abuse do not necessarily mean that no satanic cults exist or that no ritual abuse has ever occurred. Events such as the 1995 Oklahoma City bombing, the cult-related nerve gas attack on a Tokyo subway, and the horrific acts of butchery carried out by the Wisconsin murderer Jeffrey Dahmer provide painful reminders that people are capable of terrible deeds.[39] The human capacity for evil is not at issue, but the human ability to develop amnesia for repeated acts of brutality is very much in doubt. Until convincing evidence is forthcoming, I conclude that most, if not all, recovered memories of ritualistic horrors perpetrated by cults are based on illusory recollections. And since most recovered memories of satanic ritual abuse emerge only when therapy has begun, these cases lend support to the idea that false memories of brutal traumas can be created during therapy.

Because Diana Halbrooks's ritual abuse memories seemed so outlandish, her doubts about the reality of these and her other recovered recollections continued to grow. But these doubts met resistance from the people in her support group and her therapist. "I continually questioned the memories, doubted them," Diana acknowledges, "but when I questioned the therapist, he would yell at me, tell me I wasn't giving my 'little girl within' the benefit of the doubt. Tell me that I was in denial. I didn't know what to believe. But I trusted him." Eventually, most members of the support group recovered memories of ritual abuse and almost all, including Diana, were diagnosed as multiple personalities.

Diana escaped this toxic therapy and has managed to reassemble the pieces of her life. She no longer believes that her recovered memories have any basis in reality. In the world of recovered memories, people like Diana are called *retractors*. Retractors live most of their lives without any memories of abuse, proceed to recover memories at some point, and then later come to believe that those memories are inaccurate. A growing number of people are retracting their memories, but that does not necessarily mean that all their memories are illusory. A person might retract a memory because of pressure from family or friends or because the pain associated with the memory is simply too much to bear. But when the memories are as improbable as those that Diana Halbrooks recovered, the most reasonable interpretation is that the events do not have any basis in reality.

Diana shares features in common with other retractors. A recent survey of twenty women who retracted their recovered memories of sexual abuse revealed some striking similarities among them.[40] Nineteen recovered their memories during therapy, and all of them report that their therapists influenced the development of their memories. Only one of the twenty did not participate in therapy. This woman recovered her memories after reading *The Courage to Heal,* the bible of the recovery movement that has been roundly criticized for admonishing people to believe that they were abused even when they fail to remember it. Nearly all of the retractors—90 percent—reported that some sort of trance induction was used in therapy to recover memories. Hypnosis was the most common technique, reported by 85 percent of the women. Trance writing, regression, and suggestions of abuse were also widely reported. The majority of the women (70 percent) said that group therapy influenced their recovered memories. "The group progressed from eating disorders to childhood sexual abuse, to incest, to SRA [satanic ritual abuse]," recounted one retractor. "Eight out of ten members developed SRA memories, the two who didn't were told they were in denial." Another woman commented that "[i]f you don't have a memory you feel like you have to come up with one to compete with everybody."[41]

Obviously, there can be no unequivocal experimental data showing that an illusory memory of a sexual trauma can be implanted, but a clever attempt to surmount this problem in a related area was reported by Nicholas Spanos, a hypnosis researcher. Spanos and his colleagues conducted an experiment using a variant of the hypnotic age-regression technique, in which people are given suggestions to "regress" to a very young age. His subjects were given suggestions to "regress" to a past life. Roughly half of them came to believe that they had indeed lived a past life. And when Spanos suggested to some that they had suffered abuse as children in their past lives, they developed more "memories" of the abuse than people who had not been given such suggestions.[42] Because this experiment was couched in a "past lives" context, it does not settle the issue of whether a false sexual-abuse history can be implanted in adults, but the evidence is certainly consistent with that possibility.[43]

Hypnosis played a key role in Diana Halbrooks's story as well. She never remembered any sexual abuse by her father until her therapist instructed her to engage in automatic writing during a hypnotic trance. I know of no scientific evidence that writing down whatever comes to mind during a hypnotic trance promotes accurate recall of forgotten experiences. Trance writing was popular over a century ago, when it was used in séances as a tool for psychic communications. Scattered anecdotal observations suggest that trance writing may occasionally lead people to produce implicit memories of long forgotten events that seem strange and unfamiliar to them. But it is impossible to tell whether something that pops to mind during trance writing is an accurate memory of a distant event or a reflection of current concerns and fears—just as there is no way to tell (without external corroboration) whether memories recovered with the aid of hypnosis are true or false. With all the talk of satanic ritual abuse in her weekly support group, it is hardly surprising that a ritual abuse "memory" eventually popped to mind when Diana engaged in trance writing.[44]

Hypnosis stands out as a common denominator among the sample of retractors, but sharing memories in a support group is also an important tool used by therapists who believe that it is important to hunt for repressed memories of sexual abuse.[45] Discussing traumatic recollections with other abuse survivors would no doubt be reassuring and helpful when those recollections are real; the experiences of Diana and other retractors testify to the power of a group in also helping to shape and maintain memories of experiences that never occurred. Social psychologists have for decades documented and discussed similar kinds of social influences, although there has been surprisingly little work concerned specifically with social influence on memory.[46]

Guided imagery, or visualization, is another method recommended by various practitioners to retrieve repressed memories. Here, patients are encouraged to imagine abusive incidents that they seek to remember, attempting to create pictures in their minds of what might have happened. When sexual trauma has actually occurred, guided imagery can be a useful therapeutic technique. Studies by the psychologist Edna Foa and her colleagues have shown that the imaginary reliving of a rape produces a significant reduction in symptoms of post-traumatic stress disorder. But it is quite another matter to use guided imagery in an effort to dredge up a supposedly repressed memory of an event that may or may not have taken place. I have already pointed out that freely imagining an event, and then exploring it and talking about it as if it were real, is a potentially powerful means of creating the kind of subjective feeling that accompanies an authentic memory. After enough visualization and discussion, patients may be unable to sort out whether the memory has come to "feel" like a genuine one because the event actually happened or merely because they have been imagining it and talking about it. This idea receives support from studies by Ira Hyman and his colleagues that have documented that using guided imagery increases false memories of childhood events (see chapter 4). Recent PET scanning studies conducted by Stephen Kosslyn and his colleagues have shown that some of the same regions in the occipital lobes are involved in both visual imagery and perception. This may be one reason why incidents that people frequently imagine can come to feel like events that actually occurred: imagined events are generated by some of the same neural machinery that contributes to the perception of actual events.[47]

Just as there is no good evidence that techniques such as guided imagery and hypnosis can aid accurate retrieval of distant, forgotten, or repressed memories, there is no hard evidence that these techniques are specifically responsible for the creation of pseudomemories in therapy. And it is of course possible that in cases where real abuse has occurred and has been forgotten, such procedures might help some patients recover their memories. But unless a therapist can cite evidence that a specific memory-retrieval technique enhances accurate recall without promoting false recollections, it is inappropriate to continue to use unproven and potentially hazardous memory-retrieval techniques. Nonetheless, a recent survey of 145 doctoral-level psychotherapists in the United States indicates that close to one-third sometimes use hypnosis to help clients remember child sexual abuse, and about the same percentage report using guided imagery.[48]

I believe that three major conclusions are warranted concerning the likelihood of therapeutic implantation of false memories of sexual trauma. First, there is no conclusive scientific evidence from controlled research that false memories of sexual abuse can be created—nor will such evidence ever exist, because of ethical considerations. Second, there is likewise no definitive scientific evidence showing that therapy per se or specific suggestive techniques are alone responsible for the creation of inaccurate memories. Third, several separate strands, when considered together, support the conclusion that some therapists have helped to create illusory recollections of sexual abuse: the experimentally documented malleability of memory in response to suggestive influences; evidence that hypnosis can produce compelling but inaccurate pseudomemories;

failures to document satanic ritual abuse; recovery of memories for seemingly impossible events (past lives and alien abductions); growing numbers of therapy patients who have retracted their memories; the constructive nature of memory for emotional events; and the risky memory-retrieval techniques advocated by some proponents of recovered memory therapy. Yet we still lack solid data concerning the prevalance of therapy-induced pseudomemories. We simply don't yet know whether illusory memories of sexual abuse are exceedingly rare, as some clinicians have claimed, or whether they are widespread, as critics of so-called recovered memory therapy have argued. It seems unlikely, however, that they can all be written off to just a handful of wayward therapists.[49]

Viewed in a broader historical perspective, the idea that people can acquire convincing but inaccurate memories during therapy should not be all that surprising. The philosopher Ian Hacking points out that over a century ago, Pierre Janet routinely treated traumatized patients by implanting false memories to replace accurate but painful recollections of horrible events. For instance, he hypnotized one patient who was overwhelmed by childhood memories of sleeping next to a girl with an acute skin disease called impetigo on her face, leaving it covered by pustules and crusts. Janet replaced the traumatic memory with a pleasant but illusory image of a lovely face. Elizabeth Loftus described something similar in a 1982 paper, nearly a decade prior to the recovered-memories controversy. In an ironic twist, given later developments, she quoted two psychotherapists who implanted entire false histories in people as a way of making them feel better. Working with people who had been fat all their lives, they successfully implanted false childhoods in which the patients had grown up thin. The therapists noted that they "could very easily install memories in you that related to real world experiences that never occurred." "Made-up memories can change you just as well as the arbitrary perceptions that you made up at the time about 'real world events,'" they reflected. "That happens a lot in therapy."[50]

DISTINGUISHING ACCURATE AND ILLUSORY RECOLLECTIONS
The Role of Implicit Memory

If accurate recovered memories and illusory recollections of sexual trauma both exist, then an important question immediately arises: Are there any scientifically based criteria that allow us to distinguish memories of events that actually occurred from false recollections? The answer, unfortunately, is no. Laboratory studies have provided suggestive clues about differences between memories of actual events and imagined events, but there is no research that allows clinicians or scientists to judge unequivocally the historical truth of a traumatic memory recovered in therapy. Nonetheless, some therapists have offered suggestions about how to distinguish an accurate recovered memory from an illusory one.[51] One intriguing possibility involves implicit memory for forgotten traumas.

Sigmund Freud and Josef Breuer's classic studies of hysteria described patients who could not explicitly remember childhood sexual abuse, but experienced disabling fears, nagging anxieties, intrusive thoughts, or disturbing images that reflected implicit memory for the trauma. However, these cases proved difficult to interpret because independent corroboration of the event was often lacking. As I noted in chapter 4, Freud later abandoned his early belief in the reality of such traumatic experiences in favor of the idea that they are often fantasy-based false recollections.[52]

Breuer and Freud's early observations are germane to contemporary controversies because some have contended that true recovered memories—not false recollections—are nearly always preceded by behaviors and symptoms that reflect unconscious or implicit memory for repressed trauma. Lenore Terr's research with traumatized children shows that such implicit memory effects can occur. She studied twenty children who had been subjected to various kinds of traumas prior to the age of five; in almost all cases, the traumas were corroborated by eyewitnesses, police reports, or other means. Terr found that nineteen of the twenty children—including several who could not remember their traumas in words—showed the influence of the trauma in their play, fears, and other nonverbal behaviors. Terr notes that only one child—the single case of false memory in her sample—had no behavioral symptoms of trauma. This little girl had heard family members talk about the traumatic event but had not actually experienced it. If Terr's observations apply to other situations, then the presence or absence of implicit memory might indeed help distinguish between true and false recovered memories of sexual abuse.[53]

But there are problems in trying to apply this idea to individual cases in which memories of long-forgotten traumas are recovered in therapy. Some therapists include a vast range of symptoms and behaviors as possible indications that a person who has no explicit memory of abuse has nevertheless been influenced by it. These symptoms populate the notorious "checklists" for possible past abuse that have been published in various popular publications for incest survivors and that include such items as low self-esteem, sexual difficulty, eating disorders, depression, fears of abandonment, and so forth.

Here I agree with critics who maintain that such symptoms are so general that they could apply to many people.[54] To invoke implicit memory for a past experience, it is essential to demonstrate that a behavior or symptom is specifically related to that experience. With general symptoms of the kind that are described in popular checklists, it is difficult to establish causal links in individual cases, although it is of course possible that they sometimes exist. The psychiatrist Harrison Pope and his colleagues found no evidence that childhood sexual abuse is a risk factor for the eating disorder known as bulimia, even though bulimia has been often cited as a telltale sign of forgotten abuse.[55] We do not yet know whether particular kinds of behaviors and symptoms are unconscious remnants of traumatic abuse.

In some cases, however, more specific symptoms exist; patients may enter therapy with unexplained fears of or reactions to a particular situation, smell, or object. "Attraction to, avoidance of, or distress around objects or situations unexplained by your own history are warning signs of repressed memories," writes the therapist Renee Frederickson. "During sexual abuse, your mind focuses on the events and circumstances surrounding the abuse. You may bury the memory, but you store the reaction to the objects or situations that remind you of the abuse."[56]

This is a plausible suggestion. In chapter 8 we encountered instances of implicit memory for forgotten traumas in psychogenic amnesia patients, and I suggested a role for the amygdala in mediating persisting emotional aftereffects of experiences that are not recollected consciously. But it is still a long leap to interpreting a patient's unexplained fears, attractions, or dislikes as implicit memories of sexual abuse. One problem is that even a specific symptom could have any number of causes. In a repressed memory case cited by Frederickson, a patient felt an unexplained revulsion toward forks. Subsequently, she recovered a memory of her aunt abusing her with a fork. Frederickson concluded that the abusive episode is the origin of the patient's unexplained revulsion toward forks. Couldn't this be implicit memory for the abuse? Possibly. But suppose that the fork revulsion had nothing to do with sexual abuse, yet was one of the factors that encouraged the patient or the therapist to explore the possibility that she had been abused. Or suppose that the therapist focused on the meaning of this revulsion because she assumed that it was a symptom of abuse.

Then the symptom could become a focal point for constructing an illusory memory. Once therapist and patient become attached to the idea that the symptom reflects forgotten abuse, it should not be surprising when a patient starts to produce images, thoughts, and feelings that in some way relate to the symptom.

Nobody can say for sure whether such a process was operating in Frederickson's patient, but the psychiatrists Susan McElroy and Paul Keck have recently described a case in which it clearly played a role. Ms. B. sought therapy because of depression and intrusive thoughts of harming her infant. She also told the therapist that as a child she had experienced unwanted images of being raped, and wondered whether her disturbing ideas could be symptoms of unremembered sexual abuse: "The therapist responded to Ms. B. that these symptoms were 'clear evidence' that Ms. B. had in fact been sexually abused as a child, and instructed her to draw pictures of anything that came to her mind." After six months of trying, Ms. B. developed detailed recollections of sexual abuse involving her sister and brother-in-law. However, Ms. B.'s condition did not improve, her sister angrily denied the abuse, and she could find no corroborating evidence that any abuse occurred. Ms. B. finally concluded that her memories were false and sought alternative therapy. Eventually it was discovered that Ms. B.'s intrusive thoughts were attributable to an obsessive-compulsive disorder. As in similar cases I mentioned earlier, they disappeared when treated with appropriate medication.[57]

It seems likely that in some cases of recovered memories, unusual fears, attractions, and related symptoms may well turn out to be implicit memories of prior abuse. In other cases, like Ms. B.'s, such symptoms may provide a basis for creating false recollections in response to suggestive probing, rather than reflecting the influence of a traumatic memory that had been there prior to therapy.

Inferring implicit memory is a tricky business that calls for careful comparisons and systematic reasoning. Behaviors and symptoms may have many possible causes, and it is difficult to say whether one particular experience is the source of a specific behavior or symptom. In the laboratory, experimenters can control the events that give rise to implicit memories. In therapy settings where patients do not explicitly remember being abused, and where we do not even know for certain that the abusive event occurred, it is impossible to make controlled comparisons. A therapist who engages in undisciplined interpretation of fears, attractions, and other symptoms as signs of implicit memory for forgotten abuse may be taking a step down a road to disaster.

BEYOND CONTROVERSY

As I write these words the recovered memories controversy continues to rage. Yet we still have little good scientific evidence that bears directly on the key issues that I have discussed. Few times in the history of psychology or psychiatry has the ratio of data to impassioned argument been so low. If we are to find the truth, I believe that we need to recast the tone of the recovered-memories debate from its present black and white polarities to one that acknowledges more shades of gray.

For one, the notion of "false memory" itself is too coarse to do justice to the complex relations between memory and reality. When a patient remembers growing up in an abusive satanic cult that did not exist, then we have a belief that defies reality. Even if the ritual abuse memory is a metaphor for some other distressing experience, the memory is historically wrong in a way that most memories are not. But what of a woman who was emotionally brutalized by a neglectful parent, or perhaps exposed to sexually inappropriate language, behavior, or fondling, and then remembers incest when none occurred? The incest memory is illusory, and should be regarded as such, but it may capture something important about the past that should not be dismissed. Historical truth can be respected while at the same time doing justice to a patient's narrative truth. We need to recognize that memories do not exist in one of two states—either true or false—and that the important task is to examine how and in what ways memory corresponds to reality.[58]

Contrary to what some have said, there is a middle ground in the recovered-memories debate; the problem is to identify it. I believe that this is our best hope for resolving the bitter and divisive arguments that continue to rage among patients, families, and professionals. Political posturing and grand generalizations on both sides of this debate should come to an end. Risky therapeutic practices need to be stopped. Better techniques must be developed that allow us to distinguish between accurate recovered memories and illusory memories that arise in response to suggestion. Achieving these objectives should help to minimize the possibility that those who were not abused come to embrace the psychologically devastating belief that they were, reduce (and, one hopes, end) false accusations that shatter lives and families, and also maximize the credibility of the memories reported by genuine survivors of sexual abuse. Sadly, legitimate concerns about pseudomemories have probably helped create doubts about the accu-

FIGURE 9.2

Lorie Novak, "Fragments," 1987. 16½ x 22". Color photograph. Courtesy of the artist.

Novak is concerned with the nature of memories for family life, underscoring the discrepancy between our idealized versions of childhood and the more troublesome feelings that often lurk beneath the surface. In "Fragments" a Polaroid snapshot of a classic 1950s family that includes the artist as a young girl creates a nostalgic sense of a harmonious past. But the torn and fragmented images in the foreground show Novak at an older age and imply that the innocent family portrait masks a more complex and perhaps painful reality.

rate recollections of some survivors of actual abuse, an outcome that should not be tolerated by therapists, researchers, or society.

When Diana Halbrooks reflects on the peculiar memories that she now understands were illusory, she returns over and over again to a single theme: the importance of her family. Diana appreciates that there were problems in her early family life. She did not grow up in the idyllic 1950s family that served as a model for many of the post–World War II generation. Behind the veneer of smiling faces in old photographs and home movies, there were real difficulties that Diana needed to confront as an adult. (See figure 9.2.)

Diana Halbrooks came to understand that she could acknowledge a painful reality without vilifying or abandoning her parents. "We are rebuilding," she reflects, "and trying to make up for lost time, making every moment count." Not all the victims of the memory wars will be able to unite with their families again. This realization is sad as well as ironic. Our families serve as social repositories for autobiographical recollections from many times in our lives; we revisit favorite episodes, stories, and momentous occasions during holidays and other family gatherings. Yet for some patients, recovering memories of distant traumas—whether accurate or illusory—serves to disconnect them from one of their richest sources of personal history. The beginnings of our life stories are written in our families, and when we try to make sense of these stories near the ends of our lives, it is often to the family that we return.

TEN

STORIES OF ELDERS

EIGHTY-TWO-YEAR-OLD Littlejohn McCain, the central character in Howard Owen's novel *Littlejohn,* is embroiled in a struggle with memory. As he approaches the end of his life, this farmer from North Carolina is often plagued by his diminishing ability to remember his recent experiences. After forgetting frequently to turn off the burners on his stove, he becomes so flustered that he mounts a large sign on the kitchen door with the words TURN OFF BURNERS emblazoned on it. Sometimes Littlejohn forgets where he is or what he is doing, as in a jarring episode at the grocery store: "I had just put two cans of Campbell's cream of chicken soup in my cart and was looking for the self-rising flour when I just blanked out. I couldn't quite remember what I was doing there. It had happened once or twice before, but never this bad, or this public, at least. I looked around, and there at the end of the aisle was the meat counter. It seemed like I recognized it, so I went that way." After his grandson teases him about his penchant for forgetting, Littlejohn becomes flustered. "Son, if you ever live to be as old as me," he explains to the youngster, "you'll be happy if you can just remember your own name."[1]

At the same time that he is tormented by the fragility of his memory, Littlejohn is also increasingly inspired, and sometimes consumed, by its power. He spends much of his time recounting the significant events of his life, many of which seem as real in old age as they did when he was younger. Littlejohn thinks a lot about what has happened in his family: the stories his father told, the advice his mother gave, everything he learned from his uncles, aunts, and cousins. But he is especially concerned with reviewing, and attempting to understand, a family tragedy that has colored his entire life: he killed his younger brother in a hunting accident. The incident was too painful for him to face when he was younger. Like others who have lived through terrible events, he tried his best for years to avoid the wrenching memory, mostly by working endless hours on his farm: "If I kept at it, kept that ditchbank so clean you could eat out of it, kept the weeds out of the tobacco and corn, got the whole place looking better than it ever had, maybe everybody would forget some day that I'd killed my own brother. Maybe I'd forget, too."[2]

He never did forget. But it was only with the distance in time provided by old age that Littlejohn could ponder what had happened. The novel charts his battle to comprehend the haunting memory, and ultimately to place it in the perspective of the fundamentally decent life that he has led. Littlejohn reminds himself of the broader context in which the awful event occurred by turning to a symbol of the good things that happened in his life: a crepe myrtle flower that his wife cultivated when they first moved into their home. The house was later destroyed by fire, but even after selling off their land, Littlejohn saved the largest crepe myrtle and used it to help create a balanced recollection of the past: "That crepe myrtle comes out every summer all pink and beautiful, just when everything else is dying, and it helps me to remember what a fine life we had, in spite of everything."[3] We see here a kind of age-related heightening of memory's fragile power: the elderly Littlejohn is increasingly plagued by memory's failures at the same time that he takes refuge in its compelling force.

Pat Potter, an artist from Alabama who has spent a good deal of time listening to the reminiscences of elderly adults, evokes some of the qualities that are so evident in Littlejohn's recollections. In the mid–1980s, Potter mounted an ambitious artistic exploration of memory that combined painting, sculpture, and texts in a wide-ranging museum installation.[4] As part of her memory project, Potter interviewed elderly adults about their early recollections of family members and salient episodes from their lives. She attempted to convey the quality of their reminiscences by altering old photographs that depict the recollected family member or the remembered episode, using various techniques of artistic transformation, illustrated by "Overlays of Memory II" (figure 10.1).

We sometimes speak disdainfully of older adults as living in the past, implying a present that is so impoverished that elders must take refuge in the comfort provided by their idealized memories. Adult

FIGURE 10.1

Pat Potter, "Overlays of Memory II," 1985. 10 x 7". Mixed media, altered photograph image. Courtesy of the artist.

The artist portrays octogenarian Addie Butler's memory of her younger brother John as a boy. The multiple fragments of John's image are blurred and veiled, just like Addie's memory of him. At the same time, the picture of the innocent youth in knickers and dress shirt effectively communicates that this is an emotionally resonant memory for Addie. She recollects affectionately that John "was eight years younger and we would dress him up like a doll."[5] The image serves as a symbol of a distant childhood that continues to echo persistently in Addie's present. The faded qualities of Addie's recollections do not diminish their power to call forth potent feelings.

men and women often attribute episodes of forgetting to memory banks that are losing brain cells by the minute. And many people worry that all of their memory capacities will inevitably decline and then disappear as they grow older. These are all myths about aging memory that I try to set to rest in this chapter. Research in psychology and neuroscience indicates that aging does not produce an across-the-board decline in all memory functions; that memory systems do not necessarily lose significant numbers of brain cells as we age; and that when older adults focus on the past, there need not be any pathology involved. Memory is affected by aging, but the nature of the changes, and the reasons why they occur, are different from what many of us believe and fear.

AGING MEMORY
How Fragile Is It?

There are good reasons why people fear that aging inevitably brings a generalized decline in memory: decades of research leave little doubt that aging can impair memory. In experiments on aging memory, "old people" are usually healthy volunteers around seventy years of age, whereas "young people" are generally college students. Numerous experiments examining explicit memory for recently presented words, pictures, or stories have revealed that older adults usually remember less than young people. And we are all aware of the perils of Alzheimer's disease. It is easy for an older person to worry that failing to recall someone's name, or forgetting where the car keys were placed, is an early sign of descent into amnesia and dementia. The prospect of ending up like Frederick, unable to remember that you executed a golf stroke a minute ago, is dreadful.

But many of us are not aware of the single most important fact about memory and aging: the performance of older adults varies widely across different situations, ranging from perfectly normal to significantly impaired. For instance, after studying a list of familiar words, the elderly have problems remembering the words on their own ("free recall"), without any hints or cues. But they can remember the same items accurately—almost as well as college students do—when they are shown the words and asked to say which ones were on the list ("recognition"). When older people are shown two separate lists of sentences, they have a harder time than young people remembering whether a sentence appeared on the first or the second list. But when some sentences appear on the left side of a screen and others appear on the right, older adults remember where the sentences appeared just as well as young people. And when asked to carry out certain tasks at a designated time in the future, such as returning a borrowed comb or arranging an appointment, they are more likely to forget to do it than young people are. Asked to carry out other tasks at a future time, such as pushing a button whenever a certain word appears on a computer screen, however, older people remember to do it as often as do college students. If aging simply produced a general decline in memory, we would not expect to see elderly adults doing extremely well in some situations and poorly in others. Why does this happen?[6]

The aging brain provides some important clues. Overall brain mass steadily shrinks as we enter our sixties and seventies, at roughly 5 percent to 10 percent per decade. Fluid-filled ventricles enlarge, and the brain's blood flow and uptake of oxygen both decrease significantly.[7] Many researchers have long believed that aging results in a widespread loss of neurons in the cortex, the seat of our most advanced cognitive functions and the major site of memory storage. This belief is based on studies of brains examined in autopsies in which fewer numbers of neurons were found in the cortex of old people than of young people. But most of these studies were conducted decades ago, when researchers had only a limited awareness of Alzheimer's disease and may have included both healthy and diseased brains in their studies. Newer studies that have excluded brains of people with signs of Alzheimer's or other age-related brain diseases tell a different tale: loss of neurons in the cortex is either trivial or far less than what the early studies had shown. Recent research with monkeys leads to the same conclusion.[8]

In a compelling confirmation of this point, researchers carefully examined several regions of the hippocampus that are known to produce memory loss when damaged (including the CA1 field that was disrupted in the amnesic patient RB, discussed earlier). Normal aging was not associated with neuron loss in these regions, but there was considerable loss of hippocampal neurons in the brains of patients who had shown signs of Alzheimer's disease when alive.[9] This may be why an Alzheimer's patient such as Frederick is unable to remember golf shots he hit minutes earlier: numerous neurons in the hippocampus have been destroyed. However, an older adult who has difficulty with unaided recall of a recent experience, but remembers it well when given hints or cues, still has an ample supply of hippocampal neurons. Normal memory loss and amnesia due to Alzheimer's disease involve different kinds of changes in the brain. This means that the next time you forget where you put your car keys, you need not worry that you are headed toward Alzheimer's. Nor do you need to become concerned the next time you fail to come up with the name of a friend that feels like it is on the tip of your tongue. But if you forget that you possess a car or you can't remember your own name, then there is clearly cause for concern.

If normal aging results in less neuron loss from the cortex and hippocampus than was previously suspected, why do older adults have memory problems? The hippocampus does show definite signs of atrophy with aging, and abundant hippocampal atrophy is associated with low levels of explicit memory on laboratory tests. Also, aging produces marked loss of neurons in a few subcortical structures, including one I mentioned in connection with amnesic syndromes, the basal forebrain. The basal forebrain is important because it supplies the hippocampus with a chemical messenger called acetylcholine, which is known to be important for memory. As we have seen, memories are encoded by changes in the strengths of connections among neurons. Acetylcholine expedites these changes. When the basal forebrain is directly damaged, patients develop amnesia. Accordingly, a significant loss of neurons in the basal forebrain probably contributes to age-related memory difficulties.[10]

Changes in the frontal lobes provide important insights into why older adults show intact memory in some situations and substantial impairments in others. The frontal lobes appear to be hit hard during aging. Brain atrophy or shrinkage is most pronounced over frontal regions, as are reductions of blood flow and glucose utilization. These changes in the brain are mirrored in behavior. Elderly adults often perform especially poorly on cognitive tests that are failed by patients with damage to a part of the frontal lobe on the cortical surface known as the dorsolateral region. For example, when these frontal patients are given a deck of cards that contains different colors, shapes, and other features, they have problems sorting the cards by category: color, shape, and so on. So do older adults. Even when deficits that may be attributable to impaired function in other brain regions are carefully controlled for, difficulties related to the frontal lobes emerge as the most important factor in elderly adults' impaired cognitive performance on several different tests.[11] Because some areas of the frontal lobe play a critical role in remembering, we have a potentially useful handle on the variations in explicit memory that are characteristic of older adults. Rather than resulting from a general decline in all aspects of brain function, many memory problems in older adults may stem from specific impairments in the frontal lobes. If so, then older adults should have special problems with memory tasks that rely on frontal regions. The weight of the scientific evidence is consistent with this suggestion.

Let's consider the contrasts I highlighted earlier between spared and impaired memory functions in older adults. Frontal regions are more important for recall than for recognition, which could account for the fact that older adults have more problems recalling words on their own than recognizing them when shown a list. Memory for temporal order depends on frontal regions, which may explain why elderly adults have problems remembering the order in which two sentences appear. The elderly have no problems remembering whether sentences appeared on the left or right, probably because this kind of memory depends on brain regions outside the frontal lobes, which are not especially affected by aging. Older people do not remember to carry out future actions like arranging an appointment when they have to generate cues on their own, which probably maximizes demands on the frontal lobes. But when a cue word is presented, older people have no problems remembering to carry out a prescribed action, probably because the frontal lobes were not heavily taxed.[12]

Using PET scans, my colleagues and I have directly implicated specific areas within the frontal lobes in age-related memory deficits. I earlier discussed PET results showing that certain frontal regions become active when people work hard at trying to remember a recently studied word, thus demonstrating that parts of the frontal lobe are involved in strategic or effortful retrieval processes. We found that when young people were given cues and made extensive efforts to recall words they studied a few minutes earlier, areas in anterior sections of the frontal lobes became extremely active. But these areas, particularly in the right anterior frontal lobe, showed few signs of activity when older adults carried out the same recall task. It seemed as though elderly participants had difficulty starting up the retrieval process—engaging in the mental work necessary to search for and dredge up episodic memories. Yet the hippocampus became active during recall in both older and younger adults, probably reflecting a commonality in the way that older and younger people remember words from the study list.[13]

In another PET study, both older and younger adults showed right frontal lobe activation during recognition of faces they had studied earlier. Remember that older adults have less difficulty with recognition than with recall. Under the demanding conditions of a recall test, when an older person has to search for and produce the correct answer, right anterior frontal regions may not quite be up to the job of getting the retrieval process started. But when the answer is provided on a recognition test, and all the older adult has to do is say which of two faces appeared earlier, these frontal regions do contribute. Interestingly, during the initial study of the faces, old people showed reduced activity in the left inferior frontal lobe and several other structures that are important for encoding. As we saw earlier, the left inferior frontal lobe plays a role in elaborative encoding. Older adults apparently did not spontaneously elaborate on the faces when they encoded them into memory, whereas younger people did.[14]

How are age-related frontal impairments manifest in the everyday memory of older people? Recall that patients with frontal lobe damage are especially vulnerable to source amnesia: even when they can recall a newly learned fact, they have special problems recollecting who told it to them. This may be because retrieving source information requires the kind of effortful retrieval that depends on the frontal lobes. In the 1980 presidential campaign, Ronald Reagan repeatedly told a heartbreaking story of a World War II bomber pilot who ordered his crew to bail out after his plane had been seriously damaged by an enemy hit. His young belly gunner was wounded so seriously that he was unable to evacuate the bomber. Reagan could barely hold back his tears as he uttered the pilot's heroic response: "Never mind. We'll ride it down together." The press soon realized that this story was an almost exact duplicate of a scene in the 1944 film *A Wing and a Prayer*. Reagan had apparently retained the facts but forgotten their source.[15]

Evidence from several laboratory studies has linked this kind of source amnesia with frontal lobe dysfunction. For example, my colleagues and I examined whether older adults could learn fictitious "facts" such as "Bob Hope's father was a fireman." In the experiment, such information was given to old and young people by either a man or a woman. We found that the elderly have much more difficulty than the young recollecting whether the man or the woman told them the information—even when they can recall the information itself correctly. Poor source memory in the elderly is related to their performance on tests that are sensitive to deficiencies in the frontal lobes. Elderly people who perform poorly on these tests also tend to have special problems remembering source information.[16]

Source memory becomes important in everyday life when we are given personal tidbits or "inside" tips on the condition that we keep them to ourselves. Think about what is involved in staying true to your vow. You must be able to remember later whether the tidbit is a secret that you are not supposed to divulge; that is, you must accurately remember the source of your knowledge. If you retain the juicy tidbit but forget how you learned about it, you are liable to inadvertently spill your friend's secret. My colleagues and I made up various juicy tidbits of gossip and told old and young people that some tidbits were secrets that should not be disclosed, whereas others were common knowledge. Older adults had more difficulty than younger adults remembering which tidbits were secrets and which were not. This finding does not necessarily mean that you should never trust your grandmother with a secret, but you should probably handle such matters with care.[17]

Because forgetting the source of a memory opens the door to illusory recollections, older adults are especially vulnerable to certain types of memory distortions. Recall the false fame illusion I considered earlier in the book. When people are exposed in the laboratory to a made up, nonfamous name such as Sebastian Weisdorf, and later fail consciously to recollect having been exposed to this name, they sometimes believe that Sebastian Weisdorf is the name of a famous person. The only way to overcome the illusion is by recollecting the prior exposure to that name in the laboratory. The elderly are especially susceptible to the false fame effect. Because they are less able than young adults to recollect that they encountered the name in an experimental list, but still feel that they know it, they are more likely than younger adults to claim that the name is famous. Similarly, after studying such words as *taste, chocolate, candy, sugar,* and other strong associates of a nonstudied word (*sweet*), older adults are somewhat less likely than younger people to remember the words that were actually presented but are at least as likely to show false recognition of *sweet,* perhaps because they are especially prone to mixing up whether they merely thought about *sweet* or actually studied it (see chapter 4).[18]

These kinds of confusions could raise questions about the elderly person's ability to serve as an effective eyewitness. Recall that the memory of eyewitnesses can be badly skewed when they are asked misleading questions. After seeing a videotaped event, people who are asked a question about an episode that did not occur in the video sometimes incorporate this "misinformation" into their memory of the event. One reason why this occurs is that people forget the source of the misinformation; they cannot remember whether it was part of the original event or something they learned about when they were asked questions about the event. If impaired source memory makes a person vulnerable to being misled by bogus information, then elderly adults should be especially susceptible to the misinformation effect— and they are. Does this mean that an elderly adult's testimony in court should be viewed with skepticism? Not necessarily. There are large differences in levels of explicit memory among older people, and many perform just as well as, or better than, young adults. While older adults on average have difficulty remembering source information, this does not indicate that any particular elderly eyewitness is less reliable than a younger one.[19]

Recalling source information is an important component of our subjective experience of remembering past events. When we recollect who told us something, or other details of an episode, our subjective experience will likely involve "remembering." When we recall only an isolated fact, however, our subjective experience will likely involve "just knowing" that something is familiar. When asked to recollect recent episodes, older adults report less "visual reexperiencing" of the episodes than do younger adults.[20] And older adults are also less likely than younger people to say that they "remember" having encountered words or phrases they studied several minutes earlier; they tend to say that they "just know" that the item appeared earlier. This age-related deficit in the subjective experience of remembering is not just a matter of old people lacking confidence in their memories. The elderly are just as confident about their "remember" or "know" judgments as young people are; but they report fewer "remember" experiences than the young. In everyday life, this may mean that older adults' recollections of recent events will be rather sketchy and incomplete, even though they are certain that an event has occurred. As with age-related source memory problems, the frontal lobes play a role in an older person's recollective experience. Elderly adults who make many "remember" judgments tend to do better on tests that are sensitive to frontal lobe impairment than do those who make fewer "remember" judgments.[21]

All this evidence suggests that frontal lobe impairments lead to age-related difficulties in recalling and pulling together the diverse elements that constitute an everyday episode: what happened, when it happened, and who said what. The result is that older adults' recollective experience of recent events is less vivid than younger adults' recollective experience, and they are especially vulnerable to illusions of memory.

These frontally based problems also relate to the effects of aging on working memory—the mental workspace we use to hold information temporarily as we carry out ordinary cognitive tasks like reasoning and comprehending. Try to read a couple of sentences in this book while at the same time holding on to the digit sequence "5–9–4–2–8–6." To do both tasks at once, you will need to draw on all the working memory capacity you have available. When the working memory of older adults is taxed in ways similar to this, they perform much more poorly than young people.

This is probably because the frontal lobes play a key role in the working memory system, and are called on when we must actively work to maintain information across a delay. Patients who have suffered strokes or other kinds of direct damage to the frontal lobes have great difficulty when their working memories are taxed. In a PET scanning study carried out by the neuropsychologist Michael Petrides and his colleagues, healthy volunteers held in working memory recently presented pictures of designs as they tried to point to new pictures that had not been shown earlier—a task that is failed by patients with damage to dorsolateral frontal regions. Compared to a control condition, PET scans revealed activation in a specific part of the dorsolateral frontal region during the working memory task. Another PET scanning study has shown that a specific area in the lower part of the right frontal lobe becomes active when healthy people hold in working memory the location of several dots, whereas a lower part of the left frontal region becomes active when they use working memory to remember the exact shape of a geometric pattern.[22]

These linkages among the frontal lobes, working memory, and aging have been strengthened in experiments with monkeys by the neuroscientist Patricia Goldman-Rakic. When the animals view a visual pattern that suddenly disappears, and maintain a memory of its location across delays of several seconds, specific clusters of neurons in a part of the dorsolateral frontal region called the principal sulcus remain active. When the animals maintain a memory of the pattern itself, neurons just below the principal sulcus become active. These neurons seem to be "working" to allow the animal to remember the location or the pattern. Goldman-Rakic and her colleagues have recently shown that the activity of some frontal lobe neurons involved in working memory is regulated by a specific receptor for the neurotransmitter dopamine, one of the brain's major chemical messengers. Other work from Goldman-Rakic's laboratory indicates that working memory impairments in older monkeys are linked to age-related losses of this dopamine receptor.

Studies of elderly people have revealed that aging produces large decreases in precisely the same type of dopamine receptor. This suggests that age-related working memory deficits could result from low levels of dopamine receptors in frontal regions that are crucial for working memory. The idea is further buttressed by studies that have revealed working memory deficits in two other conditions that are both associated with dopamine abnormalities: schizophrenia and Parkinson's disease. Although the psychotic symptoms of schizophrenic patients and the tremors of Parkinson's patients render these conditions very different from each other and from normal aging, all three may be linked by dopamine abnormalities in the frontal lobes that result in impaired performance when working memory is needed to hold information as other cognitive activities proceed.[23]

In contrast to the problems they have when working memory is heavily taxed, older adults can remember nearly as many digits as young people when they repeat the numbers immediately and don't have to concentrate on anything else. This is probably because retaining the digit string alone involves primarily a small part of the working memory that I earlier called the phonological loop, which does not depend crucially on frontal regions.[24]

As we have seen, then, age-related changes in frontal lobe function have far-reaching consequences. There is still some good news about aging memory, however. For one, when older adults are guided to use preexisting knowledge to encode new information elaboratively and distinctively, and are later given cues that help them regenerate their encodings, age-related differences in recall memory largely disappear. As we age, we may need to do extra work both during encoding and during retrieval in order to remember recent experiences as often as we once did, but if we make the effort we will be rewarded with enhanced retention. We can still benefit from elaborative encoding when we grow old because semantic memory holds up well with age. Our abilities to call on our enormous networks of facts and associations are generally well preserved. We also retain the capacity to use our semantic knowledge to make inferences and solve problems. For example, elderly chess players are just as capable as young ones of searching their knowledge base to choose and evaluate moves. Semantic memory is not totally impervious to aging—elderly adults commonly have problems retrieving the names of people and objects—but on balance it is less affected than episodic memory.[25]

Another piece of good news is that the implicit form of memory known as priming generally holds up well as we age. This makes sense in light of everything I have just said, because the implicit memory tests that researchers use to assess priming do not require people to remember source information or to engage in strategic retrieval; instead, people are encouraged to say the first thing that pops into their minds. Many experiments have examined how aging affects priming, using tests ranging from completion of fragmented words to making decisions about quickly flashed pictures of objects. The general outcome is that older adults show either as much priming as young people or a little bit less.[26] In a recent PET scanning study, our research group investigated brain regions associated with priming in older adults. After studying a list of common words, such as *table* or *garden,* elderly adults saw three-letter word beginnings, such as tab—— and gar——, and were asked to say the first word that came to mind. With young people, priming on this stem-completion test is associated with blood flow decreases in the occipital lobes, which I earlier linked with the perceptual representation system (PRS) that plays an important role in various priming effects. Our older participants showed the same amount of priming as our younger participants, and also showed associated blood flow decreases in the occipital lobes (perhaps reflecting that the PRS had to do less work to recognize cues that had already been primed). The PRS seems to hold up well with aging.[27]

The news on procedural memory—the system that allows us to acquire various kinds of skills—is more mixed. Contrary to the cliché that we can't teach an old dog new tricks, some studies of procedural learning show that older adults can develop new skills with practice. They are even capable of acquiring some complex new implicit knowledge. For example, Darlene Howard and her associates had old and young people carry out a task I mentioned earlier (chapter 6) in which they push a button as quickly as they can whenever an asterisk appears in one of several locations on a computer screen. Unknown to the subjects, the asterisks sometimes appear, one after another, in a recurring pattern. When such a sequential pattern is present, both old and young people respond more quickly to the asterisk prompts than when no pattern is present. Yet older adults have more difficulty than young people predicting where an asterisk will appear next; they have acquired implicit but not explicit knowledge of the sequence.[28]

Other studies have shown, however, that older adults are not as adept as young people at acquiring motor skills, learning how to read upside-down words, or developing the cognitive skill involved in solving a puzzle efficiently. Part of the problem may be that older adults are generally slower than young people, and so take longer to acquire new skills. Part may also reside in the fact that some procedural memory tasks draw heavily on the frontal lobes. For instance, in a problem-solving task known as the Tower of Hanoi puzzle, people are faced with learning how to move a set of rings from one of three pegs to another peg according to specific rules. With practice, people become progressively more efficient at moving the rings using the minimum possible number of steps. Some amnesic patients can learn a simple version of this task as well as age-matched controls. But older adults require more trials than young people to solve the puzzle in the minimum number of moves—probably because learning to solve the puzzle depends on some of the effortful, strategic processes that are subserved by the frontal lobes. Just as older adults have a hard time recalling all the different parts of an episode, they may also have problems assembling all the different components of a cognitive skill. The neuropsychologist Arthur Shimamura suggests that these difficulties arise because the frontal lobes serve to inhibit thoughts and associations that are irrelevant to carrying out the task at hand. We have already seen that too much inhibition may lead to amnesia (chapter 8), but too little inhibition is also a problem. Patients with frontal lobe damage, and perhaps some elderly adults, are plagued by extraneous thoughts and associations that distract them during demanding tasks like acquiring a complex new skill or recalling multiple aspects of a past episode.[29]

Recent research has identified another, previously unsuspected, manifestation of the fact that older people often have difficulty recalling all the pieces of an episode: aging reduces the incidence of flashbulb memories. As part of a study I considered earlier on flashbulb memories of Margaret Thatcher's resignation, Martin Conway and collaborators asked elderly British adults how they learned about the news. When tested several days after the resignation, the elderly had no problems describing where they were and providing other salient details. When tested a year later, however, the recollections of only 42 percent of elderly participants met the criterion for flashbulb memories, whereas 90 percent of young people's recollections met the criterion.

The relative absence of flashbulb memories in the elderly fits well with other evidence on age-related deficits in remembering source information, because a flashbulb memory, by definition, includes details about its source. These results also suggest that as we age, we may be less likely to form and retain vivid memories of emotionally arousing events. Remarkably, next to nothing is known about encoding and retrieval of emotional memories in elderly adults. Older adults, like younger people, do remember more from the emotionally arousing parts of a story than from the mundane parts. But this may be due to the fact that the arousing parts of a story induce older adults to carry out effective semantic elaborations, because studies have also shown that the vividness of a memory in older people is not as closely related to emotional arousal as it is in young people.[30]

These studies confirm my earlier suggestion that as we age, the richness of our memories for what happened last week or last month declines. We "remember" fewer details of recent experiences and rely more on general feelings of familiarity. This may be one reason why older adults often prefer to focus on events from the distant past. Tracy Kidder's book *Old Friends,* which presents a poignant portrait of life in a nursing home for the aged, describes the day-to-day activities of a man in his nineties, Lou, who relates memories of his distant past to his roommate, Joe, or to anyone else who will listen. Yet Lou's memories of ongoing events and the tasks of daily life are spotty. He does not recall the names and functions of his many medicines, and he typically forgets earlier occasions on which he had reminisced about a particular incident, which leads to numerous retellings of the same stories. It is perhaps fitting that the fragility of his memory for recent events, which leads him to tell the same stories over and over, adds to the power of his tales about the distant past: "Heard only twice, Lou's memories could seem monotonous. Heard many times, they were like old friends. They were comforting. . . . Lou's memories contained such a density of life that in their presence death seemed impossible."[31]

REVIEWING A LIFE
Intensifying Memory's Power

Rosemary Pittman was born in 1916 on a farm in rural Illinois. She received a degree in nursing and went on to hold high-level positions in public health as well as a teaching position at the University of Washington in Seattle. Pittman occasionally dabbled in painting throughout her adult life, but did not pursue it seriously until after her retirement in 1981. She then began to feel a pressing need to conjure up, make sense of, and reexperience her past. Pittman found that she could do so most effectively by painting her recollections of the distant episodes and events that meant the most to her: childhood days on the farm, without electricity or running water; the one-room schoolhouse she attended; and cherished family moments from different times in her life. She developed rapidly as an artist, and her memory paintings became a powerful means of exploring her past experiences and understanding how they relate to her present life: "I found that while I loved much of the abstract art I was really most satisfied when I created something related to my past life and personal experiences and relationships. Art to me is a sort of therapy, a visual reminiscence." She adds that "[a]s one ages, one becomes more preoccupied with who one is than what one does. You wish to recapture those people, events and places that helped to define you as a unique person."[32] She illustrates this process in her painting "Grandchildren #1" (figure 10.2).

Pittman is one of many elderly adults who have embraced art late in life and used it as a tool to excavate and understand their memories. Indeed, the genre known as "memory painting"—depicting in paint personal recollections of one's past—is dominated by older adults who often lack formal artistic training, but who, like Pittman, have a need to recapture their personal pasts. Bluma Purmell, a memory painter in her nineties, commented: "Nine years ago, when I turned 83, I decided to become a painter. Detailed scenes were projecting themselves in my mind, windows of the past, waiting to be opened."[33] Other elderly adults have created memory sculptures, quilts, and baskets in order to represent and recapture their reminiscences.

These artistic explorations exemplify the increasing focus on the past that often accompanies aging. Upon entering the later decades of life, many people feel compelled to draw upon autobiographical memories more often and intensely than they had in earlier days. Yet most Western societies have devalued reminiscing by the use of pejorative phrases such as "living in the past" and by the characterization of reminiscence as an age-related pathology. Professionals working with the elderly were traditionally taught to discourage reminiscence. "It was even said that 'remembrance of things past' could cause or deepen depression among our residents," reflected Rose Dobrof, a social worker who worked with the institutionalized elderly during the 1960s, "and God forgive us, we were to divert the old from their reminiscing through activities like bingo and arts and crafts."[34]

Though this deeply held attitude may still be prevalent in our society, research conducted over the past several decades has shown that it represents a misguided view of aging memory. The initial seeds of change were sown during the 1960s, as gerontologists increasingly began to recognize the potential value of reminiscence in old age. Rather than denigrating the elderly adult's preoccupation with the

FIGURE 10.2

Rosemary Pittman, "Grandchildren #1," 1991. 12 x 23½". Acrylic on board. MIA Gallery, Seattle.

In each of the eighteen squares, Pittman paints a memory of an episode involving one of her grandchildren when they were young: an encounter with Santa Claus, a visit to the zoo, a walk in the stroller, and so forth. She has managed to gather up different moments in time that are important to her and to join them together in space to create a tapestry of memory. The painting is both an expression of her need to revisit her past and an aid to reviewing it further.

past, researchers began to conceptualize it as part of a life review—a reminiscence-based process of coming to terms with one's life that can aid understanding and integration of the self, and perhaps enhance preparation for death. The potential usefulness of life review was suggested by research findings indicating that older adults who tend to reminisce are less likely to exhibit depression and more likely to show signs of mental health than those who do not. This optimistic result was not, however, universally obtained. Recent evidence indicates that the adaptive benefit of reminiscing depends on the exact type of reminiscence in which an elder engages. For instance, reminiscences that either glorify the past or reflect persisting guilt over distant events are not associated with successful aging, whereas reminiscences that focus on previous plans and goals, or on reconciling past and present, are.[35]

Based on the swelling enthusiasm for the potential value of life review, and the findings that linked reminiscence with mental health in the elderly, a new wave of "reminiscence therapies" have emerged that attempt to enhance psychological functioning by promoting life review in older adults. Relatively few controlled studies have assessed the effectiveness of such therapies, so it is important not to get swept away by an uncritical acceptance of the idea that reminiscing is a kind of mnemonic panacea for the elderly. But the widespread usage of reminiscence as a therapeutic tool constitutes a recognition of memory's power in old age, and testifies to the fact that older adults are no longer encouraged to avoid or abandon their pasts.

Which aspects of their personal pasts do elderly adults remember when they engage in life review? One way that researchers have addressed this question is by using the Crovitz autobiographical cueing procedure I have described. Older adults are given familiar words such as *flag* or *run,* and then asked to provide a memory of a specific event from anytime in their lives. As you may remember from chapter 3, the typical finding with younger adults is that most memories come from the recent past, and progressively fewer come from the more distant past. Older adults, too, remember fewer and fewer personal experiences from the more and more distant past, with one curious exception: the gradual decline in memories over time shows a temporary reversal around late adolescence and early adulthood. The elderly recall more experiences from these years than from those immediately following, but then the curve resumes its gradual decline into the years of childhood.

The same sort of outcome occurs when older adults are given a different recall task. Try to remember three experiences from your life that were so compelling and so personally significant that you feel even today that you have a vivid and detailed memory of the events. When in your life did these three experiences occur? When elderly adults were asked to perform this task, they provided more vivid memories from the years of adolescence and early adulthood than from any other time period.

The enhanced memorability of experiences from late adolescence and early adulthood is an exception to the rule that memories become gradually less accessible with the passage of time. Researchers have given it a special name—the reminiscence bump—in order to highlight that this blip in the forgetting curve reflects an increased tendency to reminisce about experiences that occurred during a restricted time span.[36] The existence of the bump appears to be widespread among the elderly, as realized by Littlejohn McCain in Howard Owen's novel: "It's funny how, looking back at it, there's whole big chunks of my life that I don't remember too much about. Just work, eat and sleep. And there's places where something seemed like it was happening all the time. My fifteenth and sixteenth years was like that."[37]

There is no single, agreed-upon explanation of why the reminiscence bump occurs. I believe, however, that its nature and existence may provide clues concerning the power of the distant past in the lives of many elderly adults. To understand what the reminiscence bump may be telling us about memory and aging, we need to know more about what is remembered from the years of late adolescence and early adulthood. The oral historian Alice Hoffman and her husband, the experimental psychologist Howard Hoffman, have performed an unusual collaborative study that provides a unique window on this issue. Howard, born in 1925, was drafted at age eighteen to serve as a soldier in World War II. Over thirty years after the war's conclusion, Alice began probing Howard's memories for his wartime experiences in a series of interviews separated by intervals of several years. The Hoffmans were able to recover a company log that recorded much of what actually happened during the period, as well as other official documents and photographs that provided an external check on Howard's recollections.

For the most part, the experiences Howard remembered were recalled accurately and consistently. When asked about the same events on different occasions, separated by as much as four years, Howard remembered them in pretty much the same way. Attempts to cue Howard's memory via photographs, documents, and conversations with old army buddies yielded little above and beyond what he was able to provide on his own—a sharp contrast to the common observation that retrieval cues aid explicit memory. A subset of Howard's most salient wartime experiences had been extensively rehearsed and elaborated almost from the moment of their occurrence, a process that continued over subsequent years and decades. Other experiences that were not talked about dropped out of the picture.[38]

I have already considered the idea that extensively rehearsed and elaborated memories come to form the core of our life stories—narratives of self that help us define and understand our identity and our place in the world. The experiences of late adolescence and early adulthood—going to high school or college, beginning a job or career, entering into marriage—may provide the core of the emerging adult life story that we carry around with us, largely unchanged, for the remainder of our adult lives. For Howard Hoffman and others of his generation, the experiences of World War II no doubt played a central role in their emerging adult identities and personal myths.

We can understand more fully the power that these highly accessible life stories may wield in the psychological landscape of the elderly by considering them in relation to the problems that older people have remembering recent experiences. I have suggested that these difficulties arise, at least in part, because older adults do not recall in unison all of the sights, sounds, and meanings of ongoing episodes as effectively as they once did. But the narratives of self that were established in the distant past have been told and retold many times, making it easy for the older adults to recall together all the components of an episode. Recollecting a familiar life story probably does not require the kinds of contributions from frontal and medial temporal brain systems that are crucial to creating and accessing memories for recent experiences.

This conception of memory's fragile power in old age may shed some light on a cognitive function that older adults appear to perform more effectively than younger adults: telling stories. You may remember a favorite grandparent, aunt, or uncle whose stories of their personal past were so spellbinding that you felt as though you could sit and listen to them for hours. I can remember relishing the tales told by my grandfather Benjamin Flanzig, a Jewish immigrant from Russia who landed in New York City during the early years of the twentieth century. He was a large, strapping man who loved nothing better than captivating his grandchildren with stories of his travels as a young man, when he experienced adventures of all manner in far-off places that he described in colorful detail. We knew him as Grandpa Ben, and some of his stories verged on the unbelievable. In one of them, he was kidnapped from a train in Pennsylvania and forced to labor in a mountain camp until he managed to escape.

In another, he worked as a cowboy on a ranch in Wyoming. But even when Grandpa Ben told much more mundane tales of selling hats in "Ioway" or going to baseball games in "Cincinattuh," his memories came alive with a sparkling quality that was irresistible. The stories that my parents told of their own pasts never quite reached the magical level that Grandpa Ben seemed to achieve so effortlessly.

Recent research has confirmed what anyone who had listened carefully to my Grandpa Ben would have predicted. When older and younger adults were asked to tell some personal stories from anytime in their pasts, raters who read the narratives judged the elderly's stories to be of higher quality—more engaging and dramatic—than those of the young. In another similar study, the elderly told more complexly organized stories than did the young. When old and young adults had to retell an unfamiliar story that they had just heard for the first time, however, elderly adults recalled less of the story, told it less cohesively, and made more errors in retelling it than did the young. As long as they can tell the familiar stories that they have told many times before, older adults seem to do a better job of it than younger adults. But when they are required to tell a new story, the quality of the retelling is undermined by the sorts of explicit memory problems that I outlined earlier in the chapter.[39]

AGING STORYTELLERS
Bridging Generational Time

The storytelling abilities of elderly adults have important social and cultural implications. In many societies, the primary function of elderly adults is to pass on significant personal and cultural lore to younger members of the group—to tell stories about their own experiences and about the traditions and momentous events of the society. Because many of the autobiographical memories of the elderly and the collective memories of society derive from the remote past, older adults can draw freely on these highly elaborated and structured memories. They can use their storytelling abilities to the fullest, unimpeded by difficulties that arise when they attempt to remember recent events. This storytelling function of old people is not fully appreciated

in American and other contemporary Western societies, where negative stereotypes of aging are unfortunately all too common. It is far
more prominent in many tribal societies with richly developed oral
traditions, where the stories and knowledge of the elderly are seen as
manifestations of wisdom that command special respect.[40]

The history of Native North Americans provides a harsh contrast
between these two perspectives. Elders in Native American tribes
were traditionally viewed with deference as sources of cultural memories that provide essential guidelines for numerous aspects of tribal
life. These intergenerational memories frequently take the form of
creation stories that are passed down from generation to generation
by tribal elders, containing vital lessons about the origin of the tribe,
how to behave toward others, hunt, prepare food, relate to animals,
treat the environment, and so forth. One such creation story told by
a Seneca elder is referred to as "the remembering." People who take
to heart the lessons of the remembering prosper and lead happy lives,
but those arrogant enough to ignore the stories of their elders are ultimately doomed to repeating the mistakes of the past. "The remembering could not serve those whose self-importance had blocked the
Knowing Systems of the Ancestors who had created the memories,"
according to the elderly storyteller. "For those still living in harmony,
a new understanding had been added to the memories." N. Scott
Momaday, a Native American and one of the world's preeminent
writers, reflected on his own encounters with a storytelling tribal
elder: "It did not seem possible that so many years—a century of
years—could be so compacted and distilled. An old whimsy, a delight
in language and in remembrance, shone in her one good eye. She con-
jured up the past, imagining perfectly the long continuity of her
being."[41]

Tragically, the imposition of Western culture and religion that
destroyed so much of Native life had a devastating effect on the
respect accorded, and role played by, traditional modes of remembering that centered on the stories of elders. "With this replacing of long-
held tribal religious values," comments a prominent Native scholar,
"the Indians lost the basis of their old ways of life and, just as importantly, their old ways of remembering. . . . Protestant and Mormon
missionaries still appear to be working overtime to eradicate native
tribal religions, by seeking to subvert the long-honored wisdom of
medicine-makers and elders of tribes."[42]

The Canadian artist Carl Beam, a member of the Ojibwa tribe, has
created powerful artworks that explore the loss of memory and

decline of the storytelling elder in Native life. Beam has struggled for years to integrate his Native heritage with his experiences as a member of modern Western society, as reflected in "Remembering is sometimes quite difficult to do. . ." (figure 10.3) and "School Days" (figure 10.4).[43] Beam seeks to redress cultural amnesia by reminding Natives and non-Natives alike that it is centrally important to integrate personal and collective pasts with the concerns of the present. The decline of the aging storyteller in Native life led to a break in the chain of intergenerational memory that had disastrous consequences for many. These considerations highlight that a crucial task for elderly adults is to integrate the past with the present. In the arena of social and cultural memory, the experience and knowledge of the elder can serve as a guide to the future for succeeding generations; in the arena of personal memory, the elderly adult's life review provides an opportunity to reflect on the past in the context of the present.

This integrative role is nowhere illustrated more poignantly than by the struggles of aging survivors of the Holocaust. As they approach the conclusion of their lives, many elderly survivors have not successfully integrated the traumas of the Holocaust into a more encompassing life story. The psychotherapist Yael Danieli has written eloquently about the "conspiracy of silence" that made it difficult for survivors to integrate their Holocaust experiences with the rest of their lives. Unable to mourn their losses and to feel that others understood their experiences, the survivors' memories of the Holocaust remained cut off from other knowledge and recollections.[44]

The process of life review that is important for many elders thus becomes utterly urgent for aging Holocaust survivors. Placing these experiences in proper perspective is essential, Danieli reflects, if survivors are to understand that their feelings of helplessness do not mean that they are helpless people, or that their memories of evil events do not necessarily mean that the world is evil. Integrating traumatic experiences into a broader life story is also necessary to ensure that the intergenerational chain of memory is not broken.[45]

As the realization has dawned that only limited time remains for the last generation of eyewitnesses to the Holocaust, attempts to preserve their legacies through memorials and videotapes have become more widespread. Danieli highlights that a central preoccupation of aging survivors focuses on the intergenerational extension of remembering: "For the survivor, essential components of the aging person's preoccupation with 'Who loves me?' 'Who cares if I live' . . . are the

FIGURE 10.3

**Carl Beam, "Remembering is sometimes quite difficult to do . . . ,"
1992. 14 x 10". Mixed media on plexiglass. Courtesy of the artist.**

Beam prints the title of the piece below a degraded photographic image of an antediluvian tribal ritual—the kind of intergenerational memory that is now barely known to many younger Ojibwa. A pristine image of a feather serves as a reminder of the tribal memories that are lost to the present generation.

FIGURE 10.4

Carl Beam, "School Days," 1991. 60 x 42". Mixed media on paper. Courtesy of the artist.

Beam's own handwriting, scrawled above a faded photograph of Native children in front of a school that resembles one he attended, relates a bitter reminiscence of when his teachers commanded him to worship a new God and forget the stories of past generations passed on by his elders. Instead, he was encouraged to become a young patriot and to embrace modern technology and warfare, as alluded to by the images of tanks and trains at the bottom of the piece.

devastating questions 'Who will remember me?' 'Will the memory of my people and of the Holocaust perish?' "[46]

The need to preserve memories across intergenerational time, though accentuated in aging Holocaust survivors, is a fundamental human imperative. Remember Proust and Magnani: their unrelenting obsessions with the past emerged in part from a deep desire to impart their recollections of Combray and Pontito to a larger network of rememberers who could keep these memories alive in the future. As the psychologist Merlin Donald has argued persuasively, a crucial step in the evolution of modern culture involves its increasing reliance on "external symbolic storage" for conserving and transmitting memories across generations.[47] Beginning with the development of the earliest writing systems, and progressing more rapidly with the invention of the printing press, modern societies have relied increasingly on print and electronic media to preserve memory. It is no coincidence that the mnemonic systems I discussed in chapter 2—once essential strands in the fabric of society—largely disappeared after printed storage media became available on a widespread basis.

As reliance on external storage devices has increased, the transmission of socially significant knowledge and events has relied less and less on the autobiographical recollections of elders. This may have contributed to what has been termed a "crisis of memory."[48] Beginning in the nineteenth century and exacerbated dramatically by the recent ascendance of electronic media, the crisis of memory involves a progressive sense of disconnection from the past and traditional forms of remembering. Society's most important memories now reside in the electronic archives of the mass media, not in the heads of individual rememberers and storytellers. With such immense amounts of information electronically coded and readily available, the memory-preserving role of elders with stories to tell and knowledge to impart has been diminished considerably.

It need not be that way, however. Intensified efforts to seek and videotape the oral histories of Holocaust survivors bring the personal recollections of the elderly into direct contact with contemporary external storage technology. The autobiographical stories of these elders can perhaps achieve, through electronic recording, the kind of immortality once conferred by more traditional means of oral transmission. And preserving testimonies from thousands of rememberers can help to ensure that forgetting and distortion—which can infiltrate any individual rememberer's story—are counteracted by the overwhelming truths that emerge from core elements that are shared by numerous rememberers.

Elderly adults are also intimately involved with another form of external memory storage: family photographs. Photos serve as cues to autobiographical recollections for just about everyone—an insight not lost on film and camera merchants, who run a virtual memory industry. But older people tend to value family photos as their single most cherished possession, whereas younger people rank them as less important. Older people typically say that they cherish photos primarily because of their memory-cueing functions: photos allow the elderly to make contact with, and even relive, parts of their personal pasts. My colleagues and I have recently carried out experiments in which we have found that looking at photos enhances recollective experience in elderly adults.[49] Photographs of events and people from the past make it easier for older adults to assume their time-honored role as storytellers.

It is perhaps fitting that the external media in which we pass on our personal memories—including family photos, portraits, and other heirlooms—are in some ways characterized by the fragile power that I have focused on as such an essential feature of human memories. These physical traces of the past may fade, decay, and even change over time, but they nonetheless exude a compelling emotional aura. Ben Freeman has managed to convey this realization with uncommon eloquence and force. Once an abstract painter, Freeman found himself increasingly drawn to the old photos and family heirlooms that he collected during excursions to antique shops and flea markets. He became fascinated by what he calls "the chemistry between time and our attempts to resist its passage by immortalizing events or moments in enshrinements of objects, images, and concepts." Though faded and tarnished, the images and objects he encountered spoke with undeniable force about the people whose lives they were once part of and now commemorate. For Freeman, these externalized memories are "a crying out to the future to say that we did exist and that we were important." He describes them in a way that also fits the traces of the past that exist inside our heads. "As these enshrinements become veiled by time," Freeman observes, "they lose their clarity, definition and meaning but retain a visceral presence which carries the energy and culture of the moment in which they were created."[50]

Captivated by the physical traces of our lives that we leave behind in treasured objects, Freeman abandoned his abstract canvases and started to construct large-scale paintings that incorporate old photos, family heirlooms, and yellowing maps. They are visually stunning and emotionally resonant works that speak to many of the themes I have

FIGURE 10.5

Ben Freeman, "Commitment," 1992. 66 x 72". Mixed media. Barbara Krakow Gallery, Boston.

The centerpiece of this work is a nineteenth-century family photograph, shown both in its unadorned form and also blown up, painted over, and veiled. Fragments of the family's past surround these two images: small photos of unknown people, possibly relatives; a picture of the family residence; a bleached map of Boston, where they lived; a page torn from a farmer's almanac; and a stamped postcard with a barely decipherable message written on it. These aged objects manage to convey a feeling for the richness of a past whose particulars remain hidden from us.

considered in this book, as exemplified by his haunting painting "Commitment" (figure 10.5).

Like the objects in which we attempt to preserve the past, the fragile power of memory provides us with a general sense of who we are and where we have been, even though it hides many of the specific incidents that helped shape us. We may be profoundly moved by experiences that we remember inaccurately, or by illusory memories of events we only feared or imagined. Our thoughts and actions are sometimes influenced implicitly by incidents that we do not recollect at all. And many of the specific episodes in our lives have vanished from our memories forever. On balance, however, our memory systems do a remarkably good job of preserving the general contours of our pasts and of recording correctly many of the important things that have happened to us. We could not have evolved as a species otherwise. Memory is a central part of the brain's attempt to make sense of experience, and to tell coherent stories about it. These tales are all we have of our pasts, and so they are potent determinants of how we view ourselves and what we do. Yet our stories are built from many different ingredients: snippets of what actually happened, thoughts about what might have happened, and beliefs that guide us as we attempt to remember. Our memories are the fragile but powerful products of what we recall from the past, believe about the present, and imagine about the future.

NOTES

INTRODUCTION
Memory's Fragile Power

1. Quotes are from Márquez (1970), pp. 50, 53.
2. Bellow (1989), p. 2.
3. For evolutionary perspectives on memory, see Donald (1991), Rozin (1976), and Sherry and Schacter (1987). Adopting an evolutionary perspective need not imply that memory must be perfect or optimal. Evolutionary analyses of related abilities, such as vision (Tooby & Cosmides, 1995) and language (Pinker & Bloom, 1992), acknowledge imperfections in these processes, yet at the same time emphasize the extraordinary accomplishments of the cognitive adaptations that allow us to see and communicate.
4. The psychologists Jefferson Singer and Peter Salovey were astonished when they observed this remarkably potent influence of the past on present emotions through the agency of memory. "How could [recall of] a given memory have the affective power to induce physiological responses of such magnitude that subjects could be moved to tears, giggles, or trembling fear . . . ?" they ask. "Far from taking the phenomenon for granted, we were stunned by it." See Singer and Salovey (1993), p. 14.
5. Stadler (1990), p. 144.
6. The original statement of the implicit/explicit memory distinction was made by Graf and Schacter (1985).

   Several other distinctions in the literature are similar to the implicit/explicit distinction, including the contrast between declarative and nondeclarative memory (Squire, 1992, 1994) and direct and indirect tests of memory (Richardson-Klavehn & Bjork, 1988).

   Much of the contemporary interest in multiple memory systems derives from the distinction between episodic and semantic memory advanced by Tulving (1972), as well as from other seminal distinctions put forward during the 1970s (Hirsh, 1974; O'Keefe & Nadel, 1978). For an overview of research on memory systems, see the collection of chapters edited by Schacter and Tulving (1994).

   When discussing multiple forms of memory, it is easy to become confused by the different terms that are used by various researchers. In this book, I use the terms *implicit memory* and *explicit memory* in a descriptive manner, to refer to different ways in which the effects of prior experience can be retrieved and expressed. In contrast, I use such terms as *episodic memory, semantic memory, procedural memory, perceptual representation system,* and *working memory* to refer to underlying brain systems that are involved in implicit retrieval, explicit retrieval, or both.

7. My collection of memory-related artworks, which I have developed jointly with my wife, Susan McGlynn, formed the basis for a show and exhibition catalog at the Newton Arts Center in October 1993, entitled "Fragile Power: Explorations of Memory." All artworks reproduced in this book, except for Magritte's "The Menaced Assassin" (figure 2.2), are part of our collection. The development of this collection is discussed by White (1993) from a sociological perspective.

CHAPTER 1
On Remembering: "A Telescope Pointed at Time"

1. The *Boston Globe's* special section on the Boston Garden, including Will McDonough's column, appeared on April 30, 1995.

2. Bellow (1989), p. 53.

3. The quote is from Tulving (1983), p. 127, who provides an in-depth analysis of psychological research on episodic memory. Over a century ago, the great Harvard psychologist and philosopher William James (1890) made a similar point: "Memory requires more than mere dating of a fact in the past. It must be dated in *my* past. In other words, I must think that I directly experienced its occurrence" (p. 650). James added that personal recollections have a "warmth and intimacy" that identify them as a "property" of the self.

4. For a useful historical discussion of psychological and philosophical perspectives on subjective experiences of remembering, see Brewer (1996).

5. Walters shared her thoughts with me in an interview on August 7, 1992. The quoted material is from the exhibition catalog for "11 Artists/11 Visions: 1992" at the DeCordova Museum, Lincoln, Massachusetts.

6. Freud (1899).

7. This experiment is reported in Nigro and Neisser (1983).

8. The experiment is reported in Robinson and Swanson (1993). It is not entirely clear why switching from the field to the observer perspective, but not vice versa, influences subjective emotional experience, but Robinson and Swanson (1993, pp. 181–182) discuss several possibilities.

9. The distinction between "remembering" and "knowing" was introduced to the psychological literature by Tulving (1985). This distinction is quite similar to those between recollection and familiarity made by Mandler (1980), Jacoby and Dallas (1981), and others. The "beeper" experiment is described in Brewer (1988). More recently, Dewhurst and Conway (1994) provided evidence from a more tightly controlled series of laboratory experiments that confirms the importance of visual information in the experience of recollection.

10. For a thorough documentation of this point, see Kosslyn (1994).

11. Johnson, Raye, Wang, and Taylor (1979) showed that the more often college students imagined seeing a picture, the more often they later claimed to remember having seen it. Hyman and Pentland (1996) found that instructing people to imagine childhood events increased the likelihood that they would generate a false memory of an event that never happened (see chapter 4). Garry et al. (1996) report that imagining an event increases college students' confidence that the imagined experience happened to them.

12. The article is by Block (1995).

13. The experiment concerning the effects of briefly flashed words is described by Rajaram (1993) and the study on divided attention and memory for faces is reported by Parkin, Gardiner, and Rosser (1995). Previous studies by Gardiner and colleagues showed that dividing attention when experimental participants study a list of words reduces the likelihood of later "remembering" that the words were presented, but has little effect on "knowing" that the words were presented. Gardiner has also shown that extensive analysis of words during the study phase of an experiment enhances subsequent "remember" responses but does not increase "know" responses. Gardiner's experiments are summarized in Gardiner and Java (1993).

    On the basis of numerous findings showing that experimental manipulations affect "remember" and "know" responses differently, Gardiner and colleagues have argued for qualitative differences between the two forms of recollective experience. In contrast, Donaldson (1996) has recently contended that differences between remembering and knowing are largely quantitative, with "remember" simply indicating a stronger sense of familiarity than "know." Donaldson raises some important points, but it is not clear that his analysis accounts for all observed differences between remember and know responses.

14. This experiment is reported by Tulving (1985). People may be more likely to report "remember" experiences when they recall on their own (free recall) than in response to hints (cued recall) because a cued recall test is more likely than a free recall test to elicit weak or fragmentary traces that support "know" but not "remember" experiences.

15. For studies of partial recall and the feeling of knowing, see Brown and MacNeil (1966) and Schacter and Worling (1985).

16. Early evidence for the effects of cue familiarity on feeling of knowing was reported in the final experiment of my 1981 Ph.D. thesis research. I found that when people failed to recall a target word in response to a previously associated cue, they expressed a stronger feeling of knowing about the unrecalled target when the cue word seemed highly familiar than when the cue seemed unfamiliar. I never felt that the results of that final Ph.D. thesis experiment were quite convincing enough to merit publication, but subsequent work, described in Metcalfe, Schwartz, and Joaquim (1993), Reder and Ritter (1992), and the collection of readings in Metcalfe and Shimamura (1994), has shown clearly that cue familiarity affects feeling of knowing. In the experiments of Metcalfe and her colleagues, people were given cue words and they tried to recall previously associated target words. Several minutes before this recall test, they were shown half of the cue words while performing what was presented to them as an incidental, unrelated task. The key finding was that cue words that had been exposed during the incidental task produced stronger feeling-of-knowing experiences about unrecalled targets than did cue words that had not been exposed during the incidental task. Yet the unrecalled target information was not in fact any more accessible when the cues were familiar than when they were unfamiliar.

17. See Jacoby, Kelley, and Dywan (1989) for the idea that remembering involves attributions. For related ideas, see Johnson, Hashtroudi, and Lindsay (1993) and Ross (1989).

18. Proust's collection of novels is best known in English as *Remembrance of Things Past*. My reading and all quotes are based on D. J. Enright's recent revision of earlier translations by C. K. Scott Moncrief and then Terence Kilmartin. In the Enright translation (Proust, 1992), the series is titled *In Search of Lost Time*.

19. This quote and the following ones are from the most recently revised translation of *Swann's Way* (Proust, 1992, pp. 60–63).

20. This point is made eloquently in Shattuck's (1983) superb analysis of the role played by memory and time in Proust's work.

21. The letter is quoted in ibid., p. 46.

22. Ibid., pp. 46–47.

23. Magnani's story is told eloquently by the neurologist Oliver Sacks (1995), who was kind enough to put me in touch with Magnani.

24. Pearce (1988), p. 15.

25. Sacks (1995), pp. 175–177.

26. Ibid., p. 166.

27. Susan Schwartzenberg informed me in August 1995 that Magnani had nearly completed his ambitious kitchen renovation.

28. Sacks (1995), p. 186.

29. The terms *retrograde amnesia* and *anterograde amnesia* were coined in the late nineteenth century by the French physician Charles Azam, who described memory loss in a well-known case of multiple personality. See Hacking (1995) for a revealing treatment of Azam.

30. GR's case is described in detail by Lucchelli, Muggia, and Spinnler (1995). Quotes are from p. 170 of their article. In another case that they described, a man lost much of his personal past after sustaining a head injury and then suddenly recovered it a month later when a mistake that he made during a tennis match reminded him of a similar mistake that he had made years earlier. Lucchelli et al. also noted the similarity of their cases to a case of memory recovery after emotional trauma that my colleagues and I reported some years ago (Schacter et al., 1982). I tell this story in chapter 8. Kapur (in press) suggests that psychological factors played a role in the amnesia and recovery of GR and the other patient described by Lucchelli et al.

31. The dependence of the sense of self on memory is made forcefully by Singer and Salovey in their monograph, *The Remembered Self* (1993): "Although memory is perpetually taking snapshots of each and every experience that we encounter, there always emerges a core of slides to which we return repeatedly. This dog-eared bunch of slightly obscured or distorted images comes to form the central concerns of our personality. . . . Although these memories may contain but a kernel of their original truth and be filled with embellishments, false recollections, descriptions provided by others, and multiple events blended into seemingly singular occurrences, these characteristics in no way diminish their power in organizing who we are" (pp. 12–13).

32. Estes (1980) provides an illuminating discussion of similarities and differences between human and computer memories.

33. See Dennett (1991), pp. 210–214, and Penrose (1989), pp. 45–57, for different perspectives on Turing tests. Hodges (1983) provides an excellent biography of Turing.

34. For summaries of the strong AI perspective, see Crevier (1993) and Penrose (1989).

35. Dennett (1991), p. 431.

36. Perhaps the best known skeptic of strong AI is philosopher John Searle, who claims that a computer's ability to manipulate symbols by carrying out rule-based algorithms (i.e., calculation procedures) need not imply that the computer understands the symbols or is in any sense consciously aware of them. In a recent critique of Dennett's (1991) book published in *The New York Review of Books* ("The mystery of consciousness: Part II," November 16, 1995, pp. 54–61), Searle contends that Dennett denies the reality of the human subjective experience of consciousness—that is, Dennett is not so much saying that a computer could attain the type of consciousness experienced by humans as he is contending that human conscious experience is not what it seems to be. According to Searle (p. 58), Dennett "keeps the vocabulary of consciousness while denying its existence." In a subsequent letter to the *New York Review* (December 21, 1995, p. 83) that takes exception to a number of Searle's claims, Dennett does not dispute this characterization. At a recent conference I attended, however, Dennett stated in his presentation that he does not deny the existence of the subjective stream of consciousness, but does dispute the idea that there is a single place in the brain where consciousness can be found or a specific time at which information enters conscious-

ness ("First person plural: Philosophical problems of consciousness with clinical implications," New Traumatology Conference, Clearwater Beach, Florida, January 1996).

Other philosophers such as Colin McGinn argue that it is difficult to imagine how or why merely equipping a robot with appropriate software would or could produce conscious experience. And the Oxford mathematical physicist Roger Penrose has contended that the hallmark of computer intelligence—following rules and executing algorithms—does not depend on or even involve conscious awareness in either humans or computers. He suggests further that human consciousness is involved in "forming new judgments" in situations in which old rules do not apply: "The *judgement-forming* that I am claiming is the hallmark of consciousness is *itself* something that the AI people would have no concept how to program on a computer" (Penrose, 1989, p. 412). See also McGinn (1990) and Searle (1983).

37. It is interesting to note that Carnegie-Mellon computer engineer Hans Moravec, a noted proponent of strong AI, concedes that nonverbal, subjective reactions are relevant to a Turing test and acknowledges that they probably depend on hardware like that of the human brain: "Human communication is only language on the surface. What's below the language are these perceptual models of the world containing mythical allusions and pictures and emotions. There is much nonverbal machinery in our heads. A really insightful Turing judge would be probing for these things, asking 'How do you feel about this,' or 'Here is a situation, how does it strike you?' And I believe there is no more compact way of encoding that machinery than something analogous to the actual structures we have in our brains" (cited in Crevier, 1993, p. 272).

38. Edelman (1992), p. 238. In *Descartes' Error*, Antonio Damasio (1994) goes one step further and links conscious experience both with brain networks and with the body in which they are grounded.

CHAPTER 2
Building Memories: Encoding and Retrieving the Present and the Past

1. Roediger (1980) reviews spatial metaphors of memory, and Landauer (1975) describes the "garbage can" analogy. Koriat and Goldsmith (in press) contrast the storehouse metaphor of memory to an alternative metaphor that emphasizes how well remembered events correspond to the original experiences.

2. Neisser (1967), p. 285.

3. Ceci, DeSimone, and Johnson (1992) describe the case of Bubbles P. and report a series of experiments concerning his memory abilities. The importance of the "magic number" seven was described by Miller (1956).

4. Research concerning working memory has been pioneered by Baddeley (1986) and colleagues. Baddeley fractionates working memory into several subsystems: a central executive or limited capacity workspace and two "slave" subsystems, the phonological loop and a visuospatial sketch pad that temporarily holds nonverbal information. For studies of patients with damage to the phonological loop, see Vallar and Shallice (1990).

5. The term *depth of processing*, synonymous with *levels of processing*, was introduced to the psychological literature in a classic paper by Craik and Lockhart (1972).

6. For a discussion of these special techniques, known as *orienting tasks*, see Craik and Tulving (1975).

7. This finding was first reported by Craik and Tulving (1975). Other early experiments documenting the importance of elaborative encoding included those by Stein and Bransford (1979), which revealed that even subtle differences in the exact kind of elaboration that people perform can have a major impact on subsequent memory performance.

8. See Gardiner and Java (1993) for elaborative encoding and experiences of remembering and knowing.

9. See Nickerson and Adams (1979).

10. This rendition of the story of Simonides is based on Yates (1966), who provides a definitive history of the origins of mnemonics.

11. The story of mnemonics and the Middle Ages is beautifully told by Carruthers (1990). Scholarly discussions of visual imagery mnemonics and memory improvement can be found in Bellezza (1981) and Bower (1972). A popular treatment of how to use mnemonics to enhance memory function has been provided by Lorayne and Lucas (1974), among many others. Herrmann, Raybeck, and Gutman (1993) focus specifically on improving memory performance in students.

12. For the backlash against mnemonics, see J. Spence (1984), pp. 4 and 12.

13. For wide-ranging discussions of imagery, mind, and brain, see Kosslyn (1981, 1994).

14. SF's feats were later matched and exceeded by another Carnegie-Mellon runner, DD, who was able to achieve correct recall of 100 digits by using elaborative encoding strategies that were based on his knowledge of running times. For studies of SF and DD, see Chase and Ericsson (1981). A startling case of exceptional memory that differs from SF and DD involves a young man known as Rajan, who was able to remember the first 31,811 digits of pi! As described in a thorough analysis by Thompson, Cowan, and Frieman (1993), Rajan apparently did not use any conscious elaborative strategies. His exceptional memory, however, was specific to numbers. Thompson et al. provide a useful discussion of other mnemonists.

15. For studies of memory in chess, bridge, and other areas, see the collection of papers in Ericsson and Smith (1991).

16. For studies of memory in actors, see Noice and Noice (1996); quote is from p. 2. According to K. Anders Ericsson (1992), a leading investigator in this area, "The superior memory performance of experts appears to be a direct consequence of their normal meaningful encoding of information in their domain" (p. 169). For biographical studies of the acquisition of expertise, see Bloom (1985).

17. For a detailed history and discussion of JD, see Waterhouse (1988). For intriguing cases of twin idiot savants that resemble JD in some ways, see Sacks (1985).

18. The quoted texts are from Storr (1992), p. 6.

19. Gerald Edelman (1992) does a particularly good job of making this point, arguing that memories result from the ongoing activity of categorizing and recategorizing events in the world.

20. In a PET study, the volunteer is either injected with or inhales a radioactive isotope that is taken up into the brain. The isotope is unstable and consequently emits positrons (hence the term *positron emission tomography*) that enter into collisions with electrons. At the exact point of collision, gamma rays are emitted at a 180-degree angle to the point of collision. These gamma rays activate detectors in the scanner that later allow researchers to reconstruct the exact point of collision. Regions that are more active during a task have greater blood flow than regions that are less active, which brings a greater amount of the radioactive isotope and hence a greater number of positron/electron collisions. The detectors in the PET scanner register this enhanced activity, and these raw "PET counts" are ultimately transformed into images that depict "hot spots" in brain areas that are especially activated by a task.

Measurement of regional cerebral blood flow is just one approach to PET scanning; another approach involves the measurement of glucose uptake. The nature of PET techniques is discussed in an accessible manner by Posner and Raichle (1994). PET involves exposing people to a small amount of radiation, but the doses are so minuscule that the procedure poses no risks for volunteers.

21. For more information on Jerry Coker's life and art, see Harris (1995), which contains a brief essay of mine on the role of memory in Coker's work.

22. The study is described by Kapur et al. (1994). Each task lasted about a minute, which is the amount of time that it takes to complete a single PET scan. For the elaborative task, the volunteers decided whether familiar words shown during the one-minute scan refer to a living or a nonliving thing. To carry out this encoding task, it is necessary to consider the meaning and associative properties of each word. For the nonelaborative task, the volunteers decided whether or not each word shown during a separate one-minute scan contains an *a*. No elaborative processing is required to make this decision. Follow-up testing revealed that, as expected, people remembered more words encountered during the elaborative task than during the nonelaborative task.

23. Kapur et al.'s (1994) results with PET scanning have been confirmed by Demb et al. (1995) with functional MRI. Demb et al. found that elaborative processing is associated with blood flow increases in the left inferior frontal cortex. For a discussion of functional MRI procedures, see Posner and Raichle (1994). Positron emission tomography studies showing activation of the left inferior frontal cortex in association with semantic encoding were initially reported by Petersen et al. (1989). For encoding deficits and frontal damage, see the reviews by Schacter (1987b) and by Stuss, Eskes, and Foster (1994). As Damasio (1994) reminds us, because the frontal lobes include many different subregions, speaking in general terms about "frontal damage" is of limited value.

24. For studies concerning distinctiveness, elaborative encoding, and event-related potentials, see Fabiani and Donchin (1995).

25. Positron emission tomography data showing hippocampal contributions to encoding novel pictures are reported by Tulving et al. (1994b). Our experiment with impossible shapes is reported in Schacter, Reiman, et al. (1995). Although I refer here and elsewhere to activation or blood flow increases in the hippocampus, it must be kept in mind that limitations in the spatial resolution of the PET techniques we and others have used make it difficult to distinguish between activation in the hippocampus proper and activation in the adjacent parahippocampal gyrus. Some "hippocampal" activations fall directly on the hippocampus, others on the parahippocampal gyrus. When I refer to activation of the hippocampus, I am including both the hippocampus and parahippocampal gyrus.

26. For an overview of Semon's theory of memory, see Schacter, Eich, and Tulving (1978); for a broader treatment that delves into Semon's life and ideas in the context of the history and sociology of science, see Schacter (1982). For English translations of his work on memory, see Semon (1921, 1923).

27. Watt (1905), p. 130.

28. See Hebb (1949) for the original statement of what has come to be known as "Hebbian learning." For a modern treatment, see McNaughton and Nadel (1989), and for a review of recent evidence, see Merzenich and Sameshima (1993).

29. The classic reference on the encoding specificity principle is Tulving and Thompson (1973); see also Tulving (1983).

30. As an example, consider an experiment by Barclay et al. (1974). They required people to think about sentences such as the following: "The man lifted the piano." It is likely that you imagine someone struggling hard to budge the weighty instrument, and perhaps wonder whether he can successfully lift it alone. The experimenters showed other people a slightly different sentence: "The man tuned the piano." Here you probably imagine someone plucking the strings or testing the keyboard; you may even mentally "hear" the sound of a note. The sentence contexts induced you to encode the target word, *piano*, differently in the two examples.

After time has passed, the experimenters probed memory for the critical word (*piano*) by providing brief phrases as retrieval cues. The cue "something heavy" may remind you of a man struggling to move the piano, but it probably will not make you think of anyone plucking the strings. In contrast, the cue "something with a nice sound" will probably remind you of someone plucking the strings, but will not evoke a man attempting to move the instrument. This is exactly what happened in Barclay et al.'s study. "Something heavy" elicited good recall of *piano* only when people studied "The man lifted the piano"; conversely, "something with a nice sound" elicited good recall of *piano* only when people studied "The man tuned the piano."

31. Anderson et al. (1976).

32. For an excellent review of research on state–dependent retrieval, see Eich (1989). Eich highlights an important qualifier about state–dependent retrieval: if the experimenter provides participants with hints that help to trigger explicit memory, it no longer matters whether the drug state is the same or different at study and test. For example, if experimental volunteers who are intoxicated study a list that contains the words *peach, apple, banana, tiger, horse,* and *monkey,* a state-dependent effect will be observed when they are later asked to remember all of the words on their own—they will recall more words when they are intoxicated than when they are sober. But when the experimenter provides retrieval cues such as "fruits" and "animals" to aid recollection, a state-dependent effect is no longer observed; memory performance is about the same in intoxicated and sober conditions. Thus, reinducing a prior state of mind helps recollection in the absence of other cues, but it becomes superfluous when specific, effective cues are available.

33. This experiment was reported by Fisher and Craik (1977); a similar one was reported by Morris, Bransford, and Franks (1977).

34. The experiments showing high levels of retention after exposure to numerous words are reported by Mäntylä (1986). Studies by Shepard (1967) and Standing (1973) have shown that, when people are shown hundreds or even thousands of distinctive pictures of real scenes, they can correctly recognize the vast majority of them when tested soon after seeing the pictures. One way to think about these striking findings is that pictures of diverse real-life scenes tend to elicit highly distinctive elaborative encodings. These encodings can be reinstated easily at the time of test, because the retrieval cue (the picture itself) provides a highly specific match to the encoding. When people are tested at longer delays, however, they remember many fewer pictures or words.

35. For a review of evidence from people and animals on retrieval of seemingly forgotten memories in response to cues and reminders, see Capaldi and Neath (1995).

36. Neil's case is described in detail by Vargha-Khadem, Isaacs, and Mishkin (1994). Quotes are from pp. 692–693 of that article. The tumor was in the pineal region of the third ventricle. Although it was treated successfully, MRI scans after treatment revealed abnormalities in structures thought to be important for memory, including the left hippocampal formation, parts of the diencephalon, and the fornix, which connects the hippocampus and diencephalon.

37. Caramazza and Hillis (1991).

38. For a readable discussion of possible cellular bases of memory retrieval, see Johnson (1991). For psychological and computational theories of retrieval, see McClelland (1995) and Metcalfe (1993).

39. For a detailed elaboration of this idea, see Damasio (1989) and Damasio and Damasio (1994).

40. Tulving et al. (1994a) summarize evidence concerning right/left frontal asymmetries during retrieval.

41. In the Squire et al. (1992) study that showed hippocampal activation during retrieval, people remembered recently presented words when given three-letter word beginnings. Since that time, some experiments have revealed evidence for hippocampal activation during retrieval, but others have not. This may be because the activation of the hippocampus depends on the specific manner in which people recollect a past event

or a variety of other factors. Relevant evidence and discussion can be found in Buckner and Tulving (1995), Buckner et al. (1995), Grasby et al. (1993), Schacter, Alpert, et al. (1996), and Ungerleider (1995).

42. To disentangle retrieval effort from the subjective experience of recollection, we used a depth-of-processing manipulation. Participants saw a list of words. They engaged in deep, elaborative processing of some words and shallow processing of others. After the deep encoding task, the subjects did not have to work very hard to recall the target words, and they remembered most of them well. After the shallow encoding task, the subjects had to work quite hard to try to retrieve the items and remembered only a few of them. We performed brain scans as the subjects attempted retrieval; there were separate scans for words that had been studied in the deep encoding task and for words that had been studied in the shallow encoding task. The hippocampus was most active when people were recalling words from the deep task (which they remembered well without much effort), whereas the frontal lobes were most active when people were recalling words from the shallow task (which they remembered poorly despite considerable effort). The experiment is reported by Schacter, Alpert, et al. (1996); see also Kapur et al. (1995). A key remaining question concerns what exact features of recollection are related to hippocampal activation, and my research group is actively trying to answer it. Consistent with our results, Nyberg, MacIntosh, Houle, et al. (1996) have recently reported PET data showing a strong positive correlation between hippocampal activity and successful retrieval within individual subjects.

43. For the distinction between associative and strategic retrieval, see Moscovitch (1994).

44. The experiments on tone of voice and facial expression were conducted with Kevin Ochsner, a graduate student in my laboratory, and Kari Edwards, a psychologist at Brown University. Loftus and Palmer (1974) have reported data on cue contributions to remembering that I discuss in chapter 4.

45. See Tulving (1983) for a forceful statement of the idea that what we call a memory is a joint product of cues and engrams. Tulving applied this idea to memory distortion, offering a comment that I believe has turned out to be prescient: "memory distortions, rememberers' 'remembering' things that did not occur, could be attributed to the constructive role of retrieval information" (p. 181).

46. The classic volume on connectionism and parallel distributed processing, edited by McClelland and Rumelhart (1986), provides an excellent overview of connectionist approaches to memory. More recent developments and other perspectives can be found in Edelman (1992), Grossberg and Stone (1986), and McClelland (1995).

CHAPTER 3
Of Time and Autobiography

1. The quote is from David Bonetti's review of Mildred Howard's exhibition at the Paule Anglim Gallery, San Francisco, *Art News,* November 1991, p. 154. My discussion of Howard's family background is based on personal conversations with the artist and on two exhibition catalogs: Mildred Howard, *1991 Adaline Kent Award Exhibition,* San Francisco Art Institute, and Mildred Howard, *TAP: Investigation of Memory,* Intar Gallery, New York, 1992.

2. For an English translation of Ebbinghaus's classic monograph, see Ebbinghaus (1885/1964). In 1985, the *Journal of Experimental Psychology* devoted a special issue to the 100th anniversary of Ebbinghaus's publication featuring a lengthy retrospective by Slamecka (1985) and several commentaries. The form of the forgetting curve can be accurately described by a mathematical expression known as a power function, which simply means that the rate of forgetting is slowed down by the passage of time. Wixted

and Ebbeson (1991) provide compelling evidence on forgetting as a power function of time.

3. Crovitz and Schiffman (1974); see also Rubin (1982). In both of these studies, the shape of the curve was extraordinarily well described by a power function. For the work of Galton that Crovitz rediscovered and modified, see Galton (1879). Galton timed and noted his own associations to word cues. Unlike Crovitz, he did not specifically require the retrieval of a particular episode. Galton's paper was published six years before Ebbinghaus's book, which is generally regarded as the first experimental investigation of memory. But Galton did not use experimental controls, whereas Ebbinghaus did.

4. The study on recall of accidents is by Cash and Moss (1972) and is cited in Loftus (1982). The quote is from Cash and Moss (1972), p. 5, as cited by Loftus (1982), p. 127. Although some accident victims probably forgot to report the accident because of head injuries, this cannot explain the dramatic drop-off of recall in people interviewed nine to twelve months after the accident compared to those interviewed less than three months after the accident.

5. The interference theory of forgetting has a long and distinguished history in the experimental study of memory. See, for example, Postman and Underwood (1973).

6. The idea that all experiences are stored permanently in memory is reviewed critically by Loftus and Loftus (1980). In chapter 10, I consider an apparent exception to the rule of graded forgetting as a function of time, known as the *reminiscence bump*. Another exception is found in the work of Bahrick (1979, 1984), which indicates that some extremely well learned information enters a "permastore" in which it no longer exhibits detectable forgetting.

7. Penfield's experiments are reported in Penfield and Perot (1963) and are reviewed carefully by Loftus and Loftus (1980) and Squire (1987). The quotes from the patients are from Penfield and Perot (1963), pp. 653 and 650, respectively.

8. Penfield (1969), p. 165.

9. See Squire (1987) for similar criticisms.

10. Quotes are from Bancaud, Brunet-Bourgin, Chauvel, and Halgren (1994), pp. 78–79.

11. Neurobiological evidence for the loss of synaptic connectivity is provided by Bailey and Chen (1989).

12. Linton (1986), p. 63.

13. For Funes, see Borges (1962); the quote is from p. 112. The story of Shereshevskii is told by Luria (1968).

14. For forgetting as an adaptive response to the structure of the environment, see Anderson and Schooler (1991).

15. Excellent reviews and discussions of hypermnesia are provided by Erdelyi (1984, 1996) and Payne (1987). Hypermnesia seems to occur more readily for pictures than for words; Payne (1987) considers various possible explanations. For historical analyses of the consolidation idea, see Polster, Nadel, and Schacter (1991) and Squire (1987).

16. For reviews of amnesia following head injury, see Levin, Benton, and Grossman (1982), Russell and Nathan (1946), and Schacter and Crovitz (1977). For "the ding," see Yarnell and Lynch (1973).

17. Abel et al. (1995), p. 302. Abel et al. provide an excellent overview of the cellular aspects of research on short- and long-term memory in Aplysia, mice, and other organisms. See also Kandel, Schwartz, and Jessell (1995) and Rose (1992). New studies by Kandel's group (Bartsch et al., 1995) have shown that Aplysia can consolidate a long-term memory even after only a single burst of stimulation. This happens when cellular processes that normally suppress the rapid formation of long-term memories are prevented from doing so.

18. The law is stated and exemplified in Ribot (1882). For an informative discussion of

Ribot's ideas, see Roth (1989), and for his role in the early development of a scientific approach to memory, see Hacking (1995).

19. For the development of the famous faces test, see Butters and Albert (1982). For the television test, see Squire (1987, 1992).

20. MacKinnon and Squire (1989).

21. See Butters and Cermak (1986).

22. For animal studies of retrograde amnesia, see Zola-Morgan and Squire (1990), Cho, Beracochea, and Jaffard (1993), and Kim and Fanselow (1992).

23. For patient EH and a general discussion of face recognition problems ("prosopagnosia"), see Damasio, Tranel, and Damasio (1990). Studies of facial and object recognition deficits are well reviewed by Farah (1990). Schacter and Nadel (1991) review spatial memory deficits in patients with parietal lobe damage and Moscovitch et al. (1995) present PET data. Gardner (1975) provides an excellent introduction to patients with Wernicke's aphasia. For general discussion of principles of information storage in cortical networks, see Damasio (1989) and Mesulam (1990).

24. For neurobiological ideas about consolidation and the medial temporal region, see Damasio (1989), Squire, Cohen, and Nadel (1984), Squire (1987, 1992), and Teyler and DiScenna (1986).

25. McClelland, McNaughton, and O'Reilly (1995).

26. For visual reorganization, see Darien-Smith and Gilbert (1994).

27. See Winson (1985) and also Reiser (1990) for ideas about dreams, consolidation, and the hippocampus. The study on rats, hippocampus, and sleep is reported by Wilson and McNaughton (1994). For an experiment showing consolidation of a visual skill during REM, see Karni et al. (1994). Karni's group has provided evidence suggesting that the perceptual skill learning they observed involves changes in early visual processing stages, so the relevance of the hippocampus to observed consolidation remains to be established. To assess the issue, Karni is currently testing whether amnesic patients with damage to medial temporal structures show normal learning of this perceptual skill (Avi Karni, personal communication, June 8, 1995). Many studies have examined whether REM sleep contributes to memory consolidation, and the hypothesis has received some support, although the relevant studies are not without problems (Horne & McGrath, 1984).

28. See Allende (1995) for her deeply moving story of her life and Paula's illness. Quotes are from pp. 3 and 23.

29. For distinctions among kinds of autobiographical knowledge, see Conway and Rubin (1993). Similar distinctions have been offered by Linton (1986) and Neisser (1986). Scientific concern with everyday memories outside the laboratory among cognitive psychologists and neuropsychologists was stimulated to a large extent by an important paper by Neisser (1978). Banaji and Crowder (1989) have argued that naturalistic studies are of limited value because they sacrifice methodological rigor, but I believe that a science of memory has room for both laboratory and everyday studies.

30. Quotes from Allende (1995), pp. 83–84.

31. See Barsalou (1988) for general events as entry points into autobiographical memories. This research parallels classic work on preferred entry points into semantic knowledge (the basic level) described in Rosch et al. (1976).

32. Conway and Bekerian's (1987) research, for instance, indicates that providing lifetime periods as cues prior to probing for more specific events and episodes speeds up memory retrieval. See also Reiser, Black, and Abelson (1985).

33. For a detailed description of PS, see Hodges and McCarthy (1993).

34. Allende (1995), p. 8.

35. McAdams (1993), p. 28. For similar ideas about life stories and personal myths, see Kotre (1995), Kris (1956), Schank (1990), and Singer and Salovey (1993).

36. Price (1992).
37. For review of studies on retrospective estimates of childhood and family life, see Brewin, Andrews, and Gotlib (1993). They conclude that concerns about the unreliability of retrospective reports concerning the general character of childhood experiences are needlessly exaggerated.
38. Barclay (1986), p. 97.
39. Quotes from Isabel Allende are from an interview in the *Boston Globe* by Cynthia Dockrell, "The spirits of Isabel Allende," May 24, 1995, p. 80. Quote from *Paula's* letter is in Allende (1995), p. 322.

CHAPTER 4
Reflections in a Curved Mirror: Memory Distortion

1. Breznitz (1993), p. 179.
2. For a summary of the Walus case and a lengthy exploration of Demjanjuk, see Wagenaar (1988); quotes are from pp. 17–18. Demjanjuk's acquittal by the Israeli Supreme Court was reported by the *New York Times,* "Kin Bringing Demjanjuk Home to Face Troubles," by Stephen Labaton (September 21, 1993, p. 17A). The article also points out that "The Justice Department has said that it did nothing improper and that even if Mr. Demjanjuk was not Ivan, he was an SS guard, lied on his immigration papers to conceal his Nazi affiliation and therefore should be barred from the United States."
3. Erdelyi (1985) argues that Freud's change of view resulted from a delayed but appropriately critical analysis of the recollections presented to him in therapy and the hypnotic techniques used to elicit them. Masson (1984) contends that it was a career-saving move attributable to a failure of courage in the face of criticism, a viewpoint echoed by Herman (1992). Ofshe and Watters (1994) claim that Freud bullied his clients into generating false memories.
4. D. P. Spence (1984) provides an excellent analysis of these points. For an English translation of Freud's paper on screen memories, see Freud (1899).
5. It is curious that Bartlett's (1932) landmark experiments have never been replicated; see Gauld and Stephenson (1967).
6. See Buckhout (1974) and also Wagenaar (1988) for the Carbone misidentification and photographs of all three men. Wagenaar (1988), pp. 132–133, points out how something similar may have occurred in the Demjanjuk case.
7. Schooler and Engstler-Schooler (1990) demonstrated that encoding verbal labels impairs face and color recognition. Melcher and Schooler (1996) found the same with wine tasting. Interestingly, recognizing the taste of wine was not impaired in expert wine tasters, who had extensive experience translating taste into words. These effects may be better conceptualized as "recoding" effects than "encoding" effects, because in experiments demonstrating the distorting influences of verbal labels, people generate the labels some time after having encoded a nonverbal stimulus.
8. For the baseball experiment, see Arkes and Freedman (1984). For similar kinds of demonstrations, see Bransford and Franks (1971) and Sulin and Dooling (1974).
9. Psychologists often refer to these kinds of inferences as schema-based inferences. A *schema* refers to an organized unit of past experiences that is used to interpret and analyze a current situation; the term was introduced to psychology by Sir Frederic Bartlett (1932) in his classic monograph on remembering. See Alba and Hasher (1983) for a review of research and theory concerning schemata and memory.
10. The original "sweet" demonstration was reported by Deese (1959), who examined only recall intrusions. Newer and more compelling versions of these experiments are reported by Roediger and McDermott (1995), who provide data on recall, yes/no

recognition, and remember/know judgments. Other similar false recognition phenomena have been reported by other investigators, as reviewed in Schacter (1995a).

11. The PET study is reported by Schacter, Reiman, Curran, Yun, Bandy, McDermott, & Roediger (1996). In the follow-up study by Johnson, Nolde, Mather, Kounios, Schacter, and Curran (in press), we examined brain activity during true and false recognition using event-related potentials (ERPs). When different types of words (e.g., previously studied words, nonstudied associates of previously studied words, and unrelated nonstudied words) were tested in separate blocks, as required by PET technology, we found ERP differences between true and false recognition that resembled those seen in the PET study. But when different word types were randomly intermixed during testing, such differences were not observed. Johnson et al. (in press) provide a theoretical account of the contrasting results from different test conditions. For the study of amnesic patients, see Schacter, Verfaellie, and Pradere (1996). The idea that false recognition can be based on recalling the gist of a past experience has been developed most extensively by the cognitive psychologists Charles Brainerd and Valerie Reyna in their useful "fuzzy trace theory," which holds that accurate recollections depend on a "verbatim" or specific representation of what occurred during an episode, whereas distorted recollections depend on a gist representation. According to fuzzy trace theory, a gist representation can give rise to "vague impressions of similarity" (Brainerd, Reyna, & Brandse, 1995, p. 360) between a present event and a past one that may result in false recognition. False recognition of strong associates such as *sweet*, however, produces vivid recollections, not vague impressions of similarity. Schacter et al. (1996) suggest a modified version of the fuzzy trace idea to account for false recognition in amnesic and nonamnesic individuals.

12. For a discussion of connectionism and memory distortion, see McClelland (1995).

13. The story of Arnold is told by Geary (1994), who provides an informative analysis of the nature and functions of memory in eleventh-century Europe.

14. An early laboratory demonstration that pointed in this direction was reported by Loftus and Palmer (1974), who sought to determine whether the exact wording of a retrieval query could affect what people said that they remembered. In one experiment, they probed participants' recollection of what had happened in a film involving an automobile accident. When Loftus asked participants, "About how fast were the cars going when they smashed into each other?" they "remembered" the car going faster than when she asked, "About how fast were the cars going when they hit each other?" The idea that the properties of a retrieval cue help to shape or bias the construction of a memory allows us to make sense of these findings. The participants' interpretation of the verb "smashed" contributed significantly to their memorial experience of the initial event—perhaps as much as the fragments of experience that they retained from the film.

15. For the toothbrush and study skills experiments, see Ross and Conway (1986). The study on political attitudes is reported by Marcus (1986) and summarized by Dawes (1988, 1991), who provides a general discussion of retrospective bias. Dawes also discusses a similar outcome that was observed in a study that examined high school students' reported use of alcohol, tobacco, and illegal drugs (Collins et al., 1985). Students were interviewed initially, and then again on two separate occasions, one year and two and one half years after the initial screening. During the latter two interviews, students were asked to recall what they had said during the initial interview. Clear evidence for retrospective bias was obtained: students' memories were often more closely related to current substance use than to initially reported use. For instance, students whose drinking behavior had changed over the years of the study nevertheless "remembered" that their initial levels of alcohol use were about the same as their current levels of use. For additional relevant evidence on retrospective biases, see Ross (1989).

16. Quotes from D. P. Spence (1984), pp. 93–94.

17. Lynn and Nash (1994) conclude that both high-hypnotizable and medium-hypnotizable subjects, as assessed by standard hypnotic susceptibility scales, are "at particular risk for suggestion-related memory distortions, and these hypnotizability effects are not necessarily related to hypnotic situations."

18. The material on Spaziano and the McCawley quote come from the article by Spaziano's lawyer, Michael Mello, in the *Orlando Sentinel* (June 4, 1995, p. G1), "Did Tainted Testimony Doom Man? As Joseph Spaziano Nears the Execution, a Lawyer Questions the Evidence That Sealed His Fate." Mello points out that Spaziano was hardly a choirboy—he was a convicted rapist—but also details various kinds of potentially exonerating evidence that were withheld from the jury in addition to the information about hypnosis. A follow-up article published after Chiles granted the stay of execution on June 15, however, revealed that the governor's lawyer still believes that Spaziano is guilty ("Spaziano Guilty, Chiles' Lawyer Decides after Reviewing Case," by Michael Griffin and Beth Taylor, *Orlando Sentinel* [June 17, 1995, p. A1]). The next day, however, another article pointed out that Dilisio is now wavering about his hypnotically induced testimony ("Essay-Writing Lawyer Rejoins Killer's Case," by Beth Taylor, *Orlando Sentinel* [June 18, 1995, p. B1]). By the time he was interviewed on the June 30 edition of ABC's "World News Tonight," Dilisio had recanted his testimony completely, stating unequivocally that "At this point, I believe with all my heart that I never went to the dump with Joe Spaziano." As of late fall 1995, Spaziano's fate remains undecided.

    For useful discussions of hypnosis and the claims that have been made about it, see the chapters in Pettinati (1988).

19. A good example of how hypnosis alters a person's willingness to call mental events "memories" is provided by Dywan and Bowers (1983). They showed experimental volunteers line drawings of common objects and later tested their memory of the drawings. After testing, half the subjects were hypnotized and half were not, and another memory test was given. Dywan and Bowers found that the hypnotized subjects recovered more previously unrecalled pictures than did the nonhypnotized subjects, but they also produced even greater numbers of "false memories" of pictures that had never been presented. Dywan (1995) and Klatzky and Erdelyi (1985) provide helpful discussions of this issue. For studies on confidence and hypnosis, see Orne et al. (1984, 1988), Lynn and Nash (1994), and Sheehan (1988). Orne et al. (1988), pp. 27–28, also summarize evidence concerning imagery and hypnosis.

20. Laurence and Perry (1983) report the "noises at night" study; the quote is from p. 524. Lynn and Nash (1994), Brown (1995), and Kihlstrom (in press b) summarize the large experimental literature on hypnotically induced pseudomemories.

21. The *Frontline* show aired on April 4, 1995. Baker (1992) offers a critique of hypnotically induced "memories" of past lives and alien abductions; Spanos et al. (1991) provide relevant experimental evidence. Mack (1994) provides the perspective of a "true believer" in the reality of alien abductions, but the cases he describes of abduction memories remembered via hypnosis are quite consistent with the idea that hypnosis helped to create, rather than recover, these bizarre mental experiences.

22. Loftus (1993), p. 532; see also Loftus and Ketcham (1994). In follow-up studies, Loftus and Pickrell (1995) report that approximately 25 percent of participants generated false memories of childhood events.

23. See Hyman, Husband, and Billings (1995) for the basic false memory demonstration, Hyman and Pentland (1996) for the effects of imagining episodes, and Hyman and Billings (1995) for individual differences in false memories. In the latter study, the tendency to generate false memories was correlated significantly (+.36) with scores on the Creative Imagination Scale (Wilson & Barber, 1978), which measures vividness of

mental imagery and responsiveness to suggestion. False memory creation was also correlated significantly (+.48) with scores on the Dissociative Experience Scale (Bernstein & Putman, 1986), which measures reported tendencies toward lapses in attention and memory.

24. For experiments concerning repetition, rehearsal, and confidence, see Begg, Anas, and Farinacci (1992), Poole and White (1995), and Roediger, Wheeler, and Rajaram (1993). For the relationship between eyewitness identification and confidence, see Bothwell, Deffenbacher, and Brigham (1987), Kassin, Rigby, and Castillo (1991), and Wells (1993). In a recent review and meta-analysis on confidence/accuracy relations, Sporer et al. (1995) point out that confidence and accuracy tend to show little or no correlation in studies that include both witnesses who make positive identifications of suspects and those who are unable to choose a suspect from a lineup. However, when considering only the subset of witnesses who make positive identifications, they observed a moderate positive correlation between confidence and accuracy.

25. The final quote is from Neisser (1982), p. 159. The material from the September 15, 1973, meeting is from the Hearings before the Select Committee on Presidential Campaign Activities of the United States Senate (Ninety-third Cong., 1st sess., 1973, p. 957) and is reprinted in Neisser (1982), p. 147. For studies examining the reliability and accuracy of eyewitness testimony, see Wells (1993).

26. For discussion of memory-related issues in the Hill–Thomas case, see Pezdek and Prull (1993). Elizabeth Loftus discussed issues related to confidence and rehearsal in the O. J. Simpson case in the *Los Angeles Times* (August 25, 1995, p. B9), "The Whole Truth and Nothing but the Truth?"

27. Thompson's case is described by Read et al. (1990) as an illustration of "unconscious transference," which occurs when a witness confuses an innocent bystander with the actual criminal; see also Ross et al. (1994). Thompson (1988) himself provides an informed theoretical analysis of related memory distortions.

28. For the early Loftus experiments on eyewitness suggestibility, see Loftus, Miller, and Burns (1978); for more recent studies, see Loftus, Feldman, and Dashiell (1995).

29. McCloskey and Zaragoza (1985) provide compelling evidence that original memories are not overwritten in the Loftus paradigm. Lindsay (1990) conducted the study where people were told that the post-event narrative was false. Other evidence implicating source memory failures in eyewitness suggestibility is reported by Belli et al. (1994), Lindsay and Johnson (1989), and Zaragoza and Lane (1994).

30. Jacoby, Kelley, Brown, and Jasechko (1989).

31. See Johnson and Raye (1981), Johnson et al. (1988), and Johnson, Hashtroudi, and Lindsay (1993) for studies of reality monitoring.

32. For discussions of the social implications of source memory failures, see Johnson (1996) and Riccio, Rabinowitz, and Axelrod (1994). See Pratkanis et al. (1988) for social psychological research on source credibility and forgetting, Gilbert (1991) for studies of the bias to believe, and Begg et al. (1992) for links between source memory failure and unwarranted beliefs.

33. For review, see Friedman (1993).

34. See Brown, Rips, and Shevell (1985). For related distortions of temporal memory that have implications for survey researchers who try to estimate the frequency of crime and other social issues, see Loftus, Fienberg, and Tanur (1985).

35. Gene was one of several patients who exhibited source amnesia in the experiments reported by Schacter, Harbluk, and McLachlan (1984). The term *source amnesia* was coined by Evans and Thorn (1966) in their studies of hypnosis.

36. For source amnesia in patients with lesions restricted to the frontal lobes, see Janowsky, Shimamura, and Squire (1989); for impaired temporal memory in frontal patients, see Milner, Corsi, and Leonard (1991).

37. Moscovitch (1995), p. 228. As Moscovitch and others emphasize, confabulation is not observed in all patients with frontal lobe damage, which follows from the fact that the frontal lobes are composed of numerous subregions that perform different functions (Damasio, 1994; Shimamura, 1995). Extensive confabulation tends to be seen only when lesions penetrate to the inner (ventromedial) regions of the frontal lobes and damage the nearby basal forebrain. Perhaps related to confabulation, a recent PET study of schizophrenic patients (Silbersweig et al., 1995) revealed a relative absence of frontal lobe activity when patients experienced hallucinations, which may reflect a diminished ability to monitor the source (internal or external) of a mental event. Interestingly, the hippocampal formation was one of several structures that became extremely active during hallucinations. In view of PET data linking the hippocampal formation and explicit retrieval (Nyberg et al., 1995; Schacter, Reiman, et al., 1995; Schacter, Alpert, et al., 1996), the combination of hippocampal activation and frontal deactivation in schizophrenic patients might have contributed to their mistaking a past experience for a present one.

38. Dalla Barba (1993).

39. Talland (1965).

40. This view has been advanced by Moscovitch (1995).

41. A full report of our experiments is contained in Schacter, Curran et al. (1996). Although my interest in Frank was stimulated in part by PET scanning studies showing right frontal lobe activation during explicit retrieval, the location of Frank's lesion is posterior to the region that is typically activated in PET studies (known as area 10). Accordingly, it is difficult to say how the false recognition phenomena we have observed in Frank relate, if at all, to right frontal lobe activations in PET studies of healthy volunteers. Also, we cannot determine on the basis of this single case whether pathological false recognition is uniquely associated with right frontal damage. Indeed, Parkin et al. in press have recently reported a case of pathological false recognition after damage to the left frontal lobe. For an extended discussion of theoretical aspects of false recognition after brain damage, see Norman and Schacter (in press).

42. See Phelps and Gazzaniga (1992) and Metcalfe, Funnell, and Gazzaniga (1995). For an introduction to split-brain patients, see Gazzaniga (1985).

43. For review and discussion, see Bruck and Ceci (1995) and Nathan and Snedeker (1995).

44. In May 1995, a state court of appeals overturned the convictions of Robert Kelly, Jr., and of Kathryn Dawn Wilson and ordered new trials for them. However, several weeks later the North Carolina Supreme Court stopped this ruling and provided state prosecutors with another chance to make their case that the convictions should stand and that new trials are not warranted. The story is summarized in the *Charlotte Observer,* "Court Stops Appeals Ruling in Kelly Case, Prosecutors Get Chance for Review," by Estes Thomson (May 23, 1995, p. C4).

45. Ceci and Bruck (1995), p. 12. See also Bruck and Ceci (1995) for a detailed discussion of the Michaels case.

46. For a thorough review and discussion of children's eyewitness testimony, see Ceci and Bruck (1993, 1995).

47. For a review of these experiments, see Ceci (1995).

48. The quote is from Ceci (1995), p. 103.

49. The Sam Stone study is reported by Leichtman and Ceci (1995). I thank Michelle Leichtman and Steve Ceci for providing me with the quote from the three-year-old girl. In addition to their finding that misleading suggestions produced inaccurate recollections, they also reported that telling children in advance of his visit that Sam Stone was a bad fellow made children more likely to falsely remember things that Sam had not actually done. Children who were exposed to both advance negative information and

misleading suggestions were the most likely of all to generate mistaken recollections. In fact, over 70 percent of three- and four-year-old children said that Sam had committed misdeeds after exposure to both negative advance information and misleading suggestions. The percentage of false recalls dropped substantially when children were "gently challenged" about their memories by an interviewer who said, "You didn't really see him do anything to the book/teddy bear, did you?" Under these conditions only about 20 percent of three- and four-year-olds who received both misleading suggestions and negative advance information stuck by their false memories. Although this finding suggests that only a minority of children were totally convinced that Sam Stone had done anything to a book and teddy bear, the fact that so many children were willing to "back off" their memories in response to an interviewer further underscores the power that adult figures wield with young children and how malleable their memory reports can be.

50. Bruck et al. (1995).
51. See Fivush and Schwarzmueller (1995). Goodman et al. (1994) and Saywitz and Moan-Hardie (1994) also provide evidence for accurate memory of everyday events in young children. For a review and discussion of other studies on memory distortion in children, see Bruck and Ceci (1995) and Ceci (1995).
52. Schacter, Kagan, and Leichtman (1995).
53. For the Ingram story, see Wright's (1993) *New Yorker* article and subsequent book (Wright, 1994); see also Ofshe and Watters (1994).
54. Olio and Cornell (1995) provide a critique of Ofshe's observations and entertain alternative interpretations of his experiment with Ingram. Ingram's plight was probably also related to idiosyncratic features of his past and personality. He admitted that he was a distant, sometimes neglectful, father. Ingram was also likely more prone to suggestive influences than most people.

CHAPTER 5
Vanishing Traces: Amnesia and the Brain

1. The two rounds of golf were originally reported in Schacter (1983).
2. For a biography of HM, see Hilts (1995).
3. See Scoville and Milner (1957) for an early description of HM. Corkin (1984) provides a comprehensive review of the case.
4. See Hirsh (1974) and O'Keefe and Nadel (1978).
5. For case RB, see Zola-Morgan, Squire, and Amaral (1986). For the recent cases similar to RB, see Zola-Morgan (1996).
6. For the neurology of herpes simplex encephalitis, see Damasio and Van Hoesen (1985).
7. The case of SS is thoroughly presented by Cermak and O'Connor (1983). Damasio, Tranel, and Damasio (1989) summarize the case of Boswell.
8. This quote is from an unpublished interview that David Jane sent to me, along with a letter describing his situation, in January 1994.
9. See Jones-Gotman (1986) and Smith and Milner (1981).
10. For a review of David Jane's MRI paintings, see Hall (1993).
11. For a review of deficits associated with encephalitis, see Parkin and Leng (1993).
12. Mishkin (1978, 1982).
13. Hippocampal LTP was discovered by Bliss and Lømo (1973). Numerous experiments have since shown that hippocampal LTP possesses a number of properties that make it well suited to serve as a cellular basis for memory. For recent discussions of LTP and memory, see Bliss and Collingridge (1993) and Maren and Baudry (1995).

14. For the original cognitive map theory of hippocampal function, see O'Keefe and Nadel (1978). For recent discussions of the hippocampus and spatial memory, see Nadel (1994), Cohen, and Eichenbaum (1993), and Cave and Squire (1991). Evidence concerning the contribution of the hippocampus to recognition memory in monkeys is provided by Zola-Morgan, Squire, and Ramus (1994).

15. See Murray, Gaffan, and Mishkin (1993), Squire and Zola-Morgan (1991), and Zola-Morgan et al. (1989).

16. Butters and Cermak (1980).

17. The examples of confused Korsakoff patients are from Talland (1965), pp. 46–48.

18. The conversation with the Korsakoff patient is reported in Gardner (1975), p. 183.

19. MRI data are reported in Jernigan et al. (1991), and postmortem data are discussed by Mair, Warrington, and Weiskrantz (1979) and Victor, Adams, and Collins (1989). See also Parkin and Leng (1993).

20. This circuit is often referred to as the *Papez circuit*. Mayes (1988) and Zola-Morgan and Squire (1993) provide a good summary of pertinent observations. Although the idea of a single medial temporal-diencephalic network is attractive in its simplicity, it has been bedeviled by inconsistent and failed attempts to confirm to a simple prediction that follows from it: damage to the fornix, which connects the medial temporal and diencephalic regions, should produce amnesia. Early clinical reports failed to provide convincing evidence that damage to the fornix causes memory loss. More recent observations, however, indicate that patients with damage to the fornix do have difficulties remembering their ongoing experiences (Gaffan, Gaffan, & Hodges, 1991). But such patients appear to exhibit relatively mild memory problems, not severe and global amnesia.

    A further twist in the neuroanatomy of amnesia may help explain the apparently mild amnesia associated with fornix damage. In the early 1980s, Mortimer Mishkin (1982) emphasized that two different circuits connect the medial temporal lobe and diencephalon. One circuit includes the hippocampus and the mammillary bodies, which are connected by the fornix; the other includes the amygdala and a critical part of the thalamus (the dorsomedial nucleus), but does not involve the fornix. Profound amnesia may require damage to both circuits.

21. For the neuropathology of Alzheimer's disease, see Price and Sisodia (1992) and Van Hoesen and Damasio (1987); for genetic contributions to Alzheimer neuropathology, see Pollen (1993). Hasselmo (1994) provides an interesting theoretical analysis in which depletion of acetylcholine, a neurotransmitter that is deficient in Alzheimer patients, leads to "runaway" modification of synaptic connections, which in turn creates pathological plaques and tangles.

22. For recent evidence on semantic learning in amnesic patients and reviews of earlier studies, see Hamann and Squire (1995) and Verfaellie, Reiss, and Roth (1995). In studies that I describe in chapter 6, my colleagues and I devised techniques that allow amnesic patients to learn large numbers of new words and facts, albeit at a slower than normal rate (Glisky, Schacter, & Tulving, 1986a,b).

    For studies of remember and know responses in amnesia, see Knowlton and Squire (1995). While all researchers agree that amnesic patients have difficulty recalling contextual details of episodes, there has been debate about whether amnesic patients also lose the ability to recognize recent events on the basis of simple familiarity. Consistent with Knowlton and Squire's results, Haist, Shimamura, and Squire (1992) provide evidence that recall and recognition are similarly impaired in amnesic patients with medial temporal lobe damage. Some amnesic patients do seem to be less impaired on recognition tests than on recall tests (Hirst et al., 1988), but even these patients are seriously impaired on both types of tests. Other studies suggest that compared to people with intact memories, amnesic patients base their recognition decisions more on whatever feelings of familiarity they do possess and less on recollection of context

(Verfaellie & Treadwell, 1993). On balance, however, the evidence supports the conclusion that feelings of familiarity are impaired in amnesic patients.

23. Tulving et al. (1988) provide a detailed case study. Although we did not have MRI data available at the time, Gene has since had an MRI scan that revealed damage to the left hippocampus.

24. See Tulving (1993) for a discussion of Gene's personality, and Hayman, Macdonald, and Tulving (1993) for his semantic learning.

25. For Boswell, see Damasio et al. (1989). Cermak and O'Connor (1983) provide a general description of SS. Another well-studied encephalitic patient, known by the initials RFR, also recalls "semantic" memories of his personal past, yet cannot provide detailed recollections of particular incidents. RFR retained knowledge of words that had entered the language during time periods for which he has no episodic memories. For instance, RFR could provide adequate definitions of such terms as *AIDS* and *Thatcherism* despite his inability to recollect particular episodes from the 1980s. When presented with famous and nonfamous names and faces from the past, RFR had no difficulty telling apart the famous and the nonfamous. Although he had some problem naming pictures of famous people from the past, when RFR was given a few hints, he frequently came up with the correct answer. See Warrington and McCarthy (1988).

26. Conway (1992) offers a similar analysis. Gene and SS had damage to cortical association areas that store memories. When damage is restricted to the medial temporal lobes, more limited forms of retrograde amnesia are observed. For a recent review of different forms of retrograde amnesia, see Hodges (1995).

27. De Renzi, Liotti, and Nichelli (1987).

28. Quotes are from Hodges et al. (1992), p. 1797, who provide a thorough analysis of semantic dementias. Hodges et al. note that these patients may represent a subtype of Alzheimer's dementia.

29. For category-specific impairments, see Damasio (1990), Hillis and Caramazza (1991), and Warrington and Shallice (1984). There are a variety of theoretical interpretations of how and why category-specific impairments come about. For discussion of alternative viewpoints, see Damasio (1990), Farah and McClelland (1991), and Patterson and Hodges (1995).

30. PET data concerning identification of tools vs. objects are reported by Martin et al. (1996); Decety et al. (1994) report PET data concerning imagined movements. Martin et al. (1995) found that the left middle temporal gyrus is activated when people generate action words. For a review of brain areas implicated in different kinds of category-specific impairments, see Gainotti et al. (1995).

31. The conversational quotes are from Gardner (1975), pp. 181–182.

32. For experimental observations concerning awareness in Korsakoff patients, see Shimamura (1994).

33. For amnesia after anterior communicating artery aneurysms and basal forebrain damage, see Damasio et al. (1989) and Parkin and Leng (1993). Hanley et al. (1994) provide evidence of spared recognition relative to recall.

34. The prediction study was carried out with Elizabeth Glisky and Susan McGlynn and is reported in Schacter (1991).

35. The encephalitic patient is described by Rose and Symonds (1960), p. 195, and the diencephalic patient by Kaushall, Zetin, and Squire (1981), p. 385. For HM's awareness, see Hilts (1995), p. 140. Corkin (1984) also describes awareness in patient HM. For reviews of research on awareness of memory and other cognitive deficits, see McGlynn and Schacter (1989) and Prigatano and Schacter (1991).

36. For observations concerning transient global amnesia, see Evans (1966), Hodges and Warlow (1990), and Kritchevsky, Squire, and Zouzounis (1988).

37. For reviews, see McGlynn and Schacter (1989) and Schacter (1991).

38. Mercer et al. (1977).
39. For patient BM, see Ramachandran (1995).The quote is from pp. 35–36.
40. See Prigatano (1991), Schacter (1991), and Stuss (1991) for discussions of awareness of deficit and rehabilitation.
41. See McGowin (1993) for the story of Diana's illness.The quote is from p. 8.
42. Glenn Collins's reflections appeared in the *New York Times,* November 10, 1994, "Enduring a Disease that Steals the Soul."
43. For the relation between confabulation, frontal lobe function, and unawareness in Alzheimer's disease, see Dalla Barba et al. (in press). For a general review and discussion of awareness and Alzheimer's patients, see McGlynn and Kaszniak (1991).

CHAPTER 6
The Hidden World of Implicit Memory

1. Richardson-Klavehn and Bjork (1988), pp. 476–477, offered the opinion that research on implicit memory constitutes a "revolution in the way that we measure and interpret the influence of past events on current experience and behavior."
2. See Warrington and Weiskrantz (1968, 1974).
3. For the link between amnesia and blindsight, see Weiskrantz (1978); for a thorough treatment of blindsight, see Weiskrantz (1986). Schacter (1992) provides a review of implicit knowledge in a wide variety of neuropsychological syndromes.
4. For motor skill learning and HM, see Corkin (1968) and Milner, Corkin, and Teuber (1968). For more recent evidence showing intact learning and retention of motor skills in amnesia, see Tranel et al. (1994). For a historical review of early observations of implicit memory, see Schacter (1987a).
5. For a summary of Freudian and other early ideas about the unconscious, see Ellenberger (1970). For attempts to test these ideas experimentally, see Shevrin (1988, 1992). For the amnesic dressmaker, see Dunn (1845), and for memory versus habit, see Bergson (1911).
6. I later developed the procedures used with Mickey into the source amnesia paradigm described in chapter 4 (Schacter, Harbluk, & McLachlan, 1984).
7. The experiment is reported by Tulving, Schacter, and Stark (1982). Our finding that priming is unrelated to whether or not a person remembers having seen a word reflects a state of affairs known by the technical term *stochastic independence*. The analysis of stochastic independence subsequently became a controversial issue. For discussion, see Hayman and Tulving (1989).
8. Dannay (1980), p. 681, quoted in Brown and Murphy (1989), p. 441.
9. For the Freud quote, see Taylor (1965), p. 1113. Brown and Murphy (1989) and Marsh and Landau (1995) provide an experimental analog of unintentional plagiarism, which is sometimes referred to as *cryptomnesia*. See Baker (1992).
10. The experiments are described by Jacoby and Dallas (1981). Later studies showed that priming is also reduced when people see a word during the study phase and are later given an auditory test in which they try to identify the word when it is masked in noise. See Jackson and Morton (1984).
11. For different effects of depth of encoding effects with different test instructions, see Graf and Mandler (1984). Graf, Squire, and Mandler (1984) showed that amnesic patients' performance on the stem completion test depends critically on task instructions; see also Cermak et al. (1985) and Schacter, Bowers, and Booker (1989).The general pattern in these experiments is that asking normal subjects to think back to the study list improves recall, but has little or no effect on the performance of amnesic patients, who tend to rely on priming no matter what they are instructed to do.

12. Tulving et al. (1982), p. 341.

13. For Maine de Biran's ideas, see Maine de Biran (1929) and summaries in Schacter (1987a) and Schacter and Tulving (1994). For short-term versus long-term memory, see Baddeley (1986). For the episodic/semantic distinction, see Tulving (1972, 1983).

    Single-system alternatives to the multiple memory systems hypothesis generally focus on the kinds of encoding and retrieval processes carried out by people in different memory tasks. Representative views are discussed by Jacoby (1983), Masson and MacLeod (1992), Roediger, Weldon, and Challis (1989), and Ratcliff and McKoon (1995). Several researchers have attempted to unify the single system and multiple systems approaches, including Blaxton (1995), Gabrieli (1995), Roediger (1990), and Schacter (1990). For general discussion of memory systems, see Schacter and Tulving (1994).

14. Cohen and Squire (1980). The task of reading mirror-inverted script was developed several years earlier by Kolers (1975).

15. See Graf and Schacter (1985) for the initial distinction between explicit and implicit memory, and see Schacter (1987a) for a historical review of implicit memory. For more up-to-date reviews of implicit memory, see Roediger and McDermott (1993) and Schacter, Chiu and Ochsner (1993).

16. The finding on biasing of preferences was first reported by Kunst-Wilson and Zajonc (1980). Pendergrast (1993, pp. 267–68) describes how the Coke and popcorn incident unfolded and why it was a hoax. In fact, there is little evidence that subliminal messages affect real-world behavior (Merikle, 1988). Although laboratory studies have shown that information not registered by conscious perception can influence performance on subsequent tasks, the effects are generally short-lasting and do not support the usefulness of commercially available subliminal tapes. Curiously, however, people express considerable concern that their behavior will be influenced by subliminal messages (Wilson & Brekke, 1994, p. 124).

17. For the Boswell "treat" study, see Damasio et al. (1989); see also, Johnson, Kim, and Risse (1985) for additional evidence on implicit memory for affect in amnesic patients. The experiment using hostile words was reported by Bargh and Pietromonaco (1982). For a review of other evidence showing nonconscious shaping of preferences and feelings, see Bargh (1992), Niedenthal (1992), and Greenwald and Banaji (1995).

18. The mock operative crisis was reported by Levinson (1965). It is difficult to imagine that such an experiment would be approved by any present-day human subjects committee.

19. For evidence of improved postoperative recovery following suggestions given under anesthesia, see Evans and Richardson (1988). A critical review of early studies of memory and anesthesia is provided by Eich, Reeves, and Katz (1985). Kihlstrom and Schacter (1990) review more recent work. In our own research, we found significant priming effects with one anesthetic agent, isoflurane (Kihlstrom et al., 1990), but not with another anesthetic, sufentanil (Cork, Kilhstrom, & Schacter, 1992).

    The positive findings with anesthesia suggest that implicit memory might also be observed for information presented during ordinary sleep. Findings concerning "sleep learning" have generally been negative (see the chapters in Bootzin, Kihlstrom, & Schacter, 1990). When my colleagues and I examined whether presenting words during sleep produced priming, we found no evidence of it (Wood et al., 1992).

20. For discussion of such attributional processes, see Jacoby et al. (1989) and Kelley and Jacoby (1990). See also Squire (1995) for a useful discussion of the relation between memory distortion and implicit memory.

21. For the nineteenth-century debate over déjà vu, see Berrios (1995).

22. The work on preferences in newborn infants is reported by DeCasper and Fifer (1980) and DeCasper and Spence (1986).

23. Rovee-Collier (1993) provides a clear summary of her research.

24. The conditioning study was reported by Papousek (1967).

25. Schacter and Moscovitch (1984) discuss the development of an early memory system and possible parallels between infants and amnesics. Bachevalier, Brickson, and Hagger (1993) report that hippocampal lesions disrupt recognition memory in infant monkeys.

26. For a review of findings on recall of hidden objects in infancy, see Diamond (1990). Meltzoff (1995) provides a helpful discussion of his findings on delayed imitation of actions by nine-month-old infants. Nelson (1993) offers a useful conceptualization of the development of narrative forms of autobiographical memory. Naito and Komatsu (1993) review recent research on development of implicit and explicit memory.

   Patricia Bauer and her colleagues have provided impressive evidence for delayed imitation of event sequences in thirteen-month-old infants, reviewed by Bauer (1996). Data showing memory failure by amnesic patients on adult versions of such tasks are provided by McDonough et al. (1995). The fact that amnesic patients perform poorly does not, of course, necessarily imply that infants explicitly recall the event sequences, but it is consistent with this possibility. Assessing the implicit/explicit nature of retrieval in very young children is difficult because of their limited abilities to communicate. Interestingly, Myers, Perris, and Speaker (1994) taught ten- and fourteen-month-old infants how to operate a toy puppet and examined their behavior toward the toy on several occasions months and years later, when language skills had improved. Compared with youngsters without prior exposure to the toy, these children showed more interest in the puppet and had an easier time making it work. Yet Myers et al. observed almost no evidence of verbal recall of past episodes involving the toy, and concluded that retention was almost exclusively based on implicit memory. As Bauer (1996) notes, these findings have important implications for understanding the infantile amnesia we all have for the first two to three years of life, because they indicate that some aspects of events can be retained for long periods of time. However, these event representations may never become converted into the narrative form necessary for later recall (for observations and discussion of infantile amnesia, see Meltzoff, 1995; Pillemer & White, 1989; and Usher & Neisser, 1993).

27. See Tranel and Damasio (1985) and also Bauer (1984) for skin conductance studies of prosopagnosics; see Young (1992) for priming studies.

28. For reviews of research on memory rehabilitation after brain damage, see Glisky and Schacter (1989b) and Wilson (1987).

29. Glisky, Schacter, and Tulving (1986b). We suggested that the vanishing cues technique aids vocabulary learning because it enables amnesics to make use of priming, but other factors are also relevant. For example, Hayman et al. (1993) have found that the profoundly amnesic patient I call Gene can learn a great deal of new semantic information when he is prevented from making errors that interfere with subsequent learning (see Wilson et al., 1994 for a similar approach). Although the vanishing cues procedure does not prevent incorrect guesses, it does ensure that patients eventually provide a correct answer on every trial. Hamann and Squire (1995) have found that semantic learning in amnesic patients benefits greatly from training conditions that eliminate interference produced by previous errors, although amnesic patients still exhibit impaired semantic learning compared to control subjects.

30. For the computer learning studies, see Glisky, Schacter, and Tulving (1986a) and Glisky and Schacter (1988).

31. For the job training studies, see Glisky and Schacter (1987, 1989a). Much to our astonishment, these studies were reported as front-page news in the *Wall Street Journal* on October 5, 1993, in an article by David Stipp with the headline "Amnesia Studies Show That Brain Can Be Taught at Subconscious Level."

32. One particularly promising extension of the vanishing cues procedure is the errorless

learning technique developed by Wilson, Baddeley, Evans, and Shiel (1994).

33. We referred to this kind of rigidity as "hyperspecific learning" (Glisky et al., 1986a). For follow-up research, see Butters, Glisky, and Schacter (1993). For analogous phenomena in rats with hippocampal lesions, see Eichenbaum (1994). Hamann and Squire (1995), by contrast, observed only a nonsignificant trend for hyperspecific learning in their studies on the acquisition of new semantic knowledge in amnesic patients. Part of the reason for the difference may be that the vanishing cues procedure in our study encouraged patients to rely on priming, which is automatic and inflexible, whereas patients in Hamann and Squire's study may have relied more on residual explicit memory, which is not particularly inflexible.

34. Joanne Silver, "Show Focuses on the Diversity of Black Art" (*Boston Herald,* February 5, 1993).

35. Telephone interview with Cheryl Warrick, October 25, 1991.

36. Nancy Stapen, "Images from the Unconscious" (*Boston Globe,* October 25, 1991).

37. Some studies have shown that visual word priming is decreased when details such as typefont or typecase are changed between study and test, but others have failed to observe such effects. Marsolek, Kosslyn, and Squire (1992) discuss some of these studies and provide evidence that type-case specific priming is associated with the right cerebral hemisphere. Srinivas (1993) reports that priming of familiar pictures can be affected by changes in physical details, and Church and Schacter (1994) have shown that auditory priming can also be highly specific, affected by even small changes in the fundamental frequency of a speaker's voice. For review and discussion, see Curran, Schacter, and Bessenoff (1996) and Tenpenny (1995).

38. For WLP, see Schwartz, Saffran, and Marin (1980).

39. See, for example, Démonet et al. (1992) and Peterson et al. (1990).

40. For discussion of studies on priming of familiar pictures, see Srinivas (1993).

41. Our initial work on object decision priming is reported in Schacter, Cooper, and Delaney (1990). For studies with amnesic patients, see Schacter, Cooper, and Treadwell (1993). Other studies have revealed that amnesic patients can show intact priming for various kinds of novel perceptual information, including geometric patterns, nonsense words, and unfamiliar faces. For a recent review of these studies and their theoretical implications, see Keane et al. (1995).

42. Schacter et al. (1990) also showed that, when people are encouraged to come up with the name of an object from the real world that fits each shape, explicit memory for the objects is enhanced, but the priming effect disappears altogether. This result shows conclusively that priming of novel objects does not occur because people generate verbal labels for the objects. According to our view, the priming effect disappears when people generate verbal labels for the objects because thinking about the verbal labels distracts them from encoding the global shape of the object.

Our ideas about why there is no priming for impossible objects have been contested by Ratcliff and McKoon (1995). They suggest that on the object decision task, people show a general bias to call previously studied objects "possible." For possible objects, this bias produces priming. For impossible objects, they assert, the bias is counteracted by explicit memory for the unusual features that make these objects impossible, with the result that no priming is observed. Ratcliff and McKoon have provided some evidence that is consistent with these ideas. In a lengthy consideration of their position that attempts to clarify the issues, we have pointed out that their hypothesis does not fit in with all available data and have suggested an alternative account of their results (Schacter & Cooper, 1995).

In our first article on possible/impossible object priming (Schacter et al., 1990), we pointed out that failure to observe priming of impossible objects could be attributable to differences in size, complexity, or other features of possible and impossible objects we had not controlled. We also noted that priming of impossible objects might be observed if such features could be equated. Carrasco and Seamon (1996) recently reported that the impossible objects we used are perceived as more complex than the possible objects. When they equated perceived complexity, they found priming of both possible and impossible objects. This finding suggests that people can form some sort of structural representation of simple impossible objects.

43. For the PRS theory, see Schacter (1990) and Tulving and Schacter (1990).

44. This patient is described at length by Riddoch and Humphreys (1987).

45. For auditory priming in patient JP, see Schacter, McGlynn, Milberg, and Church (1993). For auditory priming in college students, see Church and Schacter (1994), and for auditory priming in amnesic patients, see Schacter, Church, and Treadwell (1994).

46. The first study to examine priming with PET scanning was reported by Squire et al. (1992). They found that priming was associated with blood flow decreases in extrastriate occipital cortex, but also found activation of the hippocampus during priming. This latter finding probably reflects the fact that explicit memory influenced or "contaminated" priming in Squire et al.'s experiment, as the authors themselves acknowledged. In our PET scanning study of priming (Schacter, Alpert et al., 1996), we eliminated contamination from explicit memory and also eliminated the hippocampal activation during priming. Yet we still observed blood flow decreases in extrastriate occipital regions during priming. Further evidence linking occipital cortex with visual word priming is reported by Gabrieli et al. (1995), who found impaired visual word priming in a patient with damage to the occipital cortex.

The observation that priming was accompanied by blood flow *decreases* suggests that identification of primed stimuli requires less metabolic activity and possibly fewer neurons than identification of nonprimed stimuli. This idea is supported by experiments with monkeys showing that as stimuli become increasingly familiar, the responses of some neurons in the inferior temporal cortex gradually decrease (for a review of these studies, see Desimone, Miller, Chelazzi, & Lueschow, 1995). However, priming may not always and exclusively involve blood flow decreases. Schacter, Alpert, et al. (1996) noted some priming-related increases outside the extrastriate region, and Schacter, Reiman, et al. (1995) found that priming of novel possible objects was associated with increased blood flow in inferior temporal regions (although we also noted alternative interpretations of this increase). Interestingly, Desimone et al. (1995) note that some inferior temporal neurons show enhanced responses to repeated stimuli. Ungerleider (1995) provides a thoughtful discussion of priming-related blood flow decreases in relation to animal studies and also in relation to blood flow increases and decreases in skill learning experiments.

47. For PET scanning and object decision, see Schacter, Reiman, et al. (1995). The ideas leading up to the PET study are described most fully in Cooper et al. (1992). For discussion of the role of inferior temporal and fusiform regions in object and face recognition, see Plaut and Farah (1990) and Damasio (1989).

48. The dissociations between priming and skill learning are reported by Butters, Heindel, and Salmon (1990). Impaired sequence learning and planning in cerebellar patients is reported by Grafman et al. (1994) and Pascual-Leone et al. (1993); see Salmon and Butters (1995) for review. Preserved piano playing and learning in amnesia were reported by Starr and Phillips (1970). For further discussion of the cerebellum and learning, see Thompson and Krupa (1994). Nissen and Bullemer (1987) report intact sequence learning in amnesic patients, and Rauch, Savage, et al. (in press) provide PET data. Karni et al. (1995) report the functional MRI study of finger sequences.

49. For habit learning in monkeys, see Mishkin, Malamut, and Bachevalier (1984). For impaired habit learning with basal ganglia damage, see McDonald and White (1993) and the review by Salmon and Butters (1995). For category learning in amnesia, see

Knowlton and Squire (1993) and Knowlton, Squire, and Gluck (1994). Kolodny (1994) reports that amnesic patients can show normal category learning when the task involves categorizing dot patterns. Kolodny also reports impaired category learning in amnesic patients on a more complex task involving classification of paintings by different artists. This suggests that explicit memory may be necessary for acquiring certain kinds of categorical knowledge. For preserved learning of artificial grammars in amnesic patients, see Knowlton, Ramus, and Squire (1992). Knowlton et al. based their work on the classic studies of Reber and associates showing implicit learning of artificial grammars in college students. For a review of this work, see Reber (1993).

50. For our ambiguous sentences experiment, see McAndrews, Glisky, and Schacter (1987). For other work on conceptual priming, see Blaxton (1989), Graf, Shimamura, and Squire (1985), and Hamann (1990). Some research indicates that, when priming involves acquiring new semantic associations, amnesic patients do not show intact performance (Schacter & Graf, 1986; Shimamura & Squire, 1989). The same appears to be true with some other kinds of novel associations (Kinoshita & Wayland, 1993; Schacter, Church, & Bolton, 1995).

51. See Devine (1989). For a review and discussion of implicit memory in social contexts, see Greenwald and Banaji (1995).

52. See Perfect and Askew (1994) for the experiment on advertising and implicit memory and Sanyal (1992) for a discussion of the relation between implicit memory research and consumer psychology. Wilson and Brekke (1994) introduce the idea of mental contamination and review a large body of relevant evidence.

53. For discussion of the functions of different forms of memory, and for the contrast between rapid and slow learning systems, see Sherry and Schacter (1987), Squire (1992), and McClelland et al. (1995).

CHAPTER 7
Emotional Memories: When the Past Persists

1. Interview with Melinda Stickney-Gibson, December 17, 1993.

2. All of Brown and Kulick's (1977) subjects were seven years or older at the time of the Kennedy assassination. Winograd and Killinger (1983) report that nearly everyone born in 1956 retains an assassination flashbulb, with gradually decreasing numbers of flashbulbs reported by people born in the subsequent six years.

   Although Brown and Kulick's report is generally regarded as the first investigation of flashbulb memories, Colegrove (1899) reported a similar investigation of memory for the assassination of Abraham Lincoln, with roughly similar results. For a general review of flashbulb memories, see Conway (1995).

3. The entire flashbulb memory series is reproduced in Turyn (1986).

4. For the multinational study, see Conway et al. (1994); the Loma Prieta study is described by Neisser et al. (1996); and the Olof Palme study is reported by Christianson (1989).

5. Larsen (1992) provides a detailed analysis of his memory for the Palme assassination compared to other news events and finds that mundane news events are forgotten quickly. In contrast to flashbulbs, few people can remember exactly how they learned about the news that the government finally passed its most recent budget or how they learned about who won the most recent mayoral race in their town.

6. Neisser and Harsch (1992).

7. Weaver (1993).

8. Neisser and Harsch (1992), p. 9.

9. Brewer (1992).

10. The evidence concerning contributions of rehearsal and affect to flashbulb memories is not entirely clear-cut. For example, Pillemer (1984) has reported little effect of rehearsal on memories of the Reagan assassination attempt, and Neisser and Harsch (1992) failed to find effects of rated affective arousal on retention of the *Challenger* disaster.

11. Rubin and Kozin (1984).

12. The quotes are from James (1890), p. 670, and Terr (1988), p. 103.

13. Wilkinson (1983).

14. For the Loma Prieta earthquake, see Cardena and Spiegel (1993); for Chowchilla, see Terr (1981); for the North Carolina tornado, see Madakasira and O'Brien (1987). Krystal, Southwick, and Charney (1995) summarize numerous studies of combat veterans.

15. Quotes are from Langer (1991), pp. 34–35.

16. Rivers's observation is from Barker (1991), pp. 25–26. Dr. William Rivers was an actual psychiatrist who treated protesting British poet Siegfried Sassoon. Barker's novel is a fictional account of Rivers's treatment of Sassoon and other soldiers. Rivers's actual clinical cases and views are described lucidly in Rivers (1918).

17. See, for example, van der Kolk (1994).

18. Terr (1994), p. 28.

19. Pynoos and Nader (1989), p. 238.

20. For the 1988 school shooting see Schwartz, Kowalski, and McNally (1993). For combat flashbacks, see MacCurdy (1918) and also Pendergrast (1995).

21. Frankel (1994), p. 329. See also Spiegel (1995).

22. Good (1994). For other examples of misremembered traumas, see Ceci (1995).

23. Wagenaar and Groeneweg (1988).

24. Bradley et al. (1992). For similar results, see Bradley and Baddeley (1990), Brewer (1988), and Dutta and Kanungo (1967).

25. Christianson and Loftus (1987).

26. For weapon focus, see Loftus, Loftus, and Messo (1987); see Kramer, Buckhout, and Eugenio (1990) for individual differences related to anxiety and narrowing of attention; for anxiety and memory, see Eysenck and Mogg (1992). For a review of studies on how emotion affects memory for central and peripheral information, see Heuer and Reisberg (1992).

27. Personal communication, Richard J. McNally, May 1995.

28. For memory in regalia-wearing veterans, see McNally et al. (1995). See Krystal et al. (1995) and van der Kolk (1994) for reviews of studies involving memory in Vietnam veterans with post-traumatic stress disorders. Turner (in press) discusses the experiences of individual veterans and society's reactions to the war.

29. For a review of research on overgeneral memories, see Williams (1992). Baxter et al. (1989) first reported reduced left frontal activity in depressed patients, and the finding has since been replicated by others.

30. For discussion of mood-congruent retrieval, see Bower (1992).

31. See Clark and Teasdale (1982) for mood-congruent retrieval in depressed patients and Mineka and Nugent (1995) for a review of memory biases in depression, anxiety, and related clinical conditions.

32. For depressed patients, see Lewinsohn and Rosenbaum (1987); for pain patients, see Eich, Reeves, Jaeger, and Graff-Radford (1985).

33. See Brewin, Andrews, and Gotlib (1993) for a review of relevant literature.

34. Kluver and Bucy (1937); Weiskrantz (1956).

35. Mishkin (1978); Zola-Morgan et al. (1991).

36. For excellent summaries of the role of various parts of the amygdala in fear conditioning, see LeDoux (1992, 1994).

37. See Bechara et al. (1995).

38. For a thorough review of animal research concerning stress-related hormones, the amygdala, and memory, see McGaugh (1995).

39. Markowitsch et al. (1994) report selective emotional memory loss in one of their patients, and Gloor (1992) summarizes his own and others' research on electrical stimulation of the amygdala.

    Adolphs et al. described impaired fear recognition in an Urbach-Wiethe patient with bilateral amygdala damage (1994, 1995). Adolphs et al. (1995) report that unilateral amygdala damage does not produce impaired fear recognition. Interestingly, Larry Squire has found that an amnesic patient with extensive amygdala damage has no problems recognizing fear (personal communication, October 1995). Because the patient described by Adolphs et al. had amygdala damage since birth, and Squire's patient only sustained it in adulthood, the fear recognition failure in Adolphs et al.'s patient may be attributable to an early failure to learn emotional expressions. For the PET scanning study, see Rauch, van der Kolk, et al. (in press). This study must be interpreted cautiously, because it lacked a control group. In a related study by Shin et al. (1995), the right amygdala was activated and Broca's area deactivated when Vietnam combat veterans with post-traumatic stress disorder formed mental images of recently seen combat pictures. But neither of these effects was observed in healthy combat veterans.

40. The effects of yohimbine on memory and perception in Vietnam veterans are described by Krystal et al. (1995). For evidence on catecholamines, see Yehuda et al. (1992) and Brown (1994). Krystal et al. (1995), and van der Kolk (1994) provide reviews of psychobiological aspects of post-traumatic stress disorders.

41. For the drug study, see Cahill et al. (1994); see also McGaugh (1995). For the study of the amygdala-damaged patient, see Cahill et al. (1995).

CHAPTER 8
Islands in the Fog: Psychogenic Amnesia

1. "Lumberjack" is not the patient's actual nickname. A full report of the case is provided in Schacter, Wang, Tulving, and Freedman (1982).

2. Abeles and Schilder (1935) estimate that less than 1 percent of psychiatric patients exhibit functional amnesia; Kirschner (1973) offers an estimate of between 1 percent and 2 percent. For the 14 percent estimate of amnesia during wartime, see Sargent and Slater (1941). This estimate included both extensive amnesia for the entire personal past, and more limited amnesias for particular events.

3. This case is described by Fisher (1945). For reviews of fugues and related functional retrograde amnesias, see Kihlstrom and Schacter (1995) and Schacter and Kihlstrom (1989).

4. See Kritchevsky, Zouzounis, and Squire (in press).

5. This letter was sent to me by Dr. Robert Kaye on April 29, 1986.

6. The case is reported by Treadway et al. (1992). As of the early 1990s, K. had not recovered his memories (Michael McCloskey, personal communication, December 1995). They also describe another patient who is in several respects similar to K.

7. The British psychiatrist Charles Symonds adopted the extreme view that all cases of fugue and extensive functional amnesia are consciously simulated. He claimed that a simple speech had allowed him to "cure" the approximately half-dozen patients on whom he had tried it. "I know from experience that your pretended loss of memory is the result of some intolerable emotional situation," Symonds informed his amnesic patients. "If you will tell me the whole story, I promise absolutely to respect your confidence, will give you all the help I can and will say to your doctor and relatives that I have cured you by hypnotism." This quote comes from an address Symonds gave to

the National Hospital in London on February 27, 1970. The entire address is reproduced in Merskey (1979), pp. 258–265; the simulation quote is on pp. 264–265.
Pendergrast (1995, p. 122) also cites Symonds's simulation speech. For a case in which
genuine amnesia turned into simulation, see Kopelman et al. (1994). For research on
detecting faked amnesias, see Brandt (1992) and Schacter (1986). In the latter article,
I described experiments indicating that college students who had been instructed to
feign amnesia for a specific event tended to "overdo it," and thus could be distinguished from students who had actually forgotten the event. Students who genuinely
could not remember still felt that they might recall the event if they were given cues
and hints. Simulators, by contrast, maintained that cues and hints would not help them
to remember. The general idea that simulators tend to overplay their role, behaving
"more amnesic than amnesics," is central to other techniques for detecting faked
amnesia.

8. Recent cases of functional amnesia with a history of brain injury include Akhtar, Lindsey, and Kahn (1981), Daniel and Crovitz (1986), Gudjonsson and Taylor (1985), and
Gudjonsson and Mackeith (1983).

9. For review of early studies mentioning brain injury in fugue and functional amnesia,
see Schacter and Kihlstrom (1989).

10. For amnesia after rape, see Christianson and Nilsson (1989). For reviews of limited
amnesias, see Kihlstrom and Schacter (1995), Schacter and Kihlstrom (1989), and
Spiegel (1995).

11. The 26 percent incidence of amnesia is provided by Taylor and Kopelman (1984). The
other studies are considered in an article of mine that surveys what is known about
amnesia and crime (Schacter, 1986). See also Herman (1995).

12. For alcoholic blackout, see Lisman (1974).

13. Quotes are from Moldea (1995), pp. 124–125. For a firsthand account of Sirhan's
amnesia and reenactment of the crime under hypnosis, see Diamond (1969).

14. Bower (1981) provides an early discussion of mood state–dependent retrieval. In the years
since the publication of Bower's paper, mood state–dependent retrieval has often proved
an elusive phenomenon, with a "now-you-see-it-now-you-don't" quality. Mood
state–dependent retrieval—higher levels of recall when moods match at encoding and
retrieval—is generally not as robust as mood-congruent retrieval, which I discussed in
chapter 7. In mood-congruent retrieval, information that is congruent with a particular
mood is preferentially easy to recall. Eich (1995) provides a helpful discussion.

15. All quotes are from Moldea (1995), p. 298 for Sirhan's claim of amnesia, p. 326 for the
McCowan incident, and p. 325 for Moldea's reflection.

16. Tayloe (1995).

17. Other observations sometimes cited as evidence for traumatic amnesia are likewise difficult to interpret. For example, in a thoughtful essay on trauma and memory, the psychiatrist Judith Herman (Herman, 1995) refers to Carlson and Rosser-Hogan's (1994)
study of 50 Cambodian war refugees as evidence for a link between trauma and amnesia. In that study, 90 percent of the refugees endorsed as applicable to them a check-
list item "amnesia for past traumatic experiences." This is certainly an intriguing observation, but its meaning is not entirely clear. How could a respondent know that he was
amnesic for past traumatic experiences unless he now remembered them? Exactly how
did the refugees interpret the term *amnesia* (which was translated for them into their
native Cambodian language)? And how would other nontraumatized Cambodians of
a similar age and background respond to this question? Without an appropriate control group and a better understanding of how the respondents understood the check-
list item, we simply cannot say whether this study provides any evidence of an association between trauma and amnesia.

Likewise, when arguing for the prevalence of traumatic amnesia, van der Kolk and

Fisler (1995) cite Charles Wilkinson's (1983) study of people who witnessed the collapse of the skywalks in the Kansas City Hyatt Regency. As we saw in chapter 7, nearly all of these people were plagued by intrusive recollections of the trauma; none of them reported amnesia for the horrible incident. About half of them said they attempted to avoid being reminded of the disaster and about one-third reported post-traumatic "memory difficulties," which is presumably why van der Kolk and Fisler refer to this study. But we must not confuse these effects of trauma on memory with amnesia for the traumatic episode itself.

18. See Jacobs and Nadel (1985) for a discussion of recovered childhood fears and a review of relevant animal research.

19. Solomon et al. (1987). The research study in which this patient was included revealed that eight of thirty-five Israeli soldiers who had been traumatized during the 1973 war exhibited some evidence suggesting the reactivation of trauma during the 1982 conflict. It is difficult, however, to distinguish between the idea that the second trauma reactivated some aspect of the first and the idea that the patient simply responded in a similar manner to two independent events.

20. Van Dyke, Zilberg, and McKinnon (1985), p. 1072.

21. Coriat (1907). The cause of amnesia was never conclusively determined in this case.

22. The homosexual rape case is described by Kaszniak et al. (1988), and the telephone dialing case is reported by Lyon (1985). Other clinical examples of implicit memory are reviewed by Schacter and Kihlstrom (1989) and Kihlstrom and Schacter (1995).

23. For discussions of Janet, see Ellenberger (1970), Hacking (1995), Perry and Laurence (1984), and van der Kolk and van der Hart (1989).

24. Janet (1904). The Janet quote is from Ellenberger (1970), p. 371. For Breuer and Freud's cases, see Freud and Breuer (1966).

25. Christianson and Nilsson (1989); for other cases, see Schacter and Kihlstrom (1989) and Tobias, Kihlstrom, and Schacter (1992).

26. For review and discussion of implicit emotional memory in amnesic patients, see Tobias et al. (1992).

27. For a lengthy exposition of Janet's ideas, see Janet (1907).

28. Morton Prince (1910) also viewed dissociation as a natural consequence of the architecture of cognition, as opposed to the strictly pathological process envisaged by Janet (1907). For modern perspectives on dissociation theory that bear on multiple personality patients, see Bowers (1991), Freyd (1994), Hilgard (1977), Kihlstrom (1984), and Spiegel (1991, 1994, 1995).

29. See Spiegel (1995) for a thoughtful discussion of the relation between dissociation and repression with regard to psychogenic amnesia.

30. For a recent review of inhibition, attention, and the brain, see Desimone and Duncan (1995).

31. For PET studies and inhibition, see Grasby et al. (1993) and Nyberg, McIntosh, Cabeza, et al. (1996). In these studies, there was evidence for inhibition during retrieval when a brain region showed decreased blood flow during explicit retrieval compared to a nonmemory control task. Although such blood flow decreases could be interpreted in a number of ways, analyses by Nyberg and colleagues provide convincing evidence that inhibitory processes are involved in producing them. For cognitive research on inhibitory processes in memory, see Anderson, Bjork, and Bjork (1994).

32. For research on instructed forgetting, see Bjork (1989). For tip-of-the-tongue states and inhibition, see Brown (1991).

33. See Morton (1991) for a similar idea.

34. See Putnam et al. (1986) for estimates of amnesia, and Bliss (1986) for clinical descriptions.

35. For Eve, see Thigpen and Cleckley (1957); for Sybil, see Schreiber (1973).

36. For different perspectives on dissociative disorders and children, see Donovan and McIntyre (1990) and Putnam (1993).

37. Mary Reynolds, described initially in 1816 as a case of "double consciousness," is often cited as the first case of a multiple personality. However, as Hacking (1995, p. 151) points out in his excellent historical treatment, two cases, one European and one American, were described as early as 1791. A few other scattered cases were reported during the mid-nineteenth century, until the eclectic French scholar Eugene Azam reported the landmark case of Felida X. in 1876. The patient spontaneously dissociated into different personalities, and Azam found that he could achieve the same effect through hypnosis. Shortly after the publication of Azam's case, there was a deluge of reports of similar cases in France and then America. For detailed histories of the nineteenth-century development of multiple personalities, see Hacking (1995) and Kenny (1986).

38. See Bower (1981), Kihlstrom (1984), Putnam (1993), and Spiegel (1991) for variants on the ideas discussed in this paragraph.

39. Prince (1910), p. 265. See also Coriat (1916) and Janet (1907) for similar observations.

40. For our study, see Nissen et al. (1988). All of the names of the personalities are pseudonyms.

41. Evidence of the abuse was provided both by IC's sister and her mother. IC initially did not admit to the abuse, but later conceded that it had occurred. It is not clear whether IC initially failed to remember the abuse or simply did not wish to acknowledge that it had occurred. For a full report of the IC case, see Schacter, Kihlstrom, Kihlstrom, and Kaszniak (1989).

42. Ofshe and Watters (1994), p. 239.

43. Ofshe and Watters's version of what happened in Anne Stone's case is disputed by Dr. Bennett Braun, the main psychiatrist involved in her treatment. In a June 22, 1995, article by Matt Keenan in *New City,* a Chicago magazine, Braun's attorney Debra Davy is quoted as saying that Ofshe and Watters's account of the case is "just absurd."

44. The *Frontline* documentary *Searching for Satan* was broadcast on October 24, 1995. See Coons (1994) for corroboration of sexual abuse in patients with dissociated identities and for discussion of earlier research.

45. Merskey (1992), p. 337.

46. For thoughtful discussions on the role of social and cultural factors in shaping the character of multiple personality patients, see Hacking (1995), Kenny (1986), and Mulhern (1994).

47. My discussion of glucocorticoids is based largely on Sapolsky's (1992) excellent treatment of the subject.

48. The experiments on primates are reviewed by Sapolsky (1992), pp. 269–270 and 310–311.

49. Experiments showing memory impairment as a result of injections that cause temporary elevation of glucocorticoid levels are reported by Wolkowitz et al. (1990) and Newcomer et al. (1994). In the Wolkowitz et al. study, memory impairment was reflected by increased errors of commission during recall of a word list. In the Newcomer et al. study, impairment was reflected by increased errors of omission during recall of stories. Keenan et al. (1995) report long-term effects of glucocorticoid exposure on explicit but not implicit memory.

    The evidence on reduced hippocampal volume in traumatized veterans has been reported by Bremner et al. (1993) and Gurvitz et al. (1996). In Gurvitz et al.'s sample, a strong positive correlation (+.72) was observed between degree of combat exposure and hippocampal volume, favoring the idea that traumatic stress associated with combat exposure may have indeed played a role in the reduced hippocampal volumes in combat veterans (Roger Pittman, personal communication, November 1995).

50. Bremner et al. (1993) report that veterans with post-traumatic stress disorder remembered fewer neutral words from a list than did control subjects. For studies of concen-

tration camp survivors, see Sutker, Golina, and West (1990) and Thygesen, Hermann, and Willanger (1970).

51. For studies on cortisol regulation in abused girls, see De Bellis, Lefter, et al. (1994); De Bellis, Chrousos, et al. (1994). The imaging study is reported by Stein et al. (1995), and the articles on autobiographical memory impairment in women with abuse histories are by Park and Balon (1995), and by Kuyken and Brewin (1995), who studied depressed women.

52. For a review of brain–damaged patients with so-called focal retrograde amnesias, see Hodges (1995). For ideas about binding codes and the temporal lobes, see Damasio (1989). Hunkin et al. (1995) apply Damasio's ideas to a case of focal retrograde amnesia.

53. Sapolsky (1992), p. 334. Sapolsky also points out that, perhaps ironically, people who have sustained serious brain injuries are often treated with steroids that increase glucocorticoid levels and hence may further endanger the hippocampus.

54. Some amnesic patients with medial temporal damage do have fairly extensive retrograde amnesias that extend back more than a decade. And in the syndrome of transient global amnesia, which has been linked to reduced blood flow in the hippocampus and related structures in the medial temporal lobe, some patients have been described who cannot remember personal events dating back to childhood, even though they recognize famous public figures from the distant past; see Evans, Wilson, Wraight, and Hodges (1993). See also Hodges and Warlow (1990) and Kritchevsky et al. (1988). However, when Kritchevsky et al. (in press) directly compared transient global amnesia patients with psychogenic amnesia patients, they found strikingly different results: patients with transient global amnesias recalled remote experiences more easily than recent ones, whereas patients with psychogenic amnesias showed precisely the opposite pattern. Also, the psychogenic amnesia patients had no anterograde memory problems, whereas the transient global amnesia patients did.

55. See Jacobs and Nadel (1985).

CHAPTER 9
The Memory Wars: Seeking Truth in the Line of Fire

1. Personal communication from Diana Halbrooks, April 24, 1995. All quotes attributed to Diana Halbrooks in the chapter are taken from this letter, which Diana wrote to me in response to my request for information about her story for this book. A brief description of Diana's case appeared in the *Dallas Morning News,* "Memories Almost Split This Family," by Steve Blow (May 21, 1995).

2. Cheit is quoted in Pendergrast (1995), p. 102. My discussion of Cheit's case draws both from Pendergrast, who interviewed Cheit, and from lengthy articles on May 7 and May 9, 1995, in the *Providence Journal-Bulletin,* "Bearing Witness: A Man's Recovery of His Sexual Abuse as a Child," by Mike Stanton. These articles describe in detail Cheit's search for Farmer, his one-hour phone conversation with him, and his attempts to sue Farmer and the camp that employed him. One curious feature of this conversation is that Farmer quickly admits to molesting other boys, but says he remembers Cheit only after considerable prodding. Farmer has claimed that he only admitted abusing Cheit and others to get him off the phone. Yet Cheit also discovered that Farmer had previously been forced to leave positions because he was suspected of molesting children, including one incident in which he was forced to leave town as a result of being accused of molesting a judge's son. It seems highly improbable that Cheit would have just happened to recover a memory about a man who admitted molesting children and had lost jobs because of his problem, had Cheit not been abused himself.

3. For detailed presentation of individual cases of recovered memories and their effects on families, see Goldstein and Farmer (1992, 1993), Loftus and Ketcham (1994), Ofshe and Watters (1994), and Pendergrast (1995).

4. Differing accounts of the Franklin case exist. For the defense perspective, see Loftus and Ketcham (1994), and for the prosecution perspective, see Terr (1994). MacLean (1993) provides a detailed and comprehensive journalistic account.

   The *New York Times* (April 5, 1995) reported that Franklin's conviction was overturned in part because the jury was prevented from learning that nearly every corroborated detail of Eileen Lipsker Franklin's memory was publicly available from newspaper accounts shortly after the crime.

   Terr (1994) tells the story of former Miss America Marilyn Van Derbur Atler. For Roseanne Barr, see Loftus and Ketcham (1994), p. 79. The numbers concerning the False Memory Syndrome Foundation were provided by director Pamela Freyd (personal communication, December 1995). She states that overall, about 30,000 people have asked FMSF for information. In addition to 17,000 that appear to involve repressed memory recovery by an adult, about 9,000 are inquiries from professionals, 1,500 are from people questioning their own recovered memories, and 300 are from people who have retracted their memories. The remainder are from individuals who say they have been falsely accused of abuse on a basis other than recovery of repressed memory, students, and general interest inquiries.

5. For discussion of the backlash, see Bass and Davis (1994), pp. 477–534, Herman and Harvey (1993), and Olio (1994).

6. For general reviews of the debate, see Lindsay and Read (1994) and Loftus (1993). Some sense of the passions aroused by this debate can be gleaned from the fact that a variety of journals have recently devoted entire issues to it: *Applied Cognitive Psychology* (August 1994), *Consciousness and Cognition* (September/December 1994), *International Journal of Clinical and Experimental Hypnosis* (October 1994 and April 1995), and *Psychiatric Annals* (December 1995), among others.

7. A collection of papers presented at the conference can be found in Schacter, Coyle, et al. (1995).

8. For material concerning "memories" of past lives and alien abductions, see Baker (1992), Spanos et al. (1991), and Mack (1994).

9. I made this point in a lengthy review of several books concerning recovered memories that was published in the April 1995 *Scientific American* (Schacter, 1995b). I received many letters concerning the review and was gratified that people responded positively to my attempt to alter the standard portrayal of the debate. I titled the review "Memory Wars," which provided the basis for the title of this chapter. Apparently I picked a popular title, because in fall 1995, a volume appeared entitled *The Memory Wars: Freud's Legacy in Dispute* (Crews, 1995). The volume contains critiques of recovered memory therapy by Frederick Crews that had been published previously in *The New York Review of Books,* together with responses from critics of Crews's writings.

10. The study of rape memories is reported by Tromp et al. (1995). I should note that no information was available about the relative ages of the rape memories and the other unpleasant memories that women provided. If the rape memories were older, this could be why they were less clear and vivid. Nonetheless, the data are consistent with the idea that failing to think about or talk about a traumatic experience might result in a blurry or fragmented engram. Freyd (1994) emphasizes that talking about past experiences with others is critical for creating an accessible and socially "shareable" engram. However, the social psychologist Dan Wegner has reported a series of experiments that show that sometimes people have great difficulty trying not to think about specified items. For example, experimental volunteers who are told not to think about a "white bear" end up thinking about it more than those who are not instructed to stop thinking about the word (for a review of these experiments, see Wegner, 1992).

Koutstaal and Schacter (in press) provide a lengthy discussion of intentional forgetting and voluntary thought suppression in relation to forgetting of sexual abuse. For an insightful fictional depiction of how a person goes about trying to deliberately forget painful events, see Van Arsdale (1995).

11. Berendzen's *Nightline* interview aired on May 23, 1991. The quote from his autobiographical recounting of the abuse and its consequences is in Berendzen and Palmer (1993), p. 67. There is one passage at the beginning of the book where Berendzen can be read as suggesting that his forgetting involved something more powerful than conscious suppression. Recounting the first time his mother had sexually molested him, Berendzen said that "Once it was over, it was erased" (p. xi). This could be taken to mean that he was literally unable to remember the event immediately after it occurred. But it seems more likely that it refers to his family's ability to act as if nothing had happened, which Berendzen goes on to describe.

12. For examples of such cases, see Loftus and Ketcham (1994), Ofshe and Watters (1994), Pendergrast (1995), and Yapko (1994).

13. For reviews of relevant experiments on directed forgetting, see Bjork (1989) and Johnson (1994).

14. Brewin et al. (1993) review studies showing that people are generally accurate in recollecting the general contours of childhood (see chapter 3).

15. For relevant discussions of this kind of repression, see Herman (1992), Frederickson (1992), and Terr (1994); for critiques, see Crews (1995), Loftus and Ketcham (1994), Ofshe and Watters (1994), Pope and Hudson (1995), and Pendergrast (1995).

16. These points are made forcefully by Erdelyi (1985), p. 218, who points out that when Freud "states that 'repression is the foundation stone on which the whole structure of psychoanalysis rests, the most essential part of it' . . . we are to understand that he is speaking of defense processes in general." He goes on to depict Freud's dilemma clearly: "How was repression in this general sense (subsuming a multiplicity of specific techniques) to be distinguished from the original, simplistic notion of repression as the forcing out or keeping out of some specific mental content from consciousness? It is this problem that Freud sought to resolve in his monograph, *Inhibitions, Symptoms, and Anxiety* (1926), where he proposed that the term *defense (Abwehr)* replace the by then overgrown construct of repression, and that the original term be reserved for the early, simple meaning, namely, motivated amnesia or forgetting. Although the suggestion is implemented by some later psychoanalysts . . . Freud himself did not pursue it with any consistency" (pp. 219–220).

For recent developments concerning the concept of repression that attempt to relate it to contemporary memory research, see Jones (1993).

17. For studies of repressors and memory for negative experiences, see Davis (1990) and Myers and Brewin (1994). Ramachandran (1995) describes patient BM. Holmes (1990) surveyed the research literature and concluded that no evidence for defensive repressions exists. His conclusion seems warranted, but it is questionable whether the laboratory experiments he considered are relevant to real-life traumas.

18. Erika Marquardt, artist's statement, 1992.

19. The information about the study of the Father Porter victims was provided by personal communications from Dr. Stuart Grassian, December 1994 and October 1995.

20. See, for example, Harvey and Herman (1994) for examples of sketchy partial amnesias in sexual abuse survivors.

21. See Elliott and Briere (1995). For earlier studies, see Briere and Conte (1993), Herman and Schatzow (1987), and Loftus, Polonsky, and Fullilove (1994). These studies also have various other problems (for detailed critiques, see Pope and Hudson [1995]; Kihlstrom [in press]; Lindsay and Read [1994], Ofshe and Watters [1994], and Pendergrast [1995]). To take just one example, Herman and Schatzow (1987) reported that fourteen of fifty-three clients (26 percent) who participated in a group therapy pro-

gram for incest survivors reported "severe" memory impairment for the abuse prior to memory recovery. But on average, the abuse began when these patients were under five years old. I have already pointed out that for most of us, earliest recollections begin around ages two to three, and not much is remembered until a few years later (chapter 8). The "severe" memory impairment in fourteen group therapy participants could be attributable to normal forgetting of early childhood experiences as opposed to massive repression. Finally, all retrospective studies share another methodological problem: it is not clear how accurately people can respond to such questions as "Was there ever a time when you had no memory of this event?" (Elliott & Briere, 1995, p. 635). Different people may interpret such questions differently, and it may be difficult in retrospect for people to recollect with any precision prior states of forgetting.

22. Respondents in interviews concerning sexual abuse sometimes withhold information initially (for reasons other than amnesia) that they later divulge in follow-up clarification interviews, and Williams did not report any clarification interviews. Moreover, if these respondents had been abused more than once, they might have confused this particular incident with another abuse episode. Indeed, two-thirds of the women included in the 38 percent figure remembered other episodes of abuse. For further discussion, see the critiques cited in the previous note.

23. Schooler (1994) reports that the abusive incidents JR had forgotten about apparently occurred over a period of years. When he eventually recovered the memories after seeing a movie that dealt with sexual abuse, the priest admitted the molestation. Herman and Harvey (1994) have also reported forgetting of extended abuse in the form of a composite case composed of several different patients' stories, referred to as "Emily B."

In the Williams (1994) study, Williams does provide the ages of the women who failed to recall the index hospital admission. On the one hand, these women were at the time of the index admission on average younger than women who recalled the admission (seven years old vs. nine years old), implying that normal forgetting of childhood incidents plays a role in what Williams observed. On the other hand, roughly half were seven or older when they were brought to the hospital, meaning that infantile or childhood amnesia cannot account for all of the observed forgetting. Another point is that many different kinds of abuse were experienced by the women in Williams's sample (e.g., about one-third of cases involved intercourse, whereas another one-third involved touching and fondling). We do not know whether all of the women included in the 12 percent who reported no abuse had suffered extensive and severe abuse (which, if forgotten, would imply the existence of massive repression), or whether some or all of these women endured milder forms of abuse that might be subject to "ordinary" forgetting.

Moreover, Williams (1994) found a marginally significant trend for more forceful abuse to be better remembered than less forceful abuse—the opposite of what might be expected if a repression mechanism were operating to block out the most unbearable abuse. Curiously, although Table 2 in Williams (1994, p. 1172) shows this trend, the text of Williams's paper says that "There is a tendency for the women who were subjected to more force to not recall the abuse" (p. 1172). This error was spotted by a psychology graduate student at Temple University, Evan Harrington, who discusses it in the February 1995 edition of the *FMS Foundation Newsletter*. Harrington characterizes the mistake as an undetected typo in the manuscript.

24. Williams (1995), p. 655.

25. Ibid., p. 663.

26. Ibid.

27. McNally et al. (1995) describe a directed forgetting experiment in which survivors of sexual abuse suffering from post-traumatic stress disorder, when compared to abuse survivors without post-traumatic stress disorder, showed enhanced memory for abuse-related words (e.g., incest) and were less able than controls to forget about abuse-

related words when instructed to do so. These findings are in some respects similar to memory biases observed in depression and other emotional disorders (see chapter 7); it is unclear how they relate to memory for an actual episode of abuse.

There is little scientific evidence available concerning dissociative pathology in repressed memory cases. Wakefield and Underwager (1994), p. 87, reported the results of a survey sent to accused parents who belong to the FMS Foundation. They found little evidence for a history of psychopathology in the accusers. This study is limited by the fact that it relies on the retrospective estimates of the accused. However, as the authors point out, the results are consistent with data reported by Spanos et al. (1993), who found no evidence of serious psychopathology in people who "remembered" UFO abductions.

28. Although the importance of subjective or "narrative truth" in therapy is widely acknowledged, and the reality of Ann's pain could hardly be denied, objective or "historical truth" also becomes important when, as in Ann's case, a multimillion dollar law suit is filed against the alleged perpetrators.

29. MacLean (1993), pp. 391–395, discusses the relation between repression and dissociation in the Franklin case with respect to the testimony of Dr. David Spiegel, who strongly maintained a distinction between the two.

30. MacLean's (1993) book provides the most detailed accounting available of Eileen Franklin's memory.

31. See Nash (1994) for the young man. Likewise, in the well-known case of former Miss America Marilyn Van Derbur Atler, who recovered memories of sexual abuse by her father, confirmation was provided by a sister who had always remembered her own abuse. Van Derbur Atler went public with her recovered memories in 1991, but she had initially recovered them some three decades earlier at age twenty-four, during a conversation with an old friend. She stated that the abuse by her father went on from age five until she left for college and that she had forgotten about it completely. According to Terr (1994), Van Derbur Atler "split" into a day child and a night child, and forgot about the abuse virtually as soon as it occurred. Although this may seem to be evidence for massive repression or dissociation, Pendergrast (1995) points out that it is difficult to say much about the nature of forgetting processes that took place some thirty to forty years prior to Van Derbur Atler's 1991 announcement.

In another documented case of what appears to be a recovered memory, Szajnberg (1993) described a twelve-year-old boy who entered psychoanalysis because of severe obsessive-compulsive symptoms. During the period that he was in analysis, the boy was riding with his mother and "he asked if she had ever tried to strangle him. Startled that he remembered, mother admitted that she had. Neither could recall how old he was at the time, so they drove home to comb through picture albums. They were able to date this to his seventh birthday" (p. 716).

Szajnberg treats this as recovery of a repressed memory and links it to subsequent changes in the patient's symptoms. It is unclear, however, whether and to what extent the boy had been unable to recall the incident prior to mentioning it to his mother.

32. See Williams (1995). In addition to Mary, Kim, and Tanya, Williams describes in some detail two other individual cases. Jackie was apparently told about the abuse by her mother at age seventeen. Faith appears to have always remembered at least one incident of abuse, except for intervals of forgetting that occur when she is happy. These women recollected an experience they had not thought about for years in response to retrieval cues that elicited some aspects of what they had encoded about the experience—just as in examples of nontraumatic memory I considered earlier in the book.

33. The quote is from van der Kolk (1994), p. 261. Data concerning characteristics of traumatic and nontraumatic memories are reported by van der Kolk and Fisler (1995). They note that, although it is "possible" that traumatic memories are "reflections of sensation experienced at the moment of the trauma," it is also possible that "increased

activity of the amygdala at the moment of recall may be responsible for the subjective assignment of accuracy and personal significance." Herman (1992, 1995) also provides thoughtful discussions of the relation between traumatic and nontraumatic memories.

34. For example, Frederickson (1992), p. 88, states that "the mind has a process for recording, storing, and retrieving everything that happens." She makes this statement in the context of distinguishing among five different forms of memory, noting that the mind records everything that happens "using at least one of these memory processes." Frederickson allows for some infidelity in memory records, noting that the stress of an abusive experience may cause altered perceptions, with the result that "Some aspects of imagery may be exaggerated, even though each image represents an accurate slice of the abuse" (p. 90).

35. See, for example, Frederickson (1992), Herman (1992), and Terr (1994).

36. Lipinksi and Pope (1994), p. 245.

37. Groff's decision is rendered in The State of New Hampshire Hillsborough County Superior Court, *State of New Hampshire v. Joel Hungerford* 94-S–045 through 94-S–047; *State of New Hampshire v. John Morahan* 93-S–1734 through 93–5–1936. Dalianis's November 1995 ruling is rendered in The State of New Hampshire Hillsborough Superior Court Southern District, *State of New Hampshire v. David Walters* 93-S–2111, 2112.

38. See Ofshe and Watters (1994), pp. 178–181, for a description of Lanning's findings and Young (1992) for a therapist's perspective on ritual abuse. The survey of American Psychological Association members is part of the larger report from the National Center for Child Abuse, summarized by Goodman et al. (1994). For an informative analysis of the ritual abuse phenomenon, see Nathan and Snedeker (1995).

39. Japanese sources report that over 300 people have vanished since joining the cult that has been implicated in the nerve gas attack and that they have recovered a bone-grinding machine that may have been used to dispose of the remains of the victims. The story is reported in the *Boston Globe,* "Japan Cult May Have Ground Up 300 Bodies, Media Report" (May 25, 1995).

40. Nelson and Simpson (1994).

41. Ibid., p. 126. For other compelling stories of retractors, see Goldstein and Farmer (1993) and Pasley (1994).

42. Spanos et al. (1991).

43. A survey of over 800 psychotherapists by the clinician Michael Yapko suggests that many are not familiar with, or put little stock in, well-controlled studies of hypnosis. Yapko asked respondents to indicate whether they agree or disagree with a variety of questions about hypnosis and other aspects of therapy. Forty-seven percent of the therapists agreed either slightly or strongly with the statement "Psychotherapists can have greater faith in the details of a traumatic event when obtained hypnotically than otherwise"; 31 percent agreed with the statement "When someone has a memory of a trauma in hypnosis, it objectively must have occurred"; 54 percent agreed with the statement "Hypnosis can be used to recover memories of actual events as far back as birth"; and 28 percent agreed with the statement "Hypnosis can be used to recover accurate memories of past lives." No scientific evidence exists to support any of these statements. It is somewhat reassuring that 80 percent of the respondents in Yapko's survey agreed with the statement "It is possible to suggest false memories to someone who then incorporates them as true memories." But it also implies that one-fifth of his sample believes that it is not possible to suggest false memories. See Yapko (1994, 1995) for details of the survey.

44. For an excellent historical review of trance writing, see Koutstaal (1992). Schacter (1987a) reviews early anecdotal evidence concerning implicit memory and trance or automatic writing. Studies by Pennebaker and colleagues have shown that writing about traumatic experiences can yield therapeutic benefits (for review, see Harber &

Pennebaker, 1992). However, these benefits were observed in cases where there was no question that the trauma occurred. There is a huge difference between having people write about known traumas that they explicitly remember, as Pennebaker has done, and having people hunt for repressed memories that might or might not have occurred by writing down whatever pops to mind, as was done in Diana Halbrooks's therapy. The case of Neil discussed in chapter 2—the young boy who could remember his recent experiences by writing but not talking—suggests different retrieval pathways for written and spoken materials. But Neil's case says nothing about the potential accuracy of forgotten experiences retrieved through trance writing.

45. See, for example, Bass and Davis (1988, 1994), Frederickson (1992), and Herman (1992).

46. For a collection of papers dealing with social influences on memory, see the volume edited by Middleton and Edwards (1990).

47. For therapeutic effects of imaginal reliving of actual trauma, see Foa et al. (1991). For imagining unremembered abuse, see Frederickson (1992), pp. 108–112. Hyman et al. (in press) report effects of imagery on false memory creation. For a summary of work on imagery, perception, and the brain, see Kosslyn (1994).

48. The survey of psychotherapists is reported by Poole et al. (1995). For a detailed analysis and discussion of memory techniques used in psychotherapies concerned with childhood sexual abuse, see Lindsay and Read (1996).

49. For sharply contrasting estimates of the prevalence of illusory memories of sexual abuse, see Whitfield (1995), who claims on the basis of clinical experience that false memories of sexual abuse hardly ever occur, and Pendergrast (1995), who reasons that the phenomenon has reached epidemic proportions.

50. The quotes are from a book entitled *Frogs into Princes* by therapists Bandler and Grinder (1979), p. 96. They are reproduced in Loftus (1982), p. 149. For Janet, see Hacking (1995).

51. For experimental research on distinctions between memories of real and imagined events, see Johnson et al. (1988) and Schooler, Gerhard, and Loftus (1986). For clinical suggestions concerning ways to distinguish true and false recovered memories, see Person and Klar (1994) and Terr (1994).

52. For contrasting perspectives on this point, see Masson (1984), Erdelyi (1985), and Schimek (1987).

53. See Terr (1988) on trauma and play.

54. For incisive critiques of symptom checklists, see Lindsay and Read (1994), Loftus and Ketcham (1994), Ofshe and Watters (1994), Pendergrast (1995), and Yapko (1994).

55. See Pope and Hudson (1992) and Pope et al. (1994).

56. Frederickson (1992, p. 41).

57. See McElroy and Keck (1995); quote is from p. 732.

58. For a useful philosophical discussion of subtleties regarding the relation between memory and reality, see Hacking (1995), especially chaps. 17 and 18. I should emphasize that I am *not* asserting that all recovered memories of childhood sexual abuse necessarily contain a kernel of truth, in the sense that such memories must capture something that was terribly wrong in a person's early family life. In agreement with Neisser's (1994) analysis of this issue, it seems there are many possible sources of an illusory memory of sexual abuse; a problematic early family life is only one of them.

CHAPTER 10
Stories of Elders

1. Owen (1992), pp. 15, 51.

2. Ibid., p. 97.

3. Ibid., p. 160.

4. The exhibition catalog for Overlays of Memory contains an essay by memory researcher Endel Tulving. Much of the installation is based on Tulving's ideas about forms of memory.

5. Pat Potter, personal communication, March 29, 1993.

6. For recent reviews of explicit recall and recognition deficits in elderly adults, see Craik et al. (1995) and Light (1991). For the recall versus recognition contrast, see Craik and McDowd (1987). Parkin, Walter, and Hunkin (1995) reported preserved memory for left/right location compared to impaired memory for temporal order, although they note other evidence of impaired spatial memory in older adults (see also Craik et al., 1995). McDaniel and Einstein (1992) report normal prospective remembering of a to-be-performed task in the elderly, whereas Cockburn and Smith (1991) found impaired prospective remembering in old people.

7. For a review of brain changes with aging, see Ivy et al. (1992). Jernigan et al. (1991) provide MRI evidence of age-related decreases in the volume of the medial temporal lobes and cortical association areas.

8. For a review of research on neuron loss and aging, see Albert and Moss (in press).

9. The study of hippocampal neurons is by West et al. (1994). Albert and Moss (in press) point out that studies of humans and monkeys show little or no neuron loss in the CA1, CA2, and CA3 fields that constitute the core of the hippocampus, whereas there is some evidence of neuron loss in the output pathway of the hippocampus known as the subiculum.

10. For hippocampal atrophy and memory performance, see Golomb et al. (1994). Albert and Moss (in press) review evidence on neuron loss in the basal forebrain.

11. For changes in frontal lobe physiology with age, see Bashore (1993), Ivy et al. (1992), and Mittenberg et al. (1989). For elderly adults' performance on tests sensitive to frontal lobe lesions, see Mittenberg et al. (1989), Moscovitch and Winocur (1992), and Whelihan and Lesher (1985).

12. For evidence that frontal lobes are more relevant to recall than recognition, temporal order memory than spatial memory, and certain prospective memory tasks, see the reviews by Schacter (1987b) and Shimamura (1995).

13. The PET study was carried out in collaboration with Marilyn Albert, Nat Alpert, Scott Rauch, and Cary Savage. The comparison that yielded impaired right frontal activation in older adults involved one condition where participants provided the first word that came to mind in response to three letter word beginnings, and another where they tried to remember words that had appeared in a shallow encoding condition during study list exposure. In addition to the clear-cut age-related differences in right frontal activation, there was a similar, albeit less obvious, difference in left frontal activation. Older adults also tended to show greater activation than young in Broca's area in the posterior left frontal region, which is involved in language production, perhaps reflecting a greater reliance on phonetic retrieval strategies in old than young. There were also age-related differences in a brain region known as the anterior cingulate, which is often activated when young people are required to pay active attention to a target stimulus. For discussion of the frontal and cingulate contributions to retrieval, see Buckner and Tulving (1995).

14. See Grady et al. (1995). It must be noted that, in addition to the recognition versus recall difference, this study differs from the experiment by our group in the respect that we used words and they used faces. Differences in activations could reflect word versus face differences as much as recognition versus recall differences. Interestingly, the hippocampus was among the structures that showed age-related reductions during encoding in Grady et al.'s study. Because my colleagues and I found normal activation of the hippocampus during retrieval in old people, these findings point toward possible differences in hippocampal contributions to encoding and retrieval. But again, this

possibility is tempered by differences between words and faces in the two studies.

15. See Wills (1987) for the Reagan anecdote.

16. For source memory deficits and aging, see Ferguson, Hashtroudi, and Johnson (1992), McIntyre and Craik (1987), and Schacter et al. (1991). These experiments show that older adults' recollection of source information can be more or less impaired in different experimental conditions. A recent review and meta-analysis, however, reveals that on balance source memory tends to be impaired in elderly adults (Spencer & Raz, 1995). For links between frontal lobe impairment and source memory impairments in the elderly, see Craik et al. (1990), Glisky, Polster, and Routhieaux (1995), and Schacter et al. (1991). Dywan, Segalowitz, and Williamson (1994) have recently provided electrophysiological evidence indicating that the specific aspect of frontal dysfunction associated with source recall errors in older adults is different from the specific aspect of frontal dysfunction related to performance on problem-solving tests. They also provide evidence that frontal dysfunction alone probably does not account for all of older adults' source memory problems.

17. The study on remembering confidential information was conducted in collaboration with Kathryn Angell and Susan McGlynn.

18. For false fame effects in the elderly, see Dywan and Jacoby (1990). The elderly are susceptible to a similar kind of illusion with unfamiliar faces. After having seen a photograph of a not famous face once or twice, one week later older adults are much more likely to claim that the face is famous than are young adults (Bartlett, Strater, & Fulton, 1991). The experiment on false recognition was conducted recently by Kenneth Norman and me.

19. Cohen and Faulkner (1989). In the relevant experiment, old and young adults were shown a videotape of a kidnapping. Later, some elderly adults and some young adults read a written summary of the event that contained misinformation, and others read an accurate summary. Older adults were more influenced by the misinformation than were younger adults; they frequently claimed that the misinformation was part of the original videotaped event.

20. Hashtroudi, Johnson, and Chrosniak (1990).

21. Parkin and Walter (1992).

22. For evidence concerning working memory and frontal lobe patients, see Baddeley (1986, 1994) and Shimamura (1995). The PET studies are by Petrides et al. (1993) and Smith et al. (1995). In addition to frontal-lobe activations, both studies also revealed evidence of activation in posterior cortical regions during performance of working memory tasks, particularly the parietal lobes. Based on studies of monkeys, Friedman and Goldman-Rakic (1994) have emphasized that specific areas within the frontal and parietal regions work closely together and are key elements of a distributed network of structures that subserve working memory.

23. For monkeys and working memory, see Goldman-Rakic (1994) and Wilson, O'Scalaidhe, and Goldman-Rakic (1993). The link between dopamine receptors and working memory is shown by Williams and Goldman-Rakic (1995). The specific type of dopamine receptor implicated in working memory is known as the "D1" receptor. Arnsten et al. (1994) show that the D1 receptor is implicated in the working memory deficits of aged monkeys, and de Keyser et al. (1990) provide evidence for D1 receptor depletion in the frontal lobes or elderly people. Park and Holzman (1992) report working memory deficits in schizophrenics and Bradley, Welch, and Dick (1989) show working memory deficits in Parkinson's patients.

24. For working memory and aging, see reviews by Craik et al. (1995) and Light (1991).

25. For a review of semantic memory and inference making in older adults, see Light (1991). Charness (1981) reports experiments on chess and aging. For a summary of research showing how distinctive encoding and retrieval can benefit the elderly, see Bäckman, Mäntylä, and Herlitz (1990). Name finding impairments in aging are commonly observed but are not well understood. They may relate to impaired inhibitory processes in the

elderly, which I discuss elsewhere in the chapter. Older adults are sometimes less able than young people to suppress irrelevant thoughts and ideas when carrying out a cognitive task, and this may sometimes get in the way of retrieving specific names.

26. See La Voie and Light (1994) for a systematic review of priming and aging. Howard (1996) and Davis and Bernstein (1992) also provide reviews of implicit memory and aging. I believe that some of the apparent age-related deficits in priming are attributable to the use of explicit retrieval strategies by young subjects in experiments that do not have adequate procedures for ruling out "contamination" from explicit memory (see Schacter, Kihlstrom, et al., 1993). There is also some indication of more pronounced age-related deficits when priming depends on forming novel associations during a study task. Howard, Fry, and Brune (1991) have shown that older adults do not always show normal priming of new associations on a stem completion test, although they perform well when they are given more time than the young to form novel associations. In another recent study, Schacter, Church, and Osowiecki (1994) examined auditory priming and found that older adults failed to show more priming when the speaker's voice was the same at study and test than when the speaker's voice was different between study and test; young subjects showed more priming with the same than with different voices at study and test. Hearing loss in the elderly did not account for their impaired auditory priming. However, there is reason to believe that voice-specific priming depends on forming a new association between a word and a specific speaker's voice. My colleagues and I reported normal priming of novel visual objects in older adults (Schacter, Cooper, & Valdiserri, 1992), but Lynn Cooper (personal communication, June 1995) has recently found that the priming effect decays more quickly in older than in younger adults. La Voie and Light (1994) note that meta-analytic procedures do not indicate that priming of novel is generally more impaired than simple priming of familiar words in the elderly, so the issue is not yet settled.

27. The PET study of priming and aging was conducted in collaboration with Marilyn Albert, Nat Alpert, Scott Rauch, and Cary Savage.

28. For sequence learning in the elderly, see Howard and Howard (1989).

29. For the Tower of Hanoi task in aging and amnesic patients, see the papers by Davis and Bernstein (1992) and Saint-Cyr and Taylor (1992). Howard and Wiggs (1993) provide a general discussion of procedural learning and aging, including discussion of Howard's experiments showing an intact form of implicit learning in the elderly. Fisk et al. (1994) show that older adults retain general but not specific aspects of a perceptual skill as well as young people. For discussion of general slowing and older adults, see Salthouse (1991). For discussion of inhibition and the frontal lobes, see Shimamura (1995), and for evidence linking memory impairment and impaired inhibitory processes in the elderly, see Stoltzfus et al. (1993).

30. For flashbulb memories and aging, see Cohen, Conway, and Maylor (1994). Carstensen and Turk-Charles (1994) showed that older adults remember more from the emotionally arousing parts of a story than from the neutral parts. Cohen and Faulkner (1988) failed to find an association between the vividness of a memory and emotional arousal in the elderly.

31. Kidder (1993), p. 184.

32. The quotes are from an unpublished manuscript by Rosemary Pittman, provided to me by the MIA Gallery, Seattle. For biographical information on Pittman, see Rosenak and Rosenak (1990), pp. 244–245.

33. The quote is from Hufford, Hunt, and Zeitlin (1987), p. 42, who provide numerous examples of other elderly memory painters and folk artists.

34. Dobrof (1984), p. xviii. See Kaminsky (1984) for a review of the literature on reminiscence therapy.

35. For reviews of life review and reminiscence in the elderly, see Coleman (1986), Moli-

nari and Reichlin (1985), and Thornton and Brotchie (1987). For the differential benefits of different types of reminiscence, see Wong and Watt (1991).

36. For studies of the reminiscence bump, see Fitzgerald (1988, 1992).

37. Owen (1992), p. 82.

38. The fact that cueing only rarely evoked memories of unrecalled experiences suggests that the relevant engrams had decayed or deteriorated considerably. Interestingly, the Hoffmans observed that "In order to access this [seemingly forgotten] material, it was necessary to find a very specific cue, and that seemed to be largely a hit-or-miss affair" (Hoffman & Hoffman, 1990, p. 145). This observation fits with a point that I stressed earlier: when the engram is impoverished or degraded, only a select set of highly specific cues will provide a sufficiently good match to yield a subjective experience of remembering.

39. For studies showing better storytelling in elderly people than in young people, see Kemper et al. (1990) and Pratt and Robins (1991). For age-related problems in telling unfamiliar stories, see Pratt et al. (1989). Even when they tell recently learned stories, however, the elderly manage to offset their poor memory to some extent by superimposing narrative themes, morals, or lessons on their recall of story elements to a greater degree than the young do (Adams et al., 1990; Mergler, Faust, & Goldstein, 1984/1985).

40. Schleifer, Davis, and Mergler (1992, chap. 3) address the cultural functions of storytelling in elderly adults and review relevant literature on negative stereotypes of aging in Western society. See also Mergler et al. (1984/1985). For memory and oral tradition, see Rubin (1995).

41. For "the remembering," see Sams and Nitsch (1991, p. 57). For the Momaday quote, see Hobson (1979, p. 163).

42. Hobson (1979), p. 2.

43. For a discussion of Beam's work, see Grande (1994).

44. Danieli (1988).

45. Danieli (1994).

46. Ibid.

47. See Donald (1991) for a wide-ranging discussion of external symbolic storage and the evolution of memory.

48. For a discussion of the "crisis of memory," see Lipsitz (1990).

49. For studies of cherished possessions and aging, see Kamptner (1991), Sherman and Newman (1977/1978), and Wapner, Demick, and Redondo (1990). For the film and camera memory industries, see Kuhn (1991) and Slater (1991).

The photo experiments are being conducted with Wilma Koutstaal, Marcia Johnson, Mara Gross, and Kathryn Angell. In the actual experimental paradigm, people first view videotapes of several everyday scenarios that we "staged" ourselves, each comprised of a dozen or so mini-events. In one of them, for example, a woman professor goes about her business in her office—working on a paper, talking on the telephone, lending a model brain to a colleague, and so forth. Sometime after seeing the taped scenarios, people return to the laboratory and look at photos of key moments from half of the events—the woman in the act of handing the model brain to her colleague, for instance. This is in many ways similar to an everyday situation, where you would photograph only some of the events at a party or on a trip. Later, however, we test our experimental participants' ability to recall and recognize all the events that were shown in the original videotape.

50. The quotes from Ben Freeman are in the exhibition catalog *New Artists 1994: Photography Outside Tradition* (p. 12), from the Currier Gallery of Art in Manchester, New Hampshire.

BIBLIOGRAPHY

Abel, T., Alberini, C., Ghirardi, M., Huang, Y.-Y., Nguyen, P., & Kandel, E. R. (1995). Steps toward a molecular definition of memory consolidation. In D. L. Schacter, J. T. Coyle, G. D. Fischbach, M. M. Mesulam, & L. E. Sullivan (Eds.), *Memory distortion: How minds, brains and societies reconstruct the past* (pp. 298–328). Cambridge: Harvard University Press.

Abeles, M., & Schilder, P. (1935). Psychogenic loss of personal identity. *Archives of Neurology and Psychiatry, 34,* 587–604.

Adams, C., Labouvie-Vief, G., Hobart, C. J., & Dorosz, M. (1990). Adult age group differences in story recall style. *Journal of Gerontology: Psychological Sciences, 45,* 17–27.

Adolphs, R., Tranel, D., Damasio, H., & Damasio, A. R. (1994). Impaired recognition of emotion in facial expressions following bilateral damage to the human amygdala. *Nature, 372,* 669–672.

Adolphs, R., Tranel, D., Damasio, H., and Damasio, A. R. (1995). Fear and the human amygdala. *Journal of Neuroscience, 15,* 5879–5891.

Akhtar, S., Lindsey, B., & Kahn, F. L. (1981). Sudden amnesia for personal identity. *Pennsylvania Medicine, 84,* 46–48.

Alba, J. W., & Hasher, L. (1983). Is memory schematic? *Psychological Bulletin, 93,* 203–231.

Albert, M. S. & Moss, M. B. (in press). Neuropsychology of aging: Findings in humans and monkeys. In E. Schneider & J. W. Rowe (Eds.), *The handbook of the biology of aging* (4th Ed.). San Diego: Academic Press.

Allende, I. (1995). *Paula* (Peden, M. S., Trans.). New York: HarperCollins.

Anderson, J. R., & Schooler, L. J. (1991). Reflections of the environment in memory. *Psychological Science, 2,* 396–408.

Anderson, M. C., Bjork, R. A., & Bjork, E. L. (1994). Remembering can cause forgetting: Retrieval dynamics in long-term memory. *Journal of Experimental Psychology: Learning, Memory, and Cognition, 20,* 1063–1087.

Anderson, R. C., Pichert, J. W., Goetz, E. T., Schallert, D. L., Stevens, K. V., & Trollip, S. R. (1976). Instantiation of general terms. *Journal of Verbal Learning and Verbal Behavior, 15,* 667–679.

Arkes, H. R., & Freedman, M. R. (1984). A demonstration of the costs and benefits of expertise in recognition memory. *Memory & Cognition, 12,* 84–89.

Arnsten, A. F. T., Cai, J. X., Murphy, B. L., & Goldman-Rakic, P. S. (1994). Dopamine D_1 receptor mechanisms in the cognitive performance of young adult and aged monkeys. *Psychopharmacology, 116,* 143–151.

Augustine (1907/1966). *Confessions of St. Augustine.* New York: Dutton.

Bachevalier, J., Brickson, M., & Hagger, C. (1993). Limbic-dependent recognition memory in monkeys develops early in infancy. *Neuroreport, 4,* 77–80.

Bäckman, L., Mäntylä, T., & Herlitz, A. (1990). The optimization of episodic remembering in old age. In P. B. Baltes & M. M. Baltes (Eds.), *Successful aging: Perspectives from the behavioral sciences* (pp. 118–163). Cambridge: Cambridge University Press.

Baddeley, A. (1986). *Working memory.* Oxford: Clarendon.

Baddeley, A. (1994). Working memory: The interface between memory and cognition. In D. L. Schacter & E. Tulving (Eds.), *Memory systems 1994* (pp. 351–368). Cambridge: MIT Press.

Bahrick, H. P. (1979). Maintenance of knowledge: Questions about memory we forgot to ask. *Journal of Experimental Psychology: General, 108,* 296–308.

Bahrick, H. P. (1984). Semantic memory content in permastore: 50 years of memory for Spanish learned in school. *Journal of Experimental Psychology: General, 113,* 1–29.

Bailey, C. H., & Chen, M. (1989). Time course of structural changes at identified sensory neuron synapses during long-term sensitization in Aplysia. *Journal of Neuroscience, 9,* 1774–1781.

Baker, R. (1992). *Hidden memories.* Buffalo, NY: Prometheus Books.

Banaji, M. R., & Crowder, R. O. (1989). The bankruptcy of everyday memory. *American Psychologist, 44,* 1185–1193.

Bancaud, J., Brunet-Bourgin, F., Chauvel, P., & Halgren, E. (1994). Anatomical origin of *déjà vu* and vivid "memories" in human temporal lobe epilepsy. *Brain, 117,* 71–90.

Bandler, R., & Grinder, J. (1979). *Frogs into princes: Neurolinguistic programming.* Moab, UT: Real People Press.

Barclay, C. R. (1986). Schematization of autobiographical memory. In D. C. Rubin (Ed.), *Autobiographical memory* (pp. 82–99). Cambridge: Cambridge University Press.

Barclay, J. R., Bransford, J. D., Franks, J. J., McCarrell, N. S., & Nitsch, K. (1974). Comprehension and semantic flexibility. *Journal of Verbal Learning and Verbal Behavior, 13,* 471–481.

Bargh, J. A. (1992). Does subliminality matter to social psychology? Awareness of the stimulus versus awareness of its influence. In R. F. Bornstein & T. S. Pittman (Eds.), *Perception without awareness: Cognitive, clinical, and social perspectives* (pp. 236–255). New York: Guilford Press.

Bargh, J. A., & Pietromonaco, P. (1982). Automatic information processing and social perception: The influence of trait information presented outside of conscious awareness on impression formation. *Journal of Personality and Social Psychology, 43,* 437–449.

Barker, P. (1991). *Regeneration.* New York: Penguin.

Barsalou, L. W. (1988). The content and organization of autobiographical memories. In U. Neisser & E. Winograd (Eds.), *Remembering reconsidered: Ecological and traditional approaches to the study of memory* (pp. 193–243). New York: Cambridge University Press.

Bartlett, F. C. (1932). *Remembering.* Cambridge: Cambridge University Press.

Bartlett, J. C., Strater, L., & Fulton, A. (1991). False recency and false fame of faces in young adulthood and old age. *Memory & Cognition, 19,* 177–188.

Bartsch, D., Ghirardi, M., Skehel, P. A., Karl, K. A., Herder, S., Chen, M., Bailey, C. H., & Kandel, E. R. (1995). CREB–2/ATF–4 as a repressor of long-term facilitation in *Aplysia:* Relief of repression converts a transient facilitation into a long-term functional and structural change, *Cell, 83,* 979–992.

Bashore, T. R. (1993). Differential effects of aging on the neurocognitive functions subserving speeded mental processing. In J. Cerella, J. Rybash, W. Hoyer, & M. L. Commons (Eds.), *Adult information processing: Limits on loss* (pp. 37–76). San Diego: Academic Press.

Bass, E., & Davis, L. (1988). *The courage to heal: A guide for women survivors of child sexual abuse* (1st ed.). New York: HarperPerennial.

Bass, E., & Davis, L. (1994). *The courage to heal: A guide for women survivors of child sexual abuse* (3rd ed.). New York: HarperPerennial.

Bauer, P. J. (1996). What do infants recall of their lives? Memory for specific events by one-to two-year-olds. *American Psychologist, 51,* 29–41.

Bauer, R. M. (1984). Autonomic recognition of names and faces in prosopagnosia: a neuropsychological application of the guilty knowledge test. *Neuropsychologia, 22,* 457–469.

Baxter, L. R., Jr., Schwartz, J. M., Phelps, M. E., Mazziotta, J. C., Guze, B. H., Selin, C. E., Gerner, R. H., & Sumida, R. M. (1989). Reduction of prefrontal cortex glucose metabolism common to three types of depression. *Archives of General Psychiatry, 46,* 243–250.

Bechara, A., Tranel, D., Damasio, H., Adolphs, R., Rockland, C., & Damasio, A. R. (1995). Double dissociation of conditioning and declarative knowledge relative to the amygdala and hippocampus in humans. *Science, 1995, 269,* 1115–1118.

Begg, I. M., Anas, A., & Farinacci, S. (1992). Dissociation of processes in belief: Source recollection, statement familiarity, and the illusion of truth. *Journal of Experimental Psychology: General, 121,* 446–458.

Bellezza, F. S. (1981). Mnemonic devices: Classification, characteristics, and criteria. *Review of Educational Research, 51,* 247–275.

Belli, R. F., Lindsay, D. S., Gales, M. S., & McCarthy, T. T. (1994). Memory impairment and source misattribution in postevent misinformation experiments with short retention intervals. *Memory and Cognition, 22,* 40–54.

Bellow, S. (1989). *The Bellarosa Connection.* New York: Penguin.

Berendzen, R., & Palmer, L. (1993). *Come here: A man overcomes the tragic aftermath of childhood sexual abuse.* New York: Villard.

Bergson, H. (1911). *Matter and memory* (N. M. Paul & W. S. Palmer, Trans.). London: Swan Sonnenschein.

Bernstein, E. M. and Puttnam, F. W. (1986). Development, reliability, and validity of a dissociation scale. *Journal of Nervous and Mental Disease, 174,* 727-735.

Berrios, G. E. (1995). Déjà vu in France during the 19th century: A conceptual history. *Comprehensive Psychiatry, 36,* 123–129.

Bjork, R. A. (1989). Retrieval inhibition as an adaptive mechanism in human memory. In H. L. Roediger, III, & F. I. M. Craik (Eds.), *Varieties of memory and consciousness: Essays in honour of Endel Tulving* (pp. 309–330). Hillsdale, NJ: Erlbaum.

Blaxton, T. A. (1989). Investigating dissociations among memory measures: Support for a transfer-appropriate processing framework. *Journal of Experimental Psychology: Learning, Memory, and Cognition, 15,* 657–668.

Blaxton, T. A. (1995). A process-based view of memory. *Journal of the International Neuropsychological Society, 1,* 112–114.

Bliss, E. L. (1986). *Multiple personality, allied disorders, and hypnosis.* New York: Oxford University Press.

Bliss, T. V. P., & Lømo, W. (1973). Long-lasting potentiation of synaptic transmission in the dentate area of the anesthetized rabbit following stimulation of the perforant path. *Journal of Physiology, 232,* 331–356.

Bliss, T. V. P., & Collingridge, G. L. (1993). A synaptic model of memory: Long-term potentiation in the hippocampus. *Nature, 232,* 31–39.

Block, N. (1995). On a confusion about a function of consciousness. *Behavioral and Brain Sciences, 18,* 227–287.

Bloom, B. S. (Ed.). (1985). *Developing talent in young people.* New York: Ballantine.

Bootzin, R. R., Kihlstrom, J. F., & Schacter, D. L. (Eds.) (1990). *Sleep and cognition.* Washington, DC: American Psychological Association.

Borges, J. L. (1962). *Ficciones.* New York: Grove.

Bothwell, R. K., Deffenbacher, K. A., & Brigham, J. C. (1987). Correlation of eyewitness accuracy and confidence: Optimality hypothesis revisited. *Journal of Applied Psychology, 72,* 691–695.

Bower, G. H. (1972). Mental imagery and associative learning. In L. Gregg (Ed.), *Cognition and learning and memory*. New York: Wiley.

Bower, G. H. (1981). Mood and memory. *American Psychologist, 36,* 129–148.

Bower, G. H. (1992). How might emotions affect learning? In S.-Å. Christianson (Ed.), *The handbook of emotion and memory: Research and theory* (pp. 3–31). Hillsdale, NJ: Erlbaum.

Bowers, K. S. (1991). Dissociation in hypnosis and multiple personality disorder. *The International Journal of Clinical and Experimental Hypnosis, 39,* 155–173.

Bradley, B. P., & Baddeley, A. D. (1990). Emotional factors in forgetting. *Psychological Medicine, 20,* 351–355.

Bradley, M. M., Greenwald, M. K., Petry, M. C., & Lang, P. J. (1992). Remembering pictures: Pleasure and arousal in memory. *Journal of Experimental Psychology: Learning, Memory, and Cognition, 18,* 379–390.

Bradley, V. A., Welch, J. L., & Dick, D. J. (1989). Visuospatial working memory in Parkinson's disease. *Journal of Neurology, Neurosurgery, and Psychiatry, 52,* 1228–1235.

Brainerd, C. J., Reyna, V. F. , and Brandse, E. (1995). Are children's false memories more persistent than their true memories? *Psychological Science, 6,* 359–364.

Brandt, J. (1992). Detecting amnesia's impostors. In L. R. Squire & N. Butters (Eds.), *Neuropsychology of memory* (pp. 156–165). New York: Guilford Press.

Bransford, J. D., & Franks, J. J. (1971). The abstraction of linguistic ideas. *Cognitive Psychology, 2,* 331–350.

Bremner, J. D., Randall, P., Scott, T. M., Bronen, R. A., Seibyl, J. P., Southwick, S. M., Delaney, R. C., McCarthy, G., Charney, D. S., & Innis, R. B. (1995). MRI-based measurement of hippocampal volume in patients with combat-related posttraumatic stress disorder. *American Journal of Psychiatry, 152,* 973–981.

Bremner, J. D., Steinberg, M., Southwick, S. M., Johnson, D. R., & Charney, D. S. (1993). Use of the structured clinical interview for DSM-IV dissociative disorders for systematic assessment of dissociative symptoms in posttraumatic stress disorder. *American Journal of Psychiatry, 150,* 1011–1014.

Brewer, W. F. (1988). Memory for randomly sampled autobiographical events. In U. Neisser & E. Winograd (Eds.), *Remembering reconsidered: Ecological and traditional approaches to the study of memory* (pp. 21–90). New York: Cambridge University Press.

Brewer, W. F. (1992). The theoretical and empirical status of the flashbulb memory hypothesis. In E. Winograd & U. Neisser (Eds.), *Affect and accuracy in recall: Studies of "flashbulb" memories* (pp. 274–305). New York: Cambridge University Press.

Brewer, W. F. (1996). What is recollective memory? In D. C. Rubin (Ed.), *Remembering our past: Studies in autobiographical memory*. Cambridge: Cambridge University Press.

Brewin, C. R., Andrews, B., & Gotlib, I. H. (1993). Psychopathology and early experience: A reappraisal of retrospective reports. *Psychological Bulletin, 113,* 82–98.

Breznitz, S. (1993). *Memory fields: The legacy of a wartime childhood in Czechoslovakia*. New York: Knopf.

Briere, J., & Conte, J. (1993). Self-reported amnesia for abuse in adults molested as children. *Journal of Traumatic Stress, 6,* 21–31.

Brown, A. S. (1991). A review of the tip-of-the-tongue experience. *Psychological Bulletin, 109,* 204–223.

Brown, A. S., & Murphy, D. R. (1989). Cryptomnesia: Delineating inadvertent plagiarism. *Journal of Experimental Psychology: Learning, Memory, and Cognition, 15,* 432–442.

Brown, D. (1995). Pseudomemories: The standard of science and the standard of care in trauma treatment. *American Journal of Clinical Hypnosis, 37,* 1–24.

Brown, N. R., Rips, L. J., & Shevell, S. K. (1985). The subjective dates of natural events in very-long-term memory. *Cognitive Psychology, 17,* 139–177.

Brown, P. (1994). Toward a psychobiological model of dissociation and post-traumatic stress disorder. In S. J. Lynn & J. W. Rhue (Eds.), *Dissociation: Clinical and theoretical perspectives* (pp. 94–122). New York: Guilford Press.

Brown, R., & Kulik, J. (1977). Flashbulb memories. *Cognition, 5,* 73–99.

Brown, R., & McNeill, D. (1966). The "tip-of-the-tongue" phenomenon. *Journal of Verbal Learning and Verbal Behavior, 5,* 325–337.

Bruck, M. L., & Ceci, S. J. (1995). Amicus brief for the case of *State of New Jersey v. Michaels* presented by Committee of Concerned Social Scientists. *Psychology, Public Policy and Law, 1,* 272–322.

Bruck, M. L., Ceci, S. J., Francoeur, E., & Barr, R. (1995). "I hardly cried when I got my shot": Young children's reports of their visit to a pediatrician. *Child Development, 66,* 193–208.

Buckhout, R. (1974). Eyewitness testimony. *Scientific American, 231,* 23–31.

Buckner, R. L., & Tulving, E. (1995). Neuroimaging studies of memory: Theory and recent PET results. In F. Boller & J. Grafman (Eds.), *Handbook of neuropsychology,* Volume 10 (pp. 439–466). Amsterdam: Elsevier.

Buckner, R. L., Petersen, S. E., Ojemann, J. G., Miezin, F. M., Squire, L. R., & Raichle, M. E. (1995). Functional anatomical studies of explicit and implicit memory retrieval tasks. *Journal of Neuroscience, 15,* 12–29.

Butters, M. A., Glisky, E. L., & Schacter, D. L. (1993). Transfer of new learning in memory-impaired patients. *Journal of Clinical and Experimental Neuropsychology, 15,* 219–230.

Butters, N., & Albert, M. S. (1982). Processes underlying failures to recall remote events. In L. S. Cermak (Ed.), *Human memory and amnesia* (pp. 257–274). Hillsdale, NJ: Erlbaum.

Butters, N., & Cermak, L. S. (1980). *Alcoholic Korsakoff's syndrome: An information processing approach.* New York: Academic Press.

Butters, N., & Cermak, L. S. (1986). A case study of forgetting autobiographical knowledge: Implications for the study of retrograde amnesia. In D. Rubin (Ed.), *Autobiographical memory* (pp. 253–272). New York: Cambridge University Press.

Butters, N., Heindel, W. C., & Salmon, D. P. (1990). Dissociation of implicit memory in dementia: Neurological implications. *Bulletin of the Psychonomic Society, 28,* 359–366.

Cahill, L., Prins, B., Weber, M., & McGaugh, J. L. (1994). ß-Adrenergic activation and memory for emotional events. *Nature, 371,* 702–704.

Capaldi, E. J., & Neath, I. (1995). Remembering and forgetting as context discrimination. *Learning and Memory, 2,* 107–132.

Caramazza, A., & Hillis, A. E. (1991). Lexical organization of nouns and verbs in the brain. *Nature, 349,* 788–790.

Cardena, E., & Spiegel, D. (1993). Dissociative reactions to the San Francisco Bay area earthquake of 1989. *American Journal of Psychiatry, 150,* 474–478.

Carlson, E. B., & Rosser-Hogan, R. (1994). Cross-cultural response to trauma: A study of traumatic experiences and posttraumatic symptoms in Cambodian refugees. *Journal of Traumatic Stress, 7,* 43–58.

Carrasco, M., & Seamon, J. G. (1996). Priming impossible figures in object decision test: The critical importance of perceived stimulus complexity. *Psychonomic Bulletin and Review.*

Carruthers, M. J. (1990). *The book of memory: A study of memory in medieval culture.* New York: Cambridge University Press.

Carstensen, L. L., & Turk-Charles, S. (1994). The salience of emotion across the adult life span. *Psychology and Aging, 9,* 259–264.

Cash, W. S., & Moss, A. J. (1972). *Optimum recall period for reporting persons injured in motor vehicle accidents* (DHEW-HRA No. 72–1050). Washington, DC: U.S. Public Health Service.

Cave, C. B., & Squire, L. R. (1991). Equivalent impairment of spatial and nonspatial memory following damage to the human hippocampus. *Hippocampus, 1,* 329–340.

Ceci, S. J. (1995). False beliefs: Some developmental and clinical considerations. In D. L. Schacter, J. T. Coyle, G. D. Fischbach, M.-M. Mesulam, & L. E. Sullivan (Eds.), *Memory distortion: How minds, brains, and societies reconstruct the past* (pp. 91–128). Cambridge: Harvard University Press.

Ceci, S. J., & Bruck, M. (1993). Suggestibility of the child witness: A historical review and synthesis. *Psychological Bulletin, 113*, 403–439.

Ceci, S. J., & Bruck, M. (1995). *Jeopardy in the Courtroom.* Washington, DC: APA Books.

Ceci, S. J., DeSimone, M., & Johnson, S. (1992). Memory in context: A case study of "Bubbles P.," a gifted but uneven memorizer. In D. J. Herrmann, H. Weingartner, A. Searleman, & C. McEvoy (Eds.), *Memory improvement: Implications for memory theory* (pp. 169–186). New York: Springer-Verlag.

Cermak, L. S., & O'Connor, M. (1983). The anterograde and retrograde retrieval ability of a patient with amnesia due to encephalitis. *Neuropsychologia, 21,* 213–234.

Cermak, L. S., Talbot, N., Chandler, K., & Wolbarst, L. R. (1985). The perceptual priming phenomenon in amnesia. *Neuropsychologia, 23,* 615–622.

Charness, N. (1981). Aging and skilled problem solving. *Journal of Experimental Psychology: General, 110,* 21–38.

Chase, W. G., & Ericsson, K. A. (1981). Skilled memory. In J. R. Anderson (Ed.), *Cognitive skills and their acquisition.* Hillsdale, NJ: Erlbaum.

Cho, Y. H., Beracochea, D., & Jaffard, R. (1993). Extended temporal gradient for the retrograde and anterograde amnesia produced by ibotenate entorhinal cortex lesions in mice. *Journal of Neuroscience, 13,* 1759–1766.

Christianson, S.-Å. (1989). Flashbulb memories: Special, but not so special. *Memory and Cognition, 17,* 435–443.

Christianson, S.-Å., & Loftus, E. F. (1987). Memory for traumatic events. *Applied Cognitive Psychology, 1,* 225–239.

Christianson, S.-Å., & Nilsson, L. G. (1989). Hysterical amnesia: A case of adversively motivated isolation of memory. In T. Archer & L.-G. Nilsson (Eds.), *Aversion, avoidance, and anxiety: Perspectives on aversively motivated behavior* (pp. 289–310). Hillsdale, NJ: Erlbaum.

Church, B. A., & Schacter, D. L. (1994). Perceptual specificity of auditory priming: Implicit memory for voice intonation and fundamental frequency. *Journal of Experimental Psychology: Learning, Memory, and Cognition, 20,* 521–533.

Clark, D. M., & Teasdale, J. D. (1982). Diurnal variation in clinical depression and accessibility of positive and negative experiences. *Journal of Abnormal Psychology, 91,* 87–95.

Cockburn, J., & Smith, P. T. (1991). The relative influence of intelligence and age on everyday memory. *Journal of Gerontology: Psychological Sciences, 46,* P31–P36.

Cohen, G., & Faulkner, D. (1988). Life span changes in autobiographical memory. In M. M. Gruneberg, R. N. Sykes, & P. E. Morris (Eds.), *Practical aspects of memory: Current issues and theory.* New York: Wiley.

Cohen, G., & Faulkner, D. (1989). Age differences in source forgetting: Effects on reality monitoring and on eyewitness testimony. *Psychology and Aging, 4*(1), 10–17.

Cohen, G., Conway, M. A., & Maylor, E. A. (1994). Flashbulb memories in older adults. *Psychology and Aging, 9,* 454–463.

Cohen, N. J., & Eichenbaum, H. (1993). *Memory, amnesia, and the hippocampal system.* Cambridge, MA: MIT Press.

Cohen, N. J., & Squire, L. R. (1980). Preserved learning and retention of pattern analyzing skill in amnesics: Dissociation of knowing how and knowing that. *Science, 210,* 207–210.

Colegrove, F. W. (1899). Individual memories. *American Journal of Psychology, 10,* 228–255.

Coleman, P. G. (1986). *Ageing and reminiscence processes: Social and clinical implications.* New York: Wiley.

Collins, L. N., Graham, J. W., Hansen, W. B., & Johnson, C. A. (1985). Agreement between retrospective accounts of substance use and earlier reported substance use. *Applied Psychological Measurement, 9,* 301–309.

Conway, M. A. (1992). A structural model of autobiographical memory. In M. A. Conway, D. C. Rubin, H. Spinnler, & W. A. Wagenaar (Eds.), *Theoretical perspectives on autobiographical memory* (pp. 167–193). Dordrect, The Netherlands: Kluwer.

Conway, M. A. (1995). *Flashbulb memories*. Hillsdale, NJ: Erlbaum.

Conway, M. A., & Bekerian, D. A. (1987). Organization in autobiographical memory. *Memory & Cognition, 15,* 119–132.

Conway, M. A., & Rubin, D. C. (1993). The structure of autobiographical memory. In A. F. Collins, S. E. Gathercole, M. A. Conway, & P. E. Morris (Eds.), *Theories of memory* (pp. 103–137). Hillsdale, NJ: Erlbaum.

Conway, M. A., Anderson, S. J., Larsen, S. F., Donnelly, C. M., McDaniel, M. A., McClelland, A. G. R., Rawles, R. E., & Logie, R. H. (1994). The formation of flashbulb memories. *Memory & Cognition, 22,* 326–343.

Coons, P. M. (1994). Confirmation of childhood abuse in child and adolescent cases of multiple personality disorder and dissociative disorder not otherwise specified. *The Journal of Nervous and Mental Disease, 182,* 461–464.

Cooper, L. A., Schacter, D. L., Ballesteros, S., & Moore, C. (1992). Priming and recognition of transformed three-dimensional objects: Effects of size and reflection. *Journal of Experimental Psychology: Learning, Memory, and Cognition, 18,* 43–57.

Coriat, I. H. (1907). The Lowell case of amnesia. *Journal of Abnormal Psychology, 2,* 93–111.

Coriat, I. H. (1916). *Abnormal psychology.* New York: Moffat, Yard.

Cork, R. C., Kihlstrom, J. F., & Schacter, D. L. (1992). Absence of explicit or implicit memory in patients with sufentanil/nitrous oxide. *Anesthesiology, 76,* 892–898.

Corkin, S. (1968). Acquisition of motor skill after bilateral medial temporal lobe excision. *Neuropsychologia, 6,* 255–265.

Corkin, S. (1984). Lasting consequences of bilateral medial temporal lobectomy: Clinical course and experimental findings in H.M. *Seminars in Neurology, 4,* 249–259.

Craik, F. I. M., & Lockhart, R. S. (1972). Levels of processing: A framework for memory research. *Journal of Verbal Learning and Verbal Behavior, 11,* 671–684.

Craik, F. I. M., & McDowd, J. M. (1987). Age differences in recall and recognition. *Journal of Experimental Psychology: Learning, Memory, and Cognition, 13,* 474–479.

Craik, F. I. M., & Tulving, E. (1975). Depth of processing and the retention of words in episodic memory. *Journal of Experimental Psychology: General, 104,* 268–294.

Craik, F. I. M., Morris, L. W., Morris, R. G., & Loewen, E. R. (1990). Relations between source amnesia and frontal lobe functioning in older adults. *Psychology and Aging, 5,* 148–151.

Craik, F. I. M., Anderson, N. D., Kerr, S. A., & Li, K. Z. H. (1995). Memory changes in normal ageing. In A. D. Baddeley, B. A. Wilson, & F. N. Watts (Eds.), *Handbook of memory disorders* (pp. 211–241). New York: Wiley.

Crevier, D. (1993). *AI: The tumultuous history of the search for artificial intelligence.* New York: Basic Books.

Crews, F., et al. (1995). *The memory wars: Freud's legacy in dispute.* New York: A New York Review Book.

Crovitz, H. F., & Schiffman, H. (1974). Frequency of episodic memories as a function of their age. *Bulletin of the Psychonomic Society, 4,* 517–518.

Curran, T., Schacter, D. L., & Bessenoff, G. (1996). Visual specificity effects on memory: Beyond transfer appropriate processing? *Canadian Journal of Experimental Psychology.*

Dalla Barba, G. (1993). Confabulation: Knowledge and recollective experience. *Cognitive Neuropsychology, 10,* 1–20.

Dalla Barba, G., Parlato, V., Iavarone, A., & Boller, F. (in press). Anosognosia, intrusions and "frontal" functions in Alzheimer's disease and depression. *Neuropsychologia.*

Damasio, A. R. (1989). Time-locked multiregional retroactivation: A systems-level proposal for the neural substrates of recall and recognition. *Cognition, 33,* 25–62.

Damasio, A. R. (1990). Category-related recognition defects as clues to the neural substrates of knowledge. *Trends in Neuroscience, 13,* 95–98.

Damasio, A. R. (1994). *Descartes' error: Emotion, reason, and the human brain.* New York: Putnam.

Damasio, A. R., Tranel, D., & Damasio, H. (1989). Amnesia caused by herpes simplex encephalitis, infarctions in basal forebrain, Alzheimer's disease and anoxia/ischemia. In F. Boller & J. Grafman (Eds.), *Handbook of Neuropsychology, Volume 3* (pp. 149–165). Amsterdam: Elsevier.

Damasio, A. R., Tranel, D., & Damasio, H. (1990). Face agnosia and the neural substrates of memory. *Annual Review of Neuroscience, 13*, 89–109.

Damasio, A. R., & Damasio, H. (1994). Cortical systems for retrieval of concrete knowledge: The convergence zone framework. In C. Koch & J. L. Davis (Eds.), *Large-scale neuronal theories of the brain* (pp. 61–74). Cambridge: MIT Press.

Damasio, A. R., & Van Hoesen, G. W. (1985). The limbic system and the localisation of herpes simplex encephalitis. *Journal of Neurology, Neurosurgery and Psychiatry, 48*, 297–301.

Daniel, W. F., & Crovitz, H. F. (1986). ECT-induced alteration of psychogenic amnesia. *Acta Psychiatrica Scandinavica, 74*, 302–303.

Danieli, Y. (1988). On not confronting the Holocaust: Psychological reactions to victim/survivors and their children. In *Remembering for the future: Theme II: The impact of the Holocaust on the contemporary world* (pp. 1257–1271). Oxford: Pergamon.

Danieli, Y. (1994). As survivors age: Part 1. *Clinical Quarterly, 4*, 3–7.

Dannay, R. (1980). *Current developments in copyright law.* New York: Practicing Law Institute.

Darien-Smith, C., & Gilbert, C. D. (1994). Axonal sprouting accompanies functional reorganization in adult cat striate cortex. *Nature, 368*, 737–740.

Davis, H. P., & Bernstein, P. A. (1992). Age-related changes in explicit and implicit memory. In L. R. Squire & N. Butters (Eds.), *Neuropsychology of memory* (pp. 249–261). New York: Guilford Press.

Davis, P. J. (1990). Repression and the inaccessibility of emotional memories. In J. L. Singer (Ed.), *Repression and dissociation* (pp. 387–404). Chicago: University of Chicago Press.

Dawes, R. M. (1988). *Rational choice in an uncertain world.* San Diego: Harcourt, Brace, Jovanovich.

Dawes, R. M. (1991). Biases of retrospection. *Issues in Child Abuse Accusations, 1*, 25–28.

De Bellis, M. D., Chrousos, G. P., Dorn, L. D., Burke, L., Helmers, K., Kling, M. A., Trickett, P. K., & Putnam, F. W. (1994). Hypothalamic-pituitary-adrenal axis dysregulation in sexually abused girls. *Journal of Clinical Endocrinology and Metabolism, 78*, 249–255.

De Bellis, M. D., Lefter, L., Trickett, P. K., & Putnam, F. W. (1994). Urinary catecholamine excretion in sexually abused girls. *Journal of the American Academy of Child and Adolescent Psychiatry, 33*, 320–327.

DeCasper, A. J., & Fifer, W. P. (1980). Of human bonding: Newborns prefer their mothers' voices. *Science, 208*, 1174–1176.

DeCasper, A. J., & Spence, M. J. (1986). Prenatal maternal speech influences newborns' perception of speech sounds. *Infant Behavior and Development, 9*, 133–150.

Decety, J., Perani, D., Jeannerod, M., Bettinardi, V., Tadary, B., Woods, R., Mazziota, S. C., & Fazio, F. (1994). Mapping motor representations with positron emission tomography. *Nature, 371*, 600–602.

Deese, J. (1959). On the prediction of occurrence of particular verbal intrusions in immediate recall. *Journal of Experimental Psychology, 58*(1), 17–22.

de Keyser, J., De Backer, J.-P., Vauquelin, G., & Ebinger, G. (1990). The effect of aging on the D_1 dopamine receptors in human frontal cortex. *Brain Research, 528*, 308–310.

Demb, J. B., Desmond, J. E., Wagner, A. D., Vaidya, C. J., Glover, G. H., & Gabrieli, J. D. E. (1995). Semantic encoding and retrieval in the left inferior prefrontal cortex: A functional MRI study of task difficulty and process specificity. *Journal of Neuroscience, 15*, 5870–5878.

Démonet, J.-F., Chollet, F., Ramsay, S., Cardebat, D., Nespoulous, J.-L., Wise, R., Rascol, A., & Frackowiak, R. (1992). The anatomy of phonological and semantic processing in normal subjects. *Brain, 115*, 1753–1768.

Dennet, D. C. (1991). *Consciousness explained*. Boston: Little, Brown.

De Renzi, E., Liotti, M., & Nichelli, P. (1987). Semantic amnesia with preservation of autobiographic memory. A case report. *Cortex, 23,* 575–597.

Desimone, R., & Duncan, J. (1995). Neural mechanisms of selective visual attention. *Annual Review of Neuroscience, 18,* 193–222.

Desimone, R., Miller, E. K., Chelazzi, L., & Lueschow, A. (1995). Multiple memory systems in the visual cortex. In M. S. Gazzaniga (Ed.), *The cognitive neurosciences* (pp. 475–486). Cambridge: MIT Press.

Devine, P. G. (1989). Stereotypes and prejudices: Their automatic and controlled components. *Journal of Personality and Social Psychology, 56,* 5–18.

Dewhurst, S. A., & Conway, M. A. (1994). Pictures, images, and recollective experience. *Journal of Experimental Psychology: Learning, Memory, and Cognition, 20,* 1088–1098.

Diamond, A. (1990). Developmental time course in human infants and infant monkeys, and the neural bases of inhibitory control in reaching. In A. Diamond (Ed.), *The development and neural bases of higher cognitive functions* (pp. 637–676). New York: The New York Academy of Sciences.

Diamond, B. (September 1969). Interview regarding Sirhan Sirhan. *Psychology Today,* 48–55.

Dobrof, R. (1984). Introduction: A time for reclaiming the past. In Kaminsky, M. (Ed.) (1984). The uses of reminiscence: New ways of working with older adults (pp. xvii–xix). New York: Hayworth Press.

Donald, M. (1991). *Origins of the modern mind*. Cambridge: Harvard University Press.

Donaldson, W. (1996). The role of decision processes in remembering and knowing. *Memory and Cognition.*

Donovan, D. M., & McIntyre, D. (1990). *Healing the hurt child: A developmental-contextual approach*. New York: Norton.

Dunn, R. (1845). Case of suspension of the mental faculties. *Lancet, 2,* 588–590.

Dutta, S., & Kanungo, R. N. (1967). Retention of affective material: A further verification of the intensity hypothesis. *Journal of Personality and Social Psychology, 5,* 476–481.

Dywan, J. (1995). The illusion of familiarity: An alternative to the report-criterion account of hypnotic recall. *International Journal of Clinical and Experimental Hypnosis, 53,* 194–211.

Dywan, J., & Bowers, K. S. (1983). The use of hypnosis to enhance recall. *Science, 222,* 1184–1185.

Dywan, J., & Jacoby, L. L. (1990). Effect of aging and source monitoring: Differences in susceptibility to false fame. *Psychology and Aging, 3,* 379–387.

Dywan, J., Segalowitz, S. J., & Williamson, L. (1994). Source monitoring during name recognition in older adults: Psychometric and electrophysiological correlates. *Psychology and Aging, 9,* 568–577.

Ebbinghaus, H. (1885/1964). *Memory: A contribution to experimental psychology*. New York: Dover.

Edelman, G. (1992). *Bright air, brilliant fire: The matter of mind*. New York: Basic Books.

Eich, E. (1989). Theoretical issues in state dependent memory. In H. L. Roediger, III, & F. I. M. Craik (Eds.), *Varieties of memory and consciousness: Essays in honour of Endel Tulving* (pp. 331–354). Hillsdale, NJ: Erlbaum.

Eich, E. (1995). Searching for mood dependent memory. *Psychological Science, 6,* 67–75.

Eich, E., Reeves, J. L., & Katz, R. L. (1985). Anesthesia, amnesia, and the memory/awareness distinction. *Anesthesia and Analgesia, 64,* 1143–1148.

Eich, E., Reeves, J. L., Jaeger, B., & Graff-Radford, S. B. (1985). Memory for pain: Relation between past and present pain intensity. *Pain, 23,* 375–379.

Eichenbaum, H. (1994). The hippocampal system and declarative memory in humans and animals: Experimental analysis and historical origins. In D. L. Schacter & E. Tulving (Eds.), *Memory Systems 1994* (pp. 147–202). Cambridge: MIT Press.

Ellenberger, H. F. (1970). *The discovery of the unconscious*. New York: Basic Books.

Elliott, D. M., & Briere, J. (1995). Posttraumatic stress associated with delayed recall of sexual abuse: A general population study. *Journal of Traumatic Stress, 8,* 629–648.

Erdelyi, M. H. (1984). The recovery of unconscious (inaccessible) memories: Laboratory studies of hypermnesia. In G. H. Bower (Ed.), *The psychology of learning and motivation; Advances in research and theory* (Vol. 18, pp. 95–127). New York: Academic Press.

Erdelyi, M. H. (1985). *Psychoanalysis: Freud's cognitive psychology.* New York: Freeman.

Erdelyi, M. H. (1996). *The recovery of unconscious memories: Hypermnesia and reminiscence.* Chicago: University of Chicago Press.

Ericsson, K. A. (1992). Experts' memory. In L. R. Squire (Ed.), *Encyclopedia of learning and memory* (pp. 166–170). New York: Macmillan.

Ericsson, K. A., & Smith, J. (1991). Prospects and limits in the empirical study of expertise: An introduction. In K. A. Ericsson & J. Smith (Eds.), *Toward a general theory of expertise: Prospects and limits.* New York: Cambridge University Press.

Estes, W. K. (1980). Is human memory obsolete? *American Scientist, 68,* 62–69.

Evans, C., & Richardson, P. H. (1988). Improved recovery and reduced postoperative stay after therapeutic suggestions during general anaesthesia. *Lancet, 2,* 491–493.

Evans, J., Wilson, B., Wraight, E. P., & Hodges, J. R. (1993). Neuropsychological and SPECT scan findings during and after transient global amnesia: Evidence for the differential impairment of remote episodic memory. *Journal of Neurology, Neurosurgery and Psychiatry, 56,* 1227–1230.

Evans, J. H. (1966). Transient loss of memory, an organic mental syndrome. *Brain, 89,* 539–548.

Evans, R., & Thorn, W. A. F. (1966). Two types of posthypnotic amnesia: Recall amnesia and source amnesia. *International Journal of Clinical and Experimental Hypnosis, 14,* 162–179.

Eysenck, M. W., & Mogg, K. (1992). Clinical anxiety, trait anxiety, and memory bias. In S.-Å. Christianson (Ed). *The handbook of emotion and memory: Research and theory* (pp. 429–450). Hillsdale, NJ: Erlbaum.

Fabiani, M., & Donchin, E. (1995). Encoding processes and memory organization: A model of the von Restroff effect. *Journal of Experimental Psychology: Learning, Memory and Cognition, 21,* 3–23.

Farah, M. J. (1990). *Visual agnosia.* Cambridge: MIT Press.

Farah, M. J., & McClelland, J. L. (1991). A computational model of semantic memory impairment: Modality specificity and emergent category specificity. *Journal of Experimental Psychology: General, 120,* 339–357.

Ferguson, S. A., Hashtroudi, S., & Johnson, M. K. (1992). Age differences in using source-relevant cues. *Psychology and Aging, 7,* 443–452.

Fisher, C. (1945). Amnesic states in war neuroses: The psychogenesis of fugues. *Psychoanalytic Quarterly, 14,* 437–468.

Fisher, R. P., & Craik, F. I. M. (1977). The interaction between encoding and retrieval operations in cued recall. *Journal of Experimental Psychology: Human Learning and Perception, 3,* 153–171.

Fisk, A. D., Hertzog, C., Lee, M. D., Rogers, W. A., & Anderson-Garlach, M. (1994). Long-term retention of skilled visual search: Do young adults retain more than old adults? *Psychology and Aging, 9,* 206–215.

Fitzgerald, J. M. (1986). Autobiographical memory: A developmental perspective. In D. C. Rubin (Ed.), *Autobiographical memory* (pp. 122–133). New York: Cambridge University Press.

Fitzgerald, J. M. (1988). Vivid memories and the reminiscence phenomenon: The role of a self narrative. *Human Development, 31,* 261–273.

Fivush, R., & Schwarzmueller, A. (1995). Say it once again: Effects of repeated questions on children's event recall. *Journal of Traumatic Stress, 8,* 555–580.

Foa, E. B., Rothbaum, B. O., Riggs, D., & Murdock, T. (1991). Treatment of post-traumatic stress disorder in rape victims: A comparison between cognitive-behavioral procedures and counseling. *Journal of Consulting and Clinical Psychology, 59,* 715–723.

Frankel, F. H. (1994). The concept of flashbacks in historical perspective. *The International Journal of Clinical and Experimental Hypnosis, 42,* 321–336.

Fredrickson, R. (1992). *Repressed memories.* New York: Simon & Schuster.

Freud, S. (1899). Screen Memories. In J. Strachey (Ed. and Trans.), *The standard edition of the complete psychological works of Sigmund Freud* (Vol. 3). London: Hogarth Press.

Freud, S. (1926/1959). Inhibitions, symptoms, and anxiety. In J. Strachey (Ed. and Trans.), *The standard edition of the complete psychological works of Sigmund Freud* (Vol. 20). London: Hogarth Press.

Freud, S., & Breuer, J. (1966). *Studies on hysteria* (J. Strachey, Trans.). New York: Avon.

Freyd, J. J. (1994). Betrayal-trauma: Traumatic amnesia as an adaptive response to childhood abuse. *Ethics & Behavior, 4,* 307–329.

Friedman, H. R., & Goldman-Rakic, P. S. (1994). Coactivation of prefrontal cortex and inferior parietal cortex in working memory tasks revealed by 2DG functional mapping in the rhesus monkey. *Journal of Neuroscience, 14,* 2775–2788.

Friedman, W. J. (1993). Memory for the time of past events. *Psychological Bulletin, 113,* 44–66.

Gabrieli, J. D. E. (1995). A systematic view of human memory processes. *Journal of the International Neuropsychological Society, 1,* 115–118.

Gabrieli, J. D. E., Fleischman, D., Keane, M., Reminger, S., & Morrell, F. (1995). Double dissociation between memory systems underlying explicit and implicit memory in the human brain. *Psychological Science, 6,* 76–82.

Gaffan, E. A., Gaffan, D., & Hodges, J. R. (1991). Amnesia following damage to the left fornix and to other sites. *Brain, 114,* 1297–1313.

Gainotti, G., Silveri, M. C., Daniele, A., & Giustolisi, L. (1995). Neuroanatomical correlates of category-specific semantic disorders: A critical survey. *Memory, 3,* 247–264.

Galton, F. (1879). Psychometric experiments. *Brain, 2,* 149–162.

Gardiner, J. M., & Java, R. I. (1993). Recognising and remembering. In A. F. Collins, S. E. Gathercole, M. A. Conway, & P. E. Morris (Eds.), *Theories of memory* (pp. 163–188). Hove, United Kingdom: Erlbaum.

Gardner, H. (1975). *The shattered mind: The person after brain damage.* New York: Knopf.

Garry, M., Manning, C., Lofus, E. F., & Sherman, S. J. (1996). Imagination inflation: Imagining a childhood event inflates confidence that it occurred. *Psychonomic Bulletin and Review.*

Gauld, A., & Stephenson, G. M. (1967). Some experiments related to Bartlett's theory of remembering. *British Journal of Psychology, 58,* 39–49.

Gazzaniga, M. S. (1985). *The social brain.* New York: Basic Books.

Geary, P. J. (1994). *Phantoms of rememberance.* Princeton: Princeton University Press.

Gilbert, D. T. (1991). How mental systems believe. *American Psychologist, 46,* 107–119.

Glisky, E. L., & Schacter, D. L. (1987). Acquisition of domain-specific knowledge in organic amnesia: Training for computer-related work. *Neuropsychologia, 25,* 893–906.

Glisky, E. L., & Schacter, D. L. (1988). Long-term retention of computer learning by patients with memory disorders. *Neuropsychologia, 26,* 173–178.

Glisky, E. L., & Schacter, D. L. (1989a). Extending the limits of complex learning in organic amnesia: Computer training in a vocational domain. *Neuropsychologia, 27,* 107–120.

Glisky, E. L. & Schacter, D. L. (1989b). Models and methods of memory rehabilitation. In F. Boller & J. Grafman (Eds.), *Handbook of neuropsychology, Volume 3* (pp. 233–246). Amsterdam: Elsevier.

Glisky, E. L., Polster, M. R., & Routhieaux, B. C. (1995). Double dissociation between item and source memory. *Neuropsychology 9,* 229–235.

Glisky, E. L., Schacter, D. L., & Tulving, E. (1986a). Computer learning by memory-impaired patients: Acquisition and retention of complex knowledge. *Neuropsychologia, 24,* 313–328.

Glisky, E. L., Schacter, D. L., & Tulving, E. (1986b). Learning and retention of computer-related vocabulary in memory-impaired patients: Method of vanishing cues. *Journal of Clinical and Experimental Neuropsychology, 3,* 292–312.

Gloor, P. (1992). Role of the amygdala in temporal lobe epilepsy. In J. P. Aggleton (Ed.), *The amygdala: Neurobiological aspects of emotion, memory and mental dysfunction.* New York: Wiley-Liss.

Goldman-Rakic, P. S. (1994). The issue of memory in the study of prefrontal function. In A.-M. Thierry et al. (Eds.), *Motor and cognitive functions of the prefrontal cortex* (pp. 112–121). Berlin: Springer-Verlag.

Goldstein, E., & Farmer, K. (1992). *Confabulations: Creating false memories, destroying families.* Boca Raton, FL: SIRS Books.

Goldstein, E., & Farmer, K. (1993). *True stories of false memories.* Boca Raton, FL: SIRS Books.

Golomb, J., Kluger, A., de Leon, M. J., Ferris, S. H., Convit, A., Mittleman, M. S., Cohen, J., Rusniek, H., De Santi, S., & George, A. E. (1994). Hippocampal formation size in normal human aging: A correlate of delayed secondary memory. *Learning and Memory, 1,* 45–54.

Good, M. I. (1994). The reconstruction of early childhood trauma: Fantasy, reality, and verification. *Journal of the American Psychoanalytic Association, 42,* 79–101.

Goodman, G. S., Qin, J., Bottoms, B. L., & Shaver, P. R. (1994). *Characteristics and sources of allegations of ritualistic child abuse.* Final report to the National Center on Child Abuse and Neglect.

Goodman, G. S., Quas, J. A., Batterman-Faunce, J. M., Riddlesberger, M. M., & Kuhn, J. (1994). Predictors of accurate and inaccurate memories of traumatic events experienced in childhood. *Consciousness and Cognition, 3,* 269–294.

Grady, C. L., McIntosh, A. R., Horwitz, B., Maisog, J. M., Ungerleider, L. G., Mentis, M. J., Pietrini, P., Schapiro, M. B., & Haxby, J. V. (1995). Age-related reductions in human recognition memory due to impaired encoding. *Science, 269,* 218–221.

Graf, P., & Mandler, G. (1984). Activation makes words more accessible, but not necessarily more retrievable. *Journal of Verbal Learning and Verbal Behavior, 23,* 553–568.

Graf, P., & Schacter, D. L. (1985). Implicit and explicit memory for new associations in normal subjects and amnesic patients. *Journal of Experimental Psychology: Learning, Memory, and Cognition, 11,* 501–518.

Graf, P., Shimamura, A. P., & Squire, L. R. (1985). Priming across modalities and priming across category levels: Extending the domain of preserved functioning in amnesia. *Journal of Experimental Psychology: Learning, Memory, and Cognition, 11,* 385–395.

Graf, P., Squire, L. R., & Mandler, G. (1984). The information that amnesic patients do not forget. *Journal of Experimental Psychology: Learning, Memory, and Cognition, 10,* 164–178.

Grafman, J., Litvan, I., Massaquoi, S., Stewart, J., Sirigu, A., & Hallett, M. (1992). Cognitive planning deficit in patients with cerebellar degeneration. *Neurology, 42,* 1493–1496.

Grande, J. K. (1994). *Balance: Art and nature.* Montreal, Canada: Black Rose Books.

Grasby, P. M., Frith, C. D., Friston, K. J., Bench, C., Frackowiak, R. S. J., & Dolan, R. J. (1993). Functional mapping of brain areas implicated in auditory-verbal memory function. *Brain, 116,* 1–20.

Greenwald, A. G., & Banaji, M. R. (1995). Implicit social cognition: Attitudes, self-esteem, and stereotypes. *Psychological Review, 102,* 4–27.

Grossberg, S., & Stone, G. (1986). Neural dynamics of word recognition and recall: Attentional priming, learning, and resonance. *Psychological Review, 93,* 46–74.

Gudjonsson, G. H., & MacKeith, J. A. C. (1983). A specific recognition deficit in a case of homicide. *Medicine, Science and the Law, 23,* 37–40.

Gudjonsson, G. H., & Taylor, P. J. (1985). Cognitive deficit in a case of retrograde amnesia. *British Journal of Psychiatry, 147,* 715–718.

Gurvitz, T. V., Shenton, M. E., Hokama, H., Ohta, H., Lasko, M. B., Orr, S. P., Kikinis, R., Jolesz, F. A., McCarley, R. W., & Pitman, R. K. (1996). Magnetic resonance imaging study of hippocampal volume in chronic, combat-related posttraumatic stress disorder. *Biological Psychiatry.*

Hacking, I. (1995). *Rewriting the soul: Multiple personality and the sciences of memory.* Princeton: Princeton University Press.

Haist, F., Shimamura, A. P., & Squire, L. R. (1992). On the relationship between recall and recognition memory. *Journal of Experimental Psychology: Learning Memory, and Cognition, 18,* 691–702.

Hall, C. (1993). Art and mind. *British Medical Journal, 307,* 1289.

Hamann, S. B. (1990). Level-of-processing effects in conceptually driven implicit tasks. *Journal of Experimental Psychology: Learning, Memory, and Cognition, 16,* 970–977.

Hamann, S. B., & Squire, L. R. (1995). On the acquisition of new declarative knowledge in amnesia. *Behavioral Neuroscience, 109,* 1–18.

Hanley, J. R., Davies, A.D.M., Downes, J. J., & Mayes, A. R. (1994). Impaired recall of verbal material following rupture and repair of an anterior communicating artery aneurysm. *Cognitive Neuropsychology, 11,* 543–578.

Harber, K. D., & Pennebaker, J. W. (1992). Overcoming traumatic memories. In S.-Å. Christianson (Ed.), *The handbook of emotion and memory: Research and theory* (pp. 359–387). Hillsdale, NJ: Erlbaum.

Harris, M. (1995). *Face value: The identity masks of Jerry W. Coker.* New York: Paul-Art Press.

Harvey, M. R., & Herman, J. L. (1994). Amnesia, partial amnesia, and delayed recall among adult survivors of childhood trauma. *Consciousness and Cognition, 3,* 295–306.

Hashtroudi, S., Chrosniak, L. D., & Johnson, M. K. (1990). Aging and qualitative characteristics of memories for perceived and imagined complex events. *Psychology and Aging, 5,* 119–126.

Hasselmo, M. E. (1994). Runaway synaptic modification in models of cortex: Implications for Alzheimer's disease. *Neural Networks, 7,* 13–40.

Hayman, C. A. G., & Tulving, E. (1989). Contingent dissociation between recognition and fragment completion: The method of triangulation. *Journal of Experimental Psychology: Learning, Memory, and Cognition, 15,* 228–240.

Hayman, G., Macdonald, C. A., & Tulving, E. (1993). The role of repetition and associative interference in new semantic learning in amnesia: A case experiment. *Journal of Cognitive Neuroscience, 5,* 375–389.

Hebb, D. O. (1949). *The organization of behavior.* New York: Wiley.

Herman, J. L. (1992). *Trauma and recovery.* New York: Basic Books.

Herman, J. L. (1995). Crime and memory. *Bulletin of American Academy of Psychiatry Law, 23,* 5–17.

Herman, J. L., & Harvey, M. R. (1993). The false memory debate: Social science or social backlash? *Harvard Medical School Mental Health Letter, 9,* 4–6.

Herman, J. L., & Schatzow, E. (1987). Recovery and verification of memories of childhood sexual trauma. *Psychoanalytic Psychology, 4,* 1–14.

Hermann, D., Raybeck, D., & Gutman, D. (1993). *Improving student memory.* Seattle, WA: Hogrefe & Huber.

Heuer, F., & Reisberg, D. (1992). Emotion, arousal, and memory for detail. In S.-Å. Christianson (Ed.), *The handbook of emotion and memory: Research and theory* (pp. 151–180). Hillsdale, NJ: Erlbaum.

Hilgard, E. R. (1977). *Divided consciousness.* New York: Wiley.

Hillis, A. E., & Caramazza, A. (1991). Category specific naming and comprehension impairment: A double dissociation. *Brain, 114,* 2081–2094.

Hilts, P. (1995). *Memory's ghost: The strange tale of Mr. M and the nature of memory.* New York: Simon & Schuster.

Hirsh, R. (1974). The hippocampus and contextual retrieval of information from memory: A theory. *Behavioral Psychology, 12,* 421–444.

Hirst, W., Johnson, M. K., Phelps, E., & Volpe, B. T. (1988). More on recognition and recall in amnesics. *Journal of Experimental Psychology: Learning, Memory, and Cognition, 14,* 758–762.

Hobson, G. (Ed.). (1979). *The remembered earth.* Albuquerque: University of New Mexico Press.

Hodges, A. (1983). *Alan Turing: The enigma.* New York: Simon & Schuster.

Hodges, J. R. (1995). Retrograde amnesia. In A. D. Baddeley, B. A. Wilson, & F. N. Watts (Eds.), *Handbook of memory disorders* (pp. 81–107). New York: Wiley.

Hodges, J. R., & McCarthy, R. A. (1993). Autobiographical amnesia resulting from bilateral paramedian thalamic infarction. *Brain, 116,* 921–940.

Hodges, J. R., & Warlow, C. P. (1990). The aetiology of transient global amnesia: A case-control study of 114 cases with prospective follow-up. *Brain, 113,* 639–657.

Hodges, J. R., Patterson, K., Oxbury, S., & Funnell, E. (1992). Semantic dementia: Progressive fluent aphasia with temporal lobe atrophy. *Brain, 115,* 1783–1806.

Hoffman, A. M., & Hoffman, H. S. (1990). *Archives of memory: A soldier recalls World War II.* Lexington: The University Press of Kentucky.

Holmes, D. S. (1990). The evidence for repression: An examination of sixty years of research. In J. L. Singer (Ed.), *Repression and dissociation.* Chicago: University of Chicago Press.

Horne, J. A., & McGrath, M. J. (1984). The consolidation hypothesis for REM sleep function: Stress and other confounding factors—A review. *Biological Psychology, 18,* 165–184.

Howard, D. V. (1996). The aging of implicit and explicit memory. In F. Blanchard-Fields & T. M. Hess (Eds.), *Perspectives on cognition in adulthood and aging* (pp. 221–254). New York: McGraw-Hill.

Howard, D. V., & Howard, J. H., Jr. (1989). Age differences in learning serial patterns: Direct versus indirect measures. *Psychology and Aging, 4,* 357–364.

Howard, D. V., Fry, A. F., & Brune, C. M. (1991). Aging and memory for new associations: Direct versus indirect measures. *Journal of Experimental Psychology: Learning, Memory, and Cognition, 17,* 779–792.

Hufford, M., Hunt, M., & Zeitlin, S. (1987). *The grand generation: Memory, mastery, legacy.* Seattle, WA: University of Washington Press.

Hunkin, N. A., Parkin, A. J., Bradley, V. A., Burrows, E. H., Aldrich, F. K., Jansari, A., & Burdon-Cooper, C. (1995). Focal retrograde amnesia following closed head injury: A case study and theoretical account. *Neuropsychologia, 33,* 509–523.

Hyman, I. E., Jr., & Billings, F. J. (1995). Individual differences and the creation of false childhood memories. Submitted for publication.

Hyman, I. E., Jr., & Pentland, J. (1996). The role of mental imagery in the creation of false childhood memories. *Journal of Memory and Language.*

Hyman, I. E., Husband, T. H., & Billings, F. J. (1995). False memories of childhood experiences. *Applied Cognitive Psychology, 9,* 181–197.

Ivy, G. O., MacLeod, C. M., Petit, T. L., & Markus, E. J. (1992). A physiological framework for perceptual and cognitive changes in aging. In F. I. M. Craik & T. A. Salthouse (Eds.), *The handbook of aging and cognition* (pp. 273–314). Hillsdale, NJ: Erlbaum.

Jackson, A., & Morton, J. (1984). Facilitation of auditory word recognition. *Memory and Cognition, 12,* 568–594.

Jacobs, W. J., & Nadel, L. (1985). Stress-induced recovery of fears and phobias. *Psychological Review, 92,* 512–531.

Jacoby, L. L. (1983). Remembering the data: Analyzing interactive processes in reading. *Journal of Verbal Learning and Verbal Behavior, 22,* 485–508.

Jacoby, L. L., & Dallas, M. (1981). On the relationship between autobiographical memory and perceptual learning. *Journal of Experimental Psychology: General, 110,* 306–340.

Jacoby, L. L., Kelley, C. M., & Dywan, J. (1989). Memory attributions. In H. L. Roediger III & F. I. M. Craik (Eds.). *Varieties of memory and consciousness: Essays in honor of Endel Tulving* (pp. 391–422). Hillsdale, NJ: Erlbaum.

Jacoby, L. L., Kelley, C. M., Brown, J., & Jasechko, J. (1989). Becoming famous overnight: Limits on the ability to avoid unconscious influence of the past. *Journal of Personality and Social Psychology, 56,* 326–338.

James, W. (1890). *The principles of psychology.* New York: Holt.

Janet, P. (1904). L'amnésie et la dissociation des souvenirs par l'émotion [Amnesia and the dissociation of memories by emotion]. *Journal de Psychologie Normale et Pathologigue, 1,* 417–453.

Janet, P. (1907). *The major symptoms of hysteria.* New York: Macmillan.

Janowsky, J. S., Shimamura, A. P., & Squire, L. R. (1989). Source memory impairment in patients with frontal lobe lesions. *Neuropsychologia, 27,* 1043–1056.

Jernigan, T. L., Schafer, K., Butters, N., & Cermak, L. S. (1991). Magnetic resonance imaging of alcoholic Korsakoff patients. *Neuropsychopharmacology, 4,* 175–186.

Johnson, G. (1991). *In the palaces of memory: How we build the worlds inside our heads.* New York: Knopf.

Johnson, H. M. (1994). Processes of successful intentional forgetting. *Psychological Bulletin, 116,* 274–292.

Johnson, M. K. (1996). Fact, fantasy, and public policy. In C. McEvoy & P. Hertel (Eds.), *Practical aspects of memory.* Hillsdale, NJ: Erlbaum.

Johnson, M. K., & Raye, C. L. (1981). Reality monitoring. *Psychological Review, 88,* 67–85.

Johnson, M. K., Hashtroudi, S., & Lindsay, D. S. (1993). Source monitoring. *Psychological Bulletin, 114,* 3–28.

Johnson, M. K., Kim, J. K., & Risse, G. (1985). Do alcoholic Korsakoff's patients acquire affective reactions? *Journal of Experimental Psychology: Learning, Memory, and Cognition, 11,* 22–36.

Johnson, M. K., Foley, M. A., Suengas, A. G., & Raye, C. L. (1988). Phenomenal characteristics of memories for perceived and imagined autobiographical events. *Journal of Experimental Psychology: General, 117,* 371–376.

Johnson, M. K., Nolde, S. F., Mather, M., Kounios, J., Schacter, D. L., and Curran, T. (in press). The similarity of brain activity associated with true and false recognition memory depends on test format. *Psychological Science.*

Johnson, M. K., Raye, C. L., Wang, A. Y., & Taylor, T. H. (1979). Fact and fantasy: The roles of accuracy and variability in confusing imaginations with perceptual experiences. *Journal of Experimental Psychology: Human Learning and Memory, 5,* 229–240.

Jones, B. P. (1993). Repression: The evolution of a psychoanalytic concept from the 1890's to the 1990's. *Journal of the American Psychoanalytic Association, 41,* 63–93.

Jones-Gotman, M. (1986). Memory for designs: The hippocampal contribution. *Neuropsychologia, 24,* 193–203.

Kaminsky, M. (Ed.). (1984). *The uses of reminiscence: New ways of working with older adults.* New York: Hayworth Press.

Kamptner, N. L. (1991). Personal possessions and their meanings: A life-span perspective. *Journal of Social Behavior and Personality, 6,* 209–228.

Kandel, E. R., Schwartz, J. H., & Jessell, T. M. (1995). *Essentials of neural science and behavior* (3rd ed.). Norwalk, CT: Appleton & Lange.

Kapur, N. (in press). The "Petites Madeleines" phenomenon in two amnesic patients: Sudden recovery of forgotten memories. *Brain.*

Kapur, S., Craik, F. I. M., Tulving, E., Wilson, A. A., Houle, S., & Brown, G. M. (1994). Neuroanatomical correlates of encoding in episodic memory: Levels of processing effect. *Proceedings of the National Academy of Science USA, 91,* 2008–2011.

Kapur, S., Craik, F.I.M., Jones, C., Brown, G. M., Houle, S., & Tulving, E. (1995). Functional role of prefrontal cortex in retrieval of memories: A PET study. *Neuroreport, 6,* 1880–1884.

Karni, A., Tanne, D., Rubenstein, B. S., Askenasy, J. J. M., & Sagi, D. (1994). Dependence on REM sleep of overnight improvement of a perceptual skill. *Science, 265,* 679–682.

Karni, A., Meyer, G., Jazzard, P., Adams, M. M., Turner, R., & Underleider, L. G. (1995). Functional MRI evidence for adult motor cortex plasticity during motor skill learning. *Nature, 377,* 155–158.

Kassin, S. M., Rigby, S., & Castillo, S. R. (1991). The accuracy-confidence correlation in eyewitness testimony: Limits and extensions of the retrospective self-awareness effect. *Journal of Personality and Social Psychology, 61,* 698–707.

Kaszniak, A. W., Nussbaum, P. D., Berren, M. R., & Santiago, J. (1988). Amnesia as a consequence of male rape: A case report. *Journal of Abnormal Psychology, 97,* 100–104.

Kaushall, P. I., Zetin, M., & Squire, L. R. (1981). A psychosocial study of chronic, circumscribed amnesia. *Journal of Nervous and Mental Disorders, 169,* 383–389.

Keane, M. J., Gabrieli, J. D. E., Noland, J. S., & McNealy, S. I. (1995). Normal perceptual priming of orthographically illegal nonwords. *Journal of the International Neuropsychological Society, 1,* 425–433.

Keenan, P.A., Jacobson, M. W., Soleymani, R. M., & Newcomer, J. W. (1995). Commonly used therapeutic doses of glucocorticoids impair explicit memory. *Annals of the New York Academy of Sciences, 761,* 400–402.

Kelley, C. M., & Jacoby, L. L. (1990). The construction of subjective experience: Memory attributions. *Mind & Language, 5,* 49–68.

Kemper, S., Rash, S., Kynette, D., & Norman, S. (1990). Telling stories: The structure of adults' narratives. *European Journal of Cognitive Psychology, 2,* 205–228.

Kenny, M. G. (1986). *The passion of Ansel Bourne: Multiple personality in American culture.* Washington, DC: Smithsonian Institution Press.

Kidder, T. (1993). *Old friends.* New York: Houghton Mifflin.

Kihlstrom, J. F. (1984). Conscious, subconscious, unconscious: A cognitive view. In K. S. Bowers & D. Meichenbaum (Eds.), *The unconscious reconsidered* (pp. 149–211). New York: Wiley.

Kihlstrom, J. F. (in press a). Exhumed memory. In S. J. Lynn & N. P. Spanos (Eds.), *Truth and memory.* New York: Guilford Press.

Kihlstrom, J. F. (in press b). Hypnosis, memory, and amnesia. In L. R. Squire & D. L. Schacter (Eds.), *Biological and psychological perspectives on memory and memory disorders.* Washington, DC: American Psychiatric Press.

Kihlstrom, J. F., & Schacter, D. L. (1990). Anesthesia, amnesia, and the cognitive unconscious. In B. Bonke, W. Fitch, & K. Millar (Eds.), *Memory and awareness in anesthesia* (pp. 21–44). Amsterdam: Swets & Zeitlinger.

Kihlstrom, J. F., & Schacter, D. L. (1995). Functional disorders of autobiographical memory. In A. Baddeley, B. Wilson, & F. Watts (Eds.), *Handbook of memory disorders* (pp. 337–364). Chichester: Wiley.

Kihlstrom, J. F., Schacter, D. L., Cork, R. C., Hurt, C. A., & Behr, S. E. (1990). Implicit and explicit memory following surgical anesthesia. *Psychological Science, 1,* 303–306.

Kim, J. J., & Fanselow, M. S. (1992). Modality-specific retrograde amnesia of fear. *Science, 256,* 675–677.

Kinoshita, S., & Wayland, S. V. (1993). Effects of surface features on word-fragment completion in amnesic subjects. *American Journal of Psychology, 106,* 67–80.

Kirschner, L. A. (1973). Dissociative reactions: An historical review and clinical study. *Acta Psychiatrica Scandinavica, 49,* 698–711.

Klatzky, R. L., & Erdelyi, M. H. (1985). The response criterion problem in tests of hypnosis and memory. *International Journal of Clinical and Experimental Hypnosis, 33,* 246–257.

Kluver, H., & Bucy, P. C. (1937). "Psychic blindness" and other symptoms following bilateral temporal lobectomy in rhesus monkeys. *American Journal of Physiology, 119,* 352–353.

Knowlton, B. J., & Squire, L. R. (1993). The learning of categories: Parallel brain systems for item memory and category level knowledge. *Science, 262,* 1747–1749.

Knowlton, B. J., Ramus, S. J., & Squire, L. R. (1992). Intact artificial grammar learning in amnesia: Dissociation of classification learning and explicit memory for specific instances. *Psychological Science, 3,* 172–179.

Knowlton, B. J., Squire, L. R., & Gluck, M. A. (1994). Probabilistic classification learning in amnesia. *Learning and Memory, 1,* 106–120.

Kolers, P. A. (1975). Specificity of operations in sentence recognition. *Cognitive Psychology, 7,* 289–306.

Kolodny, J. A. (1994). Memory processes in classification learning: An investigation of amnesic performance in categorization of dot patterns and artistic styles. *Psychological Science, 5,* 164–169.

Kopelman, M. D., Christensen, H., Puffett, A., & Stanhope, N. (1994). The great escape: A neuropsychological study of psychogenic amnesia. *Neuropsychologia, 32,* 675–691.

Koriat, A., & Goldsmith, M. (in press). Memory metaphors and the everyday-laboratory controversy: The correspondence versus the storehouse conceptions of memory. *Behavioral and Brain Sciences.*

Kosslyn, S. M. (1981). *Image and mind.* Cambridge: Harvard University Press.

Kosslyn, S. M. (1994). *Image and brain.* Cambridge: MIT Press.

Kotre, J. (1995). *White gloves: How we create ourselves through memory.* New York: Free Press.

Koutstaal, W. (1992). Skirting the abyss: A history of experimental explorations of automatic writing in psychology. *Journal of the History of the Behavioral Sciences, 28,* 5–27.

Koutstaal, W., & Schacter, D. L. (in press). Intentional forgetting and voluntary thought suppression: Two potential methods for coping with childhood trauma. *Review of Psychiatry.*

Kramer, T., Buckhout, R., & Eugenio, P. (1990). Weapon focus, arousal, and eyewitness memory: Attention must be paid. *Law and Human Behavior, 14,* 167–184.

Kris, E. (1956). The personal myth: A problem in psychoanalytic technique. In *The selected papers of Ernst Kris.* New Haven: Yale University Press.

Kritchevsky, M., Squire, L. R., & Zouzounis, J. A. (1988). Transient global amnesia: Characterization of anterograde and retrograde amnesia. *Neurology, 38,* 213–219.

Kritchevsky, M., Zouzounis, J. A., & Squire, L. R. (in press). Transient global amnesia and functional amnesia: Contrasting examples of episodic memory loss. In L. R. Squire & D. L. Schacter (Eds.), *Biological and psychological perspectives on memory and memory disorders.* Washington, DC: American Psychiatric Press.

Krystal, J. H., Southwick, S. M., & Charney, D. S. (1995). Post traumatic stress disorder: Psychobiological mechanisms of traumatic remembrance. In D. L. Schacter, J. T. Coyle, G. D. Fischbach, M.-M. Mesulam, & L. E. Sullivan (Eds.), *Memory distortion: How minds, brains, and societies reconstruct the past* (pp. 150–172). Cambridge: Harvard University Press.

Kuhn, A. (1991). Rememberance. In J. Spence & P. Holland (Eds.), *Family snaps: The meanings of domestic photography* (pp. 17–25). London: Virago.

Kunst-Wilson, W. R., & Zajonc, R. B. (1980). Affective discrimination of stimuli that cannot be recognized. *Science, 207,* 557–558.

Kuyken, W., & Brewin, C. R. (1995). Autobiographical memory functioning in depression and reports of early abuse. *Journal of Abnormal Psychology 104,* 585–591.

Landauer, T. K. (1975). Memory without organization: Properties of a model with random storage and undirected retrieval. *Cognitive Psychology, 7,* 495–531.

Langer, L. L. (1991). *Holocaust testimonies: The ruins of memory.* New Haven: Yale University Press.

Larsen, S. F. (1992). Potential flashbulbs: Memories of ordinary news as baseline. In E. Winograd & U. Neisser (Eds.), *Affect and accuracy in recall: Studies of "flashbulb memories"* (pp. 32–64). New York: Cambridge University Press.

Laurence, J.-R., & Perry, C. (1983). Hypnotically created memory among highly hypnotizable subjects. *Science, 222,* 523–524.

La Voie, D., & Light, L. L. (1994). Adult age differences in repetition priming: A meta-analysis. *Psychology and Aging, 9,* 539–553.

LeDoux, J. E. (1992). Emotion as memory: Anatomical systems underlying indelible neural traces. In S.-Å. Christianson (Ed.), *The handbook of emotion and memory: Research and theory* (pp. 269–288). Hillsdale, NJ: Erlbaum.

LeDoux, J. E. (1994). Emotion, memory and the brain. *Scientific American, 270,* 32–39.

Leichtman, M. D., & Ceci, S. J. (1995). The effects of stereotypes and suggestions on preschoolers' reports. *Developmental Psychology 31,* 568–578.

Levin, H. S., Benton, A. L., & Grossman, R. G. (1982). *Neurobehavioral consequences of closed head injury.* New York: Oxford University Press.

Levinson, B. W. (1965). States of awareness during general anaesthesia: Preliminary communication. *British Journal of Anaesthesia, 37,* 544–546.

Lewinsohn, P. M., & Rosenbaum, M. (1987). Recall of parental behavior by acute depressives, remitted depressives and nondepressives. *Journal of Personality and Social Psychology, 52,* 611–619.

Light, L. L. (1991). Memory and aging: Four hypotheses in search of data. *Annual Review of Psychology, 42,* 333–376.

Lindsay, D. S. (1990). Misleading suggestions can impair eyewitnesses' ability to remember event details. *Journal of Experimental Psychology: Learning, Memory, and Cognition, 16,* 1077–1083.

Lindsay, D. S., & Johnson, M. K. (1989). The eyewitness suggestibility effect and memory for source. *Memory & Cognition, 17,* 349–358.

Lindsay, D. S., & Read, J. D. (1994). Psychotherapy and memories of childhood sexual abuse: A cognitive perspective. *Applied Cognitive Psychology, 8,* 281–338.

Lindsay, D. S., & Read, J. D. (1996). "Memory work" and recovered memories of childhood sexual abuse: Scientific evidence and public, professional, and personal issues. *Psychology, Public Policy, and the Law, 1,* 846–908.

Linton, M. (1986). Ways of searching and the contents of memory. In D. C. Rubin (Ed.), *Autobiographical memory* (pp. 50–67). Cambridge: Cambridge University Press.

Lipinski, J. F., & Pope, H. G. J. (1994). Do "flashbacks" represent obsessional imagery? *Comprehensive Psychiatry, 35,* 245–247.

Lipsitz, G. (1990). *Time passages: Collective memory and American popular culture.* Minneapolis: University of Minnesota Press.

Lisman, S. A. (1974). Alcoholic "blackout": State dependent learning? *Archives of General Psychiatry, 30,* 46–53.

Loftus, E. F. (1979). *Eyewitness testimony.* Cambridge: Harvard University Press.

Loftus, E. F. (1981). Memory and its distortions. In A. G. Kraut (Ed.), *The G. Stanley Hall lecture series* (pp. 123–154). Washington, DC: American Psychological Association.

Loftus, E. F. (1993). The reality of repressed memories. *American Psychologist, 48,* 518–537.

Loftus, E. F., & Ketcham, K. (1994). *The myth of repressed memory: False memories and allegations of sexual abuse.* New York: St. Martin's Press.

Loftus, E. F., & Loftus, G. R. (1980). On the permanence of stored information in the human brain. *American Psychologist, 35,* 409–420.

Loftus, E. F., & Palmer, J. C. (1974). Reconstruction of automobile destruction: An example of the interaction between language and memory. *Journal of Verbal Learning and Verbal Behavior, 13,* 585–589.

Loftus, E. F., & Pickrell, J. E. (1995). The formation of false memories. *Psychiatric Annals, 25,* 720–725.

Loftus, E. F., Feldman, J., & Dashiell, R. (1995). The reality of illusory memories. In D. L. Schacter, J. T. Coyle, G. D. Fischbach, M. M. Mesulam, & L. E. Sullivan (Eds.), *Memory dis-*

tortion: How minds, brains and societies reconstruct the past (pp. 47–68). Cambridge: Harvard University Press.

Loftus, E. F., Fienberg, S. E., & Tanur, J. M. (1985). Cognitive psychology meets the national survey. *American Psychologist, 40,* 175–180.

Loftus, E. F., Loftus, G., & Messo, J. (1987). Some facts about "weapon focus." *Law and Human Behavior, 11,* 55–62.

Loftus, E. F., Miller, D. G., & Burns, H. J. (1978). Semantic integration of verbal information into a visual memory. *Journal of Experimental Psychology: Human Learning and Memory, 4,* 19–31.

Loftus, E. F., Polonsky, S., & Fullilove, M. T. (1994). Memories of childhood sexual abuse: Remembering and repressing. *Psychology of Women, 18,* 67–84.

Lorayne, H., & Lucas, J. (1974). *The memory book.* New York: Ballantine.

Lucchelli, F., Muggia, S., & Spinnler, H. (1995). The "Petites Madeleines" phenomenon in two amnesic patients: Sudden recovery of forgotten memories. *Brain, 118,* 167–183.

Luria, A. R. (1968). *The mind of a mnemonist: A little book about a vast memory* (L. Solotaroff, Trans.). New York: Basic Books.

Lynn, S. J., & Nash, M. R. (1994). Truth in memory: Ramifications for psychotherapy and hypnotherapy. *American Journal of Hypnosis, 36,* 194–208.

Lyon, L. S. (1985). Facilitating telephone number recall in a case of psychogenic amnesia. *Journal of Behavior Therapy and Experimental Psychiatry, 16,* 147–149.

MacCurdy, J. T. (1918). *War neuroses.* Cambridge: Cambridge University Press.

Mack, J. E. (1994). *Abduction: Human encounters with aliens.* New York: Scribner's.

MacKinnon, D., & Squire, L. R. (1989). Autobiographical memory in amnesia. *Psychobiology, 17,* 247–256.

MacLean, H. N. (1993). *Once upon a time: A true story of memory, murder, and the law.* New York: HarperCollins.

Madakasira, S., & O'Brien, K. F. (1987). Acute posttraumatic stress disorder in victims of a natural disaster. *The Journal of Nervous and Mental Disease, 175,* 286–290.

Maine de Biran. (1929). *The influence of habit on the faculty of thinking.* Baltimore: Williams & Wilkins.

Mair, W. G. P., Warrington, E. K., & Weiskrantz, L. (1979). Memory disorder in Korsakoff psychosis. A neuropathological and neuropsychological investigation of two cases. *Brain, 102,* 749–783.

Mandler, G. (1980). Recognition: The judgment of previous occurrence. *Psychological Review, 87,* 252–271.

Mäntylä, T. (1986). Optimizing cue effectiveness: Recall of 500 and 600 incidentally learned words. *Journal of Experimental Psychology: Learning, Memory, and Cognition, 12,* 66–71.

Marcus, G. B. (1986). Stability and change in political attitudes: Observe, recall, and "explain." *Political Behavior, 8,* 21–44.

Maren, S., & Baudry, M. (1995). Properties and mechanisms of long-term synaptic plasticity in the mammalian brain: Relationships to learning and memory. *Neurobiology of Learning and Memory, 63,* 1–18.

Markowitsch, H. J., Calabrese, P., Würker, M., Durwen, H. F., Kessler, J., Babinsky, R., Brechtelsbauer, D., Heuser, L., & Gehlen, W. (1994). The amygdala's contribution to memory—a study on two patients with Urbach-Wiethe disease. *Neuroreport, 5,* 1349–1352.

Márquez, G. G. (1970). *One hundred years of solitude.* New York: Avon.

Marsh, R. L., & Landau, J. D. (1995). Item availability in cryptomnesia: Assessing its role in two paradigms of unconscious plagiarism. *Journal of Experimental Psychology: Learning, Memory, and Cognition, 21,* 1568–1582.

Marsolek, C. J., Kosslyn, S. M., & Squire, L. R. (1992). Form specific visual priming in the right cerebral hemisphere. *Journal of Experimental Psychology: Learning, Memory, and Cognition, 18,* 492–508.

Martin, A., Haxby, J. V., LaLonde, F. M., Wiggs, C. L., & Ungerleider, L. G. (1995). Discrete cortical regions associated with knowledge of color and knowledge of action. *Science, 270,* 102–105.

Martin, A., Wiggs, C. L., Ungerleider, L. G., & Haxby, J. V. (1996). Neural correlates of category-specific knowledge. *Nature, 379,* 649–652.

Masson, J. M. (1984). *The assault on truth: Freud's suppression of the seduction theory.* New York: Farrar, Straus, & Giroux.

Masson, M. E. J., & MacLeod, C. M. (1992). Re-enacting the route to interpretation: Context dependency in encoding and retrieval. *Journal of Experimental Psychology: General, 121,* 145–176.

Mayes, A. R. (1988). *Human organic memory disorders.* New York: Cambridge University Press.

McAdams, D. P. (1993). *The stories we live by: Personal myths and the making of the self.* New York: Morrow.

McAndrews, M. P., Glisky, E. L., & Schacter, D. L. (1987). When priming persists: Long-lasting implicit memory for a single episode in amnesic patients. *Neuropsychologia, 25,* 497–506.

McClelland, J. L. (1995). Constructive memory and memory distortions: A parallel-distributed processing approach. In D. L. Schacter, J. T. Coyle, G. D. Fischbach, M.-M. Mesulam, & L. E. Sullivan (Eds.), *Memory distortion: How minds, brains and societies reconstruct the past* (pp. 69–90). Cambridge: Harvard University Press.

McClelland, J. L., & Rumelhart, D. E. (1986). *Parallel distributed processing: Explorations in the microstructure of cognition.* Cambridge: MIT Press.

McClelland, J. L., McNaughton, B. L., & O'Reilly, R. C. (1995). Why there are complementary learning systems in the hippocampus and neocortex: Insights from the successes and failures of connectionist models of learning and memory. *Psychological Review, 102,* 419–457.

McCloskey, M., & Zaragoza, M. (1985). Misleading postevent information and memory for events: Arguments and evidence against memory impairment hypotheses. *Journal of Experimental Psychology: General, 114,* 1–16.

McDaniel, M. A., & Einstein, G. O. (1992). Aging and prospective memory: Basic findings and practical applications. *Advances in Learning and Behavioral Disabilities, 7,* 87–105.

McDonald, R. J., & White, N. M. (1993). A triple dissociation of memory systems: Hippocampus, amygdala, and dorsal striatum. *Behavioral Neuroscience, 107,* 3–22.

McDonough, L., Mandler, J. M., McKee, R. D., Squire, L. R. (1995). The deferred imitation task as a nonverbal measure of declarative memory. *Proceedings of the National Academy of Sciences, 92,* 7580–7584.

McElroy, S. L., & Keck, P. E., Jr. (1995). Recovered memory therapy: false memory syndrome and other complications. *Psychiatric Annals, 25,* 731–735.

McGaugh, J. L. (1995). Emotional activation, neuromodulatory systems and memory. In D. L. Schacter, J. T. Coyle, G. D. Fischbach, M.-M. Mesulam, & L. E. Sullivan (Eds.), *Memory distortion: How minds, brains, and societies reconstruct the past* (pp. 255–273). Cambridge: Harvard University Press.

McGinn, C. (1990). *The problem of consciousness.* Oxford: Blackwell.

McGlynn, S. M., & Kaszniak, A. W. (1991). Unawareness of deficits in dementia and schizophrenia. In G. P. Prigatano & D. L. Schacter (Eds.), *Awareness of deficit after brain injury: Clinical and theoretical issues* (pp. 84–110). New York: Oxford University Press.

McGlynn, S. M., & Schacter, D. L. (1989). Unawareness of deficits in neuropsychological syndromes. *Journal of Clinical and Experimental Neuropsychology, 11,* 143–205.

McGowin, D. F. (1993). *Living in the labyrinth: A personal journey through the maze of Alzheimer's.* New York: Dell.

McIntyre, J. S., & Craik, F. I. M. (1987). Age differences in memory for item and source information. *Canadian Journal of Psychology, 41,* 175–192.

McNally, R. J., Lasko, N. B., Macklin, M. L., & Pitman, R. K. (1995). Autobiographical memory disturbance in combat-related posttraumatic stress disorder. *Behaviour Research and Therapy, 33,* 619–630.

McNally, R. J., Metzger, L. J., Lasko, N. B., & Pitman, R. K. (1995). Directed forgetting of trauma cues in women with histories of childhood sexual abuse. Submitted for publication.

McNaughton, B., & Nadel, L. (1989). Hebb-Marr networks and the neurobiological representation of action in space. In M. A. Gluck & D. E. Rumelhart (Eds.), *Neuroscience and connectionist theory* (pp. 1–64). Hillsdale, NJ: Erlbaum.

Melcher, J. & Schooler, J. W. (1996). The misremembrance of wines past: Verbal and perceptual expertise differentially mediate verbal overshadowing of taste. *Journal of Memory and Language.*

Meltzoff, A. N. (1995). What infant memory tells us about infantile amnesia: Long-term recall and deferred imitation. *Journal of Experimental Child Psychology, 59,* 497–515.

Mercer, B., Wapner, W., Gardner, H., & Benson, D. F. (1977). A study of confabulation. *Archives of Neurology, 34,* 429–433.

Mergler, N. L., Faust, M., & Goldstein, M. D. (1984–1985). Storytelling as an age-dependent skill: Oral recall of orally presented stories. *International Journal of Aging and Human Development, 20,* 205–228.

Merikle, P. M. (1988). Subliminal auditory messages: An evaluation. *Psychology and Marketing, 5,* 355–372.

Merskey, H. (1979). *The analysis of hysteria.* London: Baillière Tindall.

Merskey, H. (1992). The manufacture of personalities: The production of multiple personality disorder. *British Journal of Psychiatry, 160,* 327–340.

Merzenich, M. M., & Jameshima, K. (1993). Cortical plasticity and memory. *Current Opinion in Neurobiology, 3,* 187–196.

Mesulam, M.-M. (1990). Large-scale neurocognitive networks and distributed processing for attention, language, and memory. *Annals of Neurology, 28,* 597–613.

Metcalfe, J. (1993). Novelty monitoring, metacognition and control in a composite holographic associative recall model: Implications for Korsakoff amnesia. *Psychological Review, 100,* 3–22.

Metcalfe, J., & Shimamura, A. P. (Eds.). (1994). *Metacognition: Knowing about knowing.* Cambridge: MIT Press.

Metcalfe, J., Schwartz, B. L., & Joaquim, S. G. (1993). The cue familiarity heuristic in metacognition. *Journal of Experimental Psychology: Learning, Memory, and Cognition, 19,* 851–861.

Metcalfe, J., Funnell, M., & Gazzaniga, M. S. (1995). Right-hemisphere memory superiority: studies of a split-brain patient. *Psychological Science, 6,* 157–164.

Middleton, D., & Edwards, D. (1990). *Collective remembering.* London: Sage.

Miller, G. A. (1956). The magical number seven, plus or minus two: Some limits on our capacity for processing information. *Psychological Review, 63,* 81–96.

Milner, B., Corkin, S., & Teuber, H. L. (1968). Further analysis of the hippocampal amnesic syndrome: Fourteen year follow-up study of H. M. *Neuropsychologia, 6,* 215–234.

Milner, B., Corsi, P., & Leonard, G. (1991). Frontal-lobe contribution to recency judgments. *Neuropsychologia, 29,* 601–618.

Mineka, S., & Nugent, K. (1995). Mood-congruent memory biases in anxiety and depression. In D. L. Schacter, J. T. Coyle, G. D. Fischbach, M.-M. Mesulam, & L. E. Sullivan (Eds.), *Memory distortion: How minds, brains, and societies reconstruct the past* (pp. 173–196). Cambridge: Harvard University Press.

Mishkin, M. (1978). Memory in monkeys severely impaired by combined but not separate removal of amygdala and hippocampus. *Nature, 273,* 297–298.

Mishkin, M. (1982). A memory system in the monkey. *Philosophical Transactions of the Royal Society of London Series B, 298,* 85–95.

Mishkin, M., Malamut, B., & Bachevalier, J. (1984). Memories and habits: Two neural systems. In G. Lynch, J. L. McGaugh, & N. M. Weinberger (Eds.), *Neurobiology of learning and memory* (pp. 65–77). New York: Guilford Press.

Mittenberg, W., Seidenberg, M., O'Leary, D. S., & DiGiulio, D. V. (1989). Changes in cerebral functioning associated with normal aging. *Journal of Clinical and Experimental Neuropsychology, 11,* 918–932.

Moldea, D. E. (1995). *The killing of Robert F. Kennedy: An investigation of motive, means, and opportunity.* New York: Norton.

Molinari, V., & Reichlin, R. E. (1985). Life review reminiscence in the elderly: A review of the literature. *International Journal of Aging and Human Development, 20,* 81–92.

Morris, C. D., Bransford, J. D., & Franks, J. J. (1977). Levels of processing versus transfer-appropriate processing. *Journal of Verbal Learning and Verbal Behavior, 16,* 519–533.

Morton, J. (1991). Cognitive pathologies of memory: A headed records analysis. In W. Kessen, A. Ortony, & F. Craik (Eds.), *Memories, thoughts, and emotions: Essays in honor of George Mandler* (pp. 199–210). Hillsdale, NJ: Erlbaum.

Moscovitch, M. (1994). Memory and working-with-memory: Evaluation of a component process model and comparisons with other models. In D. L. Schacter & E. Tulving (Eds.), *Memory systems 1994* (pp. 269–310). Cambridge: MIT Press.

Moscovitch, M. (1995). Confabulation. In D. L. Schacter, J. T. Coyle, G. D. Fischbach, M.-M. Mesulam, & L. E. Sullivan (Eds.), *Memory distortion: How minds, brains, and societies reconstruct the past* (pp. 226–254). Cambridge: Harvard University Press.

Moscovitch, M., & Winocur, G. (1992). The neuropsychology of memory and aging. In F. I. M. Craik & T. A. Salthouse (Eds.), *The handbook of aging and cognition* (pp. 315–372). Hillsdale, NJ: Erlbaum.

Moscovitch, M., Kohler, S., & Houle, S. (1995). Distinct neural correlates of visual long-term memory for spatial location and object identity: A positron emission tomography (PET) study. *Proceedings of the National Academy of Sciences, USA, 92,* 3721–3725.

Mulhern, S. (1994). Satanism, ritual abuse, and multiple personality disorder: A sociohistorical perspective. *International Journal of Clinical and Experimental Hypnosis, 42,* 265–288.

Murray, E. A., Gaffan, D., & Mishkin, M. (1993). Neural substrates of visual stimulus-stimulus association in Rhesus monkeys. *Journal of Neuroscience, 13,* 4549–4561.

Myers, L. B., & Brewin, C. R. (1994). Recall of early experience and the repressive coping style. *Journal of Abnormal Psychology, 103,* 288–292.

Myers, N. A., Perris, E. E., & Speaker, C. J. (1994). Fifty months of memory: A longitudinal study in early childhood. *Memory, 2,* 383–415.

Nadel, L. (1994). Multiple memory systems: What and why, an update. In D. L. Schacter & E. Tulving (Eds.), *Memory systems 1994* (pp. 39–63). Cambridge: MIT Press.

Naito, M., & Komatsu, S. (1993). Processes involved in childhood development of implicit memory. In P. Graf & M. E. J. Masson (Eds.), *Implicit memory: New directions in cognition, development, and neuropsychology* (pp. 231–264). Hillsdale, NJ: Erlbaum.

Nash, M. R. (1994). Memory distortion and sexual trauma: The problem of false negatives and false positives. *The International Journal of Clinical and Experimental Hypnosis, 42,* 346–362.

Nathan, D., & Snedeker, M. (1995). *Satan's silence: Ritual abuse and the making of a modern American witch hunt.* New York: Basic Books.

Neisser, U. (1967). *Cognitive psychology.* New York: Appleton-Century-Crofts.

Neisser, U. (1978). Memory: What are the important questions? In M. M. Gruneberg, P. E. Morris, & R. N. Sykes (Eds.), *Practical aspects of memory* (pp. 3–24). London: Academic Press.

Neisser, U. (1982). John Dean's memory: A case study. In U. Neisser (Ed.), *Memory observed: Remembering in natural contexts* (pp. 139–159). San Francisco: Freeman.

Neisser, U. (1986). Nested structure in autobiographical memory. In D. C. Rubin (Ed.), *Autobiographical memory* (pp. 71–81). Cambridge: Cambridge University Press.

Neisser, U. (1994). Self-narratives: True and false. In U. Neisser and R. Fivush (Eds.), *The remembering self: Construction and accuracy in the self-narrative* (pp. 1–18). New York: Cambridge University Press.

Neisser, U., & Harsch, N. (1992). Phantom flashbulbs: False recollections of hearing the news about *Challenger*. In E. Winograd & U. Neisser (Eds.), *Affect and accuracy in recall: Studies of "flashbulb memories"* (pp. 9–31). Cambridge: Cambridge University Press.

Neisser, U., Winograd, E., Bergman, E. T., Schreiber, C. A., Palmer, S. E., & Weldon, M. S. (1996). Remembering the earthquake: Direct experience vs. hearing the news. *Memory.*

Nelson, E. L., & Simpson, P. (1994). First glimpse: An initial examination of subjects who have rejected their recovered visualizations as false memories. *Issues in Child Abuse Accusations, 6,* 123–133.

Nelson, K. (1993). The psychological and social origins of autobiographical memory. *Psychological Science, 4,* 7–14.

Newcomer, J. W., Craft, S., Hershey, T., Askins, K., & Bardgett, M. E. (1994). Glucocorticoid-induced impairment in declarative memory performance in adult humans. *Journal of Neuroscience, 14,* 2047–2053.

Nickerson, R. S., & Adams, M. J. (1979). Long-term memory for a common object. *Cognitive Psychology, 11,* 287–307.

Niedenthal, P. M. (1992). Affect and social perception: On the psychological validity of rose-colored glasses. In R. F. Bornstein & T. S. Pittman (Eds.), *Perception without awareness: Cognitive, clinical, and social perspectives* (pp. 211–235). New York: Guilford Press.

Nigro, G., & Neisser, U. (1983). Point of view in personal memories. *Cognitive Psychology, 15,* 467–482.

Nissen, M. J., & Bullemer, P. (1987). Attentional requirements of learning: Evidence from performance measures. *Cognitive Psychology, 19,* 1–32.

Nissen, M. J., Ross, J. L., Willingham, D. B., Mackenzie, T. B., & Schacter, D. L. (1988). Memory and awareness in a patient with multiple personality disorder. *Brain and Cognition, 8,* 21–38.

Noice, H., & Noice, T. (1996). Two approaches to learning a theatrical script. *Memory, 4,* 1–18.

Norman, K. A., & Schacter, D. L. (1996). Implicit memory, explicit memory, and false recollection: A cognitive neuroscience perspective. In L. M. Reder (Ed.), *Implicit memory and metacognition.* Hillsdale, NJ: Erlbaum.

Nyberg, L., McIntosh, A. R., Cabeza, R., Nilsson, L.-G., Houle, S., Habib, R., & Tulving, E. (1996). Network analysis of PET rCBF data: Ensemble inhibition during episodic memory retrieval. *Journal of Neuroscience.*

Nyberg, L., McIntosh, A. R., Houle, S., Nilsson, L.-G., & Tulving, E. (1996). Activation of medial temporal lobe structures during episodic memory retrieval.

Ofshe, R., & Watters, E. (1994). *Making monsters: False memories, psychotherapy, and sexual hysteria.* New York: Scribner's.

O'Keefe, J., & Nadel, L. (1978). *The hippocampus as a cognitive map.* Oxford: Clarendon Press.

Olio, K. A. (1994). Truth in memory. *American Psychologist, 49,* 442.

Olio, K. A., & Cornell, W. F. (1995). The facade of scientific documentation: A case study of Richard Ofshe's analysis of the Paul Ingram case. Submitted for publication.

Orne, M. T., Soskis, D. A., Dinges, D. F., & Orne, E. C. (1984). Hypnotically induced testimony. In G. L. Wells & E. F. Loftus (Eds.), *Eyewitness testimony: Psychological perspectives.* New York: Cambridge University Press.

Orne, M. T., Whitehouse, W. G., Dinges, D. F., & Orne, E. C. (1988). Reconstructing memory through hypnosis: Forensic and clinical implications. In H. M. Pettinati (Ed.), *Hypnosis and memory* (pp. 21–63). New York: Guilford Press.

Owen, H. (1992). *Littlejohn.* New York: Villard.

Papousek, H. (1967). Experimental studies of appetitional behavior in human newborns and infants. In H. W. Stevenson, E. H. Hess, & H. L. Rheingold (Eds.), *Early behavior.* New York: Wiley.

Park, S., & Holzman, P. S. (1992). Schizophrenics show spatial working memory deficits. *Archives of General Psychiatry, 49,* 975–982.

Parkin, A. J., & Leng, N. R. C. (1993). *Neuropsychology of the amnesic syndrome.* Hillsdale, NJ: Erlbaum.

Parkin, A. J., & Walter, B. M. (1992). Recollective experience, normal aging and frontal dysfunction. *Psychology and Aging, 7,* 290–298.

Parkin, A. J., Gardiner, J. M., & Rosser, R. (1995). Functional aspects of recollective experience in face recognition. *Consciousness and Cognition, 4,* 387–398.

Parkin, A. J., Walter, B. M., & Hunkin, N. M. (1995). The relationships between normal aging, frontal lobe function, and memory for temporal and spatial information. Submitted for publication.

Parkin, A., Bindschaedler, C., Harsent, L., & Metzler, C. (in press). Pathological false alarm rates following damage to the left frontal cortex. *Brain and Cognition.*

Parks, E. D., & Balon, R. (1995). Autobiographical memory for childhood events: Pattern of recall in psychiatric patients with a history of alleged trauma. *Psychiatry, 58,* 199–208.

Pascual-Leone, A., Grafman, J., Clark, K., Stewart, M., Massaquoi, S., Lou, J., & Hallet, M. (1993). Procedural learning in Parkinson's disease and cerebellar degeneration. *Annals of Neurology, 34,* 594–602.

Pasley, L. (1994). Misplaced trust: a first-person account of how my therapist created false memories. *Skeptic, 2,* 62–67.

Patterson, K., & Hodges, J. R. (1995). Disorders of semantic memory. In A. D. Baddeley, B. A. Wilson, & F. N. Watts (Eds.), *Handbook of memory disorders* (pp. 167–186). Chichester, England: Wiley.

Payne, D. G. (1987). Hypermnesia and reminiscence in recall: A historical and empirical review. *Psychological Bulletin, 101,* 5–27.

Pearce, M. (1988). A memory artist. *Exploratorium Quarterly, 12,* 12–17.

Pendergrast, M. (1993). *For God, Country, and Coca-Cola.* New York: Collier Books.

Pendergrast, M. (1995). *Victims of memory: Incest accusations and shattered lives.* Hinesburg, VT: Upper Access.

Penfield, W. (1969). Consciousness, memory, and man's conditioned reflexes. In K. Pribram (Ed.), *On the biology of learning.* New York: Harcourt, Brace & World.

Penfield, W., & Perot, P. (1963). The brain's record of auditory and visual experience. *Brain, 86,* 595–696.

Penrose, R. (1989). *The emperor's new mind: Concerning computers, minds, and the laws of physics.* New York: Penguin.

Perfect, T. J., & Askew, C. (1994). Print adverts: Not remembered but memorable. *Applied Cognitive Psychology, 8,* 693–703.

Perry, C., & Laurence, J.-R. (1984). Mental processing outside of awareness: The contributions of Freud and Janet. In K. S. Bowers & D. Meichenbaum (Eds.), *The unconscious reconsidered* (pp. 9–48). New York: Wiley.

Person, E. S., & Klar, H. (1994). Establishing trauma: The difficulty of distinguishing between memories and fantasies. *Journal of the American Psychological Association, 42,* 1055–1081.

Petersen, S. E., Fox, P. T., Posner, M. I., Mintun, M. A., & Raichle, M. E. (1989). Positron emission tomographic studies of the processing of single words. *Journal of Cognitive Neuroscience, 1,* 153–170.

Petersen, S. E., Fox, P. T., Snyder, A. Z., & Raichle, M. E. (1990). Activation of extrastriate and frontal cortical areas by visual words and word-like stimuli. *Science, 249,* 1041–1044.

Petrides, M., Alivisatos, B., Evans, A. C., & Meyer, E. (1993). Dissociation of human mid-dorsolateral from posterior dorsolateral frontal cortex in memory processing. *Proceedings of the National Academy of Sciences* (USA), *90*, 873–877.

Pettinati, H. M. (Ed.). (1988). *Hypnosis and memory.* New York: Guilford Press.

Pezdek, K., & Prull, M. (1993). Fallacies in memory for conversations: Reflections on Clarence Thomas, Anita Hill, and the like. *Applied Cognitive Psychology, 7,* 299–310.

Phelps, E., & Gazzaniga, M. S. (1992). Hemispheric differences in mnemonic processing: The effects of left hemisphere interpretation. *Neuropsychologia, 30,* 293–297.

Pillemer, D. B. (1984). Flashbulb memories of the assassination attempt on President Reagan. *Cognition, 16,* 63–80.

Pillemer, D. B., & White, S. H. (1989). Childhood events recalled by children and adults. In H. W. Reese (Ed.), *Advances in childhood development and behavior* (vol. 21, pp. 297–340). San Diego: Academic Press.

Pinker, S., & Bloom, P. (1992). Natural language and natural selection. In J. Barkow, L. Cosmides, & J. Tooby (Eds.), *The adapted mind: Evolutionary psychology and the generation of culture* (pp. 451–493). New York: Oxford University Press.

Plaut, D. C., & Farah, M. J. (1990). Visual object representation: Interpreting neurophysiological data within a computational framework. *Journal of Cognitive Neuroscience, 2,* 320–343.

Pollen, D. A. (1993). *Hannah's heirs: The quest for the genetic origins of Alzheimer's disease.* New York: Oxford University Press.

Polster, M. R., Nadel, L., & Schacter, D. L. (1991). Cognitive neuroscience analysis of memory: A historical perspective. *Journal of Cognitive Neuroscience, 3,* 95–116.

Poole, D. A., & White, L. T. (1995). Tell me again and again: Stability and change in the repeated testimonies of children and adults. In M. Zaragoza, J. R. Graham, G. C. N. Hall, R. Hirschman, & Y. S. Ben-Porath (Eds.), *Memory and testimony in the child witness* (pp. 24–43). Thousand Oaks, CA: Sage.

Poole, D. A., Lindsay, S. D., Memon, A., & Bull, R. (1995). Psychotherapy and the recovery of memories of childhood sexual abuse: U.S. and British practitioners' opinions, practices, and experiences. *Journal of Consulting and Clinical Psychology, 63,* 426–437.

Pope, H. G., Jr., & Hudson, J. I. (1992). Is childhood sexual abuse a risk factor for bulimia nervosa? *American Journal of Psychiatry, 149,* 455–463.

Pope, H. G., Jr., & Hudson, J. I. (1995). Can memories of childhood sexual abuse be repressed? *Psychological Medicine, 25,* 121–126.

Pope, H. G., Mangweth, B., Negrão, A. B., Hudson, J. I., & Cordás, T. A. (1994). Childhood sexual abuse and bulimia nervosa: A comparison of American, Austrian, and Brazilian women. *American Journal of Psychiatry, 151,* 732–737.

Posner, M. I., & Raichle, M. E. (1994). *Images of the mind.* New York: Scientific American Library.

Postman, L., & Underwood, B. J. (1973). Critical issues in interference theory. *Memory and Cognition, 1,* 19–40.

Pratkanis, A. R., Greenwald, A. G., Leippe, M. R., & Baumgardner, M. H. (1988). In search of reliable persuasion effects: III. The sleeper effect is dead: Long live the sleeper effect. *Journal of Personality and Social Psychology, 54,* 203–218.

Pratt, M. W., & Robins, S. L. (1991). That's the way it was: Age differences in the structure and quality of adults' personal narratives. *Discourse Processes, 14,* 73–85.

Pratt, M. W., Boyes, C., Robins, S., & Manchester, J. (1989). Telling tales: Aging, working memory, and the narrative cohesion of story retellings. *Developmental Psychology, 25,* 628–635.

Price, D. L., & Sisodia, S. S. (1992). Alzheimer's Disease: Neural and molecular basis. In L. R. Squire (Ed.), *Encyclopedia of learning and memory* (pp. 22–25). New York: Macmillan.

Price, R. (1992). For the family. In *Sally Mann: Immediate family*. New York: Aperture Foundation.

Prigatano, G. P. (1991). Disturbances of self-awareness of deficit after traumatic brain injury. In G. P. Prigatano & D. L. Schacter (Eds.), *Awareness of deficit after brain injury: Clinical and theoretical issues* (pp. 111–126). New York: Oxford University Press.

Prigatano, G. P., & Schacter, D. L. (Eds.). (1991). *Awareness of deficit after brain injury: Clinical and theoretical issues*. New York: Oxford University Press.

Prince, M. (1910). *The dissociation of a personality*. New York: Longman, Green.

Proust, M. (1992). *In search of lost time: Swann's way* (Moncrieff, C. K. S., Kilmartin, T., & Enright, D. J., Trans.). New York: The Modern Library.

Putnam, F. W. (1993). Dissociative disorders in children: Behavioral profiles and problems. *Child Abuse & Neglect, 17*, 39–45.

Putnam, F. W., Guroff, J. J., Silberman, E. K., Barban, L., & Post, R. M. (1986). The clinical phenomenology of multiple personality disorder: Review of 100 recent cases. *Journal of Clinical Psychiatry, 47*, 285–293.

Pynoos, R. S., & Nader, K. (1989). Children's memory and proximity to violence. *Journal of the American Academy of Child and Adolescent Psychiatry, 28*, 236–241.

Rajaram, S. (1993). Remembering and knowing: Two means of access to the personal past. *Memory & Cognition, 21*, 89–102.

Ramachandran, V. S. (1995). Anosognosia in parietal lobe syndrome. *Consciousness and Cognition, 4*, 22–51.

Ratcliff, R., & McKoon, G. (1995). Bias and explicit memory in priming of object decisions. *Journal of Experimental Psychology: Learning, Memory, and Cognition 21*, 754–767.

Rauch, S. L., Savage, C. R., Brown, H. D., Curran, T., Alpert, N. M., Kendrick, A., Fischman, A. J., & Kosslyn, S. M. (in press). A PET investigation of implicit and explicit sequence learning. *Human Brain Mapping*.

Rauch, S. L., van der Kolk, B. A., Fisler, R. E., Alpert, N. M., Orr, S. P., Savage, C. R., Fischman, A. J., Jenike, M. A., & Pitman, R. K. (in press). A symptom provocation study of posttraumatic stress disorder using positron emission tomography and script-driven imagery. *Archives of General Psychiatry*.

Read, J. D., Tollestrup, P., Hammersley, R., McFadzen, E., & Christensen, A. (1990). The unconscious transference effect: Are innocent bystanders ever misidentified? *Applied Cognitive Psychology, 4*, 3–31.

Reber, A. S. (1993). *Implicit learning and tacit knowledge: An essay on the cognitive unconscious*. New York: Oxford University Press.

Reder, L. M., & Ritter, F. E. (1992). What determines initial feeling of knowing? Familiarity with question terms, not with the answer. *Journal of Experimental Psychology: Learning, Memory, and Cognition, 18*, 435–452.

Reiser, B. J., Black, J. B., & Abelson, R. P. (1985). Knowledge structures in the organization and retrieval of autobiographical memories. *Cognitive Psychology, 17*, 89–137.

Reiser, M. F. (1990). *Memory in mind and brain: What dream imagery reveals*. New York: Basic Books.

Ribot, T. (1882). *Diseases of memory*. New York: Appleton-Century-Crofts. (Original work published 1881)

Riccio, D. C., Rabinowitz, V. C., & Axelrod, S. (1994). Memory: When less is more. *American Psychologist, 49*, 917–926.

Richardson-Klavehn, A., & Bjork, R. A. (1988). Measures of memory. *Annual Review of Psychology, 36*, 475–543.

Riddoch, M. J., & Humphreys, G. W. (1987). Visual object processing in optic aphasia: A case of semantic access agnosia. *Cognitive Neuropsychology, 4*, 131–186.

Rivers, W. H. R. (1918). The repression of war experience. *The Lancet, 1*, 173–177.

Robinson, J. A., & Swanson, K. L. (1993). Field and observer modes of remembering. *Memory, 1,* 169–184.

Roediger, H. L., III (1980). Memory metaphors in cognitive psychology. *Memory & Cognition, 8,* 231–246.

Roediger, H. L., III (1990). Implicit memory: Retention without remembering. *American Psychologist, 45,* 1043–1056.

Roediger, H. L., III, & McDermott, K. B. (1993). Implicit memory in normal human subjects. In H. Spinnler & F. Boller (Eds.), *Handbook of neuropsychology* (pp. 63–131). Amsterdam: Elsevier.

Roediger, H. L., III, & McDermott, K. B. (1995). Creating false memories: Remembering words not presented in lists. *Journal of Experimental Psychology: Learning, Memory, and Cognition, 21,* 803–814.

Roediger, H. L., III, Weldon, M. S., & Challis, B. H. (1989). Explaining dissociations between implicit and explicit measures of retention: A processing account. In H. L. Roediger III & F. I. M. Craik (Eds.), *Varieties of memory and consciousness: Essays in honor of Endel Tulving* (pp. 3–41). Hillsdale, NJ: Erlbaum.

Roediger, H. L., III, Wheeler, M. A., & Rajaram, S. (1993). Remembering, knowing, and reconstructing the past. In D. L. Medin (Ed.), *The psychology of learning and motivation: Advances in research and theory* (pp. 97–134). San Diego: Academic Press.

Rosch, E., Mervis, C., Gray, W., Johnson, D., & Boyes-Braem, P. (1976). Basic objects in natural categories. *Cognitive Psychology, 8,* 382–439.

Rose, F. C., & Symonds, C. P. (1960). Persistent memory defect following encephalitis. *Brain, 83,* 195–212.

Rose, S. (1992). *The making of memory: From molecules to mind.* London: Bantam.

Rosenak, C., & Rosenak, J. (1990). *Museum of American Folk Art encyclopedia of twentieth-century American folk art and artists.* New York: Abbeville.

Ross, D. F., Ceci, S. J., Dunning, D., & Toglia, M. P. (1994). Unconscious transference and mistaken identity: When a witness misidentifies a familiar but innocent person. *Journal of Applied Psychology, 79,* 918–930.

Ross, M. (1989). Relation of implicit theories to the construction of personal histories. *Psychological Review, 96,* 341–357.

Ross, M., & Conway, M. (1986). Remembering one's own past: The construction of personal histories. In R. M. Sorrentino & E. T. Higgins (Eds.) *Handbook of motivation and cognition* (pp. 122–144). New York: Guilford Press.

Roth, M. S. (1989). Remembering forgetting: *Maladies de la Mémoire* in nineteenth-century France. *Representations, 26,* 49–68.

Rovee-Collier, C. (1993). The capacity for long-term memory in infancy. *Current Directions in Psychological Science, 2,* 130–135.

Rozin, P. (1976). The psychobiological approach to human memory. In M. R. Rosenzweig & E. L. Bennet (Eds.), *Neural mechanisms of learning and memory* (pp. 3–46). Cambridge: MIT Press.

Rubin, D. C. (1982). On the retention function for autobiographical memory. *Journal of Verbal Learning and Verbal Behavior, 21,* 21–38.

Rubin, D. C. (1995). *Memory in oral traditions: The cognitive psychology of epic, ballads, and counting-out rhymes.* New York: Oxford University Press.

Rubin, D. C., & Kozin, M. (1984). Vivid memories. *Cognition, 16,* 81–95.

Russell, W. R., & Nathan, P. W. (1946). Traumatic amnesia. *Brain, 69,* 280–300.

Sacks, O. (1985). *The man who mistook his wife for a hat.* New York: Summit.

Sacks, O. (1995). *An anthropologist on Mars.* New York: Knopf.

Saint-Cyr, J. A., & Taylor, A. E. (1992). The mobilization of procedural learning: The "key signature" of the basal ganglia. In L. R. Squire & N. Butters (Eds.), *Neuropsychology of memory* (pp. 188–202). New York: Guilford Press.

Salmon, D. P., & Butters, N. (1995). Neurobiology of skill and habit learning. *Current Opinion in Neurobiology, 5,* 184–190.

Salthouse, T. A. (1991). *Theoretical perspectives on cognitive aging.* Hillsdale, NJ: Erlbaum.

Sams, J., & Nitsch, T. (1991). *Other council fires were here before ours.* New York: HarperCollins.

Sanyal, A. (1992). Priming and implicit memory: A review and a synthesis relevant for consumer behavior. *Advances in Consumer Research, 19,* 795–805.

Sapolsky, R. M. (1992). *Stress, the aging brain, and the mechanisms of neuron death.* Cambridge: MIT Press.

Sargent, W., & Slater, E. (1941). Amnesic syndromes in war. *Proceedings of the Royal Society of Medicine, 34,* 757–764.

Saywitz, K. J., & Moan-Hardie, S. (1994). Reducing the potential for distortion of childhood memories. *Consciousness and Cognition, 3,* 408–425.

Schacter, D. L. (1982). *Stranger behind the engram: Theories of memory and the psychology of science.* Hillsdale, NJ: Erlbaum.

Schacter, D. L. (1983). Amnesia observed: Remembering and forgetting in a natural environment. *Journal of Abnormal Psychology, 92,* 236–242.

Schacter, D. L. (1986). Amnesia and crime: How much do we really know? *American Psychologist, 41,* 286–295.

Schacter, D. L. (1987a). Implicit memory: History and current status. *Journal of Experimental Psychology: Learning, Memory, and Cognition, 13,* 501–518.

Schacter, D. L. (1987b). Memory, amnesia, and frontal lobe dysfunction. *Psychobiology, 15,* 21–36.

Schacter, D. L. (1990). Perceptual representation systems and implicit memory: Toward a resolution of the multiple memory systems debate. *Annals of the New York Academy of Sciences, 608,* 543–571.

Schacter, D. L. (1991). Unawareness of deficit and unawareness of knowledge in patients with memory disorders. In G. P. Prigatano & D. L. Schacter (Eds.), *Awareness of deficit after brain injury: Clinical and theoretical issues* (pp. 127–151). New York: Oxford University Press.

Schacter, D. L. (1992). Implicit knowledge: New perspectives on unconscious processes. *Proceedings of the National Academy of Science, USA, 89,* 11113–11117.

Schacter, D. L. (1993). *Fragile power: Explorations of memory.* Newton, MA: Newton Art Center.

Schacter, D. L. (1995a). Memory distortion: History and current status. In D. L. Schacter, J. T. Coyle, G. D. Fischbach, M.-M. Mesulam, & L. E. Sullivan (Eds.), *Memory distortion: How minds, brains and societies reconstruct the past* (pp. 1–43). Cambridge: Harvard University Press.

Schacter, D. L. (1995b). Memory wars. *Scientific American, 272,* 135–139.

Schacter, D. L., & Cooper, L. A. (1995). Bias in the priming of object decisions: Logic, assumptions, and data. *Journal of Experimental Psychology: Learning, Memory and Cognition, 21,* 768–776.

Schacter, D. L., & Crovitz, H. F. (1977). Memory function after closed head injury: A review of the quantitative research. *Cortex, 13,* 150–176.

Schacter, D. L., & Graf, P. (1986). Preserved learning in amnesic patients: perspectives from research on direct priming. *Journal of Clinical and Experimental Neuropsychology, 8,* 727–743.

Schacter, D. L., & Kihlstrom, J. F. (1989). Functional amnesia. In F. Boller & J. Grafman (Eds.), *Handbook of neuropsychology* (Vol. 3, pp. 209–231). Amsterdam: Elsevier.

Schacter, D. L., & Moscovitch, M. (1984). Infants, amnesics, and dissociable memory systems. In M. Moscovitch (Ed.), *Infant Memory* (pp. 173–216). New York: Plenum.

Schacter, D. L., & Nadel, L. (1991). Varieties of spatial memory: A problem for cognitive neuroscience. In R. G. Lister & H. J. Weingartner (Eds.), *Perspectives on cognitive neuroscience* (pp. 165–185). New York: Oxford University Press.

Schacter, D. L., & Tulving, E. (1994). What are the memory systems of 1994? In D. L. Schacter & E. Tulving (Eds.), *Memory systems 1994* (pp. 1–38). Cambridge: MIT Press.

Schacter, D. L., & Worling, J. R. (1985). Attribute information and the feeling-of-knowing. *Canadian Journal of Psychology, 39,* 467–475.

Schacter, D. L., Alpert, N. M., Savage, C. R., Rauch, S. L., & Albert, M. S. (1996). Conscious recollection and the human hippocampal formation: Evidence from positron emission tomography. *Proceedings of the National Academy of Sciences, USA, 93,* 321–325.

Schacter, D. L., Bowers, J., & Booker, J. (1989). Intention, awareness, and implicit memory: The retrieval intentionality criterion. In S. Lewandowsky, J. C. Dunn, & K. Kirsner (Eds.), *Implicit memory: Theoretical issues* (pp. 47–69). Hillsdale, NJ: Erlbaum.

Schacter, D. L., Chiu, C. Y. P., & Ochsner, K. N. (1993). Implicit memory: A selective review. *Annual Review of Neuroscience, 16,* 159–182.

Schacter, D. L., Church, B., & Bolton, E. (1995). Implicit memory in amnesic patients: Impairment of voice-specific priming. *Psychological Science, 6,* 20–25.

Schacter, D. L., Church, B., & Osowiecki, D. M. (1994). Auditory priming in elderly adults: Impairment of voice-specific implicit memory. *Memory, 2,* 295–323.

Schacter, D. L., Church, B., & Treadwell, J. (1994). Implicit memory in amnesic patients: Evidence for spared auditory priming. *Psychological Science, 5,* 20–25.

Schacter, D. L., Cooper, L. A., & Delaney, S. M. (1990). Implicit memory for unfamiliar objects depends on access to structural descriptions. *Journal of Experimental Psychology: General, 119,* 5–24.

Schacter, D. L., Cooper, L. A., & Treadwell, J. (1993). Preserved priming of novel objects across size transformation in amnesic patients. *Psychological Science, 4,* 331–335.

Schacter, D. L., Cooper, L. A., & Valdiserri, M. (1992). Implicit and explicit memory for novel objects in older and younger adults. *Psychology and Aging, 7,* 299–308.

Schacter, D. L., Coyle, J. T., Fischbach, G. D., Mesulam, M.-M., & Sullivan, L. E. (Eds.) (1995). *Memory distortion: How minds, brains, and societies reconstruct the past.* Cambridge: Harvard University Press.

Schacter, D. L., Curran, T., Galluccio, L. D., Milberg, W., & Bates, J. (1996). False recognition and the right frontal lobe: A case study. *Neuropsychologia.*

Schacter, D. L., Eich, J. E., & Tulving, E. (1978). Richard Semon's theory of memory. *Journal of Verbal Learning and Verbal Behavior, 17,* 721–743.

Schacter, D. L., Harbluk, J. L., & McLachlan, D. R. (1984). Retrieval without recollection: An experimental analysis of source amnesia. *Journal of Verbal Learning and Verbal Behavior, 23,* 593–611.

Schacter, D. L., Kagan, J., & Leichtman, M. D. (1995). True and false memories in children and adults: A cognitive neuroscience perspective. *Psychology, Public Policy, and Law, 1,* 411–428.

Schacter, D. L., Kaszniak, A. K., Kihlstrom, J. F., & Valdiserri, M. (1991). The relation between source memory and aging. *Psychology and Aging, 6,* 559–568.

Schacter, D. L., Kihlstrom, J. F., Kaszniak, A. W., & Valdiserri, M. (1993). Preserved and impaired memory functions in elderly adults. In J. Cerella, J. Rybsh, W. Hoyer, & M. L. Commons (Eds.), *Adult information processing: Limits on loss* (pp. 327–350). San Diego: Academic Press.

Schacter, D. L., Kihlstrom, J. F., Kihlstrohm, L. C., & Berren, M. B. (1989). Autobiographical memory in a case of multiple personality disorder. *Journal of Abnormal Psychology, 98* 508–514.

Schacter, D. L., McGlynn, S. M., Milberg, W. P., & Church, B. A. (1993). Spared priming despite impaired comprehension: Implicit memory in a case of word meaning deafness. *Neuropsychology, 7,* 107–118.

Schacter, D. L., Reiman, E., Uecker, A., Polster, M. R., Yun, L. S., & Cooper, L. A. (1995). Neuroanatomical correlates of memory for structurally coherent visual objects. *Nature, 376,* 587–590.

Schacter, D. L., Wang, P. L., Tulving, E., & Freedman, M. (1982). Functional retrograde amnesia: A quantitative case study. *Neuropsychologia, 20,* 523–532.

Schacter, D. L., Verfaellie, M., & Pradere, D. (1996). The neuropsychology of memory illusions: False recall and recognition in amnesic patients. *Journal of Memory and Language.*

Schank, R. C. (1990). *Tell me a story: A new look at real and artificial memory.* New York: Scribner's.

Schimek, J. G. (1987). Fact and fantasy in the seduction theory: A historical review. *Journal of the American Psychoanalytic Association, 35,* 937–965.

Schleifer, R., Davis, R. C., & Mergler, N. (1992). *Culture and cognition: The boundaries of literary and scientific inquiry.* Ithaca, NY: Cornell University Press.

Schooler, J. W. (1994). Seeking the core: The issues and evidence surrounding recovered accounts of sexual trauma. *Consciousness and Cognition, 3,* 452–469.

Schooler, J. W., & Engstler-Schooler, T. Y. (1990). Verbal overshadowing of visual memories: Some things are better left unsaid. *Cognitive Psychology, 22,* 36–71.

Schooler, J. W., Gerhard, D., & Loftus, E. F. (1986). Qualities of the unreal. *Journal of Experimental Psychology: Learning, Memory, and Cognition, 12,* 171–181.

Schreiber, F. (1973). *Sybil.* Chicago: Regency.

Schwartz, M. F., Saffran, E. M., & Marin, O. S. M. (1980). Fractionating the reading process in dementia: Evidence for word specific print-to-sound associations. In M. Coltheart, K. Patterson, & J. C. Marshall (Eds.), *Deep dyslexia* (pp. 259–269). London: Routledge & Kegan Paul.

Schwarz, E. D., Kowalski, J. M., & McNally, R. J. (1993). Malignant memories: Post-traumatic changes in memory in adults after a school shooting. *Journal of Traumatic Stress, 6,* 545–553.

Scoville, W. B., & Milner, B. (1957). Loss of recent memory after bilateral hippocampal lesions. *Journal of Neurology, Neurosurgery and Psychiatry, 20,* 11–21.

Searle, J. (1983). *Intentionality: An essay in the philosophy of mind.* Cambridge: Cambridge University Press.

Semon, R. (1904/1921). *The mneme.* London: George Allen & Unwin.

Semon, R. (1909/1923). *Mnemic psychology.* London: George Allen & Unwin.

Shattuck, R. (1983). *Proust's binoculars: A study of memory, time, and recognition in "A La Recherche du Temps Perdu."* Princeton: Princeton University Press.

Sheehan, P. W. (1988). Memory distortion in hypnosis. *International Journal of Clinical and Experimental Hypnosis, 36,* 296–311.

Shepard, R. N. (1967). Recognition memory for words, sentences, and pictures. *Journal of Verbal Learning and Verbal Behavior, 6,* 156–163.

Sherman, E., & Newman, E. S. (1977/1978). The meaning of cherished personal possessions for the elderly. *International Journal of Aging and Human Development, 8,* 181–192.

Sherry, D. F., & Schacter, D. L. (1987). The evolution of multiple memory systems. *Psychological Review, 94,* 439–454.

Shevrin, H. (1988). Unconscious conflict: A convergent psychodynamic and electrophysiological approach. In M. Horowitz (Ed.), *Psychodynamics and cognition* (pp. 117–167). Chicago: University of Chicago Press.

Shevrin, H. (1992). Subliminal perception, memory, and consciousness: Cognitive and dynamic perspectives. In R. F. Bornstein & T. S. Pittman (Eds.), *Perception without awareness: Cognitive, clinical, and social perspectives* (pp. 123–142). New York: Guilford Press.

Shimamura, A. P. (1994). The neuropsychology of metacognition. In J. Metcalfe & A. P. Shimamura (Eds.), *Metacognition: Knowing about knowing* (pp. 253–276). Cambridge: MIT Press.

Shimamura, A. P. (1995). Memory and frontal lobe function. In M. Gazzaniga (Ed.), *The cognitive neurosciences* (pp. 803–813). Cambridge: MIT Press.

Shimamura, A. P., & Squire, L. R. (1989). Impaired priming of new associations in amnesia. *Journal of Experimental Psychology: Learning, Memory, and Cognition, 15,* 721–728.

Shin, L. M., Kosslyn, S. M., McNally, R. J., Alpert, N. M., Thompson, W. L., Rauch, S. L., Macklin, M. L., & Pitman, R. K. (1995). A PET study of imagery and perception in Vietnam combat veterans with and without posttraumatic stress disorder. Submitted for publication.

Silbersweig, D. A., Stern, E., Frith, C., Cahill, C., Holmes, A., Grootoonk, S., Seaward, S., Mckenna, P., Chua, S. E., Schnorr, L., Jones, T., & Frackowiak, R. S. J. (1995). A functional neuroanatomy of hallucinations in schizophrenia. *Nature, 378,* 176–179.

Singer, J. A., & Salovey, P. (1993). *The remembered self: Emotion and memory in personality.* New York: Free Press.

Slamecka, N. J. (1985). Ebbinghaus: Some associations. *Journal of Experimental Psychology: Learning, Memory, and Cognition, 11,* 414–435.

Slater, D. (1991). Consuming Kodak. In J. Spence & P. Holland (Eds.), *Family snaps: The meanings of domestic photography* (pp. 49–59). London: Virago.

Smith, E. E., Jonides, J., Koeppe, R. A., Awh, E., Schumacher, E. H., & Minoshima, S. (1995). Spatial versus object working memory: PET investigations. *Journal of Cognitive Neuroscience, 7,* 337–356.

Smith, M. L., & Milner, B. (1981). The role of the right hippocampus in the recall of spatial location. *Neuropsychologia, 19,* 781–793.

Solomon, Z., Garb, R., Bleich, A., & Grupper, D. (1987). Reactivation of combat-related posttraumatic stress disorder. *American Journal of Psychiatry, 144,* 51–55.

Spanos, N. P., Cross, P. A., Dickson, K., & DuBreuil, S. C. (1993). Close encounters: An examination of UFO experiences. *Journal of Abnormal Psychology, 102,* 624–632.

Spanos, N. P., Menary, E., Gabora, N., DuBreuil, S., & Dewhirst, B. (1991). Secondary identity enactments during hypnotic past-life regression: A sociocognitive perspective. *Journal of Personality and Social Psychology, 61,* 308–320.

Spence, D. P. (1984). *Narrative truth and historical truth.* New York: Norton.

Spence, J. (1984). *The memory palace of Matteo Ricci.* New York: Viking.

Spencer, W. D., & Raz, N. (1995). Differential effects of aging on memory for content and context: A meta-analysis. *Psychology and Aging, 10,* 527–539.

Spiegel, D. (1991). Dissociation and trauma. In A. Tasman & S. M. Goldfinger (Eds.), *American Psychiatric Press Review of Psychiatry* (pp. 261–266). Washington, DC: American Psychiatric Press.

Spiegel, D. (Ed.). (1994). *Dissociation: Culture, mind and body.* Washington, DC: American Psychiatric Press.

Spiegel, D. (1995). Hypnosis and suggestion. In D. L. Schacter, J. T. Coyle, G. D. Fischbach, M.-M. Mesulam, & L. E. Sullivan (Eds.), *Memory distortion: How minds, brains, and societies reconstruct the past* (pp. 129–149). Cambridge: Harvard University Press.

Sporer, S. L., Penrod, S., Read, D., & Cutler, B. (1995). Choosing, confidence, and accuracy: A meta-analysis of the confidence-accuracy relation in eyewitness identification studies. *Psychological Bulletin, 118,* 315–327.

Squire, L. R. (1987). *Memory and brain.* New York: Oxford University Press.

Squire, L. R. (1992). Memory and the hippocampus: A synthesis from findings with rats, monkeys, and humans. *Psychological Review, 99,* 195–231.

Squire, L. R. (1994). Declarative and nondeclarative memory: Multiple brain systems supporting learning and memory. In D. L. Schacter & E. Tulving (Eds.), *Memory systems 1994* (pp. 203–232). Cambridge: MIT Press.

Squire, L. R. (1995). Biological foundations of accuracy and inaccuracy in memory. In D. L. Schacter, J. T. Coyte, G. D. Fischbach, M.-M. Mesulam, & L. E. Sullivan (Eds.), *Memory distortion: How minds, brains, and societies reconstruct the past* (pp. 197–225). Cambridge, MA: Harvard University Press.

Squire, L. R., & Zola-Morgan, M. (1991). The medial temporal lobe memory system. *Science, 253,* 1380–1386.

Squire, L. R., Cohen, N. J., & Nadel, L. (1984). The medial temporal region and memory consolidation: A new hypothesis. In H. Weingartner & E. Parker (Eds.), *Memory consolidation* (pp. 185–210). Hillsdale, NJ: Erlbaum.

Squire, L. R., Ojemann, J. G., Miezin, F. M., Petersen, S. E., Videen, T. O., & Raichle, M. E. (1992). Activation of the hippocampus in normal humans: A functional anatomical study of memory. *Proceedings of the National Academy of Sciences, USA, 89,* 1837–1841.

Srinivas, K. (1993). Perceptual specificity in nonverbal priming. *Journal of Experimental Psychology: Learning, Memory, and Cognition, 19,* 582–602.

Stadler, M. (1990). *Landscape: Memory.* New York: Scribner's.

Standing, L. (1973). Learning 10,000 pictures. *Quarterly Journal of Experimental Psychology, 25,* 207–222.

Starr, A., & Phillips, L. (1970). Verbal and motor memory in the amnesic syndrome. *Neuropsychologia, 8,* 75–88.

Stein, B. S., & Bransford, J. D. (1979). Constraints on effective elaboration: Effects of precision and subject generation. *Journal of Verbal Learning and Verbal Behavior, 18,* 769–777.

Stein, M. B., Koverola, C., Hanna, C., Torchia, M., & McClarty, B. (1995). Neurobiological correlates of childhood sexual abuse: II. MRI-based measurement of hippocampal volume in adult women. Submitted for publication.

Stoltzfus, E. R., Hasher, L., Zacks, R. T., Ulivi, M. S., & Goldstein, D. (1993). Investigations of inhibition and interference in younger and older adults. *Journal of Gerontology, 48,* 179–188.

Storr, R. (1992). *Dislocations.* New York: The Museum of Modern Art.

Stuss, D. T. (1991). Disturbance of self-awareness after frontal system damage. In G. P. Prigatano & D. L. Schacter (Eds.), *Awareness of deficit after brain injury: Clinical and theoretical issues* (pp. 63–83). New York: Oxford University Press.

Stuss, D. T., Eskes, G. A., & Foster, J. K. (1994). Experimental neuropsychological studies of frontal lobe functions. In F. Boller & J. Grafman (Eds.), *Handbook of Neuropsychology* (pp. 149–185). Amsterdam: Elsevier.

Sulin, R. A., & Dooling, D. J. (1974). Intrusion of a thematic idea in retention of prose. *Journal of Experimental Psychology, 103,* 255–262.

Sutker, P. B., Galina, Z. H., & West, J. A. (1990). Trauma-induced weight loss and cognitive deficits among former prisoners of war. *Journal of Consulting and Clinical Psychology, 58,* 323–328.

Szajnberg, N. M. (1993). Recovering a repressed memory, and representational shift in an adolescent. *Journal of the American Psychoanalytic Association, 41,* 711–727.

Talland, G. A. (1965). *Deranged memory: A psychonomic study of the amnesic syndrome.* New York: Academic Press.

Tayloe, D. R. (1995). The validity of repressed memories and the accuracy of their recall through hypnosis: A case study from the courtroom. *American Journal of Hypnosis, 37,* 25–31.

Taylor, K. (1965). Cryptomnesia and plagiarism. *British Journal of Psychiatry, 111,* 1111–1118.

Taylor, P. J., & Kopelman, M. D. (1984). Amnesia for criminal offences. *Psychological Medicine, 14,* 581–588.

Tenpenny, P. L. (1995). Abstractionist versus episodic theories of repetition priming and word identification. *Psychonomic Bulletin and Review, 2,* 339–363.

Terr, L. C. (1981). Psychic trauma in children: Observations following the Chowchilla school-bus kidnapping. *American Journal of Psychiatry, 138,* 14–19.

Terr, L. C. (1988). What happens to early memories of trauma? *Journal of the American Academy of Child Adolescent Psychiatry, 27,* 96–104.

Terr, L. C. (1994). *Unchained memories.* New York: Basic Books.

Teyler, T. J., & DiScenna, P. (1986). The hippocampal memory indexing theory. *Behavioral Neuroscience, 100,* 147–154.

Thigpen, C., & Cleckley, H. (1957). *The three faces of Eve.* New York: Popular Library.

Thompson, C. P., Cowan, T. M., & Frieman, J. (1993). *Memory search by a memorist.* Hillsdale, NJ: Erlbaum.

Thompson, R. F., & Krupa, D. J. (1994). Organization of memory traces in the mammalian brain. *Annual Review of Neurosciences, 17,* 519–549.

Thomson, D. M. (1988). Context and false recognition. In G. M. Davies & D. M. Thomson (Eds.), *Memory in context: Context in memory* (pp. 285–304). Chichester, England: Wiley.

Thornton, S., & Brotchie, J. (1987). Reminiscence: A critical review of the empirical literature. *British Journal of Clinical Psychology, 26,* 93–111.

Thygesen, P., Hermann, K., & Willanger, R. (1970). Concentration camp survivors in Denmark: Persecution, disease, disability, compensation. *Danish Medical Bulletin, 17,* 65–87.

Tobias, B. A., Kihlstrom, J. F., & Schacter, D. L. (1992). Emotion and implicit memory. In S.-Å. Christianson (Ed.), *The handbook of emotion and memory: Research and theory* (pp. 67–92). Hillsdale, NJ: Erlbaum.

Tooby, J., & Cosmides, L. (1995). Mapping the evolved functional organization of mind and brain. In M. S. Gazzaniga (Ed.), *The cognitive neurosciences* (pp. 1185–1197). Cambridge: MIT Press.

Tranel, D., & Damasio, A. R. (1985). Knowledge without awareness: an autonomic index of facial recognition by prosopagnosics. *Science, 228,* 1453–1454.

Tranel, D., Damasio, A. R., Damasio, H., & Brandt, J. P. (1994). Sensorimotor skill learning in amnesia: Additional evidence for the neural basis of nondeclarative memory. *Learning and Memory, 1,* 165–179.

Treadway, M., McCloskey, M., Gordon, B., & Cohen, N. J. (1992). Landmark life events and the organization of memory: Evidence from functional retrograde amnesia. In S.-Å. Christianson (Ed.), *The handbook of emotion and memory: Research and theory* (pp. 389–410). Hillsdale, NJ: Erlbaum.

Tromp, S., Koss, M. P., Figueredo, A. J., & Tharan, M. (1995). Are rape memories different? A comparison of rape, other unpleasant, and pleasant memories among employed women. *Journal of Traumatic Stress, 8,* 607–628.

Tulving, E. (1972). Episodic and semantic memory. In E. Tulving & W. Donaldson (Eds.), *Organization of memory* (pp. 381–403). New York: Academic Press.

Tulving, E. (1983). *Elements of episodic memory.* Oxford: Clarendon Press.

Tulving, E. (1985). Memory and consciousness. *Canadian Psychologist, 26,* 1–12.

Tulving, E. (1993). Self-knowledge of an amnesic individual is represented abstractly. In T. K. Srull & R. S. Wyer, Jr. (Eds.), *The mental representation of trait and autobiographical knowledge about the self* (pp. 147–156). Hillsdale, NJ: Erlbaum.

Tulving, E., & Schacter, D. L. (1990). Priming and human memory systems. *Science, 247,* 301–306.

Tulving, E., & Thomson, D. M. (1973). Encoding specificity and retrieval processes in episodic memory. *Psychological Review, 80,* 352–373.

Tulving, E., Kapur, S., Craik, F. I. M., Moscovitch, M., & Houle, S. (1994). Hemispheric encoding/retrieval asymmetry in episodic memory: Positron emission tomography findings. *Proceedings of the National Academy of Science, USA, 91,* 2016–2020.

Tulving, E., Markowitsch, H. J., Kapur, S. Habib, R., & Houle, S. (1994). Novelty encoding networks in the human brain: Positron emission tomography studies. *Neuroreport, 5,* 2525–2528.

Tulving, E., Schacter, D. L., McLachlan, D. R., & Moscovitch, M. (1988). Priming of semantic autobiographical knowledge: A case study of retrograde amnesia. *Brain and Cognition, 8,* 3–20.

Tulving, E., Schacter, D. L., & Stark, H. (1982). Priming effects in word-fragment completion are independent of recognition memory. *Journal of Experimental Psychology: Learning, Memory, and Cognition, 8,* 336–342.

Turner, F. (in press). *Echoes of combat: Trauma, memory and the Vietnam war.* New York: Anchor/Doubleday.

Turyn, A. (1986). *Missives.* New York: Alfred Van Der Marck Editions.

Ungerleider, L. G. (1995). Functional brain imaging studies of cortical mechanisms for memory. *Science, 270,* 769–775.

Usher, J. A., & Neisser, U. (1993). Childhood amnesia and the beginnings of memory for four early life events. *Journal of Experimental Psychology: General, 122,* 155–165.

Vallar, G., & Shallice, T. (1990). *Neuropsychological impairments of short-term memory.* Cambridge: Cambridge University Press.

Van Arsdale, S. (1995). *Toward amnesia.* New York: Riverhead Books.

van der Kolk, B. A. (1994). The body keeps the score: Memory and the evolving psychobiology of PTSD. *Harvard Review of Psychiatry, 1,* 253–265.

van der Kolk, B. A., & Fisler, R. (1995). Dissociation and the fragmentary nature of traumatic memories: Overview and exploratory study. *Journal of Traumatic Stress, 8,* 505–525.

van der Kolk, B. A. & van der Hart, O. (1989). Pierre Janet and the breakdown of adaptation in psychological trauma. *American Journal of Psychiatry, 146,* 1530–1540.

Van Dyke, C., Zilberg, N. J., & McKinnon, J. A. (1985). Posttraumatic stress disorder: A thirty-year delay in a World War II veteran. *American Journal of Psychiatry, 142,* 1070–1073.

Van Hoesen, G. W., & Damasio, A. R. (1987). Neural correlates of cognitive impairment in Alzheimer's disease. In *Handbook of physiology* (Vol. 5, pp. 871–898). Bethesda, MD: American Physiological Association.

Vargha-Khadem, F., Isaacs, E., & Mishkin, M. (1994). Agnosia, alexia and a remarkable form of amnesia in an adolescent boy. *Brain, 117,* 683–703.

Verfaellie, M. & Treadwell, J. R. (1993). Status of recognition memory in amnesia. *Neuropsychology, 7,* 5–13.

Verfaellie, M., Reiss, L., & Roth, H. L. (1995). Knowledge of new English vocabulary in amnesia: An examination of premorbidly acquired semantic memory. *Journal of the International Neuropsychological Society, 1,* 443–453.

Victor, M., Adams, R. D., & Collins, G. H. (1989). *The Wernicke-Korsakoff Syndrome and related neurologic disorders due to alcoholism and malnutrition* (2nd ed.). Philadelphia: Davis.

Wagenaar, W. A. (1988). *Identifying Ivan: A case study in legal psychology.* Cambridge: Harvard University Press.

Wagenaar, W. A. & Groeneweg, J. (1988). The memory of concentration camp survivors. *Applied Cognitive Psychology, 4,* 77–87.

Wakefield, H., & Underwager, R. (1994). *Return of the furies: An investigation into recovered memory therapy.* Chicago: Open Court.

Wapner, S., Demick, J., & Redondo, J. P. (1990). Cherished possessions and adaptation of older people to nursing homes. *International Journal of Aging and Human Development, 31,* 219–235.

Warrington, E. K., & McCarthy, R. A. (1988). The fractionation of retrograde amnesia. *Brain and Cognition, 7,* 184–200.

Warrington, E. K., & Shallice, T. (1984). Category specific semantic impairments. *Brain, 107,* 829–854.

Warrington, E. K., & Weiskrantz, L. (1968). New method of testing long-term retention with special reference to amnesic patients. *Nature, 217,* 972–974.

Warrington, E. K., & Weiskrantz, L. (1974). The effect of prior learning on subsequent retention in amnesic patients. *Neuropsychologia, 12,* 419–428.

Waterhouse, L. (1988). Extraordinary visual memory and pattern perception in an autistic boy. In L. K. Obler & D. Fein (Eds.), *The exceptional brain: Neuropsychology of talent and special abilities* (pp. 325–340). New York: Guilford Press.

Watt, H. J. (1905). Review of *Die Mneme*. *Archiv für die Gesamte Psychologie, 5*, 127–130.

Weaver, C. A., III (1993). Do you need a "flash" to form a flashbulb memory? *Journal of Experimental Psychology: General, 122*, 39–46.

Wegner, D. M. (1992). You can't always think what you want: Problems in the suppression of unwanted thoughts. In M. Zanna (Ed.), *Advances in experimental social psychology.* San Diego: Academic Press.

Weiskrantz, L. (1956). Behavioral changes associated with ablation of the amygdaloid complex in monkeys. *Journal of Comparative Physiological Psychology, 49*, 381–391.

Weiskrantz, L. (1978). Some aspects of visual capacity in monkeys and man following striate cortex lesions. *Archives Italiennes de Biologie, 116*, 318–323.

Weiskrantz, L. (1986). *Blindsight. A case study and implications.* Oxford: Clarendon Press.

Wells, G. L. (1993). What do we know about eyewitness identification? *American Psychologist, 48*, 553–571.

West, M. J., Coleman, P. D., Flood, D. G., & Troncoso, J. C. (1994). Differences in the pattern of hippocampal neuronal loss in normal ageing and Alzheimer's disease. *Lancet, 344*, 769–772.

Whelihan, W. M., & Lesher, E. L. (1985). Neuropsychological changes in frontal functions with aging. *Developmental Neuropsychology, 1*, 371–380.

White, H. C. (1993). *Careers & creativity: Social forces in the arts.* Boulder, CO: Westview.

Whitfield, C. L. (1995). *Memory and abuse: Remembering and healing the effects of trauma.* Deerfield Beach, FL: Health Communication, Inc.

Wilkinson, C. B. (1983). Aftermath of a disaster: The collapse of the Hyatt Regency Hotel skywalks. *American Journal of Psychiatry, 140*, 1134–1139.

Williams, G. V., & Goldman-Rakic, P. S. (1995). Modulation of memory fields by dopamine D_1 receptors in prefrontal cortex. *Nature, 376*, 572–575.

Williams, J. M. G. (1992). Autobiographical memory and emotional disorders. In S.-Å. Christianson (Ed.), *The handbook of emotion and memory: Research and theory* (pp. 451–477). Hillsdale, NJ: Erlbaum.

Williams, L. M. (1994). Recall of childhood trauma: A prospective study of women's memories of child sexual abuse. *Journal of Consulting and Clinical Psychology, 62*, 1167–1176.

Williams, L. M. (1995). Recovered memories of abuse in women with documented childhood sexual victimization histories. *Journal of Traumatic Stress, 8*, 649–674.

Wills, G. (1987). *Reagan's America: Innocents at home.* Garden City, NY: Doubleday.

Wilson, B. A. (1987). *Rehabilitation of memory.* London: Guilford Press.

Wilson, B. A., Baddeley, A., Evans, J., & Shiel, A. (1994). Errorless learning in the rehabilitation of memory impaired people. *Neuropsychological Rehabilitation, 4*, 307–326.

Wilson, F. A. W., O'Scalaidhe, S. P., & Goldman-Rakic, P. S. (1993). Dissociation of object and spatial processing domains in primate prefrontal cortex. *Science, 260*, 1955–1958.

Wilson, M. A., & McNaughton, B. L. (1994). Reactivation of hippocampal ensemble memories during sleep. *Science, 265*, 676–682.

Wilson, S. C., & Barber, T. X. (1978). The Creative Imagination Scale as a measure of hypnotic responsiveness: Applications to experimental and clinical hypnosis. *American Journal of Clinical Hypnosis, 20*, 235–249.

Wilson, T. D., & Brekke, N. (1994). Mental contamination and mental correction: Unwanted influences on judgments and evaluations. *Psychological Bulletin, 116*, 117–142.

Winograd, E., & Killinger, W. A. (1983). Relating age at encoding in early childhood to adult recall: Development of flashbulb memories. *Journal of Experimental Psychology: General, 112*, 413–422.

Winson, J. (1985). *Brain and psyche: The biology of the unconscious.* New York: Doubleday/Anchor Press.

Wixted, J. T., & Ebbensen, E. (1991). On the form of forgetting. *Psychological Science, 2*, 409–415.

Wolkowitz, O. M., Reus, V. I., Weingartner, H., Thompson, K., Breier, A., Doran, A., Rubinow, D., & Pickar, D. (1990). Cognitive effects of corticosteroids. *American Journal of Psychiatry, 147,* 1297–1303.

Wong, P. T. P., & Watt, L. M. (1991). What types of reminiscence are associated with successful aging? *Psychology and Aging, 6,* 272–279.

Wood, J., Bootzin, R. R., Kihlstrom, J. F., & Schacter, D. L. (1992). Implicit and explicit memory for verbal information presented during sleep. *Psychological Science, 3,* 236–239.

Wright, L. (1993). Remembering Satan. *The New Yorker,* May 17 and May 24, 60–81, 54–76.

Wright, L. (1994). *Remembering satan: A case of recovered memory and the shattering of an American Family.* New York: Knopf.

Yapko, M. D. (1994). *Suggestions of abuse: True and false memories of childhood sexual traumas.* New York: Simon & Schuster.

Yapko, M. D. (1995). Suggestibility and repressed memories of abuse: A survey of psychotherapists' beliefs. *American Journal of Clinical Hypnosis, 36,* 163–171.

Yarnell, P. R., & Lynch, S. (1973). The "ding": Amnesic states in football trauma. *Neurology, 23,* 196–197.

Yates, F. A. (1966). *The art of memory.* Chicago: University of Chicago Press.

Yehuda, R., Southwick, S., Giller, E. L., Ma, X., & Mason, J. W. (1992). Urinary catecholamine excretion and severity of PTSD symptoms in Vietnam combat veterans. *The Journal of Nervous and Mental Disease, 180,* 321–325.

Young, A. W., & DeHaan, E. H. F. (1992). Face recognition and awareness after brain injury. In A. D. Milner & M. D. Rugg (Eds.), *The neuropsychology of consciousness* (pp. 69–90). London: Academic Press.

Young, W. (1992). Recognition and treatment of survivors reporting ritual abuse. In D. K. Sakheim & S. Devine (Eds.), *Out of darkness.* New York: Lexington Books.

Zaragoza, M. S., & Lane, S. M. (1994). Source misattributions and the suggestibility of eyewitness memory. *Journal of Experimental Psychology: Learning, Memory, and Cognition, 20,* 934–945.

Zola-Morgan, S. (1996). Memory: Clinical and anatomical aspects. In T. E. Feinberg & M. Farah (Eds.), *Behavioral neurology and neuropsychology.* New York: McGraw-Hill.

Zola-Morgan, S., & Squire, L. R. (1990). The primate hippocampal formation: Evidence for a time-limited role in memory storage. *Science, 250,* 288–290.

Zola-Morgan, S., & Squire, L. R. (1993). Neuroanatomy of memory. *Annual Review of Neuroscience, 16,* 547–563.

Zola-Morgan, S., Squire, L. R., Alverez-Royo, P., & Clower, R. P. (1991). Independence of memory functions and emotional behavior: Separate contributions of the hippocampal formation and the amygdala. *Hippocampus, 1,* 207–220.

Zola-Morgan, S., Squire, L. R., & Amaral, D. G. (1986). Human amnesia and the medial temporal region: Enduring memory impairment following a bilateral lesion limited to field CA1 of the hippocampus. *Journal of Neuroscience, 6,* 2950–2967.

Zola-Morgan, S., Squire, L. R., Amaral, D. G., & Suzuki, W. A. (1989). Lesions of perirhinal and parahippocampal cortex that spare the amygdala and hippocampal formation produce severe memory impairment. *Journal of Neuroscience, 9,* 4355–4370.

Zola-Morgan, S., Squire, L. R., & Ramus, S. J. (1994). Severity of memory impairment in monkeys as a function of locus and extent of damage within the medial temporal lobe memory system. *Hippocampus, 4,* 483–495.

INDEX